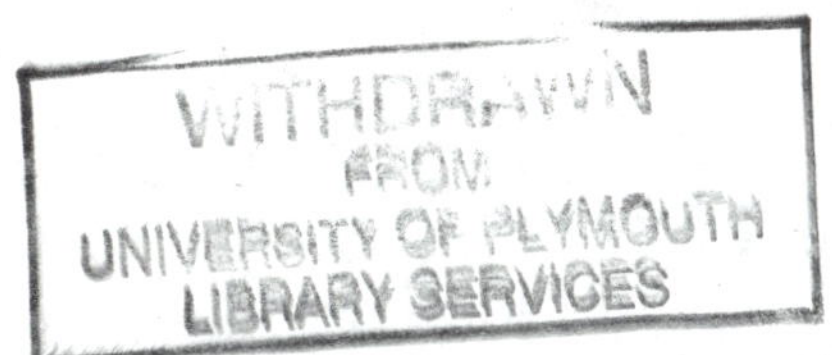

The Single Market Review

IMPACT ON COMPETITION
AND SCALE EFFECTS

PRICE COMPETITION AND PRICE CONVERGENCE

The Single Market Review series

Subseries I — Impact on manufacturing

Volume:
1 Food, drink and tobacco processing machinery
2 Pharmaceutical products
3 Textiles and clothing
4 Construction site equipment
5 Chemicals
6 Motor vehicles
7 Processed foodstuffs
8 Telecommunications equipment

Subseries II — Impact on services

Volume:
1 Insurance
2 Air transport
3 Credit institutions and banking
4 Distribution
5 Road freight transport
6 Telecommunications: liberalized services
7 Advertising
8 Audio-visual services and production
9 Single information market
10 Single energy market
11 Transport networks

Subseries III — Dismantling of barriers

Volume:
1 Technical barriers to trade
2 Public procurement
3 Customs and fiscal formalities at frontiers
4 Industrial property rights
5 Capital market liberalization
6 Currency management costs

Subseries IV — Impact on trade and investment

Volume:
1 Foreign direct investment
2 Trade patterns inside the single market
3 Trade creation and trade diversion
4 External access to European markets

Subseries V — Impact on competition and scale effects

Volume:
1 Price competition and price convergence
2 Intangible investments
3 Competition issues
4 Economies of scale

Subseries VI — Aggregate and regional impact

Volume:
1 Regional growth and convergence
2 The cases of Greece, Spain, Ireland and Portugal
3 Trade, labour and capital flows: the less developed regions
4 Employment, trade and labour costs in manufacturing
5 Aggregate results of the single market programme

Results of the business survey

EUROPEAN COMMISSION

The Single Market Review

IMPACT ON COMPETITION
AND SCALE EFFECTS

PRICE COMPETITION AND PRICE CONVERGENCE

The Single Market Review

SUBSERIES V: VOLUME 1

OFFICE FOR OFFICIAL PUBLICATIONS
OF THE EUROPEAN COMMUNITIES

KOGAN PAGE . EARTHSCAN

This report is part of a series of 39 studies commissioned from independent consultants in the context of a major review of the single market. The 1996 Single Market Review responds to a 1992 Council of Ministers Resolution calling on the European Commission to present an overall analysis of the effectiveness of measures taken in creating the single market. This review, which assesses the progress made in implementing the single market programme, was coordinated by the Directorate-General 'Internal Market and Financial Services' (DG XV) and the Directorate-General 'Economic and Financial Affairs' (DG II) of the European Commission.

This document was prepared for the European Commission

by

DRI Europe Ltd

It does not, however, express the Commission's official views. Whilst every reasonable effort has been made to provide accurate information in regard to the subject matter covered, the Consultants are not responsible for any remaining errors. All recommendations are made by the Consultants for the purpose of discussion. Neither the Commission nor the Consultants accept liability for the consequences of actions taken on the basis of the information contained herein.

The European Commission would like to express thanks to the external experts and representatives of firms and industry bodies for their contribution to the 1996 Single Market Review, and to this report in particular.

Office for Official Publications of the European Communities
2 rue Mercier, L-2985 Luxembourg
ISBN 92-827-8801-6 Catalogue number: C1-71-96-001-EN-C

Kogan Page.Earthscan
120 Pentonville Road, London N1 9JN
ISBN 0 7494 2334 X

Table of contents

List of tables

List of figures

List of abbreviations

Benelux	Economic Union of Belgium, Luxembourg and the Netherlands
CAP	Common agricultural policy
CBS	Cocoa butter substitute
CPI	Consumer price index
ECU	European currency unit
EFTA	European Free Trade Association
EU	European Union
Eurostat	Statistical Office of the European Communities
FRG	Federal Republic of Germany
IMP	Internal market programme
M&A	Mergers and acquisitions
METS	Minimum efficient technical size
NACE	General industrial classification of economic activities within the European Communities
NTB	Non-tariff barrier
NSI	National statistical institute
PPI	Producer price index
SMP	Single market programme
TPA	Third party access
VAT	Value added tax

Acknowledgements

The project was directed by Dr Elisabeth Waelbroeck-Rocha (DRI/McGraw-Hill), in coordination with Professor Elisabeth de Ghellinck (Université Catholique de Louvain). Steven Adler (Horack, Adler & Associates) coordinated the efforts of the study team from Horack, Adler & Associates.

In addition to the above, the study team also included Stéphane Gagné, Andrew Mungall and Eric Ruscher (all DRI/McGraw-Hill) and Sarah Horack (Horack, Adler & Associates). Thaitmes El Bouazzaoui (DRI/McGraw-Hill) provided production assistance.

1. Summary

This report presents the results of the study by DRI, Professor E. de Ghellinck, and Horack, Adler & Associates aimed at assessing the extent to which the single market programme has effectively resulted in the creation of pan-European markets.

If pan-European markets are defined as markets where arbitraging is not prevented by firms or governments, the aim of the 1992 programme can indeed be redefined as fostering the emergence of pan-European markets. The paragraph below taken from the European Commission report entitled 'The Economics of 1992' describes the mechanisms through which the benefits of the single market programme (SMP) were to materialize:

'The removal of barriers and the freedom of supply which businesses will enjoy as a result (of the Internal Market programme) should lead, through increased competitive pressure, to some downward convergence of prices of benefit to the customer. From the point of view of producers, the competitive pressure will be exerted first and foremost on price-cost margins, particularly in those sectors in which they held a certain monopoly power or position. Producers will also be induced – urged on by pressure on their margins – to become more efficient and thus cut their production and distribution costs. The increased pressure which will be brought to bear in this way on costs and price-cost margins will be a powerful means of causing prices to converge on levels more consistent with economic and technical efficiency'[1].

The above clearly establishes a link between the benefits of the SMP and price-cost developments.

This study evaluates the impact of the SMP on the fragmentation of geographic markets, i.e. on the extent to which the removal of non-tariff barriers between Member States has permitted enterprises to extend their activities to other markets. The study also assesses the degree to which, faced with increased competitive pressures, companies or governments have reacted with strategies or behaviours that have slowed the integration process.

The analysis was undertaken in three stages. Stage I consisted in analysing price differentials as the main indicators of evolving market integration: has there been evidence of price convergence following the launch of the single market programme, and, if so, has this price convergence taken place throughout the EU or have price disparities been reduced comparatively more in some regions or in some markets? This analysis was based on price indices for detailed product/service categories collected by Eurostat, with the help of the national statistical institutes, through regular surveys of final price levels in the 15 EU Member States. Given that market prices for specific products or services are the central indicator studied, **markets** as opposed to **sectors** are the natural unit of analysis.

The second part of the study describes the link between the creation of pan-European markets and price convergence, and discusses the expected theoretical impact on prices of increased integration according to different characteristics of the markets considered. Price convergence is, indeed, neither an end in itself nor a perfect indicator of the degree to which the SMP has

1 See European Commission [1988], 'The Economics of 1992', in *European Economy*, No 35, March 1988, Part D (The effects of market integration, p. 118).

achieved the desired objectives. Price convergence is not an end in itself because the existence of price disparities across different geographic markets is only a source of concern if it reflects market distortions or barriers to the arbitrage process. Price convergence is also neither a **necessary** nor a **sufficient** condition for demand to be transferred across markets, i.e. for markets to become pan-European. It is not a necessary condition as price convergence only occurs when consumers are both **willing** and **able** to transfer their demand between suppliers from different countries. The willingness to engage in arbitraging, however, depends on the importance of price (as opposed to, say, quality) as a choice variable, whilst the ability to engage in arbitraging is a function of the cost of arbitraging and of the existence of regulatory barriers. Price convergence is also not a sufficient condition for markets to become pan-European as uniformity of prices could result from cooperation between firms.

The analysis done in the second part of the study thus presents a theoretical framework which determines the conditions under which the SMP was expected to lead to price convergence, and then assesses the extent to which structural, behavioural or policy factors explain the observed patterns in price convergence over the period 1985 to 1993.

The third part of the study analyses the factors underlying price convergence in the EU in more detail by examining four market segments: mineral waters, white goods, construction and chocolate confectionery. The choice of the case studies was done in such a way that they would both cover sufficiently different but representative markets, and provide useful indications of the types of factors, whether structural, behavioural or policy factors, which influence price developments so that they could be incorporated in the econometric analysis (subject to data availability).

The analysis of the overall trends in price dispersion in the EU shows that:

(a) There has been a general trend towards price convergence in the EU-12 over the period 1980–93; this tendency has been more pronounced for consumer and equipment goods than for energy, services and construction (Figures 1.1 and 1.2).

(b) For energy and construction, price dispersion increased over time in the EU-12, and more so after 1985 than over the period 1980–85.

(c) The convergence in consumer products and in services prices has actually tended to accelerate following the launch of the single market programme.

(d) The tendency for prices to converge has been comparatively greater in the three Member States which joined the EU in 1989 (Greece, Portugal and Spain) than in the EU-9; this may reflect a 'catch-up' effect of integration.

(e) In the EU-15, price disparities in 1993 are not significantly greater than in the EU-12, except for food, beverages, clothing and footwear; this mainly reflects differences in the regulatory environments for these products in Austria, Finland and Sweden.

(f) Overall, neither the different levels of nor the changes in VAT rates seem to have distorted general price trends (i.e. there is no significant difference in price convergence trends including or excluding VAT) (Figures 1.3 and 1.4).

Figure 1.1. Measures of price dispersion for selected categories in 1985, prices including taxes

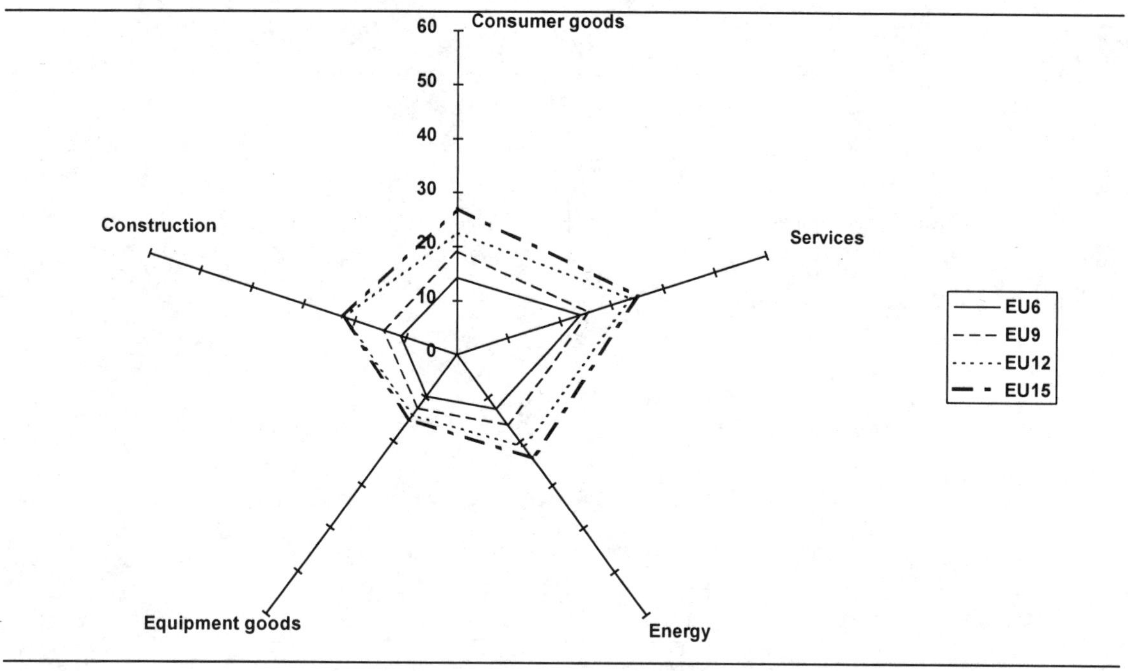

Source: DRI.

Figure 1.2. Measures of price dispersion for selected categories in 1993, prices including taxes

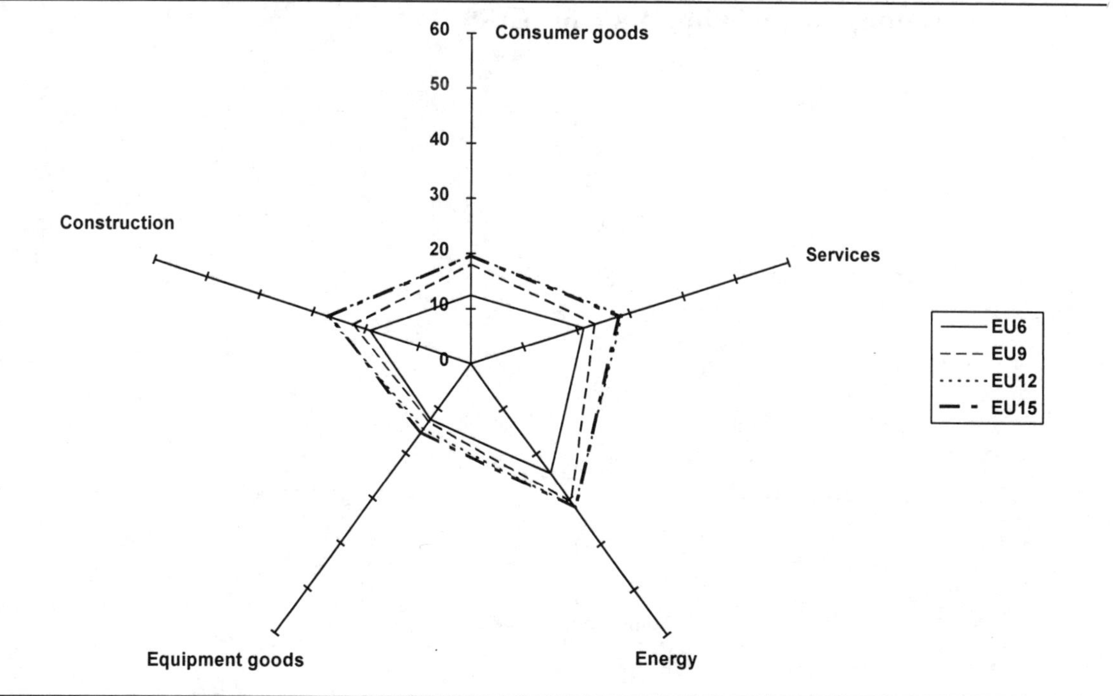

Source: DRI.

Figure 1.3. Comparison of price dispersion for consumer goods in 1985, prices including and excluding VAT for EU-9

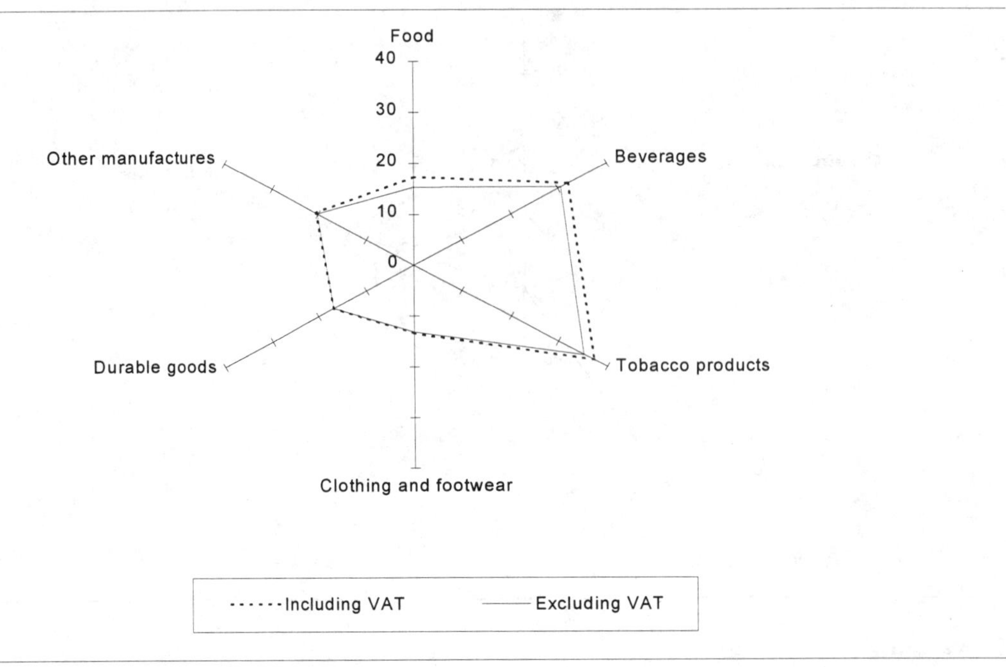

Source: DRI.

Figure 1.4. Comparison of price dispersion for consumer goods in 1993, prices including and excluding VAT for EU-9

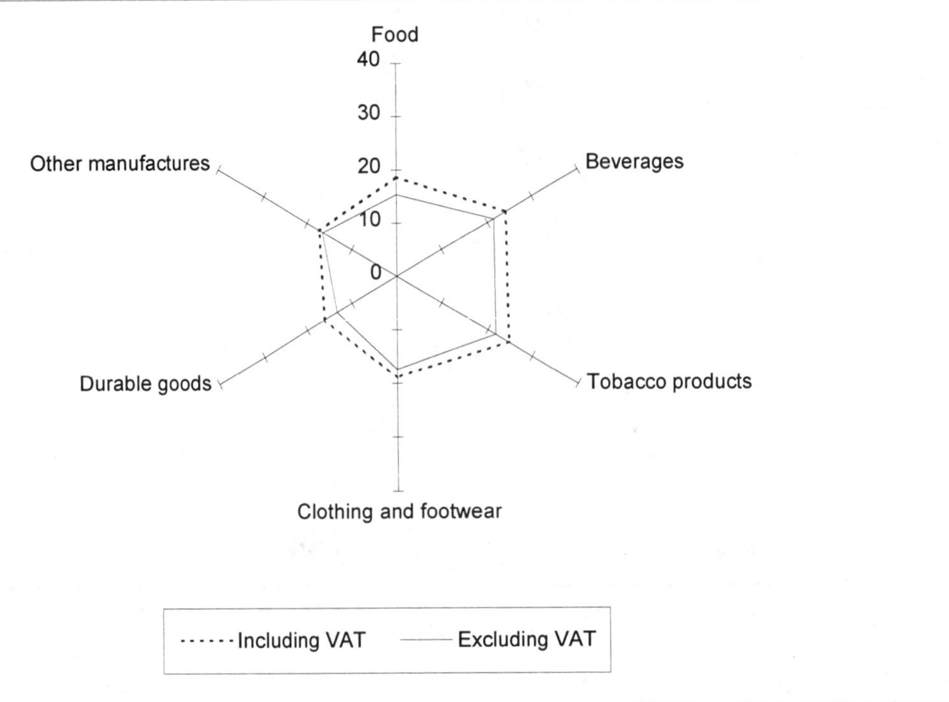

Source: DRI.

(g) Excise taxes do, however, play an important role in some product categories (notably energy products and alcoholic beverages, as well as tobacco products), increasing price disparities compared to the underlying trend in prices net of taxes.

(h) Price dispersion is lowest the more traded products/services are within the EU.

(i) The product categories which have seen the greatest convergence in prices following the launch of the single market programme correspond to highly traded sectors and, more specifically, to sectors that are more open to competition from non-EU producers; the reduction in price disparities for sectors classified as having been subject to high non-tariff barriers before the launch of the single market programme is disappointing.

(j) At the detailed product level, interesting profiles emerge: among the 10 products/services categories for which price disparities in the EU-12 were highest in 1993, there are four products/services related to health care; this reflects the fact that both pharmaceutical product prices and health care delivery prices are still highly regulated at national level. Two other product categories relate to energy, again reflecting regulatory price controls and differences in indirect tax rates, and two are national monopolies in most EU countries (water distribution and railway transport services).

(k) The number of manufactured products for which price dispersion was amongst the 50 highest in 1980 has come down significantly since; by 1993, the list of 50 consumption categories for which price disparities were highest was dominated by service sectors.

(l) In the service sectors, price convergence has been observed for most of the market services, mainly in the EU-12. In the EU-6 and EU-9 regions, convergence has taken place at a much slower rate.

(m) Disparities in price levels across the EU in most service sectors are partly explained by differences in GDP per capita (Figure 1.5). There are, however, 18 out of 37 service categories for which price disparities are not correlated to differences in GDP per capita. These include all the health care sectors but one, along with a number of regulated sectors among which are water distribution, postal services, telecommunications services and railway transport services.

(n) A statistical test has been performed to test the significance of the convergence/divergence patterns. This shows that among the 86 products/services categories for which there is a clear change in price disparities over time across the EU, there are 78 cases of statistically significant price convergence patterns, and only 8 cases of price divergence. The 78 cases of price convergence apply to goods/services which together account for 60% of total private consumption expenditure in the EU.

(o) The ranking of countries according to the lowest or highest price level is remarkably stable over time: out of 145 goods/services categories, there are only 18 for which some countries shift from being a high price to a low price country over subsequent periods, and vice versa.

(p) Exchange rate variations between 1980 and 1993 were not found to have dominated the above convergence patterns; if anything, the past changes in exchange rates have tended to increase price disparities in the EU, and not encouraged price convergence.

In the second part of the study, a theoretical framework has been developed which establishes the relationship between European integration and price convergence patterns, and highlights the role of structural, behavioural and policy factors in influencing the trend in prices as a result of integration. There can, indeed, be a number of objective factors which can account for price disparities across geographic markets for the same product at the same horizontal stage of development. Among these are differences in consumer preferences, vertical differentiation of products involving market segmentation into branded/own label products, and the existence of transport costs: these factors reflect the actual nature of the market, and are thus referred to as **structural** factors preventing price convergence. Price disparities can, however, also result from strategies of companies aimed at segmenting markets or raising barriers to entry to reduce competition. These factors, referred to as **behavioural** factors, include market sharing agreements, the control of distribution or the creation of (or increase in) barriers to entry. Finally, government policies can limit or constrain the arbitrage process by developing or maintaining a protective regulatory environment (by imposing restrictions to market access or setting strict standards that give an advantage to local firms) or creating barriers to entry (through subsidization). These policies are referred to as the **policy** factors restraining price convergence and/or the pan-Europeanization process.

Figure 1.5. Average services prices and GDP per capita in the EU-12

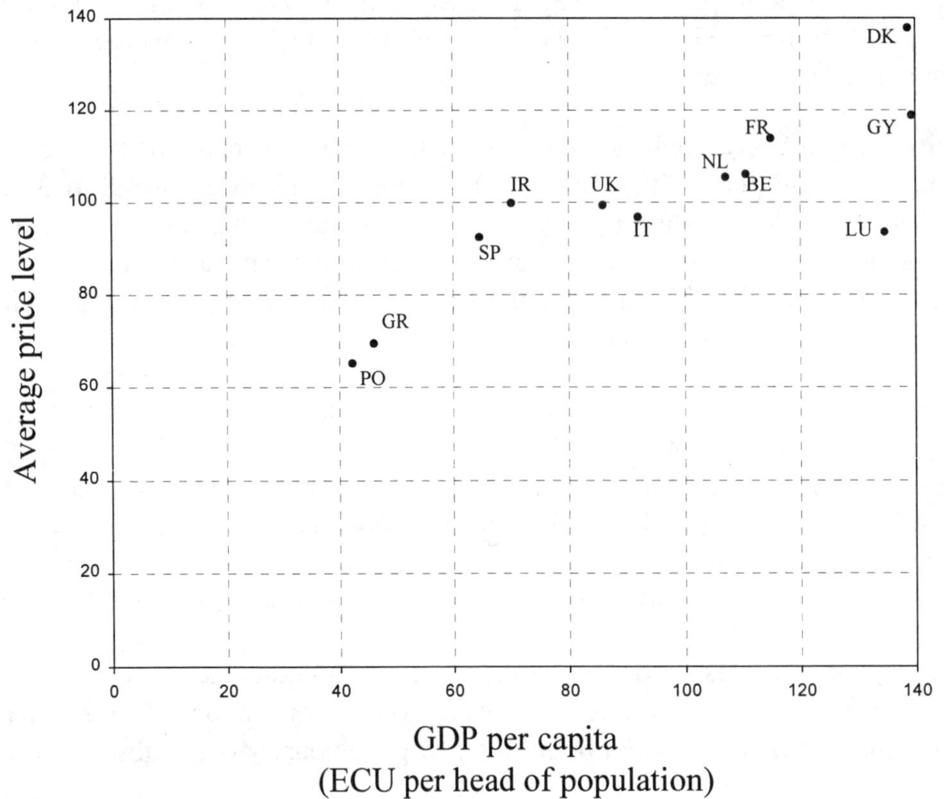

Source: DRI.

An econometric model has then been tested in order to validate the theoretical framework and shed some light on the relative importance of the structural versus the behavioural and policy factors in explaining the observed price disparities.

The results of this analysis are that:

(a) Objective factors, such as structural factors hindering the arbitraging process or leading to a competitive process based more on quality than on price, do explain a significant part of the variation in price disparity in the EU-9 across product categories, particularly for products/services intensive in R&D and advertising.

(b) In homogeneous products markets, where competition is based solely on prices, and in horizontally differentiated products markets, where competition is based both on price and on product diversity, the inception of the SMP has generally led to increased price convergence. Where increased convergence has not been observed, as in many clothing and footwear categories and for products of boilermaking, this can be associated either to remaining policy barriers (harmonization of standards not achieved, insufficient mutual recognition or incorrect interpretation of standards and norms), or to behavioural/structural factors related to the organization of distribution. In the textiles and clothing markets, for example, differences in the organization of distribution across Member States are likely to explain the remaining high price disparities.

(c) The situation is even more complex for vertically differentiated products/services. In particular, in markets intensive in both research and advertising, price disparities are relatively high and stable over time, confirming the theoretical analysis according to which vertical differentiation and barriers to entry based on high levels of endogenous costs effectively hinder the arbitrage process. Examples of vertically differentiated markets intensive in both research and advertising are heavy household appliances, televisions, electronic equipment or optical instruments and photographic material. In these markets, the econometric analysis shows that the rate of extra-EU import penetration has a positive effect on price dispersion (higher rates of extra-EU trade penetration being associated with higher coefficients of price variation), indicating that imports in these markets are generally of an intra-firm type and do not increase the competitive pressure.

(d) On the contrary, vertically differentiated products markets that are intensive in research only show a low average price disparity, suggesting that huge investments in research and development not coupled with high advertising investments compel firms to adopt pan-European strategies. Examples of such markets are tyres, inner tubes and other replacement parts for motor vehicles, other modes of transport (bicycles and motorcycles) and computers, which are markets in which price disparities have been noted to be low – and, in the case of computers, these have been further reduced between 1985 and 1993.

(e) Finally, in vertically differentiated markets in which high advertising to sales ratios reflect companies' strategies to raise barriers to entry and to increase consumers' willingness to pay by shifting the emphasis of competition from price to quality, market fragmentation typically continues to exist, along with high price disparities even after the removal of non-tariff barriers. Examples of such markets are food products such as edible oils and confectionery, and beverages such as tea and alcohol. In these markets, however, higher rates of import penetration are associated with lower levels of price disparities. The high level of price disparities in these markets compared with other markets largely reflects consumer inertia created by brand loyalty based on high advertising expenditures. Where some convergence is nevertheless observed between 1990 and 1993, this suggests a switch to pan-European brands.

(f) Disparities in fiscal policies and in consumer preferences across countries were also found to have a significant positive impact on price disparity across the EU.

(g) As suggested above, a high degree of concentration in national markets tends to favour price disparity, whereas a high degree of internationalization of the market, either through import penetration or through the presence of multinational companies within national markets, tends to decrease price disparity.

(h) The existence of high or moderate non-tariff barriers (NTBs) also explains part of the observed price disparities.

(i) Where there are no non-tariff barriers or where these are ineffective, national structures (measured by high degree of concentration in national markets) and national regulations (in particular differences in taxation) lose their effectiveness. In markets with no NTBs, thus, behavioural and policy factors are less effective in keeping markets fragmented, and it is mainly structural factors which explain price disparities where these are still observed.

(j) The effects of the SMP have either not been strong enough or have been too concentrated over the later part of the period to have induced a major shift in the estimated parameters over the period considered.

(k) Overall, about 30% of the observed variance of the dependent variable (the coefficients of price variation include taxes in the EU-9) is explained by structural and quantifiable policy factors. The remainder is due to other factors, among which are behavioural responses of firms to the rise in competition in the market, or remaining policy barriers.

(l) Among the markets in which price dispersion is least explained by the set of explanatory variables used in the regression (mainly reflecting structural factors and fiscal policy) are:

(i) fresh and frozen fish,
(ii) other seafood,
(iii) books,
(iv) preserved milk,
(v) cocoa,
(vi) condiments and sauces,
(vii) mineral waters,
(viii) alcoholic beverages,
(ix) orthopaedic and therapeutic appliances and products.

Some of these are diversified products for which differences in product quality can explain price disparities. The different organization of distribution channels for these products across

Member States can also explain some of the resistance of prices to converge. In the case of books, however, a category for which rapid price convergence has been observed since 1985 at EU-9 level, the poor fit of the regression merely indicates that there are more than structural factors which account for the rapid convergence in prices after the inception of the SMP.

There are a number of factors which could not, however, be included in the regression, due to data availability problems. With the exception of transport costs, these are mainly behavioural and policy factors. Among the factors mentioned in the theoretical framework and in the case studies as having a potentially important impact on the price convergence patterns, the following ones could play a significant role in explaining observed price disparities: asymmetries between firms, mergers and acquisitions, the nature and evolution of the distribution structure and disparities in policy regulations.

Asymmetries between firms based on historical events (such as in the European carbonated beverages market) or on strategic behaviour (such as in the ready-to-eat cereals market) may prevent arbitraging from taking place. Strategic reactions, driven by the anticipation of the completion of the single market and leading to the consolidation of market structures through mergers and acquisitions and the dominance of the market by a few big players, could also decrease the ability for buyers to engage in arbitraging. Changes in the structure of distribution (mainly through the creation of buying networks at the EU level) could, on the other hand, increase the power of retailers and allow them profitably to engage in arbitraging. These factors could not be measured through the econometric analysis, due to the unavailability of data at the relevant level of detail.

The role of the case studies which were undertaken in the last part of the study was thus to analyse in more detail the specific factors which influenced the observed trends in price convergence in a number of representative markets. The results of the case studies suggest that there are still a number of policy factors which contribute to segmenting markets, either because of differences in the regulations (e.g. product definition in the mineral water market varies between countries) or because of different degrees of stringency in their application (e.g. environmental regulation). Further harmonization of EU regulations would hence reduce such segmentation and favour the pan-Europeanization of markets.

2. Objectives of the study

This report presents the results of the study by DRI, Professor E. de Ghellinck, and Horack, Adler & Associates aimed at assessing the extent to which the single market programme has resulted in the creation of pan-European markets through an analysis of price convergence patterns.

European integration has both direct and indirect effects on the economy. The direct effects are related to the reduction in costs resulting from the removal of barriers to trade of a resource-wasting nature, whereas the indirect effects are more dynamic in nature and are consequences both of the increase in competition that results from integration, and of a better exploitation of economies of scale thanks to the fact that companies have access to a larger market. As the European economies were already largely integrated when the single market programme (SMP) was launched, the indirect effects of the SMP were expected largely to exceed the direct effects.

The completion of the single European market was thus expected, via increased competition, to lead to major improvements in both economic efficiency, and hence in the long run in consumer welfare. The paragraph below taken from the European Commission report entitled 'The Economics of 1992' describes the mechanisms through which the benefits of the single market programme (SMP) were to materialize:

'The removal of barriers and the freedom of supply which businesses will enjoy as a result (of the Internal Market programme) should lead, through increased competitive pressure, to some downward convergence of prices of benefit to the customer. From the point of view of producers, the competitive pressure will be exerted first and foremost on price-cost margins, particularly in those sectors in which they held a certain monopoly power or position. Producers will also be induced – urged on by pressure on their margins – to become more efficient and thus cut their production and distribution costs. The increased pressure which will be brought to bear in this way on costs and price-cost margins will be a powerful means of causing prices to converge on levels more consistent with economic and technical efficiency'.[2]

This study analyses whether increased economic efficiency has been achieved following the launch of the SMP by evaluating the impact of the SMP on the fragmentation of geographic markets, i.e. on the extent to which the removal of non-tariff barriers between Member States has permitted enterprises to extend their activities to other markets. Here, pan-European markets are thus defined as markets in which there are no barriers preventing companies from operating freely across the broad geographic market – in other words, markets where arbitraging is not prevented by either firms or governments.

To assess the degree of pan-Europeanization of markets as a result of the SMP, the study also seeks to identify the extent to which, faced with increased competitive pressures, companies or governments have reacted with strategies or behaviours that slowed the integration process. One of the results of the study is thus a list of markets in which it is policy factors – more

[2] See European Commission [1988], 'The Economics of 1992', in *European Economy*, No 35, March 1988, Part D (The effects of market integration, p.118).

specifically, the persistence of non-tariff barriers – or behavioural factors which have prevented pan-European markets from emerging.

The analysis of the creation of pan-European markets was done in three stages. In the first stage, the analysis of price data provided by Eurostat for 174 goods and services categories allowed the identification of both price convergence patterns across different regional groupings throughout the EU (see below), and changes in the pattern of convergence over time following the inception of the SMP. Given that market prices for specific products or services are the central indicator studied, **markets** as opposed to **sectors** are the natural unit of analysis. In the second stage, the observed price convergence patterns were analysed and related specifically to the SMP by discussing (and testing econometrically) the extent to which the observed price convergence patterns reflect structural, behavioural or policy factors. The third stage involved undertaking a number of case studies to better illustrate the factors influencing price convergence or divergence in specific market segments.

The first part of the study, the results of which are presented in Chapters 3 to 5, thus seeks to investigate:

(a) whether there has been some convergence in prices following the launch of the single market programme;

(b) whether convergence has been more pronounced in certain regions of the EU than in others – for instance, whether there is a North/South divide whereby the core EU-6 (or EU-9) Member States would have experienced a greater convergence of their prices towards the EU average than the EU-12 or the EU-15;[3]

(c) which product/service categories have price dispersion which is significantly higher (lower) than average;

(d) which product/service categories have seen the greatest convergence in prices over the past 10–15 years (traded goods? public procurement or formally regulated markets? consumer goods? equipment goods?); and among these, which are the categories for which there has been a change in trend following the launch of the single market programme;

(e) whether the price convergence and price divergence patterns that are observed are statistically significant;

(f) to what extent the convergence (or divergence) of prices across Member States reflects changes in indirect tax rates, as opposed to fundamental changes in underlying prices net of taxes;

(g) whether the observed price convergence patterns reflect or have been influenced by developments on the exchange rate front;

(h) whether there are groups of countries with significantly similar/dissimilar price structures, and whether within these groups of countries prices have evolved in a consistent way over time.

[3] For a detailed description of the four country groupings used in this study (EU-6, EU-9, EU-12 and EU-15), see box on data sources and methodology in Section 3.2.1.

Price convergence is, however, neither an end in itself nor a perfect indicator of the degree to which the SMP has achieved the desired objectives. Price convergence is not an end in itself because the existence of price disparities across different geographic markets is only a source of concern if it reflects market distortions or barriers to the arbitrage process. It is also not a perfect indicator of the degree to which the SMP has achieved the desired objective because price convergence is neither a necessary nor a sufficient condition for demand to be transferred across markets, hence leading to a pan-Europeanization of markets. Price convergence is not a **sufficient** condition for a market to be pan-European as uniformity of prices could result from a cooperation between firms: cartels or non-discriminating monopolies can indeed impose similar prices across different (fragmented) markets. Price convergence is also not a **necessary** condition as price convergence across EU countries occurs only where the 'law of one price' applies, i.e. when consumers are both willing and able to transfer their demand between suppliers from different countries. The willingness to engage in arbitraging, however, depends on the importance of price (as opposed to, say, quality) as a choice variable, whilst the ability to engage in arbitraging is a function of the cost of arbitraging and of the existence of regulatory barriers. Price disparity in a pan-European market will hence be observed either when consumers do not consider foreign production as a perfect substitute for domestic production, or when consumers are not able to engage in arbitraging. In both cases, structural, behavioural and policy factors can explain why arbitraging is not 'searched for' or not feasible.

The second part of the study (the results of which are presented in Chapters 6 through 8) thus starts by describing the link between the creation of pan-European markets and price convergence, and discussing the expected theoretical impact on prices of increased integration according to different characteristics of the markets considered. This analysis enables the identification of the markets in which price convergence was expected to be observed following the inception of the SMP, as well as those markets in which structural factors will explain the persistence of price disparities across the EU.

The analysis is then further deepened by trying to identify the relative contribution of three different types of factors – structural, behavioural and policy factors – in explaining the observed price disparities. Disparity in the pattern of preferences across countries (presence of strong national biases), vertical differentiation and market segmentation, for example, are structural factors explaining low cross-price elasticities of demand between foreign and domestic production, hence the absence of the arbitraging process. These structural factors can be reinforced by specific **behaviour of firms** and/or **policies** adopted by governments to favour national production or producers. Huge advertising campaigns by national producers, for example, or the adoption of national standards increase the costs faced by consumers when switching their demand to foreign producers. High transport costs relative to the value of the product can also decrease the size of the geographic market in which buyers search for the lowest price, hence favour a natural geographic segmentation of the market. Control of the distribution system by the sellers is yet another factor which may prevent buyers from engaging in arbitraging.

The aim of the research undertaken in the second part of the study is thus to distinguish, among the factors explaining the observed price disparities, between 'objective' factors which may be present even in markets that are pan-European, and factors reflecting barriers to the arbitraging process, which have to be removed for pan-Europeanization to materialize.

Markets characterized by those 'objective' factors will show some disparity in prices even when the single market is fully realized, whilst markets characterized by factors hindering the arbitraging process still have a potential for price convergence and increased economic efficiency.

To do this, the second part of the study:

(a) establishes the link between pan-European markets and price convergence;

(b) describes the theoretical impact of integration on prices in markets that are structurally different (i.e. which are characterized by different degrees of concentration, levels of sunk costs, degree of product differentiation, etc.);

(c) econometrically tests the relative contribution of different factors in explaining the observed convergence pattern;

(d) identifies those markets which effectively seem to have become more 'pan-European' (i.e. for which fragmentation into national markets has been reduced, permitting enterprises to extend their activities to other markets); and,

(e) among those markets in which the theoretical effects of integration on prices do not seem to have materialized, assesses whether this is due to behavioural factors (i.e. reflects the strategic responses of firms to the changes in the competitive environment – strategic responses that may in some ways have run counter to the SMP philosophy and slowed the integration process) or whether the factors underlying the observed pattern of convergence are policy factors (market deregulation being the most obvious example of a factor pushing for increased price convergence, whereas different national systems for health care clearly represent barriers to price convergence in the health services sector).

The last part of the study (Chapters 9 through 13) presents the results of four case studies designed to provide additional information on the factors underlying price convergence or divergence in four markets: soft drinks and mineral water, white goods, chocolate confectionery and construction. The case studies analyse, in each of the four markets, the extent to which the companies in these markets have become more pan-European, and the extent to which they have adopted strategies that hindered market integration. The case studies also identify the remaining barriers to pan-Europeanization in each of these particular markets, and include a discussion of the extent to which these barriers reflect structural characteristics of the market (such as differences in consumer preferences across the EU), behavioural factors (for instance, the fact that companies would adopt market segmenting strategies to differentiate themselves from competition) or policy factors (such as insufficient harmonization or implementation problems). In many ways, the case studies confirm and validate the theoretical framework presented in Chapter 6.

The remainder of this report is organized as follows: Chapter 3 describes the past trends in price convergence across regions (EU-6, EU-9, EU-12 and EU-15) for five broad product services categories (consumer goods, equipment goods, energy, construction and services) as well as for selected consumer goods categories. Chapter 3 also discusses the role of indirect taxation in influencing price convergence, and identifies the extent to which:

(a) indirect taxes (VAT and excise duties) are responsible for price differences across Member States;

(b) price convergence patterns have been influenced by the various changes in indirect tax rates that have taken place following the inception of the SMP.

Chapter 3 finally discusses the significance of high coefficients of price variation across the EU, based on a comparison of our results with those of other studies analysing price disparities across regions within the same national market.

Chapter 4 then presents the detailed trends in price convergence over time, for close to 200 goods and services categories and tests the statistical significance of the observed trends in price disparities.

In Chapter 5, we test the stability of price differentials across countries over time, and identify those groupings of countries in which prices have tended to behave in a similar way as a result of integration. Chapter 5 also discusses the possible role of exchange rate variations in influencing the observed price convergence patterns.

Chapter 6 establishes the link between pan-European markets and price convergence by discussing the theoretical impact of increased economic integration on prices in different markets. As shown in this chapter, the theoretical impact varies based on a certain set of criteria characterizing these markets in such a way that increased economic integration is not necessarily conducive to price convergence. The criteria have been classified as structural, behavioural or policy factors limiting convergence.

Chapter 7 then presents a descriptive analysis of the main factors which influenced the observed trends in prices across the EU following the inception of the SMP, by comparing the trend in price disparities for different categories of products, such as traded/non-traded products and services, products characterized by high non-tariff barriers at the start of the period, or products/services with a high import penetration rate (both intra and extra-EU import penetration rates).

In Chapter 8, a more rigorous analysis of the factors explaining the observed trends in prices is undertaken: an econometric model has been tested in order to assess the relative influence of a number of explanatory variables which reflect structural market characteristics, behavioural patterns or policy variables; and presents some conclusions.

Chapters 9 through 13 present detailed case studies for four market segments (soft drinks and mineral water, white goods, chocolate confectionery and construction) and consider the extent to which the companies in these sectors have become more pan-European, and the extent to which they have adopted strategies that hindered market integration. These case studies also identify the remaining barriers to pan-Europeanization in each of these markets, and discuss the extent to which these barriers reflect structural characteristics of the market (such as differences in consumer preferences across the EU), behavioural factors (for instance, the fact that companies would adopt market segmenting strategies to differentiate themselves from competition) or policy factors (such as insufficient harmonization or implementation problems).

Additional information on the data used, the methodology and detailed results is presented in the Appendices at the end of the report.

3. Price convergence patterns by broad products/services categories

3.1. Key results

The analysis of the observed trends in price dispersion in the EU shows that:

(a) There has been a general trend towards price convergence in the EU-12 over the period 1980–93. The tendency has been more pronounced for consumer and equipment goods, and less for energy, services and construction.

(b) For energy and construction, price dispersion has increased over time in the EU-12, and more so after 1985 than over the period 1980–85.

(c) The convergence in consumer products and services prices in the EU-12 has tended to accelerate following the launch of the SMP.

(d) The tendency for prices to converge has been comparatively greater in the three Member States which joined the EU in 1989 (Greece, Portugal and Spain) than in the EU-9; this may reflect a 'catch-up' effect of integration; the same holds for the EU-15, even though the three newer Member States only joined the EU in 1995.

(e) In the EU-15, price disparities in 1993 are not significantly greater than in the EU-12, except for food, beverages, clothing and footwear. This mainly reflects differences in the regulatory environments for these products in Austria, Finland and Sweden.

(f) Overall, neither the different levels of nor the changes in VAT rates seem to have distorted general price trends (i.e. there is no significant difference in general price convergence trends including or excluding VAT).

(g) Excise taxes have, however, played an important role in some categories (notably energy products, alcoholic beverages and tobacco products) increasing price disparities compared to prices net of taxes.

(h) The observed price disparities across Member States are significantly higher than those observed at regional level within a country.

3.2. Trends in price dispersion across regions

3.2.1. Trends for broad products and services categories

This section analyses the trend in price convergence across regions for prices inclusive of all indirect taxes (VAT plus excise duties). The analysis of the specific impact on price convergence of the changes in indirect tax rates which have been implemented over the period 1980–93 is presented in Section 3.4.

The average price dispersion indices in each of the 15 EU Member States are shown graphically in Figures 3.2.1 to 3.2.5 for five broad products or services categories. These price indices are provided by Eurostat and consist of national price indices as compared to the

EU-12 average, and not price levels. The five categories are consumer goods, services, energy, equipment goods and construction.

DATA SOURCES AND METHODOLOGY

The analysis of the price convergence across regions and over time which is presented in Chapters 3 and 4 is done at a detailed level for 174 goods and services categories, using price dispersion indices provided by Eurostat. The database supplied to DRI covers the 15 EU Member States, for the years 1980, 1985, 1990 and 1993 (Sweden and Finland are not included in the price database in 1980).

Among the 174 goods and services categories are:

consumer goods, of which there are:
- 51 food and drink products,
- 2 tobacco products,
- 8 clothing and footwear products,
- 24 durable goods,
- 18 other manufactured goods;

services;
energy products;
equipment goods;
construction.

Eurostat has devised a method to ensure the greatest degree of comparability between these categories across countries. In the case of consumer goods, the headings represent the different categories of final consumption of households by function. As for equipment goods, the headings are based on a classification by type of product which refers to the technical characteristics of products. Additional information on the database and the way price indices are constructed by Eurostat is provided in Appendix A.

Two important features of the price indices supplied by Eurostat must be underlined:

(a) The series consist of national price indices as compared to the EU-12 average, and not price levels. Detailed price levels could not be made available to DRI for confidentiality reasons. For each Member State, each product/service and each year considered, the price index is calculated in such a way as to be equal to 100 if the observed price is equal to the EU-12 average. This means that **it is possible to compare changes in price dispersion between years** but **it is impossible to compare changes in price levels over time** (in other words, it is possible to say whether prices have converged over time but impossible to say whether they have converged towards a higher or a lower average level). DRI did not receive the weights which were used to calculate the average EU-12 price for each product category.

(b) The indices are based on prices inclusive of taxes (both VAT and excise duties) for consumption goods and services and net of deductible VAT in the case of equipment goods and construction. For consumer goods, DRI calculated price indices net of taxes using a special procedure which is outlined in Appendix B. Given that the integration of European economies translated into both the removal of trade and competition hindering barriers and the harmonization of indirect taxation, dispersion in prices inclusive of taxes as well as in prices net of taxes are worth investigating.

The analysis of the trend in price disparities per category of products/services after 1980 has been done over four geographical regions, reflecting the different stages of EU integration. The first region considered is the EU-6, consisting of the six founding EU members. Another region is then defined with the following three entrants (Denmark, Ireland and the UK), called EU-9. For both the EU-6 and the EU-9, price dispersion coefficients, defined as the standard deviation of prices divided by the region's average, were calculated using final prices (including all indirect taxes) and prices net of VAT (as well as prices net of VAT and excise duties for certain products) for each of the years 1980, 1985, 1990 and 1993. A third region is then considered, consisting of the EU-12 (i.e. the EU-9 plus Spain, Portugal and Greece), for which the price dispersion coefficients based on price data net of VAT were calculated for 1990 and 1993 only, as none of these countries had fully adopted a VAT system by 1985. The fourth region covers the EU-15, i.e. the EU-12 plus the three Member States which joined the EU on 1 January 1995: Sweden, Finland and Austria. The coefficients of price variation for the EU-15 were calculated using prices including taxes for 1985, 1990 and 1993 and prices excluding VAT for 1990 and 1993. They were calculated to serve as a reference and to provide information on the degree to which increased European integration has also led to a greater convergence of these countries' prices towards the EU average.

Figure 3.2.1. Consumer goods – average price dispersion indices by country, 1993

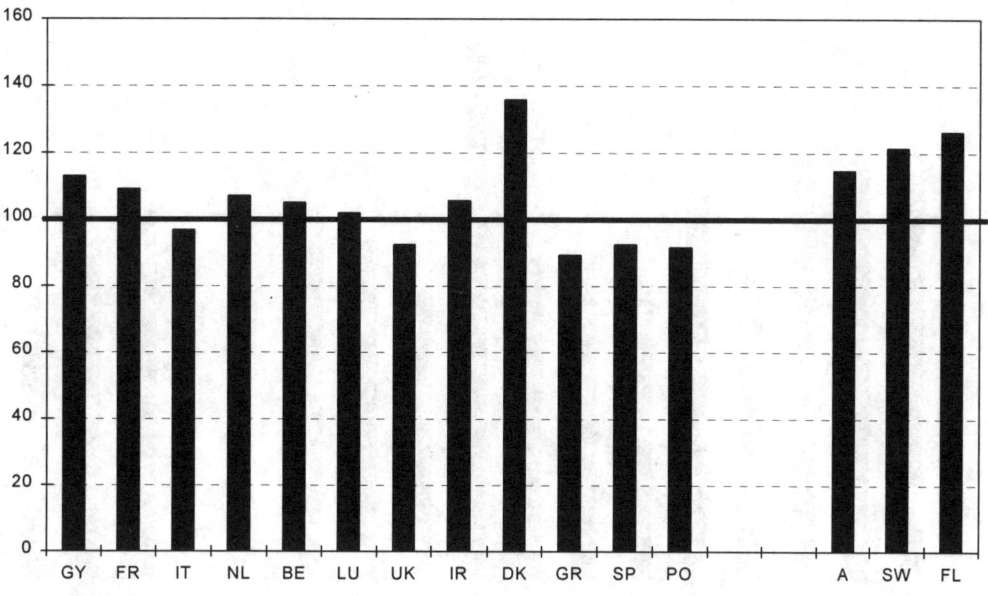

Source: DRI.

Figure 3.2.2. Services – average price dispersion indices by country, 1993

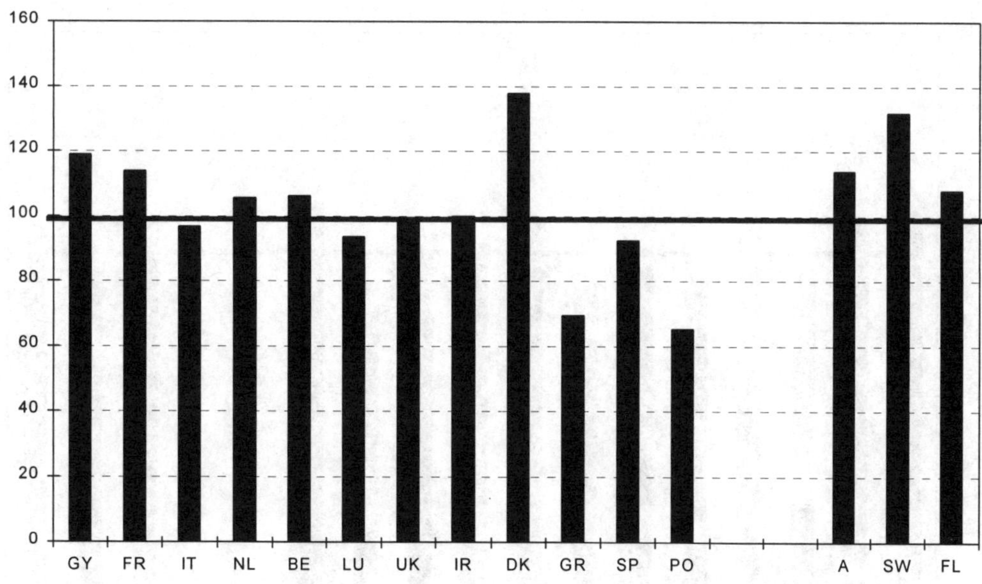

Source: DRI.

Figure 3.2.3. Energy – average price dispersion indices by country, 1993

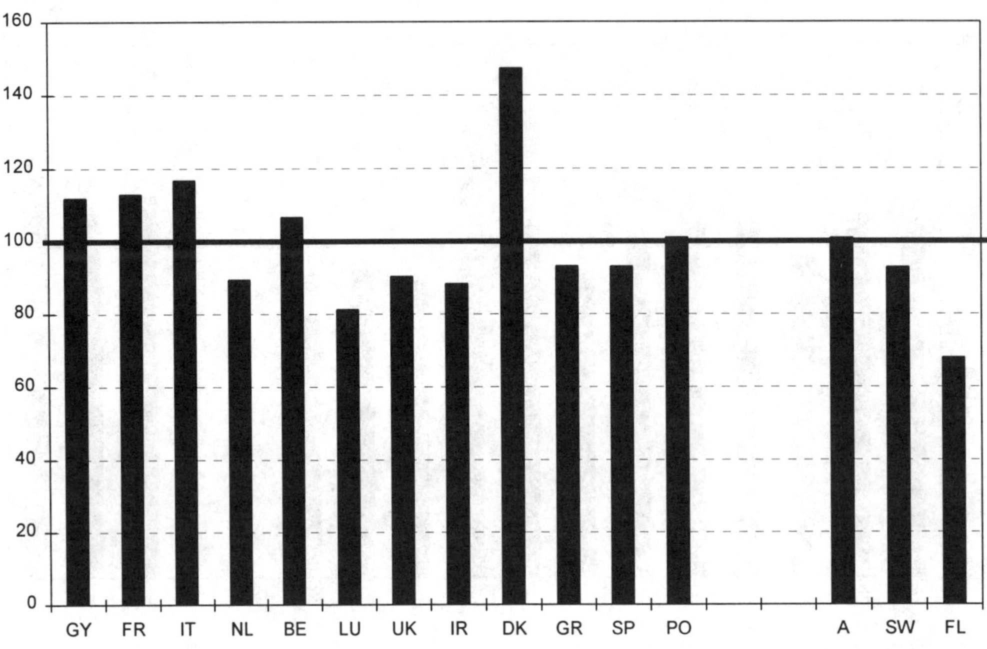

Source: DRI.

Figure 3.2.4. Equipment goods – average price dispersion indices by country, 1993

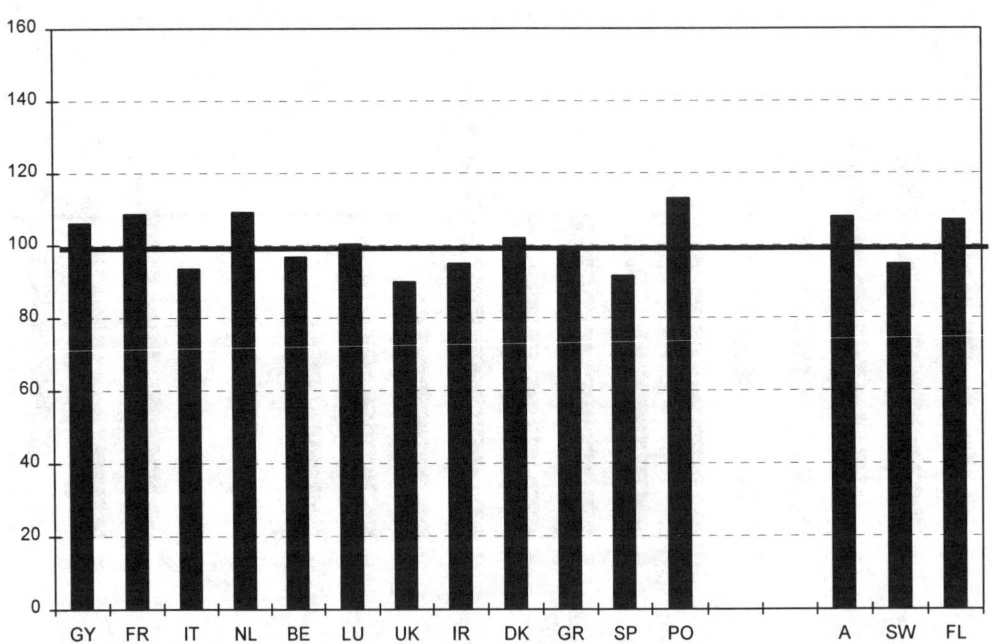

Source: DRI.

Figure 3.2.5. Construction – average price dispersion indices by country, 1993

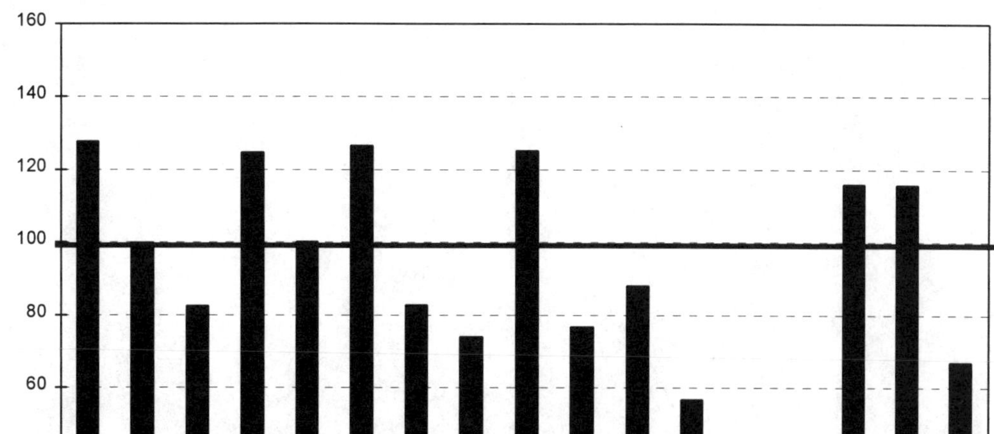

Source: DRI.

The figures reveal that price indices are generally highest in Denmark and lowest in Greece and Portugal. Price indices are visibly higher for services and construction, and lower for equipment goods, a highly traded product category. Even at this aggregate level, however, one finds that the country with the highest and lowest price respectively varies across product categories.

Whereas Portugal for instance is within 10% of the average EU price level for consumer goods, the price of services in Portugal is about 30% lower than the EU-12 average, and that of equipment goods is about 20% higher than the EU-12 average. The United Kingdom, which is one of the countries where energy and construction are cheapest, has price indices close to average for consumer goods and for services.

Figures 3.2.6 to 3.2.8 compare the coefficients of price variation for the five broad products and services categories. The graphs show the coefficient of variation of prices in the EU-6, EU-9, EU-12 and EU-15 in 1980, 1985 and 1993 respectively.[4] Both in 1980 and in 1993, one finds that the coefficient of price variation of the services, energy and, to a lesser extent, construction categories in the EU-12 is higher than that for consumer or equipment goods. For services and construction, this partly reflects the fact that these goods/services are less traded, whereas for energy the high coefficient of variation mainly reflects different pricing regulations and, as we will see in Section 3.4, differences in indirect taxation across Member States.

[4] Price data for Sweden and Finland are only available for 1985, 1990 and 1993.

Figure 3.2.6. Measures of price dispersion for selected categories 1980, prices including taxes

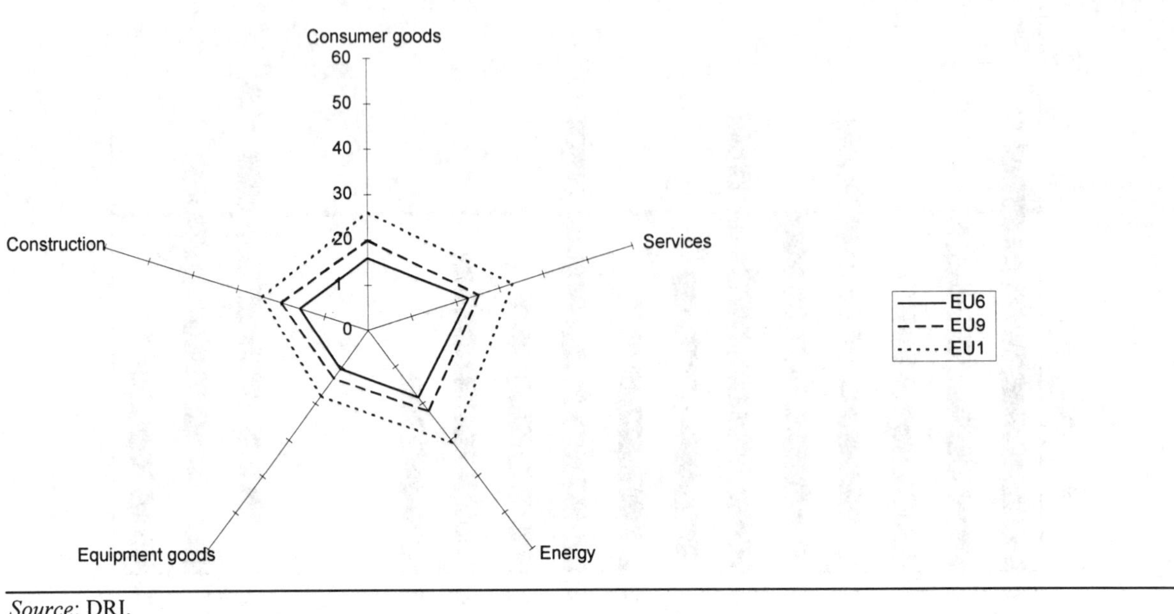

Source: DRI.

Figure 3.2.7. Measures of price dispersion for selected categories 1985, prices including taxes

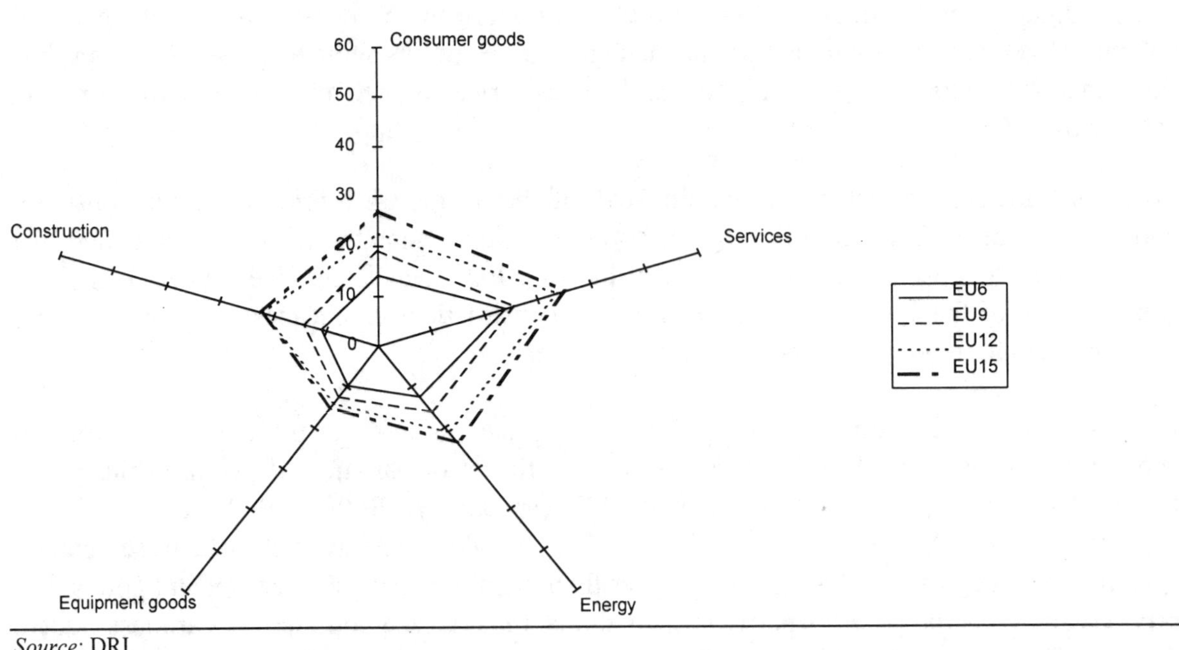

Source: DRI.

Figure 3.2.8. Measures of price dispersion for selected categories 1993, prices including taxes

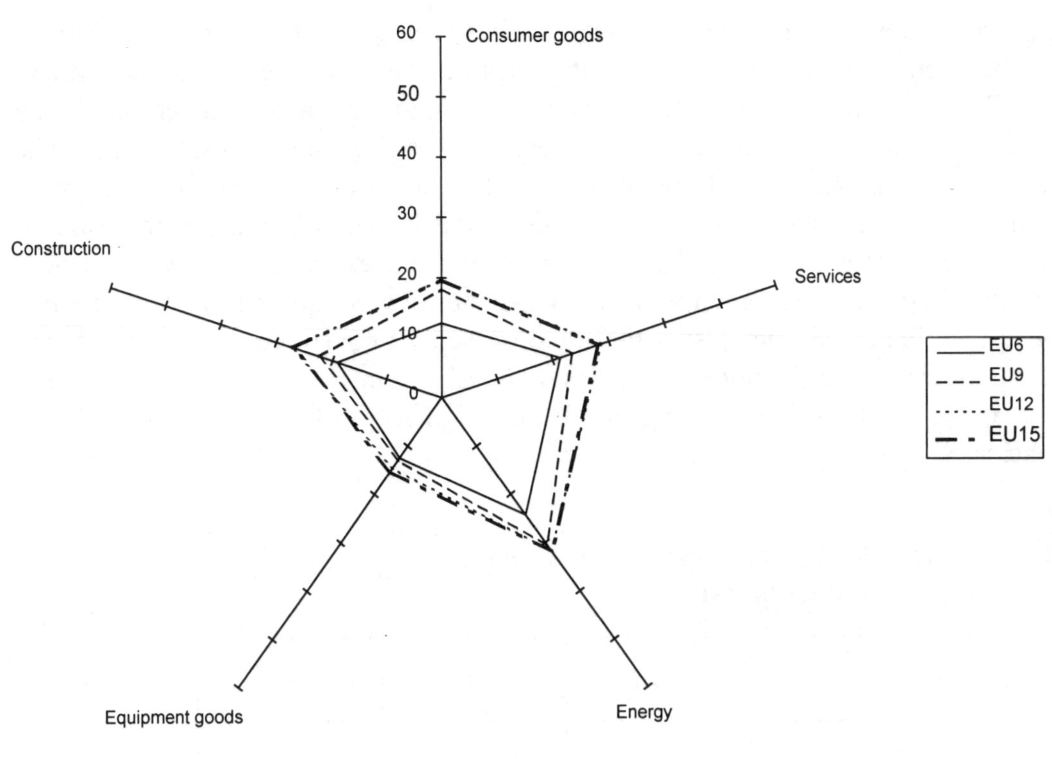

Source: DRI.

Comparing the levels of price dispersion in the EU-6, EU-9 and EU-12 in both 1980 and 1993, one also finds that price disparities increase as more Member States are taken into consideration, along a pattern which largely mirrors the different stages of EU integration: the coefficient of price variation for the six founding EU countries is systematically lower than that for the nine EU Member States (including Denmark, Ireland and the UK), and the latter is in turn lower than that for the EU-12 and the EU-15. The fact that the coefficient of variation for the EU-9 for most non-traded goods categories is significantly higher than in the EU-6 is explained by the fact that prices in Denmark are generally well above the EU average, whereas in the UK, another country in the EU-9 grouping which was not in the EU-6 category, prices are generally well below the EU-12 average.

The inclusion of the three subsequent EU members, Greece, Spain and Portugal, further increases price disparities as these three countries have price levels that are more concentrated towards the lower end of the price range.

The inclusion of the three latest EU Member States (Finland, Sweden and Austria) further raises the coefficient of variation for the less traded product categories, but less so for consumer and equipment goods, sectors for which markets were already well integrated at the European (and global) level at the start of the period (Figures 3.2.7 and 3.2.8).

Interestingly, although in 1980 the differences in the coefficients of variation of the EU-6, EU-9 and EU-12 are similar for all product categories (with the exception of services – see Figure 3.2.6), this is no longer the case in 1985 or 1993 (Figures 3.2.7 and 3.2.8). This reflects the fact that the integration of European markets – which proceeded at different rates for different categories of products and services – has affected the trend in prices over time in different ways.

Comparing Figures 3.2.6 and 3.2.8 indicates that there has been a reduction in price disparities in the EU-12 between 1980 and 1993 for all categories of products except construction and energy. In 1993, price dispersion in the EU-12 is still very high (and much higher than in the EU-6) for energy products and, to a lesser extent, for services and construction. The comparison of the two graphs also shows that the reduction in price dispersion was more pronounced in the EU-12 than in either the EU-6 or the EU-9, indicating some kind of 'catching-up' effect of the prices of the three newer Member States. In the EU-15 also, prices have tended towards greater convergence for the consumer and equipment goods categories and for services, but increased price disparities are observed for construction. It is interesting to see that for most categories the price disparities in the EU-15 in 1993 are of the same order of magnitude as for the EU-12, indicating an already high level of integration of markets before membership.

Table 3.2.1. Coefficients of price variation for selected groupings (prices including taxes)

	1980	1985	1990	1993
EU-6				
Consumer goods	15.9	14.2	13.5	12.4
Services	22.7	23.9	20.0	21.3
Energy	18.4	12.5	19.4	24.3
Equipment goods	10.5	9.7	11.6	12.5
Construction	15.7	11.0	14.0	19.1
EU-9				
Consumer goods	19.9	19.1	20.3	18.0
Services	25.2	25.6	24.6	23.4
Energy	22.1	16.1	24.7	30.6
Equipment goods	13.1	12.5	12.2	12.9
Construction	20.1	14.4	16.5	22.4
EU-12				
Consumer goods	26.0	22.5	22.8	19.6
Services	33.0	33.7	31.8	28.6
Energy	30.8	21.1	28.0	31.7
Equipment goods	18.0	14.0	13.1	14.5
Construction	24.4	22.1	23.5	27.4
EU-15				
Consumer goods	..	27.0	25.9	19.6
Services	..	35.2	35.9	28.1
Energy	..	23.7	27.5	31.9
Equipment goods	..	15.0	14.2	15.3
Construction	..	22.4	23.5	27.0

Source: DRI.

In all four regional aggregates, the reduction over time in price disparities was most pronounced for consumer goods. For equipment goods, the coefficient of price variation in the EU-12 in 1993 was lower than in 1980, but among the EU-6 countries there has been an increase in price dispersion which brought all three regional coefficients of variation to the same level in 1993 (Table 3.2.1).

In the EU-15, where price disparities were notably larger than in the EU-12 up to 1990, there has also been a strong trend towards convergence after 1990 for consumer goods and services, partly due to changes in indirect taxation and partly to changes in the regulatory environment to prepare these economies for membership, or at least benefit from the effects of increased integration within the EU-12 (changes in agricultural policy regimes, among others).

For equipment goods, a highly traded product category, price disparities between the three newer Member States and the EU-12 were already low in 1990, and have increased slightly, albeit not significantly, between 1990 and 1993, in line with the trend in the three other regions.

3.2.2. Energy

Figures 3.2.6 to 3.2.8 showed that price disparities for energy products in the EU-12 were amongst the highest of all product/services categories in both 1980 and 1993. Figure 3.2.9 compares the average energy price indices across countries in 1985 and 1993, with EU-12 = 100 in both cases. Between 1985 and 1993, price disparities in the EU-12 and in the EU-15 have increased, as confirmed in Table 3.2.1. By 1993, the average energy price in Denmark had risen well above the EU average – whereas in Luxembourg the energy price was nearly 20% below the EU-12 average, less than in Greece and Spain.

Figure 3.2.9. Comparison of average price dispersion indices for energy, 1985 and 1993

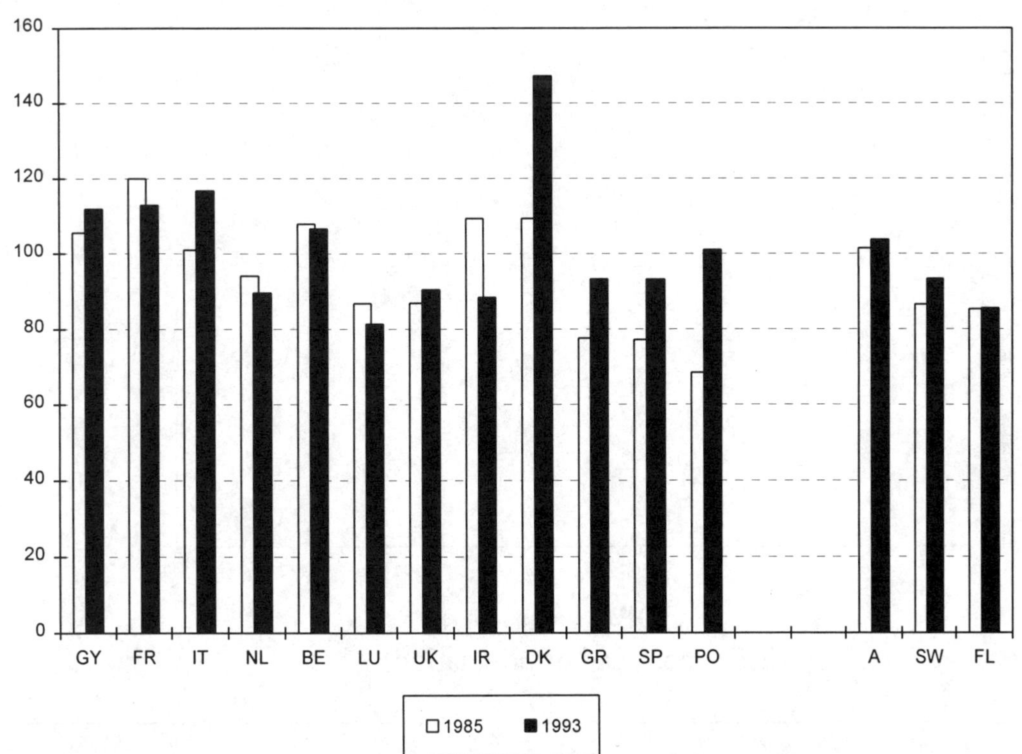

Source: DRI.

Table 3.2.1 reports that the coefficient of variation of prices for energy products decreased between 1980 and 1985 in the three first regions, but resumed an upward trend thereafter, rising well above the 1980 level in both the EU-6 and the EU-9. In the EU-15 also, price disparities for energy increased between 1985 and 1990. This reflects the fact that the fall in energy prices in 1986 was passed on to final consumer prices in different ways in different EU Member States; the fact that energy markets are not yet fully liberalized; and the existence of different levels of indirect taxation, as will be seen in Section 3.4.

3.2.3. Services

For services, there has been some convergence both of EU-12 price levels towards the EU-9 level, and of EU-9 price levels towards the EU-6 price level over the period 1980–93, but the convergence has been slow compared to that for consumer goods (Figures 3.2.6 to 3.2.8).

In the EU-15, the coefficient of variation of services prices remained stable between 1985 and 1990, indicating no trend towards integration, contrary to what happened within the EU-12. There was, however, a 'catch-up' effect after 1990, with the price disparities in the EU-15 falling to the level of the EU-12.

Figure 3.2.10. Relationship between average services prices and GDP per capita in the EU-12

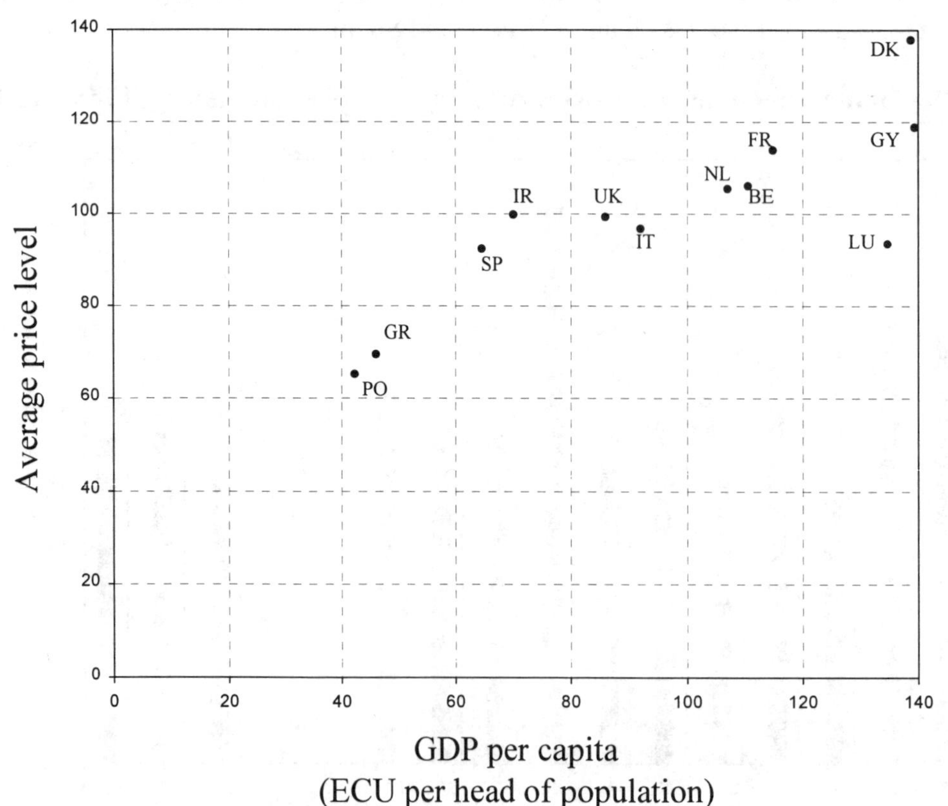

Source: DRI.

As illustrated in Figure 3.2.10, price levels in the services sectors are strongly correlated with GDP per capita, so that the convergence of service prices across the EU-12 is likely to have been slowed by persisting differences in GDP per capita across Member States.

Services are, indeed, markets in which there are important structural barriers to arbitrage. Chapters 6 through 8, however, demonstrate that there are also other factors explaining the high price dispersion for services, and that there are service categories for which the high level of price disparities observed here does reflect economic inefficiencies.

3.2.4. Equipment goods

The equipment goods category is one characterized by low price disparities across regional aggregates, largely reflecting the highly traded nature of this product category. Whereas in the EU-9, EU-12 and EU-15 the average coefficient of price variation for equipment goods ranges from 13 to 15 and has remained stable between 1985 and 1993, in the EU-6 the average level of price dispersion has tended to increase over time – possibly reflecting increased product/equipment diversity.

3.2.5. Construction

The trend in price disparities over time in the construction sector is similar in all four country groupings. During the first part of the 1980s construction prices tended to converge, but between 1985 and 1993 these prices have tended to diverge. This evolution of price disparities is somewhat surprising as the increased mobility of workers should have increased convergence of construction costs. The increase of price disparities noted between 1985 and 1993 is particularly significant among the core EU-6 countries: whereas the coefficient of variation of construction prices increased by 20.5% in the EU-15 (24% in the EU-12), it increased by 73.6% in the EU-6, from 11.0 to 19.1. Price disparities across the different regional groupings increased between the EU-6 and the EU-9, and more significantly between the EU-9 and the EU-12. However, they remained stable between the EU-12 and the EU-15, reflecting a convergence of EU-15 price levels towards the EU-12 price level.

Price data for construction are, however, not necessarily strictly comparable across countries, as there can be differences in the types of construction or materials used in different regions which make it difficult to ensure that the price data are really reliable and comparable across different geographic dimensions. Moreover, construction is essentially a ‘service’ activity which is local in nature and thus not influenced by (or responsive to) the same forces as the manufactured goods sectors. The choice of construction for one of the case studies (see Chapter 12) was thus motivated in part by the observation that price dispersion variation seems to have increased between 1985 and 1993 (contrary to what is observed in other markets and despite efforts to further integrate the EU market by liberalizing public procurement and harmonizing social regulations to some extent), and in part by the desire to check the validity of the information conveyed by the Eurostat price data through other sources.

The construction case study which is presented in Chapter 12 confirms the fact that the price developments as given by Eurostat are representative of underlying trends in construction markets across the EU. The case study indeed reports a number of factors explaining persisting price disparities in this sector, among which are differences in building efficiency and in management efficiency across countries (efficiency of design, clarity of instructions, buildability, use of plant and industrialized methods). Other factors limiting price convergence are (often structural) barriers to trade in raw materials, and the mainly local nature of the business which implies that the Public Works Directive[5] has only had a limited impact on prices across markets.

3.2.6. Consumer goods

This section looks at the trend in prices for selected consumer products in more detail, breaking down the 'consumer goods' category into food, beverages, tobacco, clothing and footwear, durable consumer goods and other manufactured products. Figures 3.2.11 to 3.2.13 compare the coefficient of variation of prices inclusive of taxes in 1980, 1985 and 1993 respectively, again in the four regional aggregates.

Figure 3.2.11. Measures of price dispersion for consumer goods 1980, prices including taxes

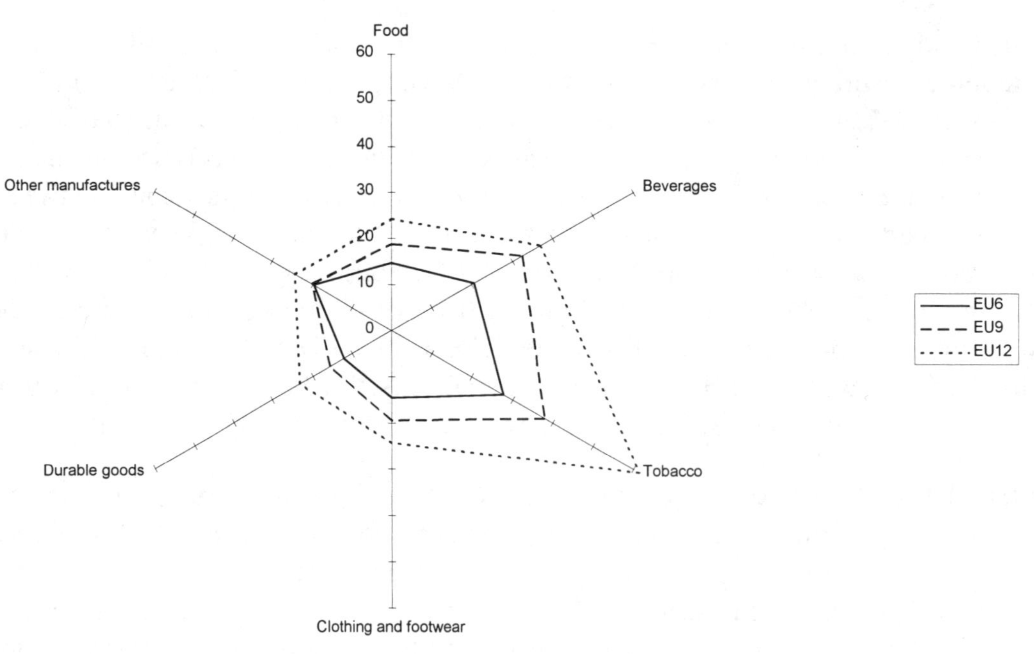

Source: DRI.

[5] Council Directive 93/37/EEC of 14 June 1993 concerning the co-ordination of procedures for the award of public works contracts (OJ L 199, 9.8.1993, p. 54).

Figure 3.2.12. Measures of price dispersion for consumer goods 1985, prices including taxes

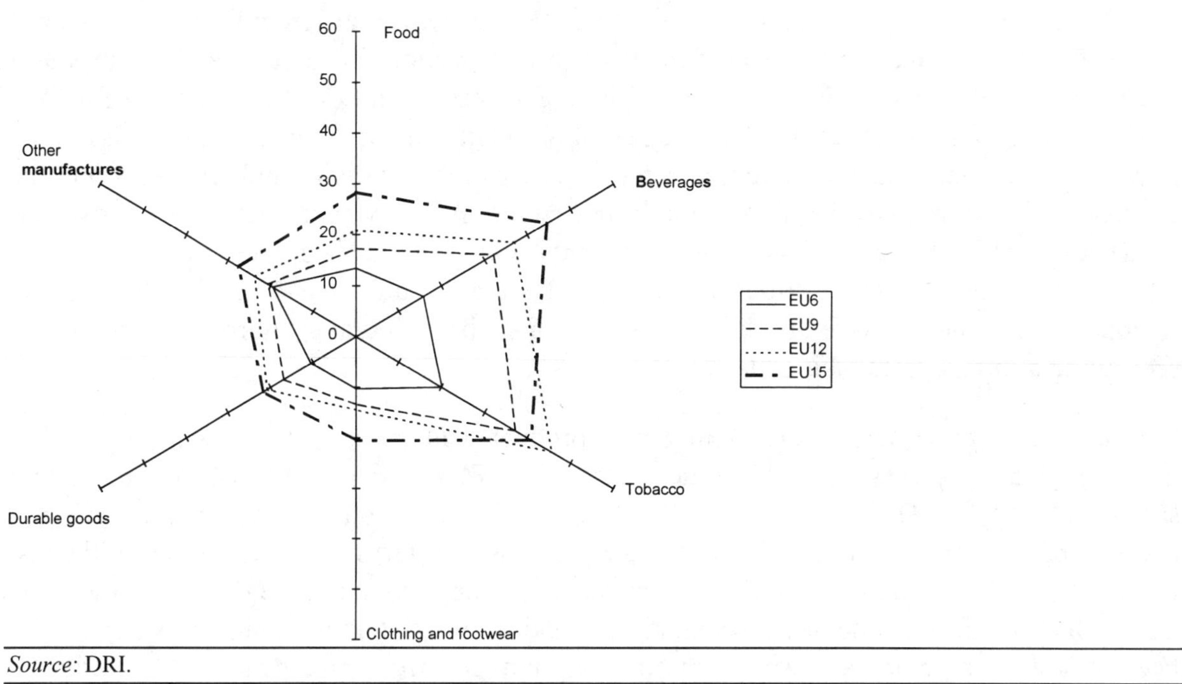

Source: DRI.

Figure 3.2.13. Measures of price dispersion for consumer goods 1993, prices including taxes

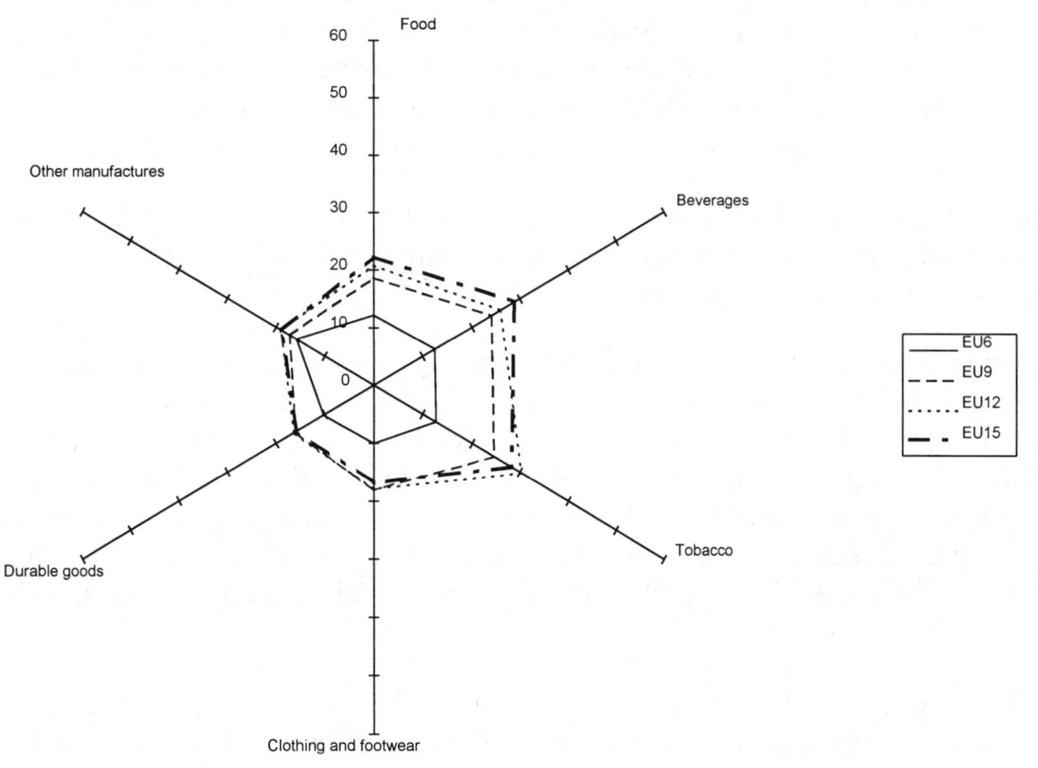

Source: DRI.

Looking at the price dispersion pattern in 1980, one finds a very high coefficient of variation for tobacco products in the EU-6, EU-9 and EU-12, followed by beverages (for the EU-9 and EU-12) and, particularly in the EU-6, by 'other manufactures'. This essentially still holds true in 1985. In the EU-15, the structure of prices in 1985 is, however, different from that observed in the EU-12, with much higher coefficients of price variation for beverages, food products and clothing and footwear (Figure 3.2.12). The higher coefficient of price variation for food products in the EU-15 reflects the high degree of protection against import competition in the three newer Member States, whereas that for beverages reflects higher indirect taxes and the existence of state monopolies for alcoholic beverages. As shown in Section 3.4, however, where the coefficients of variation for prices with and without VAT and excise duties are compared, the high price disparities for alcoholic beverages in the EU-15 also reflect market segmentation strategies of the key producers, i.e. behavioural patterns of companies preventing arbitrage from taking place.

For the durable goods and other manufactured products categories, both of which are highly traded product categories, price disparities between the EU-15 and the EU-12 were much less significant in 1985. The same does not hold for textiles and clothing. In 1985, the price of textiles and clothing products in Sweden and Finland was in fact much higher than in the rest of the EU. By 1993, price disparities for this product category had come down significantly. This reflects the fact that neither Sweden nor Finland are major textile producers, so they have been somewhat more liberal towards imports from non-EU origin than the EU-12 countries.

By 1993, price disparities in the EU-12 were reduced in most of the consumer goods categories – most notably for tobacco products and for beverages – but had not changed significantly for 'other manufactured goods', a category for which the price dispersion was already low at the start of the period. This reflects the highly traded nature of this product category. Another highly traded product category with low price dispersion at the start of the period is the durable goods category, which includes miscellaneous household items such as personal care products, books, brochures and printed material, tyres and replacement parts for motor vehicles, pharmaceutical products and other miscellaneous products (see Appendix F).

The most notable change in price dispersion between 1980 and 1993 in the EU-12 has taken place in the tobacco and beverages categories, both of which had a particularly high price dispersion at the beginning of the period.

In terms of convergence across regional groupings, this has been most notable again for beverages and for tobacco products (Figures 3.2.11 to 3.2.13). Generally speaking, the convergence of EU-12 prices towards the EU-9 has been faster than between the EU-9 and the EU-6, indicating price rigidities in the UK, Denmark and Ireland which prevented the adjustment of prices towards the EU-6 price range from taking place as quickly as for the three other EU members. The more detailed analysis of price dispersion indices in Chapter 4 illustrates the nature of the rigidities and identifies the sub-markets in which these are taking place.

In the EU-15, price disparities were, as noted earlier, comparatively high in the food and beverage categories until 1985. In the former EFTA countries, the food sector has been highly protected from import competition, which has prevented arbitrage from taking place. In the case of beverages, the higher price level which is observed in the three newer Member States is partly explained by higher taxes on alcoholic beverages.

Figure 3.2.13 shows that, between 1985 and 1993, increased European integration led to some convergence of prices in the three newer Members States towards the EU-12 average, even though these countries were not yet EU members. Convergence was particularly notable for food products, and for clothing and footwear.

3.3. Trends in price convergence over time

Comparing the overall trend in the coefficients of variation for prices inclusive of taxes over the period 1980 to 1993 across the broad product/services categories, one finds that among the core group of EU-6 countries prices have converged more or less continuously throughout the period 1980–93, with the exception of beverages for which there was a temporary increase in price dispersion in 1990 (Figures 3.3.1 to 3.3.5).

Looking at the EU-9 or at the EU-12 regional groupings, however, one finds that convergence has only been significant for beverages and tobacco products. Although clothing and footwear prices seemed to converge between 1980 and 1985, the trend was then interrupted and price dispersion increased more or less continuously after that. The trend for food products also points towards increased divergence over the period 1985–90; however, this was followed by a timid trend towards convergence after 1990.

Figure 3.3.1. Measures of price dispersion, prices including taxes: the case of food products

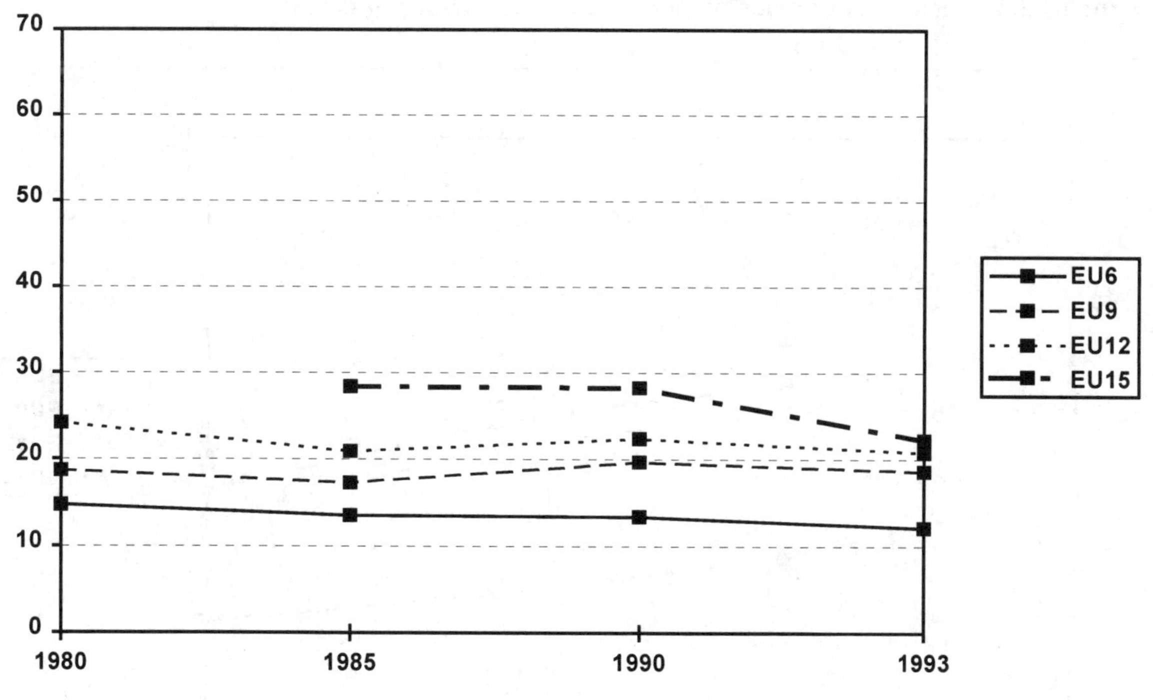

Source: DRI.

Figure 3.3.2. Measures of price dispersion, prices including taxes: the case of beverages

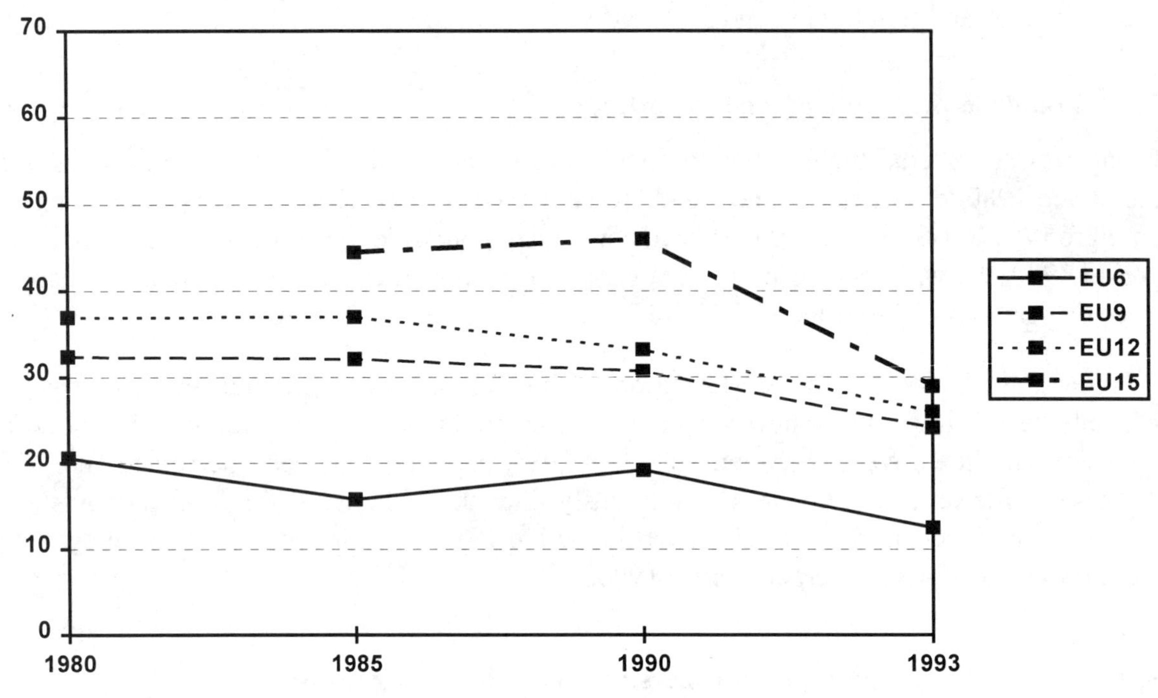

Source: DRI.

Figure 3.3.3. Measures of price dispersion, prices including taxes: the case of tobacco products

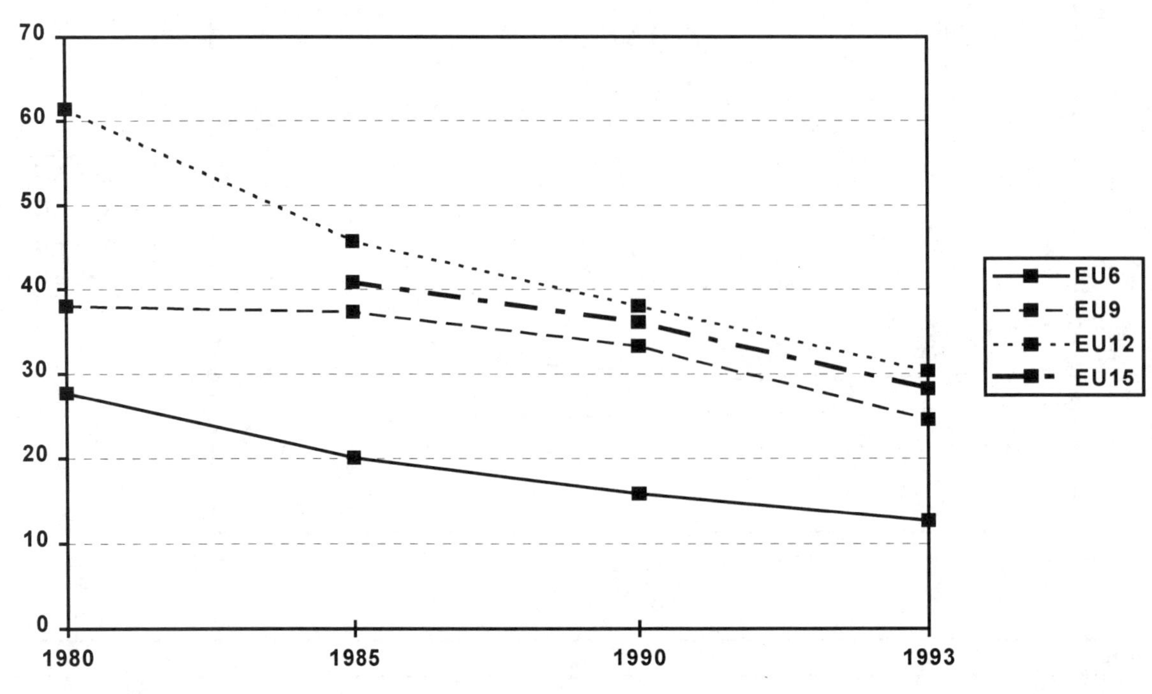

Source: DRI.

Figure 3.3.4. Measures of price dispersion, prices including taxes: the case of clothing and footwear

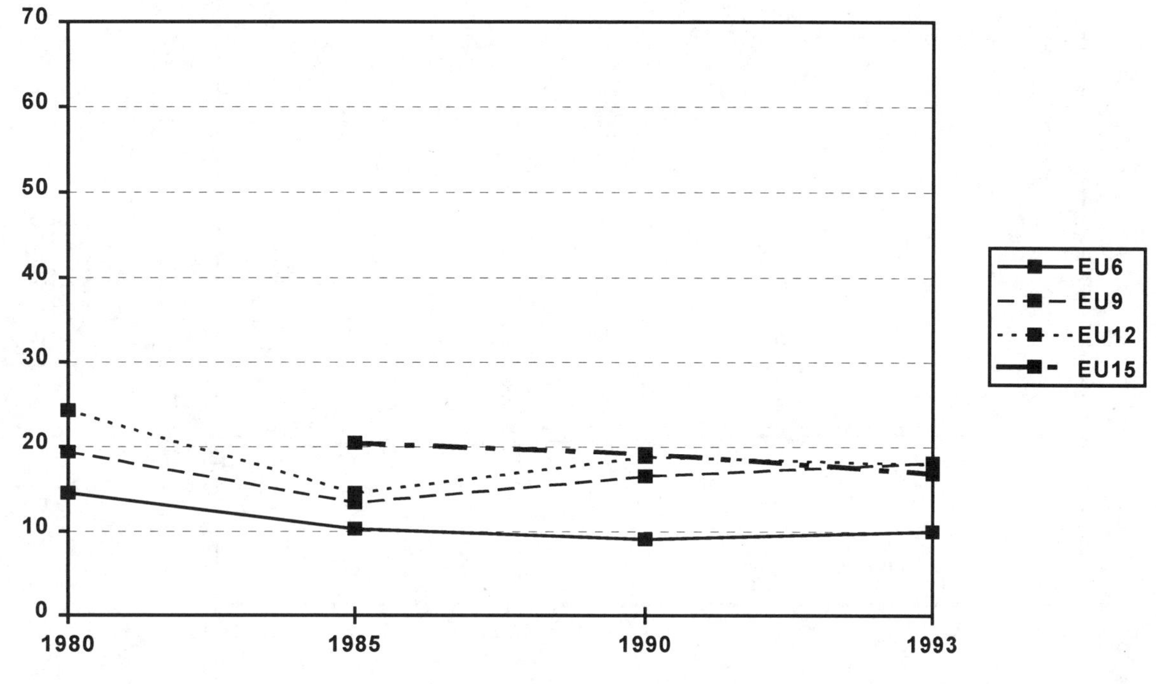

Source: DRI.

Figure 3.3.5. Measures of price variation, prices including taxes: the case of durable consumer goods

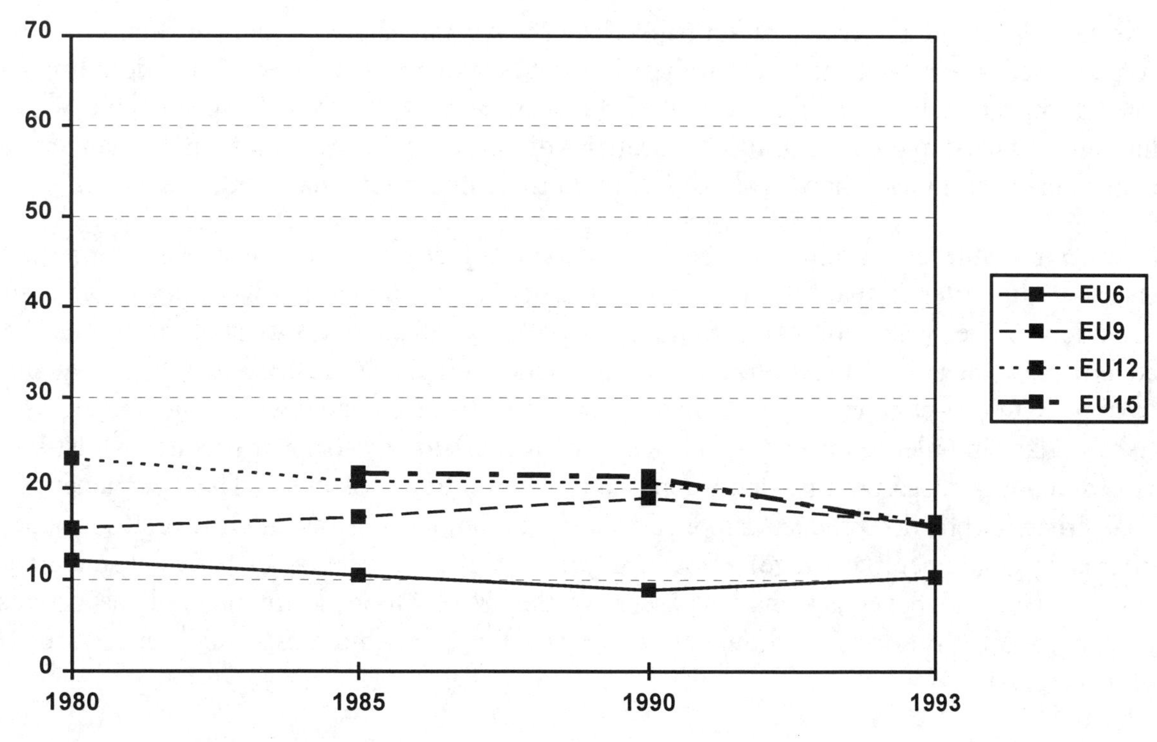

Source: DRI.

Figure 3.3.6. Measures of price variation, prices including taxes: the case of other manufactured products

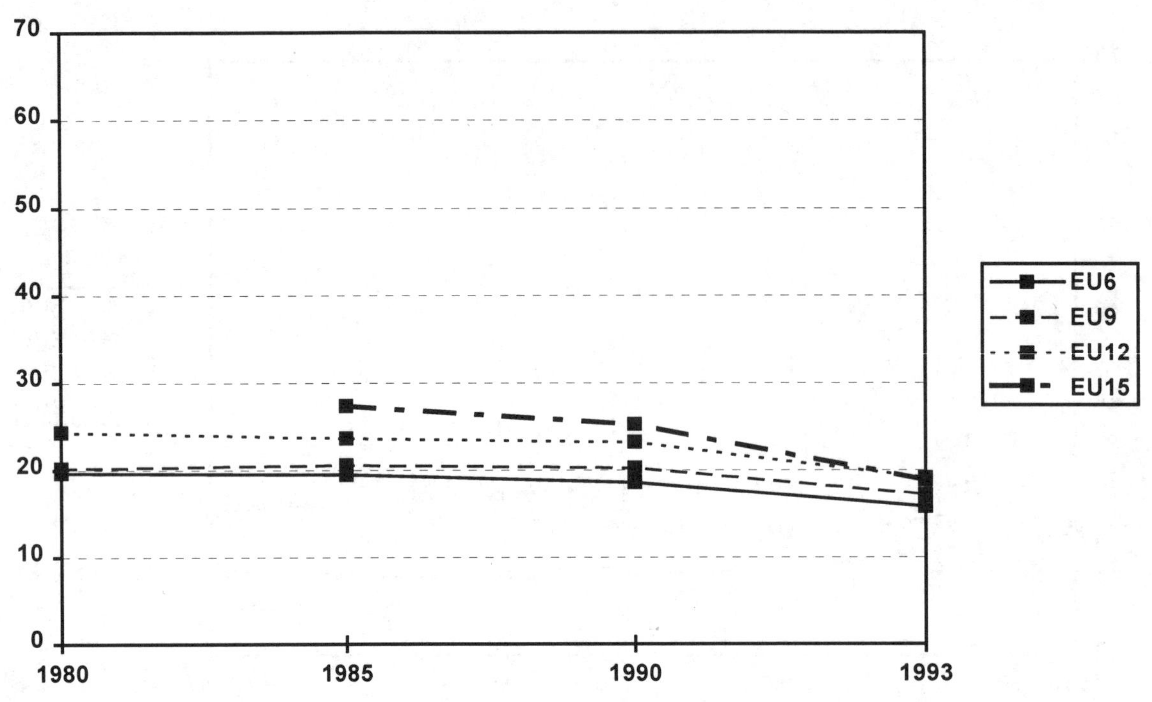

Source: DRI.

In the EU-15, the general trend between 1985 and 1993 has been for an increased convergence of price levels towards the EU-12, particularly pronounced over the period 1990–93.

The fact that food product prices in the EU-12 have not shown a notable trend towards convergence may reflect the fact that there has not been a notable increase in trade following integration but rather a reorganization of the sector across the broader geographic region through ownership restructuring, relocation of production activities and changes in management. All these changes are slower to translate into prices than trade effects.

Another possible explanation for the lack of convergence of prices in the food products category after 1986 is that, in this segment, the nature of competition has changed after the inception of the SMP. Following Sutton,[6] in presence of endogenous sunk costs (such as advertising expenditures) and once a minimal market size is reached, competition may shift from price to non-price variables. A limited number of firms compete with escalating levels of fixed outlays in order to increase consumers' willingness to pay for their product, whilst low-priced non-advertised products are offered to price-sensitive consumers. This emergence of a dual structure (branded products supplied by a small number of firms and low-priced products offered by a competitive fringe) associated with a higher dispersion of prices characterizes several food and beverages markets, such as the frozen food sector, as well as cereals, prepared soups, soft drinks and mineral waters (for the last, see the case study in Chapter 10 of this report).

---

6 See Sutton, J. [1991], *Sunk Costs and Market Structure*, MIT Press.

A third possible explanation for the absence of price convergence at the EU-12 level in the food product category is that the reorganization of the retail sector and the emergence of hypermarkets may themselves have led to greater price disparities. This observation is substantiated by a cross-border study of price levels[7] which notes that price dispersion in selected consumer markets was higher in France, where there is a higher density of hypermarkets, than in Belgium.

Finally, one has to note that the period 1985 to 1990 was one of relatively buoyant economic growth, so that the failure of food and other consumer product prices to converge to a lower level over that period possibly reflects demand/supply tensions in markets with not yet fully integrated (pan-European) supply. Consumers indeed tend to attach more importance to quality as opposed to price in periods of economic growth, whilst recession makes them more price sensitive.

3.4. The role of indirect taxation (VAT and excise duties)

3.4.1. General results

This section looks at the possible contribution of indirect taxes in influencing price disparities between EU countries. More precisely, it identifies the extent to which:

(a) indirect taxes (VAT and excise duties) are responsible for price differences across Member States;

(b) convergence/divergence of prices across Member States is explained by changes in indirect tax rates as opposed to fundamental movements in underlying prices net of taxes;

(c) price convergence/divergence patterns have been influenced by the numerous changes in indirect tax rates which have taken place following the inception of the SMP.

Coefficients of price dispersion based on price indices net of VAT were calculated for the EU-6 and EU-9 for all four years (1980, 1985, 1990, 1993), and for the EU-12 and the EU-15 for the last two years of data.[8] Dispersion coefficients were calculated net of VAT only for consumer goods and services, as prices for construction and equipment goods were provided to DRI already net of deductible VAT. The calculation of price dispersion coefficients based on prices net of VAT and excise duties was also done for the key product categories that are effectively subject to excise duties. These are alcoholic beverages, tobacco products and energy products.

The general assessment of the role of indirect taxes reveals that, while they significantly increase price disparities for some product/service categories, they do not appear to have altered overall price convergence or divergence trends between 1980 and 1993. There is no significant difference in price convergence/divergence patterns including or excluding indirect taxes.

---

7 See Centre Régional de la Consommation Nord-Pas de Calais [1994], *Etude de prix transfrontalière Belgique – France – Royaume-Uni en 1993 et 1994.*

8 See Appendix B for the description of the method used to calculate price indices net of VAT and excise duties.

Table 3.4.1. Spearman rank correlation using price dispersion coefficients over selected time periods for the EU-9

	With VAT	Without VAT
EU-9 (80) – EU-9 (85)	0.54	0.57
EU-9 (85) – EU-9 (90)	0.69	0.72
EU-9 (90) – EU-9 (93)	0.65	0.65
EU-9 (80) – EU-9 (90)	0.50	0.55
EU-9 (80) – EU-9 (93)	0.45	0.45
EU-9 (85) – EU-9 (93)	0.53	0.53

Source: DRI.

This is demonstrated by the fact that the ranking of all product/service categories based on their coefficient of price dispersion is very similar whether these coefficients are calculated based on prices including VAT or on prices net of VAT. This was verified by calculating Spearman rank correlations between the ranking of product/service categories based on coefficients of price variation including and excluding VAT. The results, presented in Tables 3.4.1 and 3.4.2, indicate that the changes in VAT rates which occurred in the EU countries from 1985 to 1993 and which were spurred by harmonization efforts have had a limited influence on the ranking of products and services based on price dispersion coefficients. The products and services with the highest coefficients calculated with prices including VAT remain more or less the same when VAT is excluded from prices.

Table 3.4.2. Spearman rank correlation using price dispersion coefficients for the EU-9

	EU-9 – EU-9 (no VAT)
1980	0.97
1985	0.96
1990	0.96
1993	0.93

Source: DRI.

3.4.2. Indirect taxation and convergence patterns

The actual comparison of the trend over time in the coefficients of variation between 1980 and 1993 for prices net of VAT and for prices including VAT reveals that changes in VAT rates in the EU countries over the period 1985 to 1993 have not had a major 'distortive' effect on the convergence pattern of final selling prices of broad product/service categories (see Figure 3.4.1 and Table 3.4.3). Prices of consumer goods and services converge regardless of whether prices include VAT or are net of VAT, while the strong pattern of increasing price disparities for energy from 1985 to 1993 is not altered by the inclusion or exclusion of VAT.

Figure 3.4.1 also shows that differences in VAT structures between Member States mainly influence the relative dispersion of the prices of consumer goods and energy products, as opposed to that of services. Overall, differences in VAT rates have increased price disparities of consumer goods and energy, as their coefficients of variation for prices including VAT are higher than for prices net of VAT.

Figure 3.4.2 further details the consumer products category in Figure 3.4.1 and indicates that, in 1985, differences in VAT rates across countries have mostly accentuated the underlying price disparities for food products, beverages and tobacco products, but less so for clothing and footwear, durable goods and other manufactures. By 1993 compared to 1985, the coefficients of variation of prices net of VAT for most of the six product categories were all much lower than for prices including VAT, indicating that the changes in VAT rates which were implemented from 1985 to 1993 were not sufficient fully to coincide with the underlying convergence of prices net of VAT (see Figure 3.4.3).

Table 3.4.3. Coefficients of price variation for selected groupings (based on prices including and excluding VAT)

	1980		1985		1990		1993	
	Incl. VAT	Excl. VAT	Incl. VAT	Excl. VAT	Incl. VAT	Excl. VAT	Incl. VAT	Excl. VAT
EU-6								
Consumer goods	15.9	15.7	14.2	14.2	13.5	13.4	12.4	12.6
Services	22.7	23.1	23.9	24.6	20.0	20.2	21.3	21.7
Energy	18.4	17.2	12.5	10.4	19.4	18.8	24.3	23.4
EU-9								
Consumer goods	19.9	18.8	19.1	17.7	20.3	18.5	18.0	16.6
Services	25.2	25.7	25.6	25.2	24.6	23.7	23.4	23.3
Energy	22.1	20.5	16.1	13.3	24.7	22.6	30.6	27.4
EU-12								
Consumer goods	..	..	..	..	22.8	21.8	19.6	18.4
Services	..	..	..	..	31.8	30.9	28.6	28.4
Energy	..	..	..	..	28.0	26.8	31.7	24.7
EU-15								
Consumer goods	..	..	..	..	25.9	24.6	19.6	18.4
Services	..	..	..	..	35.9	37.4	28.1	28.4
Energy	..	..	..	..	27.5	26.3	31.9	30.7

Source: DRI.

These results also imply that while differences in VAT rates across countries generally tend to augment price disparities, they only account for a small portion of the price dispersion (except for certain product categories, as will be seen in the next section). It is thus clear that price differences between EU countries stem mainly from factors other than indirect taxation, and that price convergence patterns are explained more by movements in underlying prices net of taxes than by changes in VAT rates. In summary, changes in VAT rates, which were characterized by harmonization efforts at the EU level following the establishment of the SMP, do not appear to have altered general price convergence trends from 1985 to 1993.

Figure 3.4.1. Comparison of price dispersion for consumer goods, services and energy products, EU-9

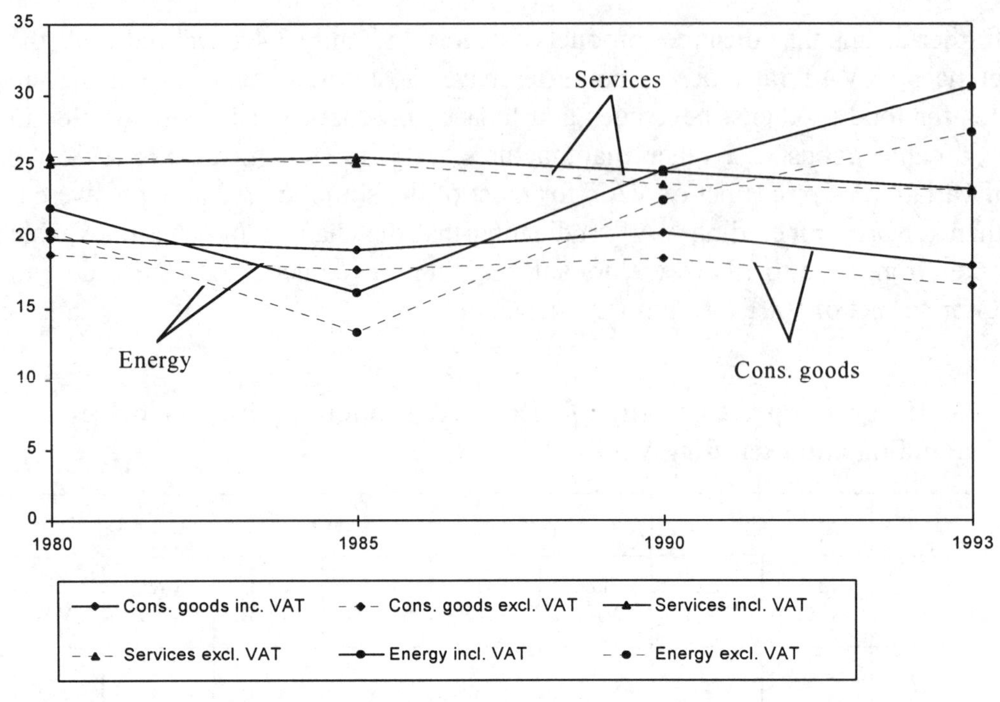

Source: DRI.

Figure 3.4.2. Comparison of price dispersion for consumer goods in 1985, prices including and excluding VAT for the EU-9

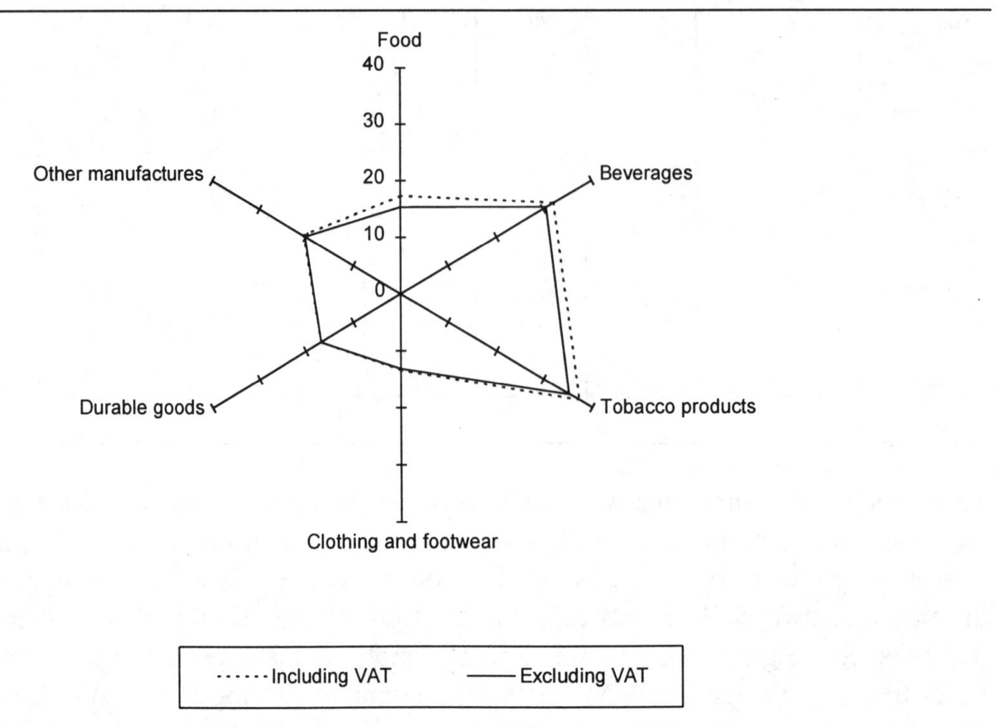

Source: DRI.

Figure 3.4.3. Comparison of price dispersion for consumer goods in 1993, prices including and excluding VAT for the EU-9

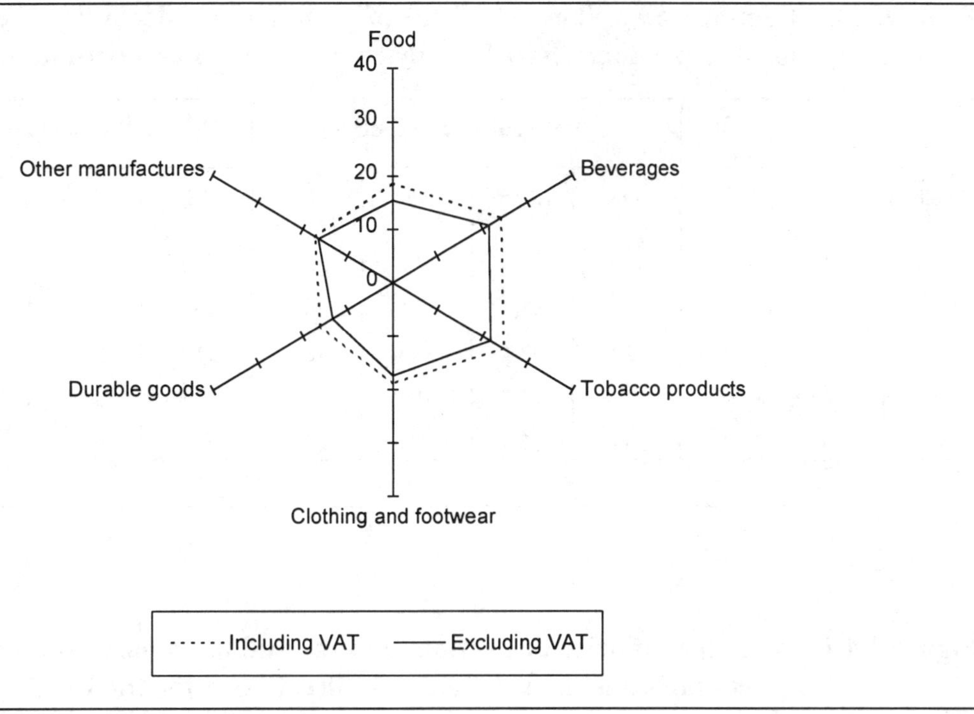

Source: DRI.

3.4.3. Impact of indirect taxes for detailed product categories

There are, however, a few detailed product items for which indirect taxes account for a significant part of price dispersion. This is particularly the case for products subject to excise duties. Excise taxes indeed play an important role in the case of tobacco products and for some energy products and alcoholic beverages, significantly increasing price disparities as compared to the trend in prices net of taxes.

When the coefficients of variation of prices excluding VAT and excise duties are compared with those for prices including VAT and excise duties in the EU-9 over the period 1985 to 1993, it appears that indirect taxes on alcoholic beverages significantly raise the average coefficient of price variation for these products. For beer, for example, the coefficient of variation based on prices inclusive of taxes in 1985 was 35% higher than for prices net of taxes. In 1985, VAT and excise duties accounted for a quarter of the dispersion in beer prices and close to a fifth of the dispersion in wine prices. Changes in VAT and excise rates after 1985 have, however, reduced the distortive effect of these indirect taxes from a price convergence point of view. Indirect taxes on beer and wine indeed explained a less important share of the price dispersion in 1993 (19.0%) than in 1985 (15.3%) (see Figure 3.4.4a). As for alcohol and other alcoholic beverages, indirect taxes have not significantly altered the convergence pattern of their prices from 1985 to 1993 (see Figure 3.4.4b).

Regarding tobacco products, the impact of indirect taxes on price dispersion is similar to that on beer and wine prices, meaning that changes in indirect tax rates after 1985 have led to a reduction of the importance of indirect taxation as a cause for price dispersion. Whereas indirect taxes explained 20% of the dispersion in tobacco products prices across EU countries in 1985, they accounted for only 16.6% of the dispersion in prices in 1993.

Table 3.4.4. Comparison of the coefficients of variation for alcoholic beverages and tobacco products, based on price indices with and without indirect taxes

	CV including taxes – EU-9				CV excl. VAT and excise duties – EU-9			
Product	**1980**	**1985**	**1990**	**1993**	**1980**	**1985**	**1990**	**1993**
Alcohol	39.3	33.6	33.0	34.4	36.5	30.7	29.6	31.3
Wine	48.9	47.9	40.8	30.7	46.9	38.8	33.0	26.0
Beer	22.6	32.4	25.3	18.9	21.5	24.1	19.3	16.2
Other alcoholic beverages	24.2	36.7	31.3	17.9	21.9	34.2	28.4	15.0
Tobacco products	38.0	37.3	33.3	24.6	35.7	29.9	26.4	20.5

Source: DRI.

Figure 3.4.4a. Measures of price dispersion for wine and beer, based on prices including and excluding indirect taxes for the EU-9

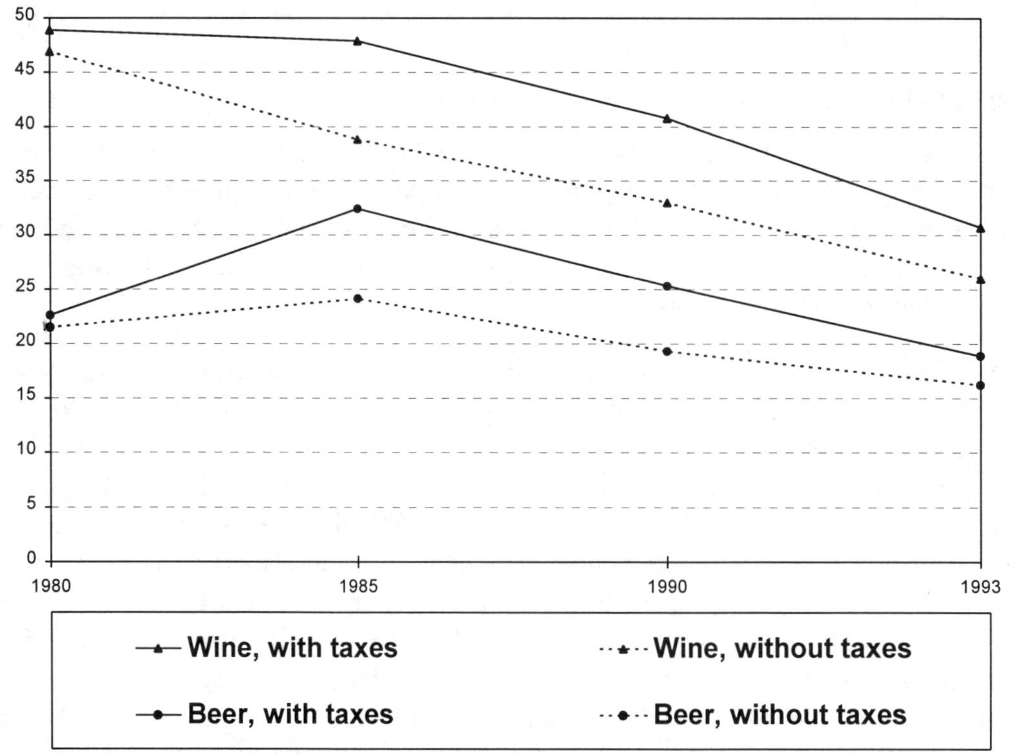

Source: DRI.

Figure 3.4.4b. Measures of price dispersion for alcohol and other alcoholic beverages, based on prices including and excluding indirect taxes for the EU-9

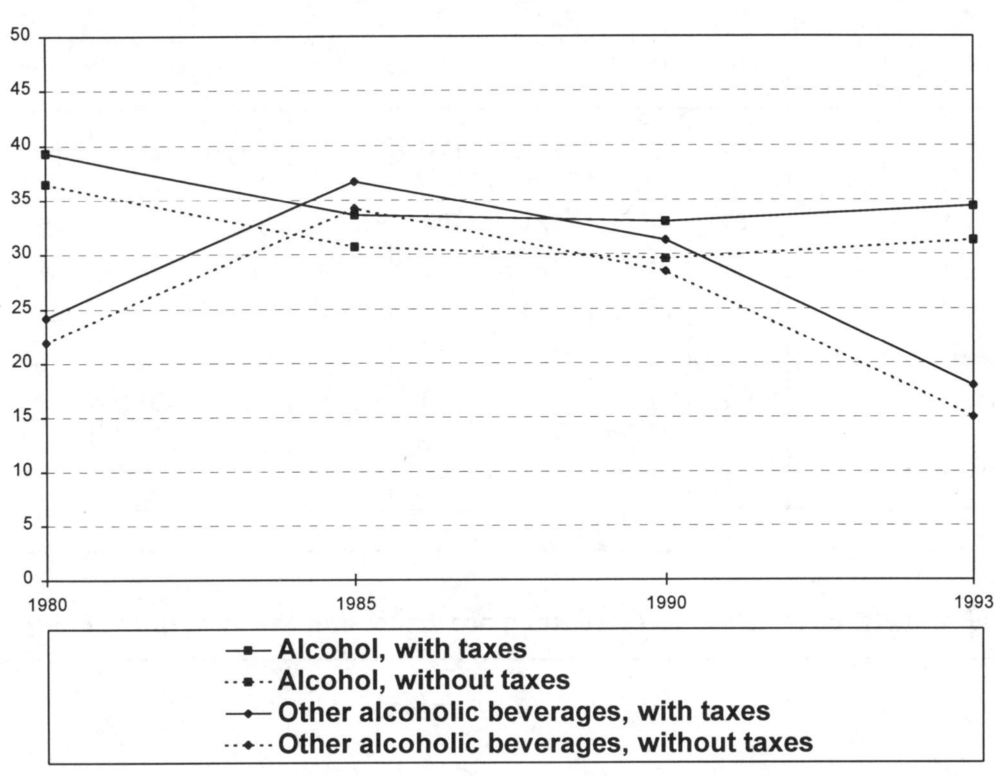

Source: DRI.

Comparing the price dispersion coefficients of energy products and motor vehicle fuels including all indirect taxes and excluding VAT and excise duties shows that indirect taxes have had a major impact on the price dispersion pattern of heating oil, but less so for the other products (Table 3.4.5). For example, the trend in price dispersion for electricity distribution, for which price disparities increased between 1985 and 1993, is very similar whether prices are considered including or excluding taxes. The price disparities for natural gas are lower for prices net of taxes than for prices including all taxes in all years considered, but the trend in convergence over time is similar for both series. The same applies in general to coal, coke and other solid fuels (except for 1990) and liquefied gas (except for 1985).

However, for heating oil and other heating fuels, although price disparities based on prices net of taxes increased consistently after 1985 (the coefficient of variation rising from 8.7 in 1985 to 31.3 in 1993), indirect taxes have been a significant additional source of divergence, with the coefficient of variation including taxes rising from 13.2 in 1985 to 47.5 in 1993. While indirect taxes accounted for 25% of the dispersion in heating oil prices in 1985, they were responsible for 34% of the price dispersion in 1993.

Turning to other product categories for which some difference in the average coefficient of variation of price was observed when prices were calculated respectively with or without VAT, one can draw a list of those products/services for which indirect taxation contributed strongly to price dispersion.

Table 3.4.5. Comparison of the coefficients for energy products and fuels and lubricants for motor vehicles, based on price indices with and without indirect taxes

	CV incl. taxes – EU-9				CV excl. VAT and excise duties – EU-9			
	1980	**1985**	**1990**	**1993**	**1980**	**1985**	**1990**	**1993**
Electricity	25.2	12.5	15.6	20.1	24.9	11.2	15.1	20.1
Natural gas	34.9	25.6	36.4	40.9	30.8	22.7	33.4	36.1
Liquefied gas	21.7	11.7	24.3	24.5	23.1	13.9	21.1	21.8
Heating oil and other heating fuels	8.7	13.2	35.6	47.5	6.6	8.7	24.1	31.3
Coal, coke and other solid combustibles	21.8	14.7	18.0	29.4	20.1	12.6	23.2	28.7
Fuels and lubricants for motor vehicles	11.6	10.9	12.8	9.3	9.5	8.6	11.4	10.1

Source: DRI.

Figure 3.4.5. Products for which VAT increases price dispersion the most in the EU-9

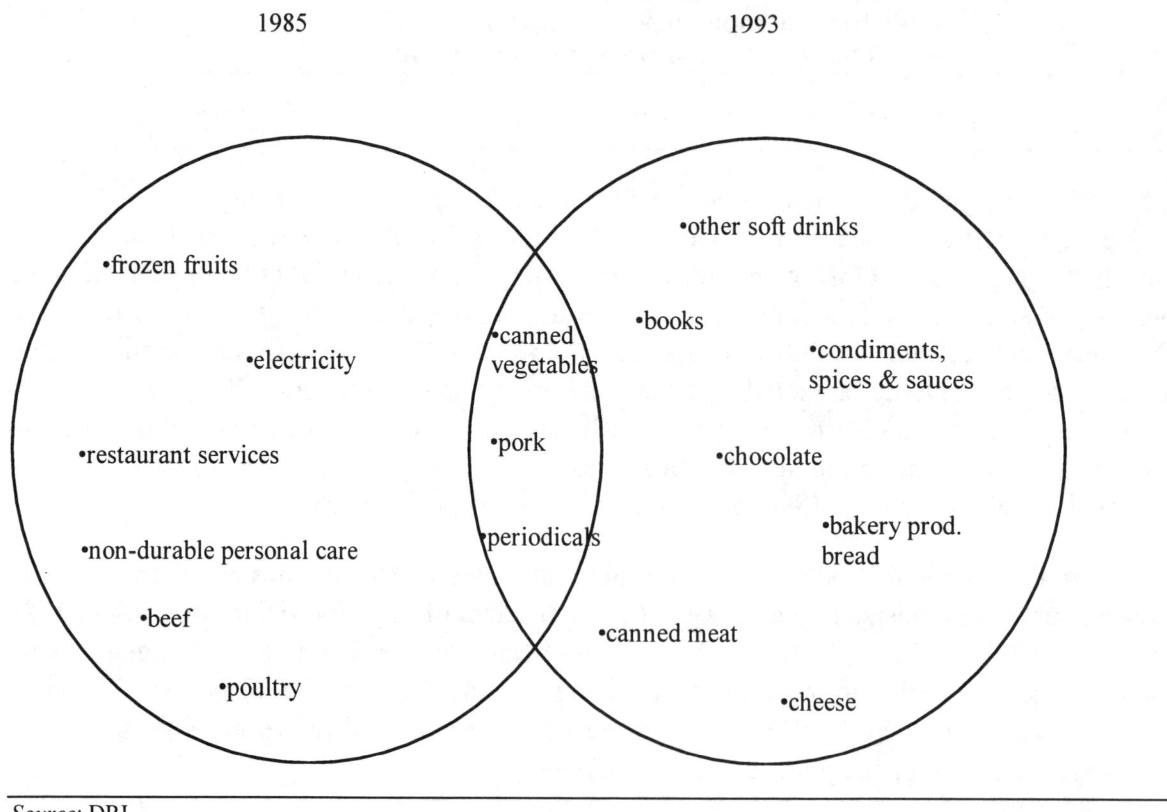

Source: DRI.

Figure 3.4.5 shows the list of products for which the coefficient of price variation measured on the basis of prices net of VAT was at least 25% lower than that based on prices including VAT, in 1985, in 1993 and in both years. These are products for which differences in VAT rates across countries create or augment underlying price disparities. These are canned vegetables, pork meat and periodicals and newspapers. Another product category for which the influence of taxation on price disparities is high in 1985 and 1993 is meat preparations – although the difference in the coefficient of variation for that category was just under 25% in 1985. Other product categories are unrelated.

All of the above are thus products for which differences in taxation across countries leads to higher price disparities than would otherwise be observed – hence creating an 'artificial' incentive for consumers to arbitrate across markets.

Another interesting situation is that wh en differences in national indirect taxation reduce price dispersion, and thus prevent consumers from arbitrating across markets – hence not putting pressure on the 'higher cost' producer to increase production efficiency. If, indeed, price disparities across countries are reduced by taxation, as illustrated in Figure 3.4.6 below in the case of two countries A and B, producers in country B will be able to survive or remain competitive even though their production costs may be notably higher than in country A.

Figure 3.4.6. The mechanisms of arbitrage when indirect tax rates differ significantly across countries

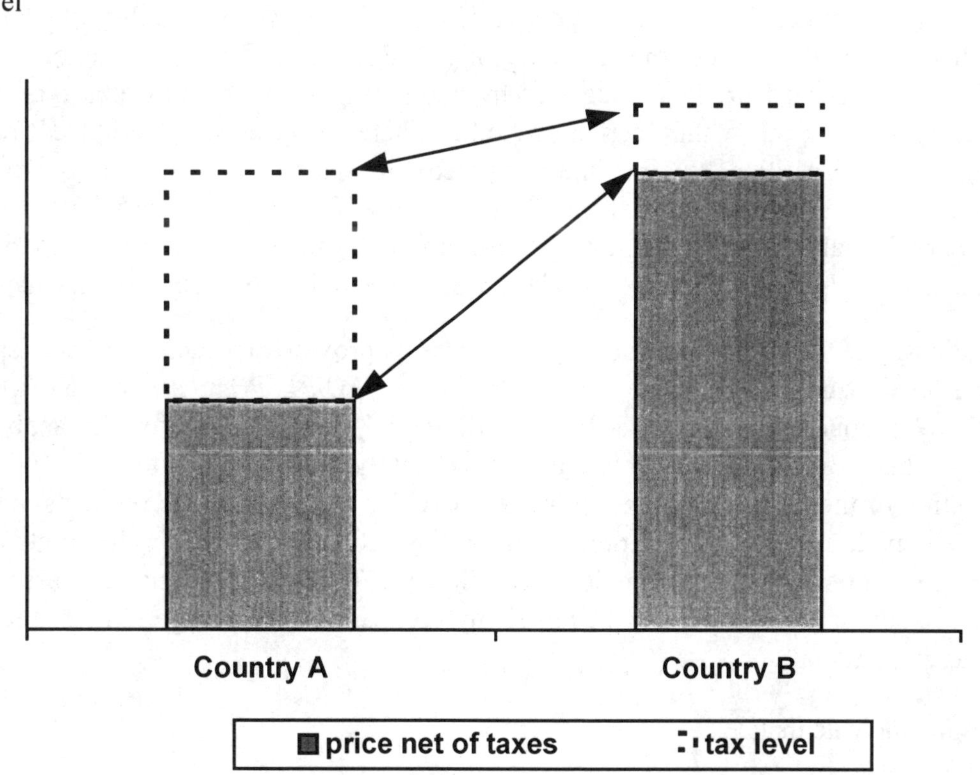

Source: DRI.

In 1993, there were nine product/services categories for which differences in indirect taxation eliminated or significantly reduced consumers' incentives to engage in arbitrage (defined as categories for which the coefficient of variation of prices net of taxes was at least 15% higher than that including taxes). These were, in decreasing order:

(a) flowers and other recreation articles,
(b) orthopaedic and other equipment,
(c) restaurant services,
(d) furniture,
(e) milk products,
(f) other dairy products,
(g) men's footwear,
(h) sugar.

Interestingly, restaurant services is one of the categories for which indirect taxation increased price dispersion in 1985, and is also a category in which producers have been complaining about the distortive effect on competition of indirect taxation.[9]

3.5. The significance of high coefficients of price variation: comparison with price disparities at regional level

As noted in Chapter 2, price convergence is neither a necessary nor a sufficient condition for markets to be pan-European. Structural factors related to the nature of the market can indeed explain why the 'law of one price' may not apply even in geographic markets in which there are no tariff or non-tariff barriers to trade. Although Chapter 6 reviews those factors in more detail, here we briefly discuss the relevance of the high coefficients of variation observed in the EU-12 for selected product categories by comparing them to those observed in studies done at regional level within certain Member States. These studies indeed reveal that important price disparities are sometimes observed within a given country, despite the absence of any objective factor preventing firms from operating freely across the whole market. This literature review also provides interesting explanations for the observed price disparities, some of which also apply to the whole of the EU. These are tested econometrically in Chapter 8.

Two studies, one for France and another for Germany, provide measures of price disparities at regional level within the EU. The first, published in *INSEE Première* (No 69, May 1990) covers 368 products considered as being sufficiently homogeneous for the analysis to be relevant. These 368 products represent approximately 60% of the items included in the construction of the French consumer price index (CPI). For each of the products, a survey of prices was made in 24 agglomerations of more than 100,000 people, in 20 points of sale in each agglomeration. The total sample thus includes 170,000 data points. The assessment of the importance of price disparities was made by comparing the average price of the products across agglomerations.

The results indicate that:

(a) There is an 8.5% difference in the general price level between the most expensive (Paris) and least expensive (Caen) agglomeration.

[9] See DRI [1995], 'Survey of the trade association's perceptions of the effects of the single market', report prepared for the European Commission (DG III).

(b) The maximum price dispersion for food products is 13%, with Ajaccio and Bastia reporting the highest prices.

(c) For clothing, the price disparity across agglomeration is 16%, but some caution has to be exerted as the products are not necessarily homogeneous.

(d) For other manufactured products, the maximum dispersion is 4%; this partly reflects that about one quarter of the products in this category are subject to uniform prices throughout the country. This is the case, in particular, for electricity, natural gas, pharmaceutical products, automobiles, tobacco products and magazines.

(e) For services (excluding rent) the maximum dispersion is 11%; this is low compared to the price dispersion observed at the EU-12 level but is, again, partly explained by the fact that the services prices are set at national level. This is the case in particular for postal services, health services, or air transport.

Among the services with the largest price disparities within France are water, urban transport, and vehicle repair.

Finally, the study notes a strong stability in these price dispersion patterns compared to 1985 when the previous survey was conducted.

The second study, for Germany ('Zwischenörtlicher Vergleich des Verbraucherpreisniveaus in 50 Städten', *Wirtschaft und Statistik*, 1994/6), relates to a 1993 survey of prices in 50 cities. About 400 goods and services were considered, and 932 points of sale were surveyed. These were divided into five categories based on the size of the agglomeration, the average purchasing power of the population in the region and an East–West divide.

The results indicate that:

(a) The maximum price disparity observed when all goods and services are considered together is 12%; this is higher than in France but is not surprising given the inclusion of the new *Länder*. On average, the price level in the new *Länder* is 6% below that of the former FRG (mainly because of lower service prices in eastern Germany).

(b) For durable consumer goods, price disparities across agglomeration are generally low, when one compares both cities of different sizes and eastern and western Germany (with average prices of 98.2 to 99.4 in western Germany and 98.0 to 98.8 in eastern Germany).

(c) For non-durable consumer goods, however, differences are more pronounced, both between agglomerations of different sizes (with the average price level growing with the size of the agglomeration) and between East and West.

(d) The greatest price disparities are, however, observed for services, again both between agglomerations of different sizes and between East and West.

These two studies are thus consistent with our general finding (confirmed in Chapter 7) that price disparities are higher for less tradeable products and services. Both studies, however, also point to significantly lower price disparities in many markets in which we find a high coefficient of price variation at the EU level, as for energy or a number of service categories for which prices are sometimes set at national level. With these exceptions, price disparities within countries do seem to be well below the levels observed at EU-12 level for most goods/services categories.

Another comparison can be made between the average level of price disparities across countries within the EU and across regions within a single country, by calculating the same coefficients of variation as used elsewhere in this report based on regional price data for Germany. The resulting coefficients of variation for 14 products/services categories and the aggregate price level are presented in Table 3.5.1.

Table 3.5.1. Coefficient of price variation for Germany, 1993

	West Germany	East Germany	Germany
Food, drink and tobacco	2.7	2.5	5.0
Clothing and footwear	1.7	2.1	1.8
Energy and water distribution	5.6	6.6	6.5
Electricity	8.5	7.2	10.1
Gas	18.6	28.1	26.2
Water distribution	23.0	20.8	22.2
Cleaning equipment and products	1.8	1.3	2.9
Healthcare and cosmetics products	3.9	5.2	8.8
Telecommunications services	1.9	1.8	2.8
Education, entertainment	2.2	1.3	3.7
Goods with administrative prices	3.6	3.5	6.4
Equipment goods	0.7	0.6	0.7
Consumption goods	2.2	1.2	3.3
Services	4.5	4.5	9.1
Total all goods	1.3	0.8	1.8

Source: Statistisches Bundesamt (1994), 'Zwischenörtlicher Vergleich des Verbraucherpreisniveaus in 50 Städten', *Wirtschaft und Statistik*, June.

Overall, we observe high price disparities in both the eastern and the western part of the country for gas and water, but comparatively low coefficients of variation of prices within each region for the other product categories. When calculated by combining price data from East and West, the results show higher price disparities at the national level for nearly all products/services categories, and most notably for health care, for goods with administrated prices and for services, but the coefficients of variation for these products/services categories are still below the levels observed at the EU level in Table 3.2.1 (or in Table 4.2.1 in the next chapter).

The next chapter reviews the level of price disparities and the average price convergence patterns of detailed products/services market segments.

4. Price convergence patterns by detailed products/ services categories

4.1. Key results

This chapter attempts to shed more light on the developments that were outlined in Chapter 3, by looking at the trends in price disparities in more detailed product/service market segments.

The main results are as follows:

(a) At the product level, interesting profiles emerge: among the 10 products/services categories for which price disparities in the EU-12 were highest in 1993 are four products/services related to health care. This reflects the fact that both pharmaceutical product prices and health care delivery prices are still highly regulated at national level. Two other product categories with high price dispersion are energy products, again reflecting regulatory price controls and differences in indirect tax rates. Two (water distribution and railway transport services) are national monopolies in most EU countries.

(b) The number of manufactured products for which price dispersion was amongst the 50 highest in 1980 has come down significantly since then. By 1993, the list of 50 consumption categories for which price disparities were highest was dominated by services (as opposed to manufacturing) sectors.

(c) In the services sectors, price convergence has been observed for most of the 'market' services, mainly in the EU-12. In the EU-6 and EU-9 regions, convergence took place at a much slower rate.

(d) Differences in GDP per capita explain disparities in price levels across the EU in many services sectors. There are, however, 18 out of 37 service categories for which price disparities are not correlated to the differences in GDP per capita: these include all the health care services but one, along with a number of regulated activities among which are water distribution, postal services, telecommunications services and railway transport.

(e) Convergence of prices in the EU-12 towards the EU-6 has been fastest for the durable consumer products and a number of market services, and slowest for tobacco products and alcoholic beverages in general. For energy, the trend was for increased price disparities in all three regions, but a much stronger increase in price disparities in the EU-6 and EU-9 than in the EU-12. The same holds for health care.

(f) A statistical test has been performed to test the significance of the convergence/divergence patterns. This shows that among the 86 products/services categories for which there is a clear change in price disparities over time across the EU, there are 78 cases of statistically significant price convergence patterns, and only 8 cases of price divergence. The 78 cases of price convergence apply to goods/services which together account for 60% of total private consumption expenditure in the EU.

(g) The ranking of countries according to the lowest or highest price level is remarkably stable over time: out of 145 goods/services categories, there are only 18 for which some countries shift from being a high price to a low price country over subsequent periods, and vice versa.

Before analysing the trends in price dispersion across detailed product categories, and identifying which products/services have a coefficient of variation or a convergence pattern which is significantly different from the other products in the same category, let us highlight a few general results.

4.2. Ranking of products/services based on the level of price dispersion

Table 4.2.1 shows the coefficients of variation of prices for the EU-12 as a whole, based on prices inclusive of VAT and excise duties for the years 1980, 1985, 1990 and 1993. Table 4.2.2 compares the coefficients of variation in the EU-9 in 1993 for prices including taxes, prices net of VAT and prices net of VAT and excise duties.

Table 4.2.1. Coefficients of variation in the EU-12 (based on prices including taxes, except for equipment goods and construction)

	1980	1985	1990	1993
1. TOTAL CONSUMER GOODS	28.2	25.9	26.0	23.2
A. Consumer goods, excluding energy and services	26.0	22.5	22.8	19.6
1.1. Food	24.2	20.9	22.4	20.8
Rice	22.8	10.4	14.5	13.0
Flour, other cereals	28.9	18.6	29.1	22.8
Bread, cakes and biscuits	22.4	20.1	19.7	20.5
Pasta, noodles	23.7	13.1	24.3	17.0
Beef	28.4	21.0	23.1	20.9
Veal	26.3	21.9	24.0	26.3
Pork	18.8	18.8	19.4	24.5
Mutton, lamb and goat meat	26.2	20.8	24.5	25.3
Poultry	19.2	21.1	16.6	23.0
Delicatessen	20.3	11.3	19.7	17.2
Meat preparations, other meat products	22.5	18.5	22.8	23.7
Fish and other seafood	21.7	19.1	23.4	17.2
Fresh milk	19.0	16.9	15.2	11.8
Preserved milk, other milk products	23.4	24.2	26.8	19.1
Cheese	21.2	12.7	17.5	18.5
Eggs	20.2	16.2	20.4	17.1
Butter, animal and vegetable fats	26.2	19.4	24.4	20.8
Edible oils	38.3	36.3	47.9	37.2
Fresh fruits	20.9	28.2	25.4	21.0
Dried fruits	23.7	23.4	28.4	22.1

Table 4.2.1. Coefficients of variation in the EU-12 (based on prices including taxes, except for equipment goods and construction) (cont.)

	1980	1985	1990	1993
Fruits preserved, frozen, and as juice	16.8	18.0	17.1	22.9
Fresh vegetables	35.1	36.7	25.7	26.8
Vegetables frozen, preserved, soups	25.2	22.6	23.6	22.7
Potatoes	31.8	26.5	35.7	39.9
Sugar	32.6	18.4	8.4	10.6
Jams, honey, syrups, ice cream	29.8	20.4	21.5	14.2
Chocolate and confectionery	23.1	23.0	23.1	25.5
1.2. Beverages	36.9	37.0	33.2	26.0
Coffee and cocoa	20.2	11.7	22.5	18.7
Tea	48.6	28.0	35.8	37.6
Mineral water and other soft drinks	39.4	30.9	28.2	21.8
Liqueurs and spirits	44.3	36.8	36.4	37.3
Beer	29.6	42.3	30.1	20.4
Wine and other alcoholic drinks	46.6	54.8	44.5	29.1
1.3. Tobacco products	61.4	45.7	38.0	30.3
Cigarettes	60.0	46.6	37.9	31.3
Other tobacco products	86.0	37.9	38.9	19.7
1.4. Clothing and footwear	24.3	14.5	18.8	17.9
Men's clothing	23.0	11.9	18.4	16.8
Women's clothing	22.9	12.8	16.6	16.5
Children's clothing	34.8	16.6	21.3	19.1
Clothing accessories	23.4	21.2	23.6	17.8
Men's, children's footwear	24.1	16.2	21.8	21.4
Women's footwear	21.5	18.9	20.7	22.3
1.5. Durable goods	23.3	20.8	20.7	16.4
Furniture and furnishings	16.7	10.1	11.9	7.7
Floor coverings	17.0	15.1	19.5	16.4
Household textiles	19.0	17.7	26.5	27.4
Refrigerators, freezers, washing machines	20.2	17.2	15.5	11.7
Cookers, heating appliances	29.8	28.8	12.7	16.5
Cleaning equipment, sewing machines	41.3	17.4	16.2	14.4
Glassware and tableware	24.0	25.1	25.4	25.1
Other domestic utensils	23.6	16.4	26.6	18.5

Table 4.2.1. Coefficients of variation in the EU-12 (based on prices including taxes, except for equipment goods and construction) (cont.)

	1980	1985	1990	1993
Motor vehicles, motorcycles, bicycles	30.9	28.9	26.6	21.0
Televisions and radios, tape and cassette recorders	24.8	26.8	20.6	11.1
Photographic and cinematographic equipment	14.9	24.1	19.7	19.9
Records, tapes, cassettes	16.9	12.8	11.0	12.5
Other leisure and recreational goods (incl. computers)	17.9	11.3	14.4	12.6
1.6. Other manufactures	24.4	23.7	23.2	19.1
Domestic electrical accessories	18.3	27.6	25.9	21.7
Non-durable household articles	16.7	19.2	17.0	13.3
Medicines, pharmaceuticals	35.6	38.2	41.6	40.5
Orthopaedic, therapeutic appliances and products	32.4	24.6	21.8	22.1
Tyres, inner tubes, replacement parts for motor vehicles	18.1	12.1	15.9	14.9
Fuels and lubricants for motor vehicles	13.7	13.1	16.1	8.4
Books, brochures, other similar printed matters	66.5	58.0	32.1	17.6
Periodicals, newspapers	24.6	19.4	21.9	19.2
Toiletries, perfumes	19.7	17.9	19.7	10.3
Jewellery, watches, alarm clocks	29.7	27.4	14.9	24.5
Travel goods and other personal articles	21.9	18.5	15.4	11.9
Writing and drawing equipment and supplies	30.0	17.7	25.0	19.7
Plants and animals	20.8	27.4	31.8	13.7
B. Energy	30.8	21.1	28.0	31.7
Electricity	30.2	15.1	17.4	20.7
Town gas and natural gas	47.0	32.6	42.5	42.3
Heating oil and other heating fuels	18.7	13.6	32.9	45.5
Coal, coke and other solid combustibles	25.8	27.4	31.0	33.6
C. Services	33.0	33.7	31.8	28.6
Repairs to clothing	28.0	26.9	14.3	23.3
Repairs to footwear	32.3	27.6	30.1	33.3
Household repairs and maintenance expenses	27.3	24.0	25.6	23.9
Water distribution charges	52.1	48.2	41.5	49.9
Repairs to household textiles	35.8	23.0	24.2	29.2
Repairs to electrical appliances	31.4	46.7	42.6	31.7
Repairs to other appliances	52.2	43.0	54.9	24.0
Laundry and dry cleaning services	29.5	40.5	50.1	18.0
Domestic services	34.9	33.6	35.1	34.7

Table 4.2.1. Coefficients of variation in the EU-12 (based on prices including taxes, except for equipment goods and construction) (cont.)

	1980	1985	1990	1993
Medical services	36.1	33.6	35.3	36.3
Car repairs and expenses	30.3	28.0	33.1	36.4
Local transport services	37.8	36.8	30.0	31.5
Rail, road transport services and other transport services	29.3	37.5	30.3	32.5
Postal services	22.8	25.9	22.6	17.5
Telephone, telegraph, telex services	41.5	43.8	39.0	31.4
Repairs to recreational goods	29.0	37.5	35.3	30.7
Expenditure related to recreational activities	45.5	36.1	36.6	26.3
Tuition costs	57.1	57.8	40.2	33.0
Hairdressers, beauticians services	31.6	31.8	33.5	32.7
Expenditure in restaurants, cafes	29.1	28.0	23.9	22.6
Expenditure in hotels and other accommodations	25.4	30.2	20.6	22.7
Financial and legal services	28.5	43.4	41.0	26.5
Other services	37.8	37.1	38.9	32.6
2. EQUIPMENT GOODS	18.0	14.0	13.1	16.5
Structural metal products	15.5	10.0	13.5	18.9
Products of boilermaking	25.6	21.7	11.4	25.2
Tools and finished metal articles	20.3	14.1	23.8	26.9
Agricultural machinery and tractors	20.0	11.5	8.7	13.4
Machine tools for metal working	17.7	14.3	17.2	17.6
Machinery for mining, metallurgy, building, etc.	14.1	9.6	9.3	16.2
Textile machinery	19.1	18.3	12.9	16.7
Machinery for food, chemicals, packaging	10.9	16.2	10.7	15.4
Machinery for working wood, paper	17.3	10.2	14.6	20.7
Other machines and mechanical equipment	11.6	8.1	10.4	18.2
Office and data processing machinery	11.9	10.8	10.8	10.8
Precision instruments	19.3	13.3	14.1	19.2
Optical instruments, photographic equipment	19.6	13.3	14.1	19.2
Electrical equipment, including lighting	16.4	7.6	14.3	15.2
Telecommunications equipment, meters	15.7	12.6	19.2	12.9
Electronic equipment, radios and televisions	23.3	14.1	17.1	15.3
Motor vehicles and engines	22.2	19.8	9.8	8.5
Ships	27.4	22.1	17.5	7.5
Trains, railway equipment	32.4	32.6	21.7	10.6
Aircraft, helicopters, aeronautical equipment	22.9	22.6	17.5	7.5
Other transport equipment	22.6	20.6	16.7	6.6

Table 4.2.1. Coefficients of variation in the EU-12 (based on prices including taxes, except for equipment goods and construction) (cont.)

	1980	1985	1990	1993
3. CONSTRUCTION	24.4	22.1	23.5	27.4
Housing	24.6	24.9	24.5	30.2
Non-residential buildings	22.9	21.3	21.3	25.0
Civil engineering works	26.5	15.7	25.0	24.2

Source: DRI.

Table 4.2.2. Comparison of coefficients of price variation in the EU-9 in 1993 (price including and excluding taxes)

	Taxes included	Without VAT	Without VAT and excise duties
1. TOTAL CONSUMER GOODS			
A. Consumer goods, excluding energy and services			
1.1. Food			
Rice	13.3	13.0	..
Flour, other cereals	22.0	17.6	..
Bread, cakes and biscuits	19.6	13.9	..
Pasta, noodles	19.1	17.8	..
Beef	16.5	12.6	..
Veal	20.5	16.0	..
Pork	19.8	14.6	..
Mutton, lamb and goat meat	17.8	16.6	..
Poultry	21.1	17.3	..
Delicatessen	18.1	16.3	..
Meat preparations, other meat products	18.0	16.5	..
Fish and other seafood	16.2	14.1	..
Fresh milk	11.7	14.0	..
Preserved milk, other milk products	15.2	17.6	..
Cheese	17.5	12.0	..
Eggs	14.5	13.0	..
Butter, animal and vegetable fats	16.3	16.0	..
Edible oils	33.0	27.2	..
Fresh fruits	14.2	11.7	..
Dried fruits	24.7	19.9	..

Table 4.2.2. Comparison of coefficients of price variation in the EU-9 in 1993 (price including and excluding taxes) (cont.)

	Taxes included	Without VAT	Without VAT and excise duties
Fruits preserved, frozen, and as juice	23.1	18.9	..
Fresh vegetables	20.4	15.9	..
Vegetables frozen, preserved, soups	20.5	15.2	..
Potatoes	35.3	31.8	..
Sugar	7.3	8.5	..
Jams, honey, syrups, ice cream	15.5	12.2	..
Chocolate and confectionery	28.0	21.3	..
1.2. Beverages			
Coffee and cocoa	18.7	16.9	..
Tea	34.5	32.8	..
Mineral water and other soft drinks	22.0	17.1	..
Liqueurs and spirits	34.4	30.8	31.3
Beer	18.9	18.7	16.2
Wine and other alcoholic drinks	25.3	22.8	19.3
1.3. Tobacco products			
Cigarettes	25.2	22.4	20.8
Other tobacco products	18.9	18.5	17.7
1.4. Clothing and footwear			
Men's clothing	18.9	18.8	..
Women's clothing	18.0	18.7	..
Children's clothing	20.0	18.2	..
Clothing accessories	16.9	17.4	..
Men's, children's footwear	17.7	19.6	..
Women's footwear	14.7	16.7	..
1.5. Durable goods			
Furniture and furnishings	6.1	7.4	..
Floor coverings	16.3	17.3	..
Household textiles	21.7	21.0	..
Refrigerators, freezers, washing machines	13.2	14.0	..
Cookers, heating appliances	16.3	15.3	..
Cleaning equipment, sewing machines	14.2	14.8	..
Glassware and tableware	18.0	18.1	..

Table 4.2.2. Comparison of coefficients of price variation in the EU-9 in 1993 (price including and excluding taxes) (cont.)

	Taxes included	Without VAT	Without VAT and excise duties
Other domestic utensils	15.6	14.7	..
Motor vehicles, motorcycles, bicycles	23.4	20.8	..
Televisions and radios, tape and cassette recorders	12.1	12.0	..
Photographic and cinematographic equipment	11.9	10.8	..
Records, tapes, cassettes	13.7	12.7	..
Other leisure and recreational goods (incl. computers)	12.1	11.6	..
1.6. Other manufactures			
Domestic electrical accessories	14.4	13.0	..
Non-durable household articles	10.1	10.3	..
Medicines, pharmaceuticals	32.3	30.0	..
Orthopaedic, therapeutic appliances and products	14.0	17.4	..
Tyres, inner tubes, replacement parts for motor vehicles	16.2	16.4	..
Fuels and lubricants for motor vehicles	9.3	9.0	..
Books, brochures, other similar printed matters	16.7	11.7	..
Periodicals, newspapers	18.6	13.8	..
Toiletries, perfumes	10.8	8.6	..
Jewellery, watches, alarm clocks	24.3	25.4	..
Travel goods and other personal articles	11.7	10.8	..
Writing and drawing equipment and supplies	14.5	14.2	..
Plants and animals	13.2	16.9	..
B. Energy			
Electricity	20.1	17.8	20.1
Town gas and natural gas	39.0	33.1	29.9
Heating oil and other heating fuels	47.5	46.4	31.3
Coal, coke and other solid combustibles	29.4	26.5	28.7
C. Services			
Repairs to clothing	23.8	24.0	..
Repairs to footwear	22.9	21.3	..
Household repairs and maintenance expenses	15.5	16.5	..
Water distribution charges	42.3	40.4	..
Repairs to household textiles	23.6	21.9	..
Repairs to electrical appliances	20.4	20.6	..
Repairs to other appliances	11.6	11.9	..

Table 4.2.2. Comparison of coefficients of price variation in the EU-9 in 1993 (price including and excluding taxes) (cont.)

	Taxes included	Without VAT	Without VAT and excise duties
Laundry and dry cleaning services	19.5	20.4	..
Domestic services	29.6	26.6	..
Medical services	36.0	37.3	..
Car repairs and expenses	28.7	28.0	..
Local transport services	18.2	18.2	..
Rail, road transport services and other transport services	24.5	23.5	..
Postal services	17.2	18.1	..
Telephone, telegraph, telex services	31.1	31.8	..
Repairs to recreational goods	27.4	31.7	..
Expenditure related to recreational activities	21.4	20.3	..
Other services	25.9	24.4	..
Tuition costs	31.4	34.6	..
Hairdressers, beauticians services	26.9	25.5	..
Expenditure in restaurants, cafes	16.4	16.3	..
Expenditure in hotels and other accommodations	18.2	14.1	..
Financial and legal services	20.0	21.5	..
2. EQUIPMENT GOODS			
Structural metal products	..	14.7	..
Products of boilermaking	..	24.7	..
Tools and finished metal articles	..	23.2	..
Agricultural machinery and tractors	..	13.6	..
Machine tools for metal working	..	13.1	..
Machinery for mining, metallurgy, building	..	13.7	..
Textile machinery	..	18.8	..
Machinery for food, chemicals, packaging	..	17.0	..
Machinery for working wood, paper	..	17.0	..
Other machines and mechanical equipment	..	14.3	..
Office and data processing machinery	..	11.0	..
Precision instruments	..	15.0	..
Optical instruments, photographic equipment	..	15.0	..
Electrical equipment, including lighting	..	13.2	..
Telecommunications equipment, meters	..	8.9	..
Electronic equipment, radios and televisions	..	16.6	..
Motor vehicles and engines	..	8.1	..
Ships	..	6.7	..

Table 4.2.2. Comparison of coefficients of price variation in the EU-9 in 1993 (price including and excluding taxes) (cont.)

	Taxes included	Without VAT	Without VAT and excise duties
Trains, railway equipment	..	11.1	..
Aircraft, helicopters, aeronautical equipment	..	6.7	..
Other transport equipment	..	5.7	..
3. CONSTRUCTION			
Housing	..	24.9	..
Non-residential buildings	..	20.5	..
Civil engineering works	..	19.0	..

Source: DRI.

Ranking the coefficients of variation in decreasing order for the year 1993 (see Appendix E.1), the 10 product categories which show the highest price dispersion (based on prices including VAT) were, in decreasing order of price dispersion:

(a) potatoes;

(b) other medical and paramedical services;

(c) water distribution charges;

(d) nurse services;

(e) heating oil and other heating fuels;

(f) town gas and natural gas;

(g) other pharmaceutical products;

(h) legal services;

(i) railway transport;

(j) general practitioner medical services.

Among these 10 categories, four are related to health care. This reflects the fact that both pharmaceutical product prices and health care delivery prices are still highly regulated across the EU. Two other product categories in this list are energy products, again reflecting regulatory price controls and differences in taxation. Two are national monopolies in most EU countries (water distribution and railway transport services). The only item which does not fall in one of these categories is potatoes.

Classifying the top 50 market segments for which price dispersion was highest in the EU-12 in 1993 based on certain key market features, such as the general sector to which they belong and the degree of regulatory price control or public ownership, one finds the results in Table 4.2.3.

Among the 50 markets in which price dispersion in the EU-12 was highest in 1993, only 10 were manufactured products (assuming potatoes, meat products and dried vegetables are 'agricultural' products). The two types of pharmaceutical products (medicines and other pharmaceutical products) were included in the 'health care related consumption items' category. Among the 10 manufactured products in the list of 50 products/services with highest price disparities in 1993, two were alcoholic beverages, i.e. products on which excise duties are high and account for higher price disparities at EU level. The other eight manufactured products items in the top 50 list are, in decreasing order of price dispersion, edible oils, cutlery, cigarettes, other animal fats, confectionery, household textiles, mineral water and lenses and glasses.

Table 4.2.3. Top 50 markets for which price dispersion was highest in 1993 (based on prices including taxes)

	1993	1980
National monopoly or regulated prices	8	5
Health care related consumption items	6	6
Agricultural products	7	7
Energy	4	2
Manufactured products	10	15
Other services	15	15

Source: DRI.

Table 4.2.3. also shows that the list of 50 markets in which price dispersion was highest in 1993 is dominated by service categories. In fact, about half of the service categories are in the list of top 50 sectors when ranked based on the highest price dispersion.

In contrast, among the 10 markets with lowest coefficient of price variation in 1993 one finds:

(a) furniture;

(b) fuels and lubricants for motor vehicles;

(c) durable and semi-durable personal care products;

(d) washing machines and dryers;

(e) cleaning equipment;

(f) other important leisure durable goods (including personal computers);

(g) televisions;

(h) non-durable personal care products;

(i) sugar;

(j) other personal articles, nec.

Most of the above categories are highly traded goods in markets dominated by a few large players strongly competing against each other. Still, this condition (being a highly traded good in a competitive market characterized by a high degree of concentration) is not sufficient to ensure price homogeneity across markets. There are, indeed, other product categories in our list which share the same characteristics but nevertheless have fairly different prices across the EU. One example is light bulbs and electrical accessories, whose dispersion coefficient was 21.7 in 1993, more than twice that for televisions. A similar observation has been made by IFAV[10] who looked at price dispersion at a regional level in Germany and a few other countries, and who noted fairly high prices differences for video and audio cassettes. The organization of distribution can, indeed, play a major role, as will be confirmed in Chapters 6 and 8 and in the case studies.

Comparing the list of 50 products/services with the highest coefficient of variation in 1993 with a similar list for 1980 (Appendix E.2), one finds that there have indeed been major differences in convergence patterns, with a number of manufacturing sectors disappearing from the list. Most notably this includes books and magazines, which ranked third in 1980 (i.e. had the third highest coefficient of price dispersion in the EU-12), children's clothing, which ranked 24th, ice cream (25th), other cereal based products (27th), sugar (36th), and motor vehicles (39th).

Although mineral waters were still in the top 50 list in 1993, the coefficient of variation of this segment did fall significantly, from 59.2 in 1985 in the EU-12 to 26.8 in 1993 in the same geographical area, as did its ranking (from 2nd to 47th).

To test the correlation between the ranking of product/service categories based on the coefficient of variation in different years or across different country groupings, Spearman rank correlation coefficients were calculated which are presented in Tables 4.2.4 to 4.2.5. Table 4.2.4 shows the rank correlation coefficient for the EU-6/EU-9, EU-9/EU-12 and EU-12/EU-15 groupings, for all four years considered. Two observations can be drawn from this table. First, the ranking of products based on the coefficient of variation is more similar between the EU-9 and the EU-12 and between the EU-15 and the EU-12 than between the EU-9 and the EU-6. This confirms an observation made in Sections 3.2 and 3.3, namely that overall price disparities between the EU-9 and the EU-6 are higher than between the EU-12 and the EU-9. The three countries, Denmark, Ireland and the UK, have indeed shown a more modest convergence of their prices towards the EU level following membership (despite the implementation of the single market programme) than the three following EU members, Greece, Spain and Portugal.

The second observation from Table 4.2.4 is that, overall, there has been no significant increase in correlation between the rankings for the EU-6 and for the EU-9 over time, as the Spearman rank correlation coefficient is about the same in 1993 as in 1980 or 1985. The same holds for the correlation between the ranking of coefficients of variations for the EU-9 and EU-12. For the EU-15, on the other hand, the rank correlation coefficient is much higher in 1993 than in either 1985 or 1990, indicating a price structure in 1993 more in line with the EU-12 price structure than in the mid-1980s.

[10] Institut für Angewandte Verbraucherforschung [1994], 'Cross-border price comparison', study prepared for the European Commission (Consumer Policy Service).

Table 4.2.4. Spearman rank correlation coefficient for selected geographic areas

	1980	1985	1990	1993
EU-6 – EU-9	0.74	0.73	0.70	0.71
EU-9 – EU-12	0.89	0.83	0.86	0.88
EU-12 – EU-15	..	0.79	0.86	0.92

Source: DRI.

Table 4.2.5 compares the ranking of the coefficients of variation within the EU-9 for prices including taxes to those for prices excluding VAT. The results indicate the following:

(a) Over the period 1985–90, the final product prices have moved closer together than during the 1980–85 or 1990–93 periods; this is mirrored in the fact that the ranking of products based on the highest coefficient of variation is similar in 1990 to the 1985 ranking (with a Spearman correlation coefficient of 0.69 for prices including taxes, and 0.72 for prices net of taxes). This period was in fact characterized by rapidly decelerating inflation throughout the EU, which seems to have influenced all products in a similar way. The changes in relative price trends were more dissimilar both before 1985 (when inflation rates were themselves dissimilar across countries and markets were not yet well integrated) and after 1990, when the SMP started to have more significant effects on prices, affecting different consumer markets in different ways depending on the dates of implementation of key measures and delays in responses of companies to the announced changes.

(b) The low coefficient of rank correlation for the EU-9 (80)–(93) comparison indicates that the changes in relative price dispersion were cumulative over time, so that the ranking of products/services based on the highest coefficient of variation is very different in 1993 from what it was in 1980.

Table 4.2.5. Spearman rank correlation coefficient over selected time periods

	With VAT	Without VAT
EU-9 (80) – EU-9 (85)	0.54	0.57
EU-9 (85) – EU-9 (90)	0.69	0.72
EU-9 (90) – EU-9 (93)	0.65	0.65
EU-9 (80) – EU-9 (90)	0.50	0.55
EU-9 (80) – EU-9 (93)	0.45	0.45
EU-9 (85) – EU-9 (93)	0.53	0.53

Source: DRI.

4.3. General patterns of price convergence over time, for detailed product/service categories

The following sections look at the trend in the coefficient of variation over time in the EU-12, by product or by market segment and identify, within the different families of products/services, those items for which price developments have been significantly different from the average for that category. In other words, knowing that food prices, for example, have converged in the EU-12 over the period 1985–93, for which product categories has this convergence been most notable? The analysis also seeks to identify those products for which prices have actually diverged over the period considered. To do this, we will refer to the broad product categories that were defined in Figures 3.2.1 and 3.3.1.

4.3.1. Food products

As discussed previously, the food products category is one for which price dispersion has always been comparatively low within the EU-12. This is nevertheless a product category in which price convergence has taken place between 1980 and 1993. Price convergence was, however, relatively more pronounced in the EU-12 than in the EU-6, as the countries in the EU-6 grouping were already highly integrated in the early 1980s, such that their coefficient of price variation was already low (at 13.5 in 1985 compared with 20.9 for the EU-12 in the same year).

Some resistance to price convergence nevertheless appears to have taken place in the EU-9, where price disparities between 1985 and 1990 increased before being partly offset between 1990 and 1993 (Figure 3.3.5).

Within the food products category there are, however, a number of products or market segments for which the developments in price disparities, both over time and across different geographical areas, vary significantly from the average pattern for other food products. Figure 4.3.1 identifies these sectors by showing the set of products for which the price convergence pattern varies significantly from the average, and by distinguishing those products for which the price dispersion in 1985 was significantly higher than (i.e. more than 20% above) the average coefficient of variation for all the food products category, as well as those categories for which price disparities were about average (i.e. within 20% of the average), or significantly less than average (taken to be at least 20% lower than the average coefficient of variation for food products in 1985).

Taking one of these boxes, for example the top right hand box in Figure 4.3.1, one finds that 'other seafood' products had a comparatively high coefficient of variation in 1985, which means that prices were very different across Member States. Between 1985 and 1993, however, the price dispersion had been reduced by more than the average for other food products. Hence, even if the coefficient of price variation for this product was still high in 1993 (in fact, for other seafood products the rate of decrease was such that the coefficient of price variation was equal to 14.9 in 1993 compared to an average of 20.8 for all food products), the changes have nevertheless taken place in the right direction, i.e. towards a progressive reduction of price disparities across the EU-12.

Taking another example from Figure 4.3.1, the products in the box in the top left hand corner indicate those products (spices and sauces, in this case) which have experienced greater price convergence than average over the period considered, despite the fact that the coefficient of price variation for those products was already comparatively low at the beginning of the period (i.e. in 1985).

The box that is most interesting in terms of identifying the market segments in which the single market failed to achieve the desired effects is the lower right hand box, which shows a set of products which displayed a high price dispersion before the launch of the SMP, and for which price dispersion has further increased (or for which price convergence has been particularly slow, compared to the average for this category). An obvious question is why has price dispersion for this particular set of products increased (or, why has price convergence taken place at a slower than average rate)?

Two other boxes which deserve more in-depth analysis are the lower left hand boxes which include a set of sectors/product categories which showed an average or below average price dispersion at the beginning of the period, and for which price convergence has been slower than for the average of the food category.

Figure 4.3.1. Pattern of price convergence for selected food products 1985–93, EU-12

Convergence between 85-93 in the EU-12			
Strong convergence	Spices, sauces, condiments	Fresh milk Other milk products except cheese Sugar Meat preparations, other meat products	**Other seafood** Dried or smoked fish Preserved milk Fresh fruits, fresh vegetables **Ice cream**
Convergence close to average	Eggs	Dried fruits Butter Vegetables preserved, prepared Bread Cakes and biscuits Other cereal based products Beef Poultry Chocolate	Confectionery
Slow convergence or divergence	Jams, honey, syrups Rice *Flour* Pasta, noodles Delicatessen Fresh, frozen Fish Cheese *Frozen vegetables* Products derived from potatoes	Veal Pork Mutton, lamb and goat meat Margarine Other animal or veg. fats Fruits frozen, preserved Other fresh or frozen meat	Preserved, prepared fish and other seafood Edible oils Dried vegetables Potatoes
	Below Average	Average	Above Average

Coefficient of variation in 1985

Source: DRI.

In Figure 4.3.1 we indicated in italics those products for which the increase in price dispersion is such that in 1993 the coefficient of variation of that product is more than 20% greater than the average for all food products. Indeed, beyond trying to understand why prices have converged less (or diverged) between 1985 and 1993, it is important to see how different prices are at the end of the period, i.e. has the price dispersion coefficient moved towards the average coefficient of price variation, or does it now exceed the average coefficient of variation for that product category by a significant amount (taken as 20%)?

In Figure 4.3.1, we find that among the 10 products which showed a significantly higher price dispersion than average in 1985, half also experienced a greater price convergence than average, and thus saw their coefficient of variation decrease after 1985. These are other seafood, dried or smoked fish, canned milk, fresh fruits and vegetables and ice cream. The trend is particularly notable for ice cream, whose coefficient of variation was 28.7 at the start of the period (compared to an average figure for food products of 20.9), and which came down to 17.7 in 1993, less than the EU average for food products of 20.8 in that year. The strong convergence of ice cream prices at the EU level can probably be attributed to the increased globalization of the sector through ownership restructuring, increased penetration of non-EU players in the EU market and increased overall concentration of production in the hands of a few big players. Through the mechanisms of competition, price convergence has thus been intensified, particularly after 1990 (Figure 4.3.2).

Figure 4.3.2. Measures of price dispersion for selected food products, based on prices including taxes, EU-12

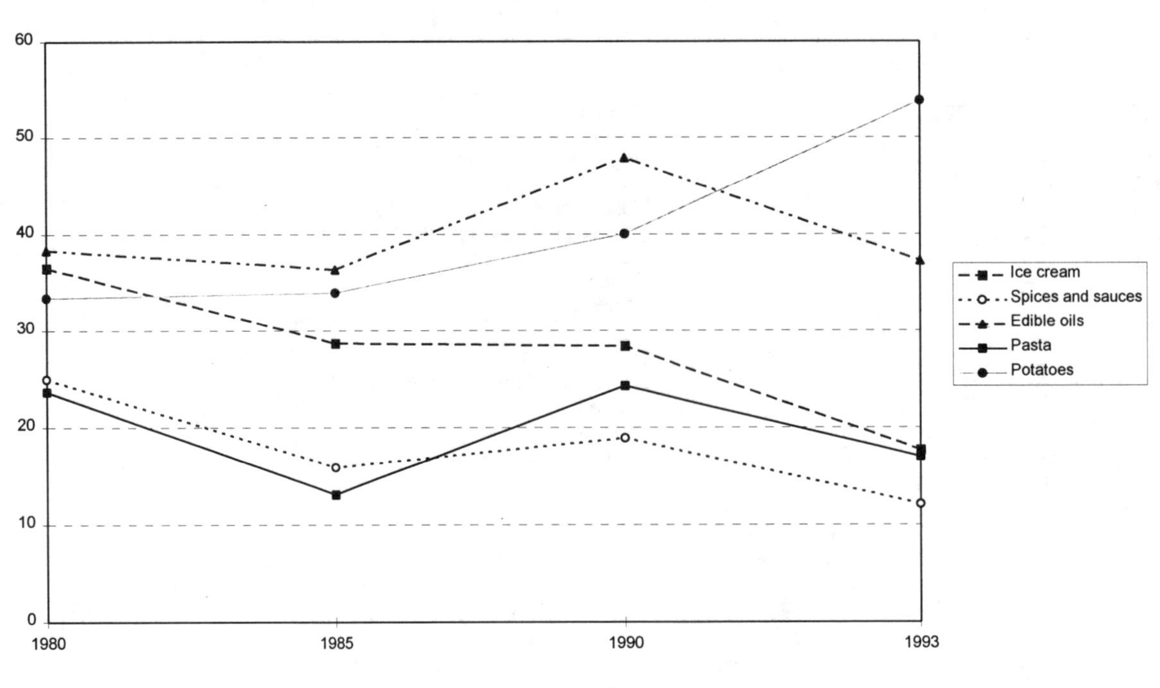

Source: DRI.

Another food product for which the rate of price convergence has been such that the coefficient of variation in 1993 had fallen below the average for all food products is other seafood.

In contrast, among the other five products for which the coefficient of price variation in 1985 was particularly high (preserved or prepared fish and other seafood, along with edible oils, dried vegetables, potatoes and confectionery), four experienced a further widening of price disparities after 1985. Among these, the most extreme case is that of potatoes. Interestingly, the margarine and edible oils markets reported only a slow price convergence over the period (i.e. less than average), even though these are products for which companies claim there has been a severe increase in price-based competition following the launch of the SMP due to the process of concentration involving the large distribution chains. The perceived upward pressure on costs of heightened environmental regulations related to packaging may actually have limited the downward price convergence, compared to what would otherwise have been observed as a result of increased competition.

Altogether, out of the 42 food products considered in this study, 27 reported an increase in price dispersion between 1985 and 1993, whereas the average trend for all food products is one of stability.

4.3.2. Beverages

The beverages category is one in which price dispersion at the EU-12 level has traditionally been very high, for a number of reasons which relate partly to the fact that these products are less traded than most manufactured products (because of high transport costs), and partly to the fact that this category includes alcoholic beverages which are subject to very different indirect tax regimes across countries.

Between 1985 and 1993, there has nevertheless been a notable trend towards price convergence in the EU-12, with the coefficient of variation of beverages inclusive of all taxes falling from 37 (in 1985) to 26 (in 1993).

Looking at the trend in convergence for detailed product categories (Figure 4.3.3), one finds that although the coefficient of price dispersion for mineral waters remains high in 1993 (at 26.8), there has nevertheless been a major reduction in price disparities across the EU despite the fact that this is a sector in which trade is generally limited to cross-border regions. The rate of convergence for other soft drinks, which covers all carbonated beverages except water, was, in contrast, slower than average. The other soft drinks market is nevertheless one in which price disparities have always been comparatively low, due to the market's dominance by a few multinationals in strong competition with one another.

The difference in both the level and the trend in price disparities in the mineral waters and other soft drinks segment is nevertheless very interesting, as the mineral water market is also dominated by a few large players and the product is difficult (costly) to carry over long distances. This is the subject of one of the case studies included in Chapter 10, which shows that the enlargement of the market for mineral waters following the removal of NTBs justified a shift from horizontally differentiated products to vertically differentiated products, with market dualization and an increase in competition in both the branded and non-branded segments of the market. Whereas in the case of other soft drinks the market was already a relatively mature market with vertically differentiated products before the launch of the SMP.

Figure 4.3.3 also indicates that the growing level of concentration in the beer market seems to have favoured a comparatively faster convergence of beer prices than of the prices of other types of alcoholic beverages such as wine and alcohols.

Figure 4.3.3. Pattern of price convergence for selected beverages 1985–93, EU-12

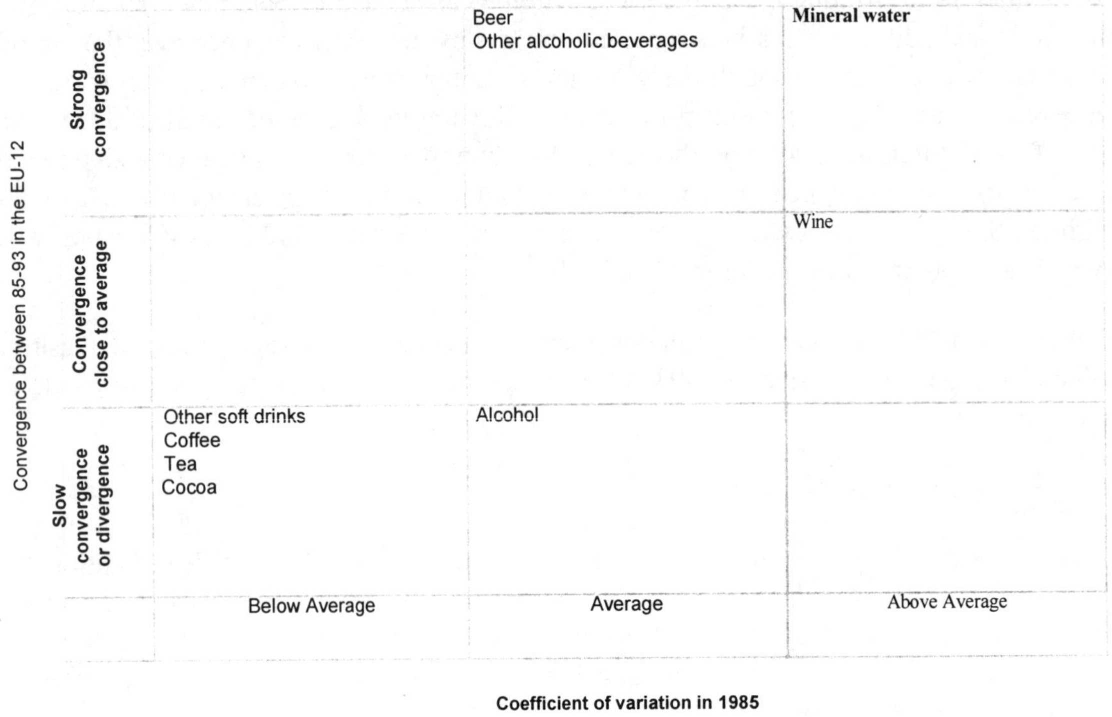

Convergence between 85-93 in the EU-12	Below Average	Average	Above Average
Strong convergence		Beer Other alcoholic beverages	**Mineral water**
Convergence close to average			Wine
Slow convergence or divergence	Other soft drinks Coffee Tea Cocoa	Alcohol	

Coefficient of variation in 1985

Source: DRI.

4.3.3. Tobacco

Figure 4.3.4. Pattern of price convergence for tobacco products 1985–93, EU-12

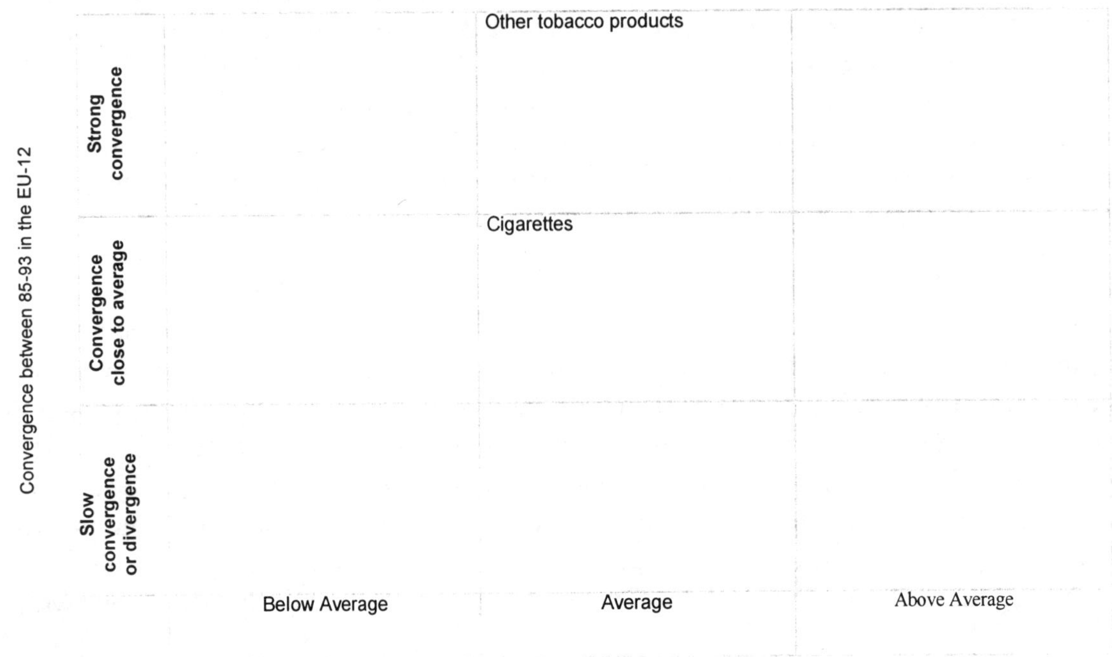

Source: DRI.

The tobacco products grouping contains only two products: cigarettes and other tobacco products. Because of the important relative weight of cigarettes in the total category, the results for tobacco products as a whole largely reflect price dispersion patterns for cigarettes. It is thus not surprising to find cigarettes in the centre box of Figure 4.3.4. Interestingly, however, we see in Figure 4.3.4 that the price of other tobacco products has tended to converge slightly more rapidly than that of cigarettes.[11]

4.3.4. Clothing and footwear

The clothing and footwear category is an interesting category as this is a market segment for which prices have not evolved homogeneously across the EU-12.

The markets in which prices have converged fastest over the period considered are babies' clothing and accessories for clothing, two segments characterized by a comparatively high price dispersion at the beginning of the period (1985). In both cases, one can indeed speak of price convergence over the period, in sharp contrast with the trend for the rest of the category, given the overall pattern of increased price disparities on textiles, clothing and footwear across the EU-12 (see Figure 4.3.5).

Figure 4.3.5. Pattern of price convergence for clothing and footwear products 1985–93, EU-12

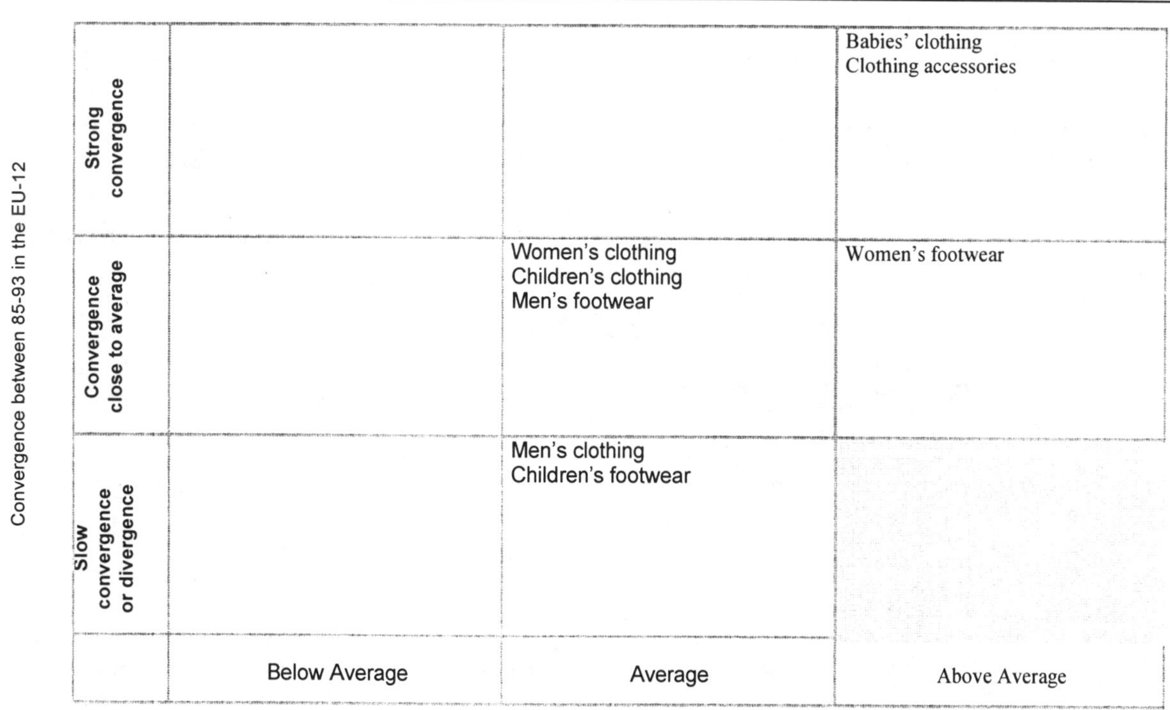

Source: DRI.

[11] One should note, however, that the tobacco products price indices are among the few price indices for which the data supplied by Eurostat seemed suspicious (mainly in the case of Portugal). A correction for all questionable data points was applied, which is described in Appendix A.2. The correction procedure was, however, found not to affect the results presented in this chapter.

4.3.5. Durable consumer goods

The durable consumer goods category is one of the most interesting consumer goods categories, as it includes a number of markets in which the degree of concentration has increased following the launch of the SMP, due to intensive M&A activity and globalization trends. Most of the products in this category are highly traded goods, for which the rate of penetration of extra-EU imports has also increased at a rapid rate.

Overall, the coefficient of variation of prices including taxes in the EU-12 has decreased consistently since 1980, falling from 23.3 in 1980 to 20.8 in 1985, 20.7 in 1990 and 16.4 in 1993. Similar trends are observed for the coefficients of variation net of VAT.

Figure 4.3.6 shows the set of products within the durable consumer goods categories for which the price convergence between 1985 and 1993 has been faster or slower than average, taking into account the relative degree of price dispersion at the beginning of the period.

Figure 4.3.6. Pattern of price convergence for durable consumer goods 1985–93, EU-12

Convergence between 85-93 in the EU-12			
Strong convergence	Other important leisure durable goods (incl. personal computers)	Cleaning equipment Televisions Washing machines, tumble dryers	Gardening equipment Radio equipment Record players, tape and cassette recorders Cookers and stoves
Convergence close to average	Furniture and furnishings		Heating and air conditioning appliances Motor vehicles Cutlery Photographic and cinematographic equipment
Slow convergence or divergence	Refrigerators, freezers Floor coverings Other household appliances *Glassware and tableware* Non-electrical kitchen utensils *Other modes of personal transport* Records, cassettes, tapes Sports equipment Games and toys Films and other photographic supplies Household textiles	*Glassware and tableware*	Cutlery
	Below Average	Average	Above Average

Coefficient of variation in 1985

Source: DRI.

Among the products for which the SMP seems to have worked best (in terms of reducing price disparities) are radio equipment, record players, tape and cassette recorders, along with televisions, washing machines and personal computers. It is interesting to see that the cut-throat competition which has taken place in the computer market translated into a strong convergence of prices of this product category, even though the coefficient of variation was already comparatively low at the beginning of the period. The same holds for musical instruments, another key product in the other important leisure items category, a market in which EU producers have been losing market share to imports and have been forced to focus on niche segments to survive.

However, there are a number of market segments for which price disparities were low at the beginning of the period but increased significantly after 1985, or have not decreased in line with the trend for other durable goods. For fridges and freezers, floorings, other household appliances, records, cassettes, magnetic tapes and other similar products, as well as films and other photographic supplies, the coefficient of price variation in 1993 in the EU-12 was virtually the same as in 1985, whereas for the other categories (sporting goods or games and toys) there has even been a rise in price dispersion between the two years. In one case, other means of personal transport, the rise in price disparities was so strong that the coefficient of variation in 1993 had risen more than 20% above the average for all durable consumer goods sectors. For the other products in the list, the coefficient of price dispersion in 1993 was about the same or marginally higher than in 1985. It is interesting to note the presence of domestic electrical appliances in that box. The market for electrical appliances for consumer use is indeed one in which the SMP has reportedly led to a greater harmonization of the technical aspects of products, an increasing internationalization of brands, an upsurge in M&A activity and the development of more homogeneous channels of distribution. The trend in price indicators confirms the industry's own view that the market was already highly integrated in 1985, and that the differences in standards and norms in this market segment were not important barriers to trade.[12] This is further discussed in Chapter 11, where the white goods market is the subject of one of the case studies done to clarify the underlying factors influencing prices. The absence of price convergence for the other products in this box nevertheless contrasts with the average trend for durable consumer goods, even though it is not worrying in itself, given that the total coefficient of price variation is still comparatively low.

The absence of price convergence – in fact, the increase in price disparities – in the sporting goods and toys markets is particularly surprising, as these are also highly traded products for which competition from non-EU-based producers has increased notably over the period. As will be seen in Chapter 6, market dualization and changes in the organization of distribution may have contributed to the observed increase in price dispersion across the EU.

There is a third set of market segments which is worth commenting on, and this is the set of products which displayed high price variation at the start of the period and whose prices have failed to converge significantly after the inception of the SMP. This category, on the right hand side of Figure 4.3.6, includes heating and air conditioning appliances, photographic equipment and motor vehicles. In the first two cases, increased diversity of products and market dualization were likely strategies adopted by firms in response to the rise in competition, whereas in the case of motor vehicles the absence of price convergence across the EU is a direct reflection of the fact that this market is still constrained by a number of non-tariff barriers: from quotas on imported vehicles to national regulatory standards (many of which are related to safety) and exclusive dealership networks.

[12] See DRI [1995], 'Survey of the trade association's perceptions of the effects of the single market', report prepared for the European Commission (DG III).

For cutlery, finally, the particular organization of distribution within the EU again seems to account for the persisting price disparities as this is a market segment in which high price variations have also been observed at regional level (see the study on France mentioned in Section 3.5).

4.3.6. Other manufactured products

The other manufactured products category also contains a number of interesting market segments, as it includes books, brochures and other similar printed material – one of the categories for which price disparities were highest before the launch of the SMP – along with pharmaceutical products, fuels and lubricants for motor vehicles and other personal consumption items.

Figure 4.3.7. Pattern of price convergence for other manufactures 1985–93, EU-12

Convergence between 85-93 in the EU-12	Below Average	Average	Above Average
Strong convergence	Fuels and lubricants for motor vehicles Durable and semi-durable personal care products Non-durable personal care products	Other non-durable household articles Flowers, other recreational goods Other personal articles nec	Books, brochures, other similar printed material
Convergence close to average	Cleaning and maintenance products Articles for travelling and personal luggage	Light bulbs and electrical accessories Orthopaedic, therapeutic products Jewelry, watches, precious stones	
Slow convergence or divergence	Tyres, inner tubes, replacement parts for motor vehicles Paper and drawing supplies	Other pharmaceutical products Lenses and glasses Periodicals, newspapers	Medicines

Coefficient of variation in 1985

Source: DRI.

On average in the EU-12, the coefficient of price dispersion in the other manufactured goods category has been going down more or less continuously since 1980, decreasing from 24.4 in 1980 to 23.7 in 1985, 23.2 in 1990 and 19.1 in 1993. (The change in the coefficient of variation over time is illustrated in Figure 3.3.6.) Price convergence thus appears to have accelerated a few years after the launch of the SMP.

In the category of products for which price dispersion was significantly higher than average in 1985 there are only two items: books, brochures and similar printed material, and medicines (Figure 4.3.7). For books, brochures and other printed material, the coefficient of variation has been reduced dramatically after the inception of the SMP, coming down from 58 to 17.8. For medicines, on the other hand, although the coefficient of price variation at the beginning of the period was already high (at 40.5 in 1985), it continued to increase between 1985 and 1993, rising to 43.4 in 1993, more than twice the average coefficient of variation for the other manufactured goods category (Figures 4.3.8 and 4.3.9).

However, there are a number of products whose coefficient of price variation was low at the start of the period, and which nevertheless experienced a pronounced trend towards (increased) price convergence after 1985. These are fuel and lubricants for motor vehicles, durable and semi-durable personal care products, and non-durable personal care products (in the top left hand corner of Figure 4.3.7). Each of these three market segments has been characterized by globalization trends both in manufacturing and in distribution which have seemingly translated into a more rapid convergence of prices across the EU.

Outliers in terms of price convergence patterns, apart from medicinal products and other pharmaceutical products, include lenses and glasses and periodicals and newspapers, two product categories for which the coefficient of variation in 1993 is significantly higher than the average for this category. The list of products for which price disparities have increased in the EU-12 after 1985 also includes tyres, inner tubes and replacement parts for motor vehicles, and paper and drawing supplies. For tyres, inner tubes and replacement parts for motor vehicles, the growth in the coefficient of variation was only moderate, so that at the end of the period the coefficient of price dispersion was still lower than the average for other manufactured consumer products, but the same does not hold for paper and drawing supplies, for which the coefficient of price dispersion was more than 20% above the average for the category in 1993.

Figure 4.3.8. Measures of price dispersion for selected manufactured products in 1985 (prices including taxes)

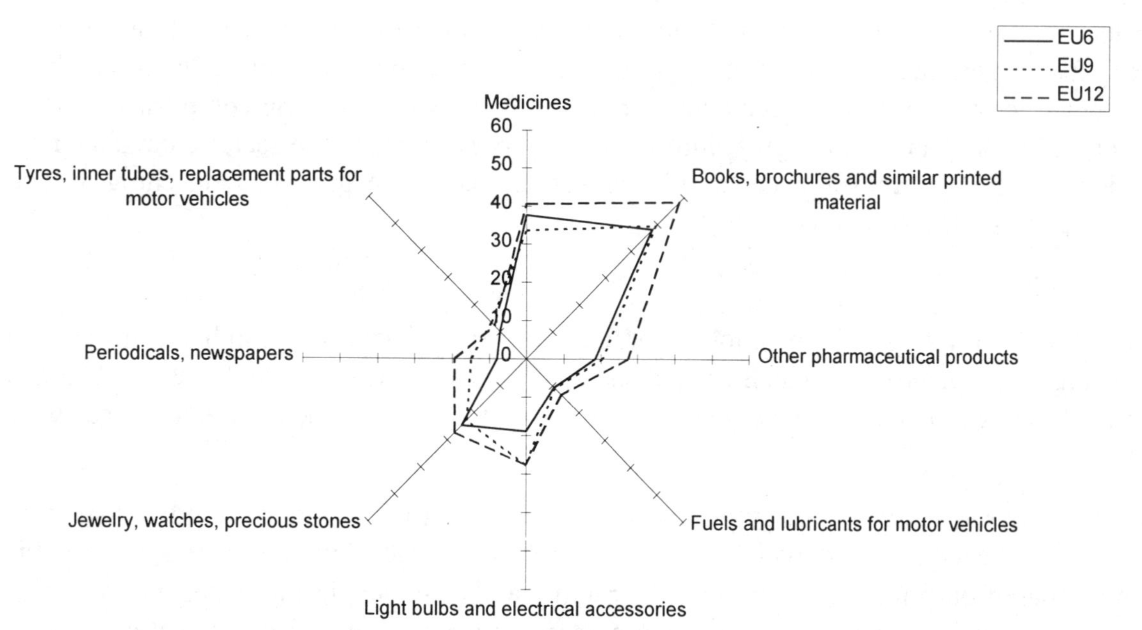

Source: DRI.

Figure 4.3.9. Measures of price dispersion for selected manufactured products in 1993 (prices including taxes)

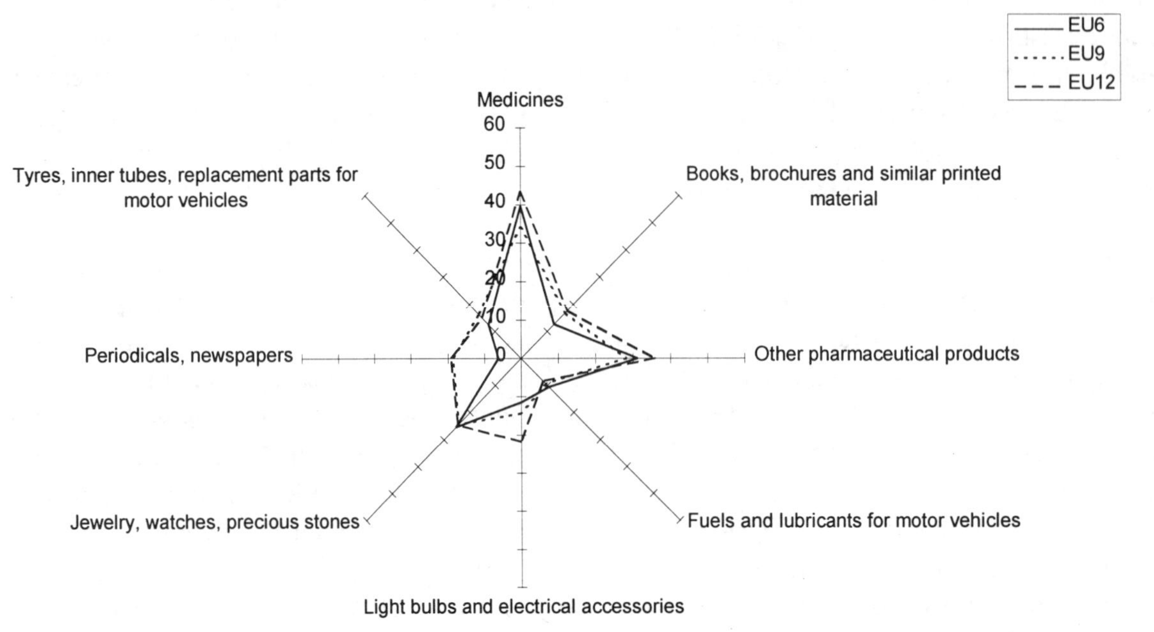

Source: DRI.

Finally, the two boxes in the top left of Figure 4.3.7 list the products which had an average or less than average price dispersion at the start of the period, and for which price disparities have been reduced significantly following the launch of the SMP. This includes other non-durable household articles, along with non-durable personal care products such as soaps as detergents, or perfumery and cosmetics. In the latter case, standards harmonization may have contributed to other observed price convergence patterns by encouraging companies to adopt pan-European strategies, although according to the professionals in the sector a key factor for the downward price convergence in this market has been the growing concentration and increased power of distributors.

4.3.7. Energy

Figure 4.3.10 shows a similar positioning of the key energy products. As indicated in Section 3.2, energy is a category for which price disparities increased significantly between 1985 and 1993, following a period of convergence between 1980 and 1985 when crude oil prices were high.

Figure 4.3.10 shows which energy products contribute most to the increased price dispersion of the whole category, and which have seen prices diverge comparatively less than the average (based on prices including taxes). Significantly, the single fuel category for which price disparities have increased more than average is heating oil and other heating fuels, a product for which the coefficient of variation was comparatively low at the start of the period.[13] This indicates different possible rates of adjustment of energy prices to consumers

[13] Looking at Figure 4.3.9, it appears that fuel and lubricants, on the other hand, do not show a similar rise in price disparities. The coefficient of variation evolves from 13.1 in 1985 to 8.4 in 1993.

following the 1986 oil price collapse. For other fuel categories, prices inclusive of VAT and excise duties have tended to diverge somewhat less than the average for all energy prices to consumers – even though the overall pattern still shows an increase in the coefficient of variation from 21.1 in 1985 to 31.7 in 1993.

Figure 4.3.10. Pattern of price convergence for energy products 1985–93, EU-12

Convergence between 85-93 in the EU-12	Below Average	Average	Above Average
Strong convergence	Electricity	Liquefied gas	Town gas and natural gas Coal, coke and other solid combustibles
Convergence close to average			
Slow convergence or divergence	Heating oil and other heating fuels		

Coefficient of variation in 1985

Source: DRI.

4.3.8. Services

The results for services are particularly important to analyse in more detail, given that the dominant pattern at EU-12 level in this category has been a slow convergence. On average, the coefficient of variation for services was 33.7 in 1985 in the EU-12, and it decreased to 28.6 in 1993, still a very high figure when compared to an average coefficient of variation for food products of 20.8 in 1993, and for clothing and footwear of 17.9. Within the EU-6, which includes economies which have a longer history of economic integration than the EU-12, the coefficient of variation for services was 21.3 in 1993, which compares with figures of 12.1 for food products and 10.0 for clothing and footwear. The difference between the coefficient of variation for services and for traded goods thus appears to increase the more integrated the economies are, despite efforts to the contrary (through the liberalization of several services markets in the EU).

Among the services whose prices have tended to converge faster than average, there are a number of sectors with a high degree of public ownership, in some cases national monopolies. In the top three boxes in Figure 4.3.11 are, for example, postal services, other (personal) transport services, and telephone, telegraph and telex services. In the case of postal services, the rapid convergence of prices in the EU-12 has taken place despite the fact that price dispersion at the beginning of the period was already low. The arrival of new suppliers in the market (private courier services) and market pressures from the demand side (such as the extension of re-mail, a practice by which private companies offer a cross-border mail service to benefit from lower fees), along with increased competition from telecom services (E-mail) have put downward pressure on prices in this market and have forced a rationalization of the organization of production. In the case of telephone, telegraph and telex services the coefficient of variation was very high at the beginning of the period (43.8, compared to an average for all services of 33.7), but the trend in price convergence was so strong that the coefficient of price variation had fallen to 31.4 in 1993, only 10% above the average for services of 28.6. The progressive liberalization of telecom markets and the entry of new suppliers in the EU market largely accounts for this increased convergence of prices.

Figure 4.3.11. Pattern of price convergence for services 1985–93, EU-12

Convergence between 85-93 in the EU-12	Below Average	Average	Above Average
Strong convergence	Postal services Service in restaurants	Other transport services Expenses for sporting events and activities Banking, insurance and other financial services	Repairs to heating, kitchen appliances Repairs to glassware, tableware Laundry and dry cleaning services Telephone, telegraph and telex services Tuition costs Legal services
Convergence close to average	Repairs to clothing	Repairs to furniture, furnishings, floorings Specialist medical services Local transport services Repairs to recreational articles Expenses for cultural events and activities Expenditures in cafes, bars Hotel and other lodging expenses	Railway, road and other transport services Charges for radio, television use
Slow convergence or divergence	**Repairs to household textiles** **Other household services** **Dental services** **Other expenses related to personal transport** General household maintenance costs	Expenditures in canteens **Repairs to footwear** Domestic services **General medical services** **Vehicle maintenance costs** **Other services nec** **Hairdressers, beauticians services** **Other expenses related to transport services**	**Water distribution charges** **Nurse services** **Other medical and paramedical services**

Coefficient of variation in 1985

Source: DRI.

At the other extreme (in the bottom three boxes in the chart) one finds a number of service categories whose prices have converged less than average, some of which have even experienced increased price divergence between 1985 and 1993. Among these are most of the services related to health care (such as nurse services and other medical and paramedical services, for which the coefficient of variation was already very high at the start of the period, along with general medical services, and dental services). In only two of these 14 service categories do we actually see some trend, albeit slow, towards convergence. These two service categories are general maintenance costs and domestic services. In each of the 12 other cases, the dominant pattern over the period 1985–93 has been increased price disparities across the EU-12. This trend has been so pronounced in the case of the four services in the lower right hand corner of Figure 4.3.11 that their coefficient of variation had become significantly higher than average in 1993.

As reported above, many health services have seen their prices diverge in the EU-12 over the period 1985–93, despite increased European integration. To see the extent to which the persistent high price disparities reflect differences in average purchasing power in the 12 Member States, we have run a number of regressions to test if the variation between the national price indices per category of services is related to the disparity in GDP per capita. The results of these regressions are presented in Table 4.3.1. Figures 4.3.12 and 4.3.13 illustrate the trend in two specific and highly contrasted market segments.

Overall, it appears that the difference in average service prices across countries is significantly related to GDP per capita, implying that service prices will tend to be higher in economies with a higher nominal GDP per capita, and lower in economies with a low level of GDP per capita (all regressions were made for the year 1993). Looking at the results for detailed service categories, however, shows some striking results (Table 4.3.1). For most market service categories, we find that the disparity in price indices in the EU-12 is indeed positively related to differences in levels of GDP per capita. The service sectors for which the disparity in GDP per capita explains almost all the variations in price indices are insurance, banking and other financial services (see Figure 4.3.13), repairs to household textiles, charges for radio and television use, hairdressers, beauticians and other similar services, shoe repairs and general household maintenance costs, among others. Significantly, a number of transport service sectors also show a positive relation between price indices and GDP per capita: this is notably the case for local transport services and other expenses related to transport services.

In total, among the 37 service categories, there are 19 cases for which the relatively high level of price disparities in the EU reflects at least in part differences in GDP per capita.

There are, however, 18 other service categories for which price disparities are not explained by the differences in GDP per capita. These include all the health care service sectors but one (the exception being other medical and paramedical services), along with a number of regulated sectors such as water distribution, postal service, telephone, telegraph and telex, and railway and other transport services. Figure 4.3.12 illustrates this in the case of medical services provided by general practitioners.

The inclusion in this list of service sectors such as expenses for sporting events, or expenses for cultural events and activities, may reflect different cultural policies across the EU.

Comparing the list of sectors for which price disparities are explained at least in part by differences in GDP per capita helps to put some results in Figure 4.3.11 in a broader perspective. In particular, the absence of price convergence over time in sectors such as repairs to household textiles, other household services, other expenses on personal transport, vehicle maintenance costs or shoe repair may simply reflect the persisting differences in GDP per capita within the EU-12.

The case of telephone, telegraph and telex services, and that of postal services are again particularly interesting, in that for both sectors there was a positive correlation between the price level of these services across the EU-12 and GDP per capita in 1985, but this link had disappeared in 1993. This indicates that the internationalization of these services (and, in the case of telephone services, increased competition) has led to such a convergence in these services prices at EU level that the link with GDP per capita is no longer relevant.

Table 4.3.1. Econometric estimation of price dispersion for services based on differences in GDP per capita in 1993

Service type	Coefficient		T stat. for b	R^2
	a	b		
All services	56.7	0.48	10.4	0.19
Not significant				
Railway and road transport services	35.1	0.64	2.14	0.24
Hotel and other lodging expenses	60.2	0.35	2.05	0.23
Legal services	35.0	0.59	2.00	0.22
Tuition costs	45.2	0.48	1.99	0.21
Specialist medical services	149.4	-0.52	-1.94	0.20
Repairs to heating, kitchen appliances	52.5	0.45	1.80	0.17
Repairs to clothing	76.3	0.40	1.77	0.16
Other expenses related to personal transport	56.1	0.43	1.73	0.15
Repairs to furniture, furnishings, floorings	56.8	0.46	1.67	0.14
Postal services	76.7	0.21	1.43	0.09
Dental services	84.5	0.30	0.94	-0.01
Laundry and dry cleaning services	84.8	0.14	0.87	-0.02
Expenses for sporting events and activities	117.8	-0.16	-0.69	-0.05
General medical services	169.3	-0.33	-0.65	-0.06
Expenses for cultural events and activities	69.2	0.14	0.62	-0.06
Expenses in canteens	77.8	0.20	0.63	-0.06
Telephone, telegraph and telex services	87.9	0.07	0.25	-0.09
Nurse services	130.8	-0.10	-0.17	-0.10
Significant				
Repairs to household textiles	24.6	0.67	5.35	0.72
Insurance, banking and other financial services	57.6	0.41	5.38	0.72
Repairs to footwear	20.8	1.01	5.33	0.71
Charges for radio and television use	16.1	0.96	5.11	0.69
Hairdressers, beauticians services	21.5	0.86	4.99	0.68
General household maintenance costs	43.6	0.62	4.83	0.67
Other transport services	48.9	0.54	4.74	0.66
Water distribution charges	-18.8	1.59	4.24	0.61
Local transport services	29.8	0.83	4.27	0.61
Vehicle maintenance costs	15.9	0.79	3.78	0.55
Repairs to glassware, tableware, etc.	45.2	0.51	3.55	0.51
Other expenses related to transport services	25.9	0.68	3.55	0.51
Expenses in cafes, bars	40.9	0.74	3.48	0.50
Other services nec	44.4	0.69	3.36	0.48
Domestic services	29.4	0.76	3.18	0.45
Expenses in restaurants	76.1	0.29	3.06	0.43
Other household services	47.2	0.57	2.40	0.30
Repairs of recreational goods	49.6	0.58	2.36	0.29
Other medical and paramedical services	14.3	0.99	2.26	0.27

Source: DRI.

Figure 4.3.12. Relation between price dispersion for general practitioner medical services and GDP per capita, prices including taxes in 1993, EU-12

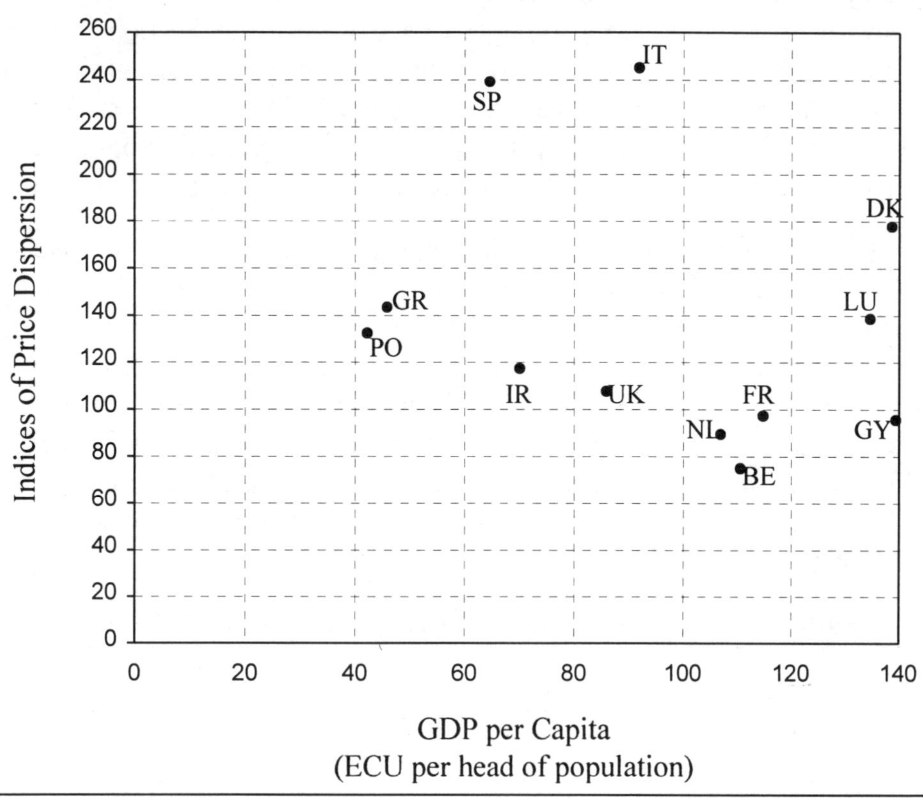

Source: DRI.

Figure 4.3.13. Relation between price dispersion for insurance, banking and other financial services and GDP per capita, prices including taxes in 1993, EU-12

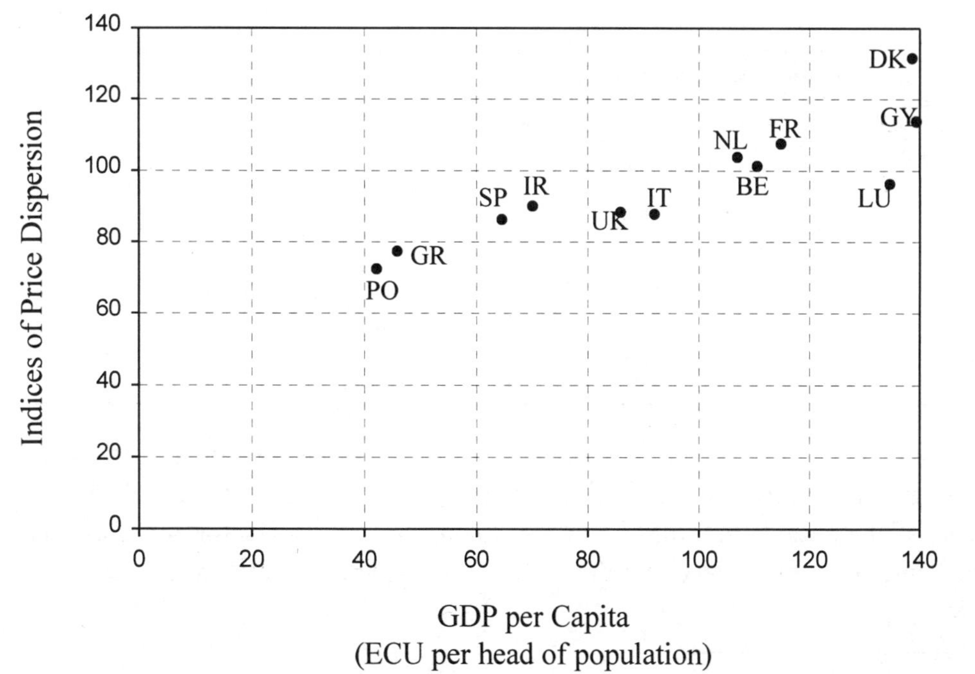

Source: DRI.

4.3.9. Equipment goods

The average coefficient of variation for equipment goods in the EU-12 in 1985 was, at 14.0, the lowest of all product categories considered. This reflects the fact that investment goods are and have always been a highly traded product category. Still, in Section 3.2 we saw that following an initial phase during which price convergence increased across the EU-12, there has been a change in the trend, with price disparities increasing again after 1990. It is thus important to look at the behaviour of prices within more detailed product categories to identify the market segments which account for the increased divergence after 1990.

Figure 4.3.14 groups the different types of investment goods according to the value of the coefficient of variation in 1985 (compared to the average coefficient for the category) and to the speed of convergence in prices between 1985 and 1990. Clearly, there are a number of highly traded equipment categories for which price dispersion was higher than average in 1985, and which have experienced a very significant reduction in price disparities after that. This includes most of the transport equipment sectors (including motor vehicles,[14] trains and railway rolling stock, aerospace equipment and other transport equipment) and textile machinery. On these markets, thus, the on-going globalization of companies has translated into reduced price disparities at EU-12 level.

Figure 4.3.14. Pattern of price convergence for equipment goods 1985–93, EU-12

Convergence between 85-93 in the EU-12	Below Average	Average	Above Average
Strong convergence	Office and data processing machinery	Machinery for food, chemicals, rubber, packaging Telecom equipment, meters	Textile machinery Motor vehicles and engines Ships Trains, railway equipment Aircraft, helicopters, aeronautical equipment Other transport equipment
Convergence close to average		Agricultural machinery and tractors Electronic equipment, radio and television	
Slow convergence or divergence	Structural metal products Machinery equipment for mining and metallurgy, building and civil engineering Machinery for working wood, paper Other machinery and mechanical equipment Electrical equipment including lighting	Tools and finished metal articles Machine tools for metal working Precision instruments Optical instruments, photographic material	Products of boilermaking

Coefficient of variation in 1985

Source: DRI.

The trend towards price convergence is also highly notable for computers (office and data processing machines), even though prices for this product category were already very similar at the start of the period (in 1985). This is consistent with the observation already made for consumer durable goods that computer prices for consumers have converged at a rapid rate after 1985.

[14] It is interesting to note that at the consumer level, the coefficient of variation for motor vehicles was above the average but did not show a particular trend towards convergence between 1985 and 1993.

There is, however, a category for which the price dispersion at the beginning of the period was high and further increased between 1985 and 1993: this is boilers. The boiler sector was one of the sectors identified by Buigues et al.[15] likely to be most affected by the SMP. Over the past decade, the market for boilers has experienced strongly increased competition from non-EU suppliers, which have forced EU producers to rationalize production, invest in automation and emphasize quality as a competitive factor. The heightening of environmental and safety standards has further contributed to this increased emphasis on quality, and on the development of custom-tailored products. This is likely to have led to increased product diversification and hence explains the absence of price convergence in this market.

Other troublesome sectors, i.e. sectors for which price dispersion increased, include all those in the lower left hand corner of Figure 4.3.14. In all these segments, price disparities in the EU-12 have increased at such a rate between 1985 and 1993 that the coefficient of price variation in 1993 is much higher than the average for all investment goods sectors. The reason may again be a tendency to develop more customized machinery, though this assertion ought to be verified.

4.3.10. Construction

The results for the construction sector are presented in Figure 4.3.15. On average, prices in this sector have tended to diverge over time in the EU-12, coming from an average dispersion level in 1985 of 22.1 and rising to 27.4 in 1993. The two construction market segments which experienced a greater price divergence than average include roads, bridges and tunnels, and agricultural buildings. In the first case, the result is somewhat surprising given that this is a public procurement market in which one would have expected to see price convergence following the liberalization of public procurement and as a result of the increasingly pan-European strategies of the larger EU construction companies. Worker mobility has also increased significantly in the sector, thanks to the new rules facilitating the movement of persons across the EU, which have made it possible for the large construction companies to increase their 'outsourcing' of labour by hiring people on fixed term contracts from the lower wage Community regions.

This factor alone should already have led to an increased convergence of construction costs for large projects, such as for public works or roads, bridges and tunnels. The case study on construction, however, provides a different insight, and identifies a number of remaining non-tariff barriers which explain the low degree of pan-Europeanization of this sector. These mainly relate to the local nature of the business, to differences in management contracting practices, to the small size of several projects allied with high tendering costs, and, in some cases, to behavioural practices which have effectively slowed the integration process by limited competition (for example, through collusive tendering or clubbing).

[15] See Buigues, P. and Ilzkovitz, A. [1988], 'The sectoral impact of the internal market', European Commission document, Vol. 2, No 335.

Figure 4.3.15. Pattern of price convergence for construction costs 1985–93, EU-12

Convergence between 85-93 in the EU-12	Below Average	Average	Above Average
Strong convergence		Housing, multi-family Non-commercial buildings	
Convergence close to average		Housing, single family Industrial buildings Commercial buildings Other communications works	
Slow convergence or divergence	Roads, bridges, tunnels	Agricultural buildings	

Coefficient of variation in 1985

Source: DRI.

4.4. Analysis of price disparities between the EU-6 and the EU-12

This section investigates the trend in price dispersion across different regional groupings, to test whether price convergence has been more (or less) pronounced in certain groups of countries (for instance, in the EU-6 or in the EU-9) than in the whole of the EU. In fact, one observes a generally stronger convergence of prices in the EU-12 than in either the EU-6 or the EU-9, with even a slight resistance to convergence in the EU-9 in selected market segments (most notably energy).

Figure 4.4.1 illustrates the typical price convergence patterns of different product/services segments both between 1985 and 1993 and across different geographical markets. As in the figures presented in Section 4.3, the vertical axis indicates whether the convergence over time of the given product in the EU-12 has been comparatively slow (maybe even a price divergence was observed), about average for this product category, or faster than average. On the horizontal axis the box has been divided into three segments to indicate the degree to which absolute price disparities in the EU-12 have come closer to those in the EU-6 (which are generally lower).

The list of products in the top right hand corner are thus products for which price disparities have been reduced most, both over time and between regions. They are, in some way, the 'success sectors' from the point of view of price convergence. In the lower left hand box are products for which price disparities have not been reduced significantly (and may even have increased) over time in the EU-12, and for which the dispersion between the EU-6 and EU-12 prices has also increased. Note that the dispersion between the EU-6 and EU-12 prices may have increased because prices have converged in the EU-6 and not in the EU-12, or because they have effectively diverged in the EU-12.

In the lower right hand box are products for which price disparities have not been reduced over time in the EU-12, but for which the coefficients of variation for the EU-6 and EU-12 have moved closer together. In most cases, the sectors have been characterized by increased price disparities within the EU-6. Finally, in the top left hand corner are products for which price convergence has been comparatively important over time, but for which price disparities between the EU-6 and the EU-12 have increased. Again, this includes mainly sectors for which the reduction of price disparities in the EU-6 has been greater than that observed in the EU-12.

Below, we look at the pattern of price convergence of each of the main product/service categories in the EU-6 and EU-12.

Figure 4.4.1. Typical price convergence patterns over time and across regional groupings, 1985–93

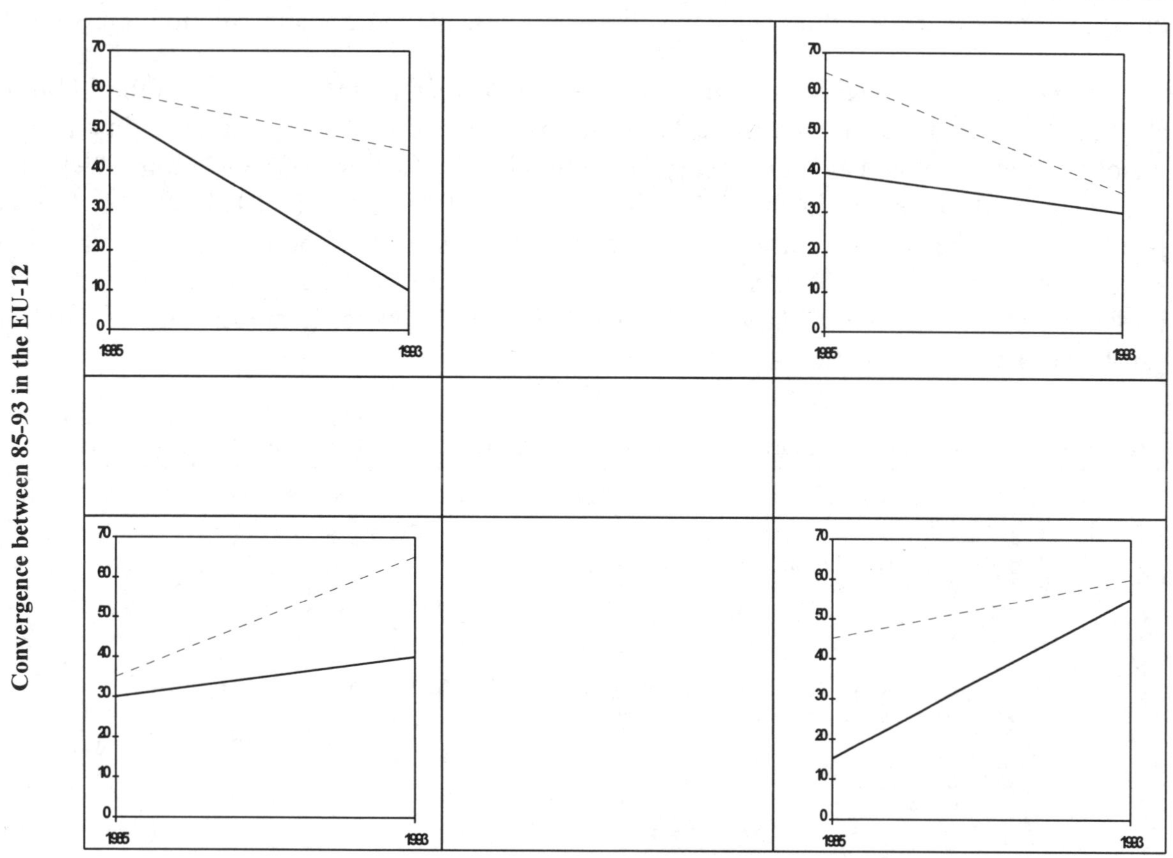

———— =EU 6, ...= EU12

Source: DRI.

4.4.1. Food products

In the food sector, the average coefficient of variation in the EU-12 was 20.9 in 1985, 54% higher than that in the EU-6. By 1993, the difference between the coefficients of variation in the EU-12 and EU-6 had increased to 72%, due to a slower convergence of prices in the EU-12 than in the EU-6.

Having this average pattern for all food products in mind, we see in Figure 4.4.2 that there are a number of products for which prices in the EU-12 did converge towards the EU-6 average over time: these are the products in the top right hand corner, namely fresh milk, dried or smoked fish, other seafood, preserved milk and meat preparations and other meat products. Similarly, convergence in the EU-6 was comparatively slow (compared to the EU-12) in the rice, pasta, pork and delicatessen markets, among others (in the lower right hand corner of Figure 4.4.2).

If 'problem' markets are identified as markets in which reductions in price disparities in the EU-12 have been slow both over time and compared to the trend in the EU-6 (i.e. markets in the lower left hand corner of Figure 4.4.2) and for which price dispersion was high at the beginning of the period, comparing Figure 4.3.1 with Figure 4.4.2 shows two markets fitting this definition: dried vegetables and confectionery. These are indicated in bold in Figure 4.4.2.

Price dispersion in the sugar confectionery market is lower in the EU-12 than in the EU-9 in all years but 1980, and lower than in the EU-6 in 1985. Slow convergence over time across regions comes from increased dispersion in the EU-9 (from 28.9 in 1985 to 32.6 in 1993) and huge decreased dispersion in the EU-6 (from 31.7 in 1985 to 9.5 in 1993). Sutton [1991] points out that the structure of supply and distribution as well as the nature of competition varies a lot between the UK, Germany, France and Italy in the sugar confectionery market. Furthermore, import penetration was less than 10%. Until 1990 at least, this market was not pan-European even in the EU-6.

Figure 4.4.2. Price convergence across regional groupings – the case of food products

Convergence between 85-93 in the EU-12	Slow convergence	Convergence close to average	Strong convergence
Strong convergence	Fresh vegetables Sugar *Ice cream* *Spices, sauces, condiments* Other milk products except cheese	Fresh fruits	Fresh milk *Dried or smoked fish* *Other seafood* *Preserved milk* Meat preparations, other meat products
Convergence close to average	Cakes and biscuits Other cereal based products Poultry Eggs Dried fruits Chocolate	Bread Edible oils	Beef Butter Vegetables preserved, prepared
Slow convergence or divergence	Flour Veal Other fresh or frozen meat Frozen fruits **Dried vegetables** Jams, honey, syrups Prepared fish and other seafood **Confectionery** Fresh, frozen fish Margarine	Mutton, lamb and goat meat Cheese Potatoes	Rice Pasta, noodles Pork Delicatessen Frozen vegetables Products derived from potatoes Other animal and veg. fats

Convergence between the EU-6 and the EU-12 (85-93)

Source: DRI.

For comparison, the products for which price disparities were comparatively high at the beginning of the period but have fallen rapidly, both in the EU-12 and in the EU-6, are indicated in italics in Figure 4.4.2. These can be called ‘successes’ of increased European integration. This category includes the ice cream market, a segment in which the average degree of concentration has increased, but so has the degree of competition as a result amongst other of increased import penetration from non-EU producers.

4.4.2. Beverages

Doing the same exercise for the nine products in the beverages category, one finds first of all that the average price dispersion for beverages in the EU-12 compared to the EU-6 has decreased between 1985 and 1993. Whereas in 1985 the average coefficient of variation for beverages was, at 37.0, more than 130% higher than that for the EU-6, this difference had shrunk slightly in 1993, to 118%.

Looking at Figure 4.4.3, we find that the only product for which price disparities in the EU-12 had fallen significantly more rapidly than both the average for beverages and EU-6 price disparities, is wine. To some extent, this reflects an increased harmonization of indirect tax rates on wine across the EU, as confirmed by the comparison of coefficients of price variation for wine prices including and excluding taxes. For mineral water, a product for which the coefficient of variation in 1985 was very high, and for which a rapid decrease in price dispersion was observed in the EU-12 between 1985 and 1993, we see that the reduction in the EU-12 was similar to that in the EU-6. The same holds for beer and other alcoholic beverages. On the other hand, alcohols posted a slow reduction of price disparities either over time or across geographical areas, starting from a relatively high coefficient of variation at the start of the period.

Figure 4.4.3. Price convergence across regional groupings – the case of beverages

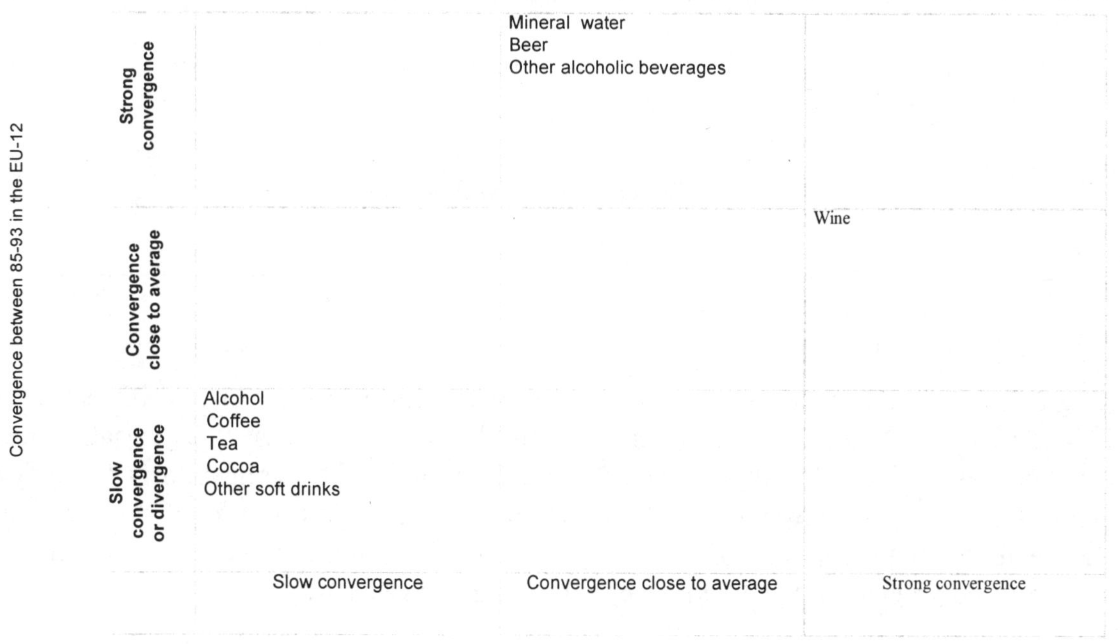

Source: DRI.

4.4.3. Tobacco

For the tobacco category as a whole, the reduction in overall price dispersion in the EU-12 between 1985 and 1993 has been slightly less than that in the EU-6, though not significantly so. In 1985, the coefficient of variation for the EU-12 was, at 45.7, 127% higher than that for the EU-6. In 1993, the coefficient of variation for the EU-12 had come down to 30.3, but that in the EU-6 had fallen a little more rapidly so that the difference between the two increased to 139%.

Figure 4.4.4 shows that the convergence of prices for the EU-12 was relatively stronger than for the EU-6 for other tobacco products.

Figure 4.4.4. Price convergence across regional groupings – the case of tobacco products

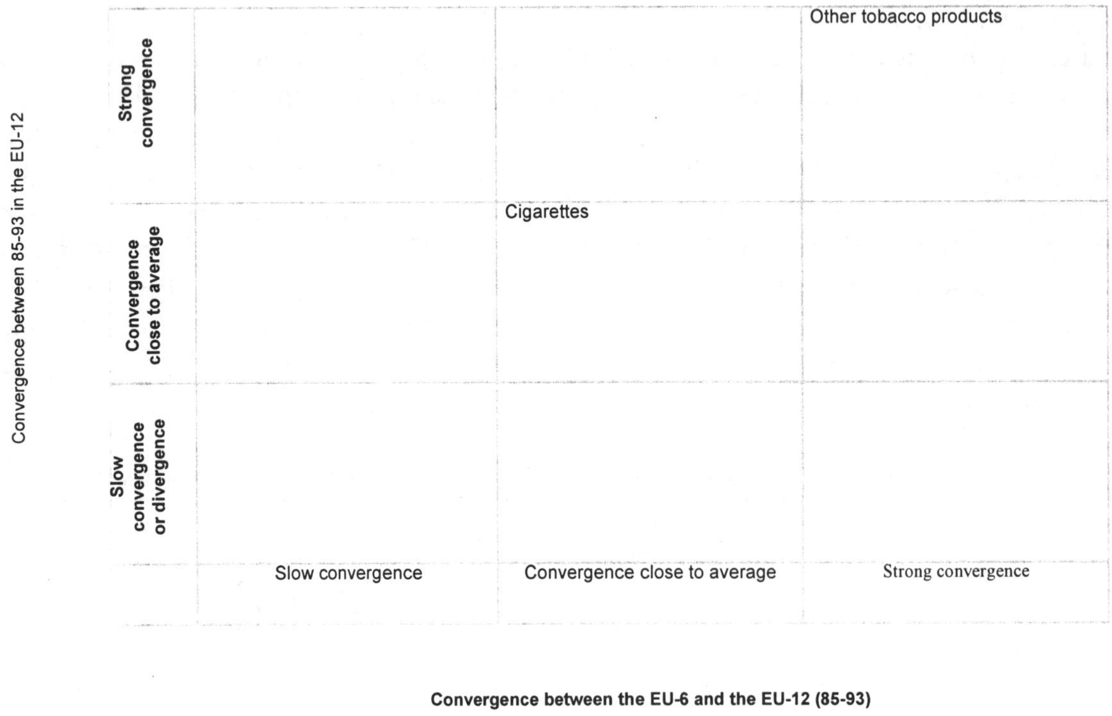

Source: DRI.

4.4.4. Clothing and footwear

Clothing and footwear is a category for which the coefficient of price variation increased in the EU-12 between 1985 and 1993, whereas in the EU-6 this coefficient of variation has always been low, and has actually remained stable over time. The implication is that price dispersion has increased between the EU-6 and the EU-12. Figure 4.4.5 shows that it is mainly the footwear product categories, along with men's clothing, which account for the non-convergence (in fact, for the divergence) in prices in the EU-12.

Figure 4.4.5. Price convergence across regional groupings – the case of clothing and footwear

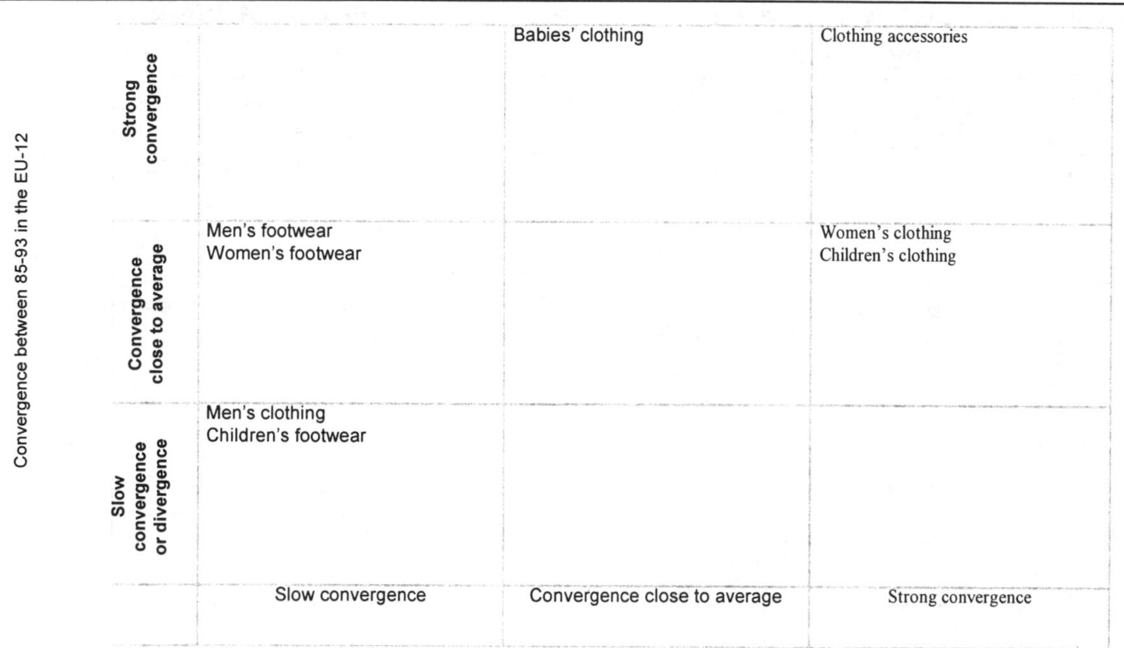

Source: DRI.

4.4.5. Durable consumer goods

The average coefficient of variation for durable consumer goods in the EU-12 was 20.8 in 1985, about twice the level of the coefficient in the EU-6. By 1993, the coefficient of variation for the EU-12 had fallen to 16.4, and the difference between that and the EU-6 had shrunk to 60%, indicating a 'catching-up' effect of the EU-12 prices towards the EU-6 average, reflecting either increased (extra-EU) trade, increased European integration or both.

In general, convergence between the EU-12 and the EU-6 has been most pronounced for all the heavy consumer appliances such as washing machines and dryers, cookers and stoves, cleaning equipment, refrigerators and freezers, and heating and air conditioning appliances. All these markets are characterized by strong brand name presence, and have become more pan-European as a result of increased European integration. In contrast, among the product categories for which EU-12 convergence towards the EU-6 has been comparatively less pronounced are a host of miscellaneous products such as sports equipment, games and toys, glassware and tableware or other household appliances, which are typically less homogeneous product categories (both at the supply and the demand levels) and less concentrated markets. Producers have responded to the increase in competition by developing new products, focusing on certain niches and, in general, attempting to distinguish themselves from competitors by phasing non-price competitiveness factors. One interesting case is that of computers, for which price disparities in the EU-12 have decreased comparatively slower than in the EU-6. In fact, the coefficient of variation for this product category in the EU-6 had fallen to a remarkably low level of 4.1 in 1993, one of the lowest coefficients of variation of categories. Within the EU-12, computer and musical instruments price divergence has nevertheless also been reduced significantly to 10.1 – even if not as rapidly as in the EU-6.

Figure 4.4.6. Price convergence across regional groupings – the case of durable consumer goods

Convergence between 85-93 in the EU-12

Strong convergence	Other important leisure durable goods (incl. personal computers)	Gardening equipment Radio equipment Televisions	Washing machines and dryers Cookers and stoves Cleaning equipment *Record players, tape and cassette recorders*
Convergence close to average	Photographic and cinematographic equipment	Furniture and furnishings Motor vehicles	Heating and air conditioning appliances
Slow convergence or divergence	Household textiles Other household appliances Glassware and tableware Other modes of personal transport Sports equipment Games and toys Floor coverings	Film and other photographic supplies Cutlery	Refrigerators, freezers Non-electrical kitchen ustensils Records, cassettes, tapes
	Slow convergence	Convergence close to average	Strong convergence

Convergence between the EU-6 and the EU-12 (85-93)

Source: DRI.

4.4.6. Other manufactured products

Price disparities on other manufactured goods in the EU-12 and in the EU-6 respectively have been reduced in a similar way between 1985 and 1993. In 1985, the average coefficient of variation for this product category in the EU-12 was 21.5% higher than in the EU-6, and in 1993 the difference between the two was at 20.9%, about the same.

It is interesting to note that the rate of convergence of prices for books, brochures and similar printed material, which has already been identified as impressive for the EU-12, has actually been even more impressive in the EU-6, since this product category is listed in the upper left hand corner of Figure 4.4.7. This is essentially explained by market deregulation within the EU-6, and the changes in the organization of distribution, with the development of large specialized book stores.

For periodicals and newspapers, however, convergence has been slow, both over time and across regions.

Another interesting sector in this category is medicines: at the EU-12 level, this sector was seen to be characterized by a high coefficient of variation and no evidence of price convergence over time. In Figure 4.4.7, we see that the trend in convergence in the EU-6 has not been significantly different from that in the EU-12, i.e. there is no convergence.

Figure 4.4.7. Price convergence across regional groupings – the case of other manufactured goods

Convergence between 85-93 in the EU-12

	Slow convergence	Convergence close to average	Strong convergence
Strong convergence	Flowers, other recreational goods Books, brochures, other similar printed material Durable and semi-durable personal care products Non-durable personal care products		Other non-durable household articles Fuels and lubricants for motor vehicles Other personal articles nec
Convergence close to average	Light bulbs and electrical accessories Orthopaedic, therapeutic products Articles for travel and personal baggage		Cleaning and maintenance products Jewelry, watches, precious stones
Slow convergence or divergence	Periodicals, newspapers	Medicines Tyres, inner tubes, replacement parts for motor vehicles	Other pharmaceutical products Lenses and glasses Paper and drawing supplies

Convergence between the EU-6 and the EU-12 (85-93)

Source: DRI.

4.4.7. Energy

The energy products category is characterized by increasing price disparities over time within a given region, but some convergence of prices across regions. In 1993, the coefficient of variation of energy prices in the EU-12 was 30% higher than in the EU-6, which compares with a figure of close to 70% in 1985. The main reason for this is the particularly rapid increase in price disparities within the EU-6, as indicated by a coefficient of variation which increased from 12.5 in 1985 to 24.3 in 1993 (for prices including taxes).

Looking at Figure 4.4.8, one sees that increased price disparities across regions were particularly significant for heating oil and other heating fuels, and for natural gas. The first of these two categories was characterized by very low price dispersion at the EU-6 level in 1985, increasing significantly after that. Electricity prices also had a relatively low coefficient of variation at the beginning of the period, and have experienced less increase in price disparities either over time or across regions than the other fuel types.

Figure 4.4.8. Price convergence across regional groupings – the case of energy

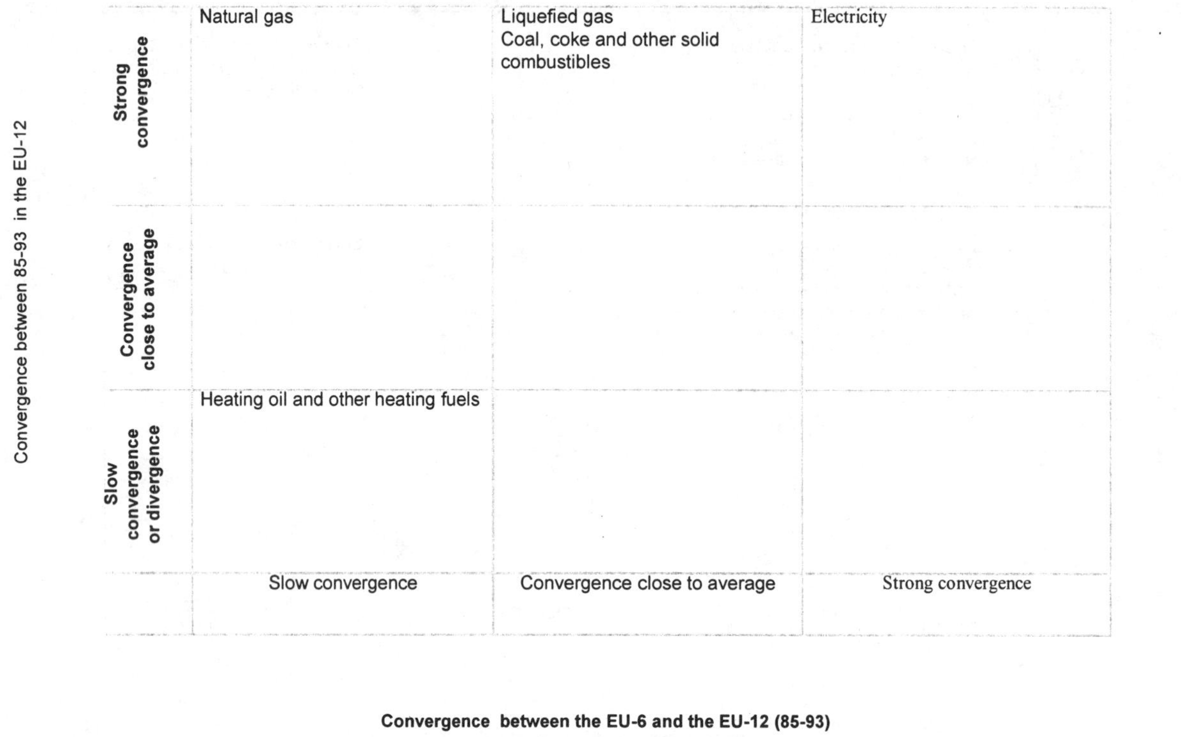

Convergence between 85-93 in the EU-12

	Slow convergence	Convergence close to average	Strong convergence
Strong convergence	Natural gas	Liquefied gas Coal, coke and other solid combustibles	Electricity
Convergence close to average			
Slow convergence or divergence	Heating oil and other heating fuels		

Convergence between the EU-6 and the EU-12 (85-93)

Source: DRI.

4.4.8. Services

Within the services category, price convergence has been relatively slow over time in the EU-12. Even so, the trend in the EU-12 was more pronounced than in the EU-6 (which has a longer history of integration), so that the general trend is for a faster reduction in price dispersion for services in the EU-12 than in the EU-6.

Figure 4.4.9. groups the services according to whether these individual services have experienced faster or slower price convergence in the EU-12 than in the EU-6.

Significantly, among the four services (in italics) which recorded comparatively high price dispersion at the beginning of the period and which have since 1985 experienced both rapid convergence in prices over time in the EU-12 and convergence between the EU-12 and the EU-6 levels, is 'repairs to heating and kitchen appliances'. This is a service which is generally provided by the manufacturing companies themselves, and these have already been found to have become more pan-European (based on price trends). Another service for which the same pattern is observed is telephone, telegraph and telex services. In contrast, there are two market segments which were characterized by high price dispersion in 1985 and no convergence over time in the EU-12, for which we find also no trend towards convergence between the EU-12 and the EU-6: these two segments are water distribution and other medical and paramedical services. In both cases, price disparities in 1993 were found to be positively correlated with differences in GDP per capita level across the EU. For other medical services, price disparities in the EU-6 have increased in such a way that the overall difference between the coefficient of variation in the EU-6 and EU-12 has come down. Section 4.3 has already shown that in 1993 there was no apparent correlation between price levels for these segments of health care and GDP per capita by Member State, so that this absence of convergence strictly reflects differences in the regulatory environment for health care across Member States.

Figure 4.4.9. Price convergence across regional groupings – the case of services

Convergence between 85-93 in the EU-12 (rows) / Convergence between the EU-6 and the EU-12 (85-93) (columns)

	Slow convergence	Convergence close to average	Strong convergence
Strong convergence	Other transport services Tuition costs Banking, insurance and other financial services Expenditures in restaurants Repairs to glassware, tableware Expenses for sporting events and activities		*Repairs to heating, kitchen appliances* *Laundry and dry cleaning services* Postal services *Telephone, telegraph & telex services* *Legal services*
Convergence close to average	Repairs to furniture, furnishings, floorings Charges for radio, television use Expenditures in cafes, bars Hotel and other lodging expenses	Local transport services	Specialist medical services Railway, road and other transport services Repairs to recreational articles Expenses for cultural events and activities Repairs to clothing
Slow convergence or divergence	Repairs to footwear **Water distribution charges** Domestic services **Other medical and paramedical services** Other expenses related to transport services Expenses in canteens		General household maintenance costs Repairs to household textiles Other household services General medical services Dental services Nurse services Vehicle maintenance costs Other expenses related to personal transport Other services nec Hairdressers, beauticians services

Convergence between the EU-6 and the EU-12 (85-93)

Source: DRI.

4.4.9. Equipment goods

The average price dispersion for equipment goods was low at the beginning of the period (with a coefficient of variation of 14.0 in the EU-12 and 9.7 in the EU-6), but increased between 1990 and 1993 in both the EU-6 and the EU-12, and between 1985 and 1990 in the EU-6. As a result, although absolute price dispersion had increased in both regions in 1993, the trend was less pronounced in the EU-12 than in the EU-6 (price dispersion increased faster within the six core countries than in the EU-12).

The products for which the convergence trend was most pronounced are, significantly, aerospace equipment and boats, along with office and data processing equipment and machinery for food, chemical and rubber processing. Boilers, a market segment characterized by a high price dispersion and a large increase in price disparities over time in the EU-12, has experienced an even stronger increase in price disparities within the EU-6 countries, such that the difference between the coefficient of variation of the EU-12 and the EU-6 was smaller in 1993 than in 1985.

Other machine types for which prices in the EU-6 tended to diverge particularly rapidly after 1985 are machine tools for metal working, machinery for working wood and other machinery. On the other hand, for both telecommunications equipment and for trains and railway equipment the pan-Europeanization of markets has meant a relative convergence of prices both over time and across regions.

Figure 4.4.10. Price convergence across regional groupings – the case of equipment goods

Convergence between 85-93 in the EU-12	Slow convergence	Convergence close to average	Strong convergence
Strong convergence	Telecom equipment, meters Trains, railway equipment	Textile machinery Other transport equipment	Machinery for food, chemicals, rubber, packaging Office and data processing machinery *Ships* *Aircraft, helicopters, aeronautical equipment* Motor vehicles and engines
Convergence close to average	Agricultural machinery and tractors	Electronic equipment, radio and television	
Slow convergence or divergence	Structural metal products Machinery equipment for mining, metallurgy, building and civil engineering Electrical equipment, including lighting Tools and finished metal articles	Precision instruments Optical instruments, photographic material	Products of boilermaking Machine tools for metal working Machinery for working wood, paper Other machinery and mechanical equipment

Convergence between the EU-6 and the EU-12 (85-93)

Source: DRI.

4.4.10. Construction

The market for construction has also been characterized by increased price dispersion in the EU-12, particularly among the core EU-6 countries. Whereas the coefficient of variation of construction prices increased by 24% in the EU-12 (from 22.1 to 27.4) between 1985 and 1993, the same coefficient in the EU-6 increased by 73.6%, from 11.0 to 19.1.

As indicated in Figure 4.4.11, however, there was no significant difference in the pattern of convergence over time of the different types of construction services between 1985 and 1993.

Figure 4.4.11. Price convergence across regional groupings – the case of construction

Convergence between 85-93 in the EU-12	Slow convergence	Convergence close to average	Strong convergence
Strong convergence		Housing, multi-family Non-commercial buildings	
Convergence close to average		Housing, single family Commercial buildings Other communications works Industrial buildings	
Slow convergence or divergence		Agricultural buildings Roads, bridges, tunnels	

Convergence between the EU-6 and the EU-12 (85-93)

Source: DRI.

4.5. Statistical significance of price convergence/divergence patterns

This section tests the statistical significance of the price convergence/divergence patterns which were described in Sections 4.3 and 4.4. To do this, a test on the equality over time of the variance of price indices has been performed, using a χ^2 distribution. The test was applied to the variance of the price indices of all consumer goods and services (145 categories) across the EU-12, over four time periods: 1980 and 1985, 1980 and 1993, 1985 and 1993, 1990 and 1993. The description of the statistical test which was performed is presented in Appendix D.

The results show that there are 86 products/services categories out of 145 for which the price variances are significantly different in at least one of the four periods considered. Within that group of 86 products/services, 78 are price convergence cases, while 8 relate to price divergence cases.[16] The 78 consumer products/services which show a statistically significant price convergence pattern account on average for about 60% of total private consumption expenditures (i.e. expenditures on 145 consumer goods and services) at the EU-12 level in the four years considered (1980, 1985, 1990 and 1993). As for the eight consumer products/services which display a statistically significant price divergence pattern, they represent an average of 6% of total private consumption expenditures across the EU-12. Thus, the consumer products/services for which we observe a statistically significant price pattern over time (convergence or divergence) together account for two thirds of total private consumption expenditures in EU-12 countries.

16 Note that the test which was performed was constructed in such a way that there is a bias for divergence cases (see Appendix D), so the fact that there are only eight statistically significant cases of price divergence among the 145 categories is particularly interesting.

The above test for the equality of the variance of price indices over time is, however, not able to detect the cases where a given disparity of prices across the EU-12 countries, measured by a constant coefficient of variation, is consistent with a substantial country mobility within the price indices distribution. Indeed, high price countries in one period can become low price countries in the next period (and vice versa) while the coefficient of price variation measured between these countries remains constant over time. In other words, it is also important to verify if, for some products or services, countries jump from the low to the high side (or vice versa) of the distribution over different sub-periods, while the overall price variation across countries remains stable.

To look at the mobility of the EU-12 countries over time according to their price indices, Spearman rank correlation tests were carried out on all products/services (with the exception of the 13 equipment goods) over three time periods: 1980 and 1985, 1985 and 1990, 1990 and 1993. The tests reveal that 18 products/services categories are characterized by a significant mobility in the ranking of countries over time, as their Spearman rank correlation coefficients are never statistically significant. In other words, there are only 18 products/services categories out of 145 for which some countries shift from being a comparatively low price country to being a comparatively high price country over subsequent time periods.

Furthermore, within that group of 18 products/services categories, there are only four for which we find both evidence of country mobility and a constant price variance over time (i.e. a non-statistically-significant change in price variances over time). These are the following: repairs to furniture, furnishings and floorings, other household appliances (such as small electrical kitchen appliances), tyres and replacement parts for motor vehicles, and other expenses related to personal transport. For these products/services, the fact that there is no convergence (or divergence) pattern of prices after inception of the SMP is thus not a sign of price rigidities, as the ranking of countries within the distribution shows a large mobility over time. It can thus be inferred that, in the case of these four products/services, further integration of the EU economies will probably not lead to a significant price convergence, but that the absence of price convergence at the EU-12 level is not a cause of concern.

The Spearman tests also reveal that 31 products/services for which there was no statistical evidence of convergence or divergence patterns (i.e. for which the price variances seem stable over time) are characterized by statistically significant rank correlation between the different time periods considered (1980 and 1985, 1985 and 1990, 1990 and 1993). For these products/services, thus, prices in the different countries evolve in the same direction over time so as to preserve the ranking of countries. In other words, there is a strong stability over time in the ranking of countries.

Table 4.5.1 lists these 31 products/services which show no particular convergence/divergence pattern but a high rank correlation of countries over time, and shows the maximum and minimum values of their price variance at the EU-12 level over the four years analysed.

Table 4.5.1. List of products/services for which the test of equality of the price indices variance is never significant and for which the Spearman rank correlation test is always significant (low country mobility)

Product/services	Range of price indices variance (across the EU-12)
Edible oils	2,750 – 4,500
Medicines	1,400 – 3,500
Potatoes	1,360 – 3,440
Alcohol	1,500 – 2,715
Railway and road transport services	1,100 – 2,700
Liquefied gas	840 – 2,800
Local transport services	1,000 – 2,200
Other expenses related to personal transport	1,100 – 2,000
Expenditures in cafes, bars	1,100 – 1,900
Telephone, telegraph and telex services	1,000 – 1,800
Hairdressers, beauticians and other similar services	1,100 – 1,300
Repairs to footwear	860 – 1,400
Other expenses related to transport services	700 – 1,200
Veal	700 – 1,100
Fresh fruits	550 – 1,100
Housing – single family	600 – 1,000
Beef	500 – 967
Mutton, lamb and goat meat	570 – 890
Housing – multi-family	600 – 700
Bread	500 – 800
Articles for travelling and personal luggage	450 – 830
Commercial buildings	350 – 900
Poultry	300 – 700
Women's footwear	410 – 580
Clothing accessories	300 – 600
Men's footwear	300 – 600
Eggs	300 – 470
Other fresh or frozen meat	360 – 900
Chocolate	670 – 720
Postal services	310 – 610
Expenses for cultural events and activities	660 – 1,050

Source: DRI.

Among these products/services, concerns about the dual problem of price rigidity and lack of price convergence should be specifically directed at the products/services which show a high and unchanging variance. Table 4.5.1 reveals that edible oil, alcohol, potatoes, medicines, liquefied gas, local transport services and railway and road transport services all fall into this category. For these products/services, there are thus factors which have hindered any price evolution between countries at the EU level.

Interestingly, the list of products/services in Table 4.5.1 contains eight food products which have the attribute of being highly unprocessed. Their presence in this list corroborates the findings of a study by Rogers and Jenkins [1995] which shows that there exists a long-term, stationary relationship between common-currency price of goods classified as homogeneous auction goods (e.g. eggs, oranges, apples, poultry, chuck roast, bananas, bakery products and dairy products).[17] This finding is indeed concordant with our observation that the Spearman rank correlation test is always significant for this type of food product. Similarly, a study by Engel [1993] shows that these goods are characterized by a higher volatility of prices over time relative to other goods' prices in the same country than the volatility of their prices relative to the prices of the same type goods in another country.[18] In Table 4.5.1, the eight food products considered are in fact characterized by a relatively low variance of their price indices across the EU-12.

[17] See Rogers, J. and Jenkins, M. [1995], 'Haircuts or hysteresis? Sources of movements in real exchange rates', *Journal of International Economics*, Vol. 38, pp. 339–360.

[18] See Engel, C. [1993], 'Real exchange rates and relative prices: an empirical investigation', *Journal of Monetary Economics*, Vol. 32, pp. 35–50.

5. Price patterns across countries and the role of exchange rates

The previous two chapters examined price convergence/divergence patterns across regions and over time, both for broad products/services categories (Chapter 3) and for detailed product/service categories (Chapter 4). This chapter carries the analysis one step further by looking more closely at the price convergence patterns of different countries within the EU-12, over the period 1985–93. In particular, this chapter examines the extent to which convergence or divergence patterns over the period 1985 to 1993 may reflect or have been influenced by volatile developments on the exchange rate front during the 1980s and 1990s. This chapter also seeks to identify groups of countries which seem to have similar price structures, or for which prices have varied in a consistent way over the period considered.

5.1. Key results

The analysis undertaken in this section shows that:

(a) The observed price convergence and price divergence patterns are not mainly reflective of developments on the exchange rate front. If, for some products, past changes in exchange rates within the EU may have influenced the observed price convergence pattern, in the vast majority of cases past changes in exchange rates have, on the contrary, favoured an increased divergence of prices, rather than the observed price convergence.

(b) Looking at groupings of countries/products with comparable prices (i.e. with prices within 30% of the lowest national price), one finds that the number of 'low price discrepancy' cases grows over time, which is consistent with a price convergence pattern. The share of 'low discrepancy' cases rises from 25% in 1980 to 37% in 1985, 33% in 1990 and 34% in 1993.

(c) There are two product categories which show a significant increase in the number of low discrepancy cases over time (i.e. increased convergence towards the lower price): these are consumer durable goods and equipment goods; for food products, the pattern is less clear cut, with an increase in price convergence in the period 1980–85 followed by increased divergence in the 1985–90 period, then again increased convergence.

(d) The analysis undertaken to identify groupings of countries in which prices have tended to behave in a similar way over time allows the identification of two broad groups of countries: Germany, the Netherlands, Belgium, Luxembourg and Denmark (over the entire period), and Italy, Portugal and Greece from 1985 onwards. Spain also behaves similarly to the three later countries from 1990 onwards.

(e) These results confirm that geographical proximity is a crucial factor in explaining similarities (or dissimilarities) in price convergence patterns.

5.2. The role of exchange rates

Table 5.2.1 illustrates the high variability of exchange rates over the different sub-periods considered in our study. Changes in exchange rates were particularly important over the period 1980–85, with Portugal and Greece, in particular, experiencing major depreciations of their currency against the ECU. Currency fluctuations remained important in subsequent periods, however, with Greece, Spain and Italy experiencing depreciations of their currency ranging from 15.2% in the case of Spain to 33.3% in the case of Greece over the period 1990–93. It is, therefore, important to investigate the extent to which the price convergence/divergence patterns which were described in the two previous chapters might actually reflect (or have been influenced by) underlying variations in exchange rates.

Table 5.2.1. Variation of EU currencies against the ECU, 1980–93 (percentages)

Time period	D	F	I	NL	B	L	UK	IRL	DK	GR	E	P
1980–85	11.8	-15.8	-21.8	9.0	-10.6	-10.6	1.6	-5.8	-2.4	-77.9	-29.5	-87.3
1985–90	7.8	-1.7	-5.1	7.9	5.5	5.5	-21.2	-7.3	2.0	-90.5	-0.2	-39.0
1990–93	5.6	4.1	-21.0	5.9	4.6	4.6	-9.3	-4.2	3.3	-33.3	-15.2	-4.0

Source: *European Economy* (1995), No 60, Table 56.

Our interest in analysing the role of exchange rates on price convergence/divergence patterns is reinforced by the findings of an analysis of the surveys of car price differentials in the EU carried out by the European Commission. This survey of car prices represents one of the rare comprehensive public sources of information on product prices in the EU at such detailed level. Recent analyses of these data show that there is a clear correlation between currency fluctuations and changes in the relative price levels of cars in certain Member States (see the box opposite).

Here, since we are working with national price indices relative to the EU average and not with price levels, we are unable to tackle directly the problem of the impact of exchange rate variations on price dispersion by applying different exchange rates, as it is done with the surveys of car price differentials. Another approach has thus been developed: in Section 5.2.1, we discuss the theoretical conditions under which exchange rate fluctuations would lead to price convergence. In a second step (Section 5.2.2), we test if these conditions are met in our sample. The main conclusions are that, even if for some products exchange rate variations could have explained the observed pattern of price convergence, in the vast majority of cases, exchange rate fluctuations are likely to have favoured price divergence rather than price convergence.

5.2.1. Theoretical impact of exchange rate variations on price convergence/divergence patterns

Table 5.2.1 shows that the number of countries which have seen their currency devaluate against the ECU from 1980 to 1993 is greater than the number of countries which saw their currency appreciate relative to the ECU. Germany and the Netherlands are the two countries whose currency appreciated the most against the ECU over the whole period, while countries whose currency depreciated the most are Italy, Ireland, Greece, Spain and Portugal. The remaining countries show contrasting variations. Thus, it is clear that the depreciation of certain national currencies against the ECU represents the most important source of exchange rate variation during the time period that we are examining. For this reason, in presenting the theoretical framework we will focus on the expected impact of exchange rate variations on price dispersion in the EU in the case of devaluations. The results in the case of revaluations are, however, symmetric.

European Commission surveys of car price differentials between Member States

In its policy to improve price transparency for the benefit of consumers, the European Commission has carried out since 1993 biannual surveys of car price differentials between EU Member States. Prices that are surveyed relate to the prices of top-selling car models in EU countries manufactured by European and Japanese car producers. The prices are recommended retail prices which are adjusted for equipment differences and compiled in local currencies, both before and after tax. Therefore, they do not reflect the discount policies that may be pursued to different degrees from one Member State to another. In all surveys, Denmark and Greece are excluded, due to their specific taxation policies which drive down pre-tax car prices to levels which do not reflect normal economic conditions.

To compare car price differentials between Member States, national prices are converted into ECU and price differential indices are calculated using the lowest national price as a reference which is taken as being equal to 100. Thus, car price disparities across Member States are estimated on the basis of an index equal to 100 for the lowest national price (denominated in ECU).

Here are the main findings to be reported from the surveys:

There exists a clear correlation between the changes in the relative price levels of cars and currency devaluations in certain Member States. The May 1993 survey reports that Italy, Spain, the United Kingdom and Ireland (where devaluations had occurred since July 1992) were the five lowest-priced car markets in the European Union, with Germany and France being the highest. However, the Commission warns that it is not possible to distinguish between the purely mechanical effects of the devaluations on the car prices in ECU and the effects of the commercial policies adopted by car manufacturers.

In the November 1993 survey, the Commission reports that there were further notable exchange rate movements which were relevant to Spain and Portugal where devaluations occurred. In November, these two countries were the lowest-priced car markets, while Germany, having a strong currency, was the highest. The survey reveals that overall car price differences were higher than they were in May 1993. However, if monetary fluctuations related to the devaluations of the currencies of Spain and Portugal are excluded, manufacturers have tended to reduce price differentials for most of their models. This is reflected by the fact that if the effects of exchange rate movements are taken out, about 90% of all car price differentials covering both European and Japanese models are contained in the 20% margin above the lowest national price.

In the May 1995 survey, the Commission reports that price differentials for the models examined have risen dramatically since the November 1994 survey. More than half of the models have price differences that are outside (higher) the 20% margin above the lowest national price. The survey indicates that exchange rate movements were generally moderate between November 1994 and May 1995, except for the Italian lira which depreciated by 13.5% against the ECU. The survey points out that the strong depreciation of the lira is reflected by the fact that for 51 out of 75 models, Italy has become the Member State with the lowest prices, hence contributing to the increase in price differentials during the time period considered. On the other hand, the survey notes that car manufacturers have generally increased prices in countries which traditionally figure among those with the highest prices, such as Germany, France and Belgium. Thus, price gaps between Member States with stronger currencies are substantially smaller.

Table 5.2.2 summarizes the analysis presented in this section by showing the impact of an exchange rate depreciation on price convergence patterns, depending on whether the country whose currency depreciates is a high or a low price country, and depending on whether imports represent a high or a low share of domestic consumption.

Table 5.2.2. Impact of exchange rate variations on price convergence

<table>
<tr><th></th><th colspan="2">Impact on prices</th></tr>
<tr><td rowspan="2">Low import penetration
or
High import penetration with sticky prices</td><td colspan="2">Stable prices in local currency
(no imported inflation)
Decreasing prices in ECU</td></tr>
<tr><td>Low relative price
Case A: Price divergence</td><td>High relative price
Case B: Price convergence</td></tr>
<tr><td rowspan="2">High import penetration with exchange rate pass-through</td><td colspan="2">Prices in local currency increase
Prices in ECU decrease</td></tr>
<tr><td>Case C: Price divergence</td><td>Case D: Indeterminate</td></tr>
</table>

Source: DRI and E. de Ghellinck.

Let us first consider the case of a country with a low rate of import penetration. In this case, national prices essentially reflect the price of domestically produced goods. Under the hypothesis that domestic policies limit the imported inflation effect of devaluations (a realistic assumption in all EU Member States over the period considered), and given that the import penetration ratio is by assumption low, prices in national currency can be considered as essentially stable and prices in ECU decrease following a devaluation of the country's currency.

If prices in the devaluating country were already low before the depreciation (compared with the EU average), the devaluation then leads to an increased price dispersion across EU countries (Case A). In contrast, if the devaluating country was a comparatively high price country before the devaluation, the latter tends to reduce price dispersion across EU countries (Case B).

Symmetrically, in the case of a revaluation, price disparities across the EU will tend to increase if the revaluation takes place in a (comparatively) high price country, and price convergence will be observed if the revaluation takes place in a low price country.

When the rate of import penetration is high, national prices reflect a combination of the prices of domestically produced goods and of imported goods. In that case, to assess the impact on price convergence of exchange rate variations, one has to take into account importers' pricing policy, and the degree of pass-through of exchange rate variations onto final prices.

Two extreme cases can be considered:

(a) When exchange rate variations are small, sticky prices can reasonably be assumed (no change in local currency prices), hence the results developed above remain valid.

(b) When exchange rate variations are large, however, as has been the case for the southern countries' currencies and for the pound sterling between 1985 and 1990, producers from the countries whose currency depreciates theoretically enjoy a strong competitive advantage as their prices in foreign currencies fall. The degree to which the price of domestically produced goods expressed in foreign currency – in this case in ECU – decreases, however, depends on the degree of pass-through of the devaluation on prices. Indeed, in the case of a devaluation, the price of imported goods in local currency increases, unless importers totally absorb the impact of the devaluation by reducing profit margins.

If importers do not pass through the total impact of the devaluation on prices expressed in local currency, i.e. if their mark-up decreases in the case of devaluation, we are in a situation of sticky prices and the prices of domestic producers will not change or will change very little. In this case, we are again in a similar situation to Cases A and B above, in that domestic prices in local currency do not change and domestic prices in ECU decrease; hence across the EU prices converge if the devaluating country was a comparatively high price country, and diverge if the devaluating country was a comparatively low price country.

If, however, importers pass through the exchange rate variation onto their prices (i.e. assumption of constant mark-up), domestic product prices in local currency increase and domestic prices in 'foreign' currencies decrease, but much less than under the assumption of a falling mark-up. Assessing the impact on the price convergence pattern in this case becomes extremely difficult, as it depends on a number of factors among which is the relative sensitivity of prices in national currency to the exchange rates. And, in the case of conversions to the ECU, a further element of complexity is added by the fact that the ECU rate is determined by a basket of currencies which fluctuate in different ways. In general, the exchange rate variations of a given country against the ECU are lower than the bilateral exchange rate variations (on which firms' pricing behaviour is based), the more so the smaller the country; hence the impact of the devaluation on price convergence/divergence patterns is indeterminate (Cases C and D).

As will be noted in Section 5.2.2, however, a number of empirical studies point to an incomplete pass-through of price rises by importers, or to a relative stickiness of prices in terms of the currency of the country in which the good is sold (as discussed in Engel and Rogers [1994]).

5.2.2. Observed impact of exchange rates variation on price convergence/divergence patterns

According to the theoretical discussion in Section 5.2.1 above, to be able to evaluate the impact of exchange rate variations on price dispersion across EU countries one needs to know:

(a) Are the countries whose currency depreciates high price or low price countries?

(b) What is the import share of domestic consumption?

(c) Are import prices flexible or sticky?

The answer to the first question is provided by an analysis of the ranking of countries on the basis of national price indices (Tables 5.2.3 and 5.2.4).

In the top part of Table 5.2.3, we list the number of cases (i.e. products/services categories) for which each particular country was the lowest price country of the EU-12 in the year considered.

Table 5.2.3. Number of country/product combinations for which a given country posts the lowest price

	D	F	I	NL	B	L	UK	IRL	DK	GR	E	P
All categories												
1980	0	1	14	3	0	1	2	6	3	31	38	74
1985	6	1	14	13	9	10	19	7	2	22	19	51
1990	14	3	2	10	3	5	22	10	0	33	7	61
1993	2	2	9	6	9	4	40	12	3	36	13	37
Total all years	22	7	39	32	21	20	83	35	8	122	77	223
1980												
Food products	0	0	0	1	0	0	1	1	0	7	7	25
Beverages	0	0	2	0	0	0	0	1	0	1	1	4
Tobacco products	0	0	0	0	0	0	0	0	0	1	1	0
Clothing and footwear	0	0	2	0	0	0	0	1	1	1	0	3
Durable consumer goods	0	0	0	1	0	0	0	0	0	2	14	7
Other manufactured products	0	0	2	1	0	0	1	0	0	3	4	7
Energy	0	0	1	0	0	0	0	0	0	1	1	2
Services	0	0	4	0	0	1	0	1	2	7	0	21
Equipment goods	0	1	0	0	0	0	0	2	0	4	9	5
Construction	0	0	3	0	0	0	0	0	0	4	1	0
1985												
Food products	2	1	2	5	2	1	7	3	0	2	5	12
Beverages	0	0	2	0	2	0	1	0	0	0	4	0
Tobacco products	0	0	0	0	0	1	0	0	0	0	1	0
Clothing and footwear	0	0	0	0	0	0	2	3	0	0	0	3
Durable consumer goods	2	0	6	4	0	1	4	0	0	3	2	2
Other manufactured products	1	0	1	1	1	0	1	0	1	4	2	6
Energy	0	0	0	0	0	1	0	0	0	1	1	2
Services	0	0	2	2	2	0	1	0	0	8	3	19
Equipment goods	1	0	1	1	2	6	3	0	1	3	1	1
Construction	0	0	0	0	0	0	0	1	0	1	0	6
1990												
Food products	5	1	0	4	0	0	8	3	0	5	1	15
Beverages	0	1	1	0	0	0	0	1	0	2	2	2
Tobacco products	0	0	0	0	0	0	0	0	0	1	0	1
Clothing and footwear	0	0	0	0	0	0	3	2	0	1	1	1
Durable consumer goods	2	0	0	2	0	1	7	2	0	0	0	9
Other manufactured products	1	1	0	2	0	0	1	0	0	6	0	7
Energy	0	0	0	1	0	1	0	0	0	3	0	0
Services	0	0	1	0	1	2	3	0	0	10	0	18
Equipment goods	6	0	0	1	2	1	0	1	0	4	3	2
Construction	0	0	0	0	0	0	0	1	0	1	0	6
1993												
Food products	2	0	0	5	2	0	10	5	1	6	3	7
Beverages	0	0	0	0	0	0	2	1	0	1	2	3
Tobacco products	0	0	0	0	0	0	0	0	0	1	1	0
Clothing and footwear	0	0	0	0	0	0	5	0	0	1	0	2
Durable consumer goods	0	0	3	1	0	0	10	1	0	1	2	6
Other manufactured products	0	1	2	0	0	1	3	3	0	8	0	0
Energy	0	0	1	0	0	0	0	0	0	1	1	2
Services	0	0	1	0	3	3	3	2	0	13	1	11
Equipment goods	0	1	2	0	4	0	6	0	2	3	3	0
Construction	0	0	0	0	0	0	1	0	0	1	0	6

Source: DRI.

Table 5.2.4. Number of country/product combinations for which a given country posts the highest price

	D	F	I	NL	B	L	UK	IRL	DK	GR	E	P
All categories												
1980	14	17	4	13	11	7	28	9	47	14	0	8
1985	6	12	16	2	12	6	12	15	60	14	9	10
1990	6	9	22	6	7	9	4	7	71	9	21	3
1993	11	21	10	5	11	12	2	10	67	9	4	12
Total all years	37	59	52	26	41	34	46	41	245	46	34	33
1980												
Food products	2	5	0	2	2	1	4	1	23	1	0	1
Beverages	3	0	0	0	0	0	1	4	1	0	0	0
Tobacco products	0	0	0	0	0	0	0	0	0	0	0	2
Clothing and footwear	0	0	0	0	0	2	0	0	6	0	0	0
Durable consumer goods	1	2	0	1	1	1	3	1	1	9	0	4
Other manufactured products	2	3	2	2	1	0	2	2	3	0	0	1
Energy	1	1	0	0	0	0	1	0	2	0	0	0
Services	4	4	1	3	7	3	6	1	8	0	0	0
Equipment goods	1	2	1	3	0	0	5	0	3	4	0	0
Construction	0	0	0	2	0	0	6	0	0	0	0	0
1985												
Food products	2	1	5	0	3	2	3	5	10	7	0	4
Beverages	0	2	1	0	0	0	0	0	6	0	0	0
Tobacco products	0	0	0	0	0	0	2	0	0	0	0	0
Clothing and footwear	0	0	2	0	1	0	0	0	4	0	1	0
Durable consumer goods	0	1	4	0	2	0	1	5	9	2	0	0
Other manufactured products	1	1	0	0	1	1	1	0	5	3	2	3
Energy	0	0	0	0	0	0	0	3	2	0	0	0
Services	3	1	0	1	1	1	5	2	15	2	3	3
Equipment goods	0	5	1	1	4	2	0	0	7	0	1	0
Construction	0	1	3	0	0	0	0	0	2	0	2	0
1990												
Food products	3	1	3	1	3	2	3	1	18	4	3	0
Beverages	0	0	1	0	0	0	0	0	7	0	1	0
Tobacco products	0	0	0	0	0	1	1	0	0	0	0	0
Clothing and footwear	0	0	3	0	1	0	0	0	4	0	0	0
Durable consumer goods	0	1	4	0	2	0	0	2	11	1	1	2
Other manufactured products	0	2	3	1	0	0	0	0	7	1	4	0
Energy	0	0	0	0	0	0	0	3	1	0	1	0
Services	1	2	3	3	1	5	0	1	13	2	5	1
Equipment goods	2	3	3	1	0	1	0	0	8	0	3	0
Construction	0	0	2	0	0	0	0	0	2	1	3	0
1993												
Food products	4	2	4	1	5	3	2	3	14	2	0	2
Beverages	1	1	0	0	0	0	0	0	7	0	0	0
Tobacco products	0	1	0	0	0	1	0	0	0	0	0	0
Clothing and footwear	0	3	0	0	2	0	0	0	2	0	0	1
Durable consumer goods	1	1	1	0	0	0	0	1	15	0	1	4
Other manufactured products	1	2	0	0	1	1	0	0	8	1	1	3
Energy	0	0	0	0	0	0	0	3	2	0	0	0
Services	2	5	1	4	1	4	0	2	11	4	1	2
Equipment goods	1	5	2	0	2	3	0	1	6	1	0	0
Construction	1	1	2	0	0	0	0	0	2	1	1	0

Source: DRI.

We find that:

(a) In 1980, Portugal has 74 product categories for which it has the lowest price among the EU-12; this is followed by Spain (38 product categories), Greece (31 product categories) and Italy (14 product categories). Taking Greece, Spain and Portugal together, these three countries account for 143 (out of 174) of the cheapest price cases in 1980, for 92 of the cheapest price cases in 1985, for 101 in 1985 and for 86 in 1993.

(b) In 1993, it is the UK that has the highest number of product categories having the lowest price in the EU (40 cases), followed by Portugal (37 cases), Greece (36 cases), Spain (13 cases) and Ireland (12 cases).

Hence, despite the huge depreciations of the three southern countries' currencies against the ECU over the period 1980–93, the number of product categories for which these countries have the lowest price thus decreases, strongly so in the case of Spain from as early as 1985, and between 1990 and 1993 in the case of Portugal. Greece, on the other hand, shows a relatively constant number of lowest price cases over the period (mainly in services). In contrast, the UK (where the number of lowest price cases increases from 2 in 1980 to 40 in 1993) and to a lesser extent Ireland (which goes from 6 cases in 1980 to 12 cases in 1993) show an increasing number of cases where they are the lowest price country over the period.

The remainder of Table 5.2.3 shows the number of cases for which each country displays the lowest price of all EU countries, by broad product/services category. As indicated in Table 5.2.3, Portugal is clearly a country which is characterized by a low price of services (compared to other EU countries). Portugal also has the highest number of lowest price cases for food products (especially in 1980, with 25 product categories out of 42) and for construction (from 1985). In the case of services and construction, this mainly reflects low labour costs. Spain concentrates 14 cheapest price cases (out of 24 product categories) in durable goods in 1980. Greece reports 10 lowest price cases in 1990 and 13 in 1993 (out of 36 categories) for services, and 8 cases (out of 18 categories) for other manufacturing products in 1993.

Table 5.2.4 shows information similar to that presented in Table 5.2.3 for the highest price countries. Here, we find that:

(a) With the exception of Denmark, which shows the highest number of product categories with the highest price of all EU countries in all four years considered, the distribution of high price cases across countries is more even than in the lowest price cases.

(b) The evolution over time reveals a decreasing number of highest price cases for the UK (28 in 1980, 2 in 1993) and an increasing number of highest price cases for Italy (4 cases in 1980 and 10 in 1993). Furthermore, despite a revaluation of the DM against the ECU of 11.8% and of the Dutch guilder against the ECU of 9% between 1980 and 1985, the number of highest price cases in these two countries has decreased over this period (from 14 to 6 in the case of Germany and from 13 to 2 in the case of the Netherlands).

Confronting the results presented in Tables 5.2.3 and 5.2.4 with the analysis in Section 5.2.1 leads us to the following important remarks:

(a) In 1980, the lowest price countries are Portugal, Spain, Greece and Italy, whereas the high price countries are Denmark, France and Germany. In 1993, the low price countries are

Portugal, Greece and UK, while the high price countries remain Denmark, France and Germany. Hence, exchange rate variations should have favoured price divergence over that period, except for the UK (where construction, equipment goods and services are product categories with relative high prices in 1980). What we observed, however, in Chapters 3 and 4, was a general price convergence pattern, therefore not due to exchange rate variations.

(b) The overall depreciation against the ECU of the currencies of the usually low price countries (respectively the appreciation of the currencies of the typically high price countries) has not translated into an increasing number of cases where the country is the lowest price country (respectively an increasing number of cases where the country is the highest price country).

(c) The UK has clearly shifted from being a relatively high price country in 1980 (there were 28 products/services categories for which it was the most expensive country and 2 cases for which it was the cheapest) to becoming a relatively low price country in 1993 (2 cases where it was the most expensive and 40 cases where it was the cheapest). The trend was particularly pronounced for food products (10 product categories out of 42) and for durable goods (10 product categories out of 24).

(d) Italy, in contrast, which is often pointed out as having gained an unfair competitive advantage through competitive devaluations (especially after July 1992), shows a less clear pattern over the period: Italy was the lowest price country in 14 cases in 1980 and 1985, in 2 cases in 1990 and in 9 cases in 1993, whereas it was the most expensive country in 4 cases in 1980, 16 cases in 1985, 22 cases in 1990 and 10 in 1993.

(e) This finding is consistent with that by Jacquemin and Sapir [1996]. The authors present a principal component and cluster analysis based on structural characteristics which show that 'what strongly emerges is a North–South rift, with Italy in an unstable position between the two clusters'.

(f) Ireland also shows a mixed situation, with both high relative EU prices in certain products/services categories (energy and food in 1985 and 1993, beverages in 1980 and durable goods in 1985) and low prices in other categories or at different points in time (food).

The second element that needs to be considered to evaluate the impact of exchange rate variations on price dispersion is the share of imports in domestic consumption. This element cannot be dealt with in a totally satisfactory way here, given that information on the share of imports in final consumption is not available at the level of detail considered in this study. A first (rough) approximation can nevertheless be made by making a distinction between tradeable and non-tradeable products/services (the latter group including mainly services and construction): pricing behaviour of importers indeed only matters for tradeable goods.

The third question concerns the impact of changes in exchange rates on the pricing behaviour of export and import firms. Empirical studies measuring the degree of pass-through of exchange rate fluctuations in foreign currency prices suggest that the dollar price of US manufactured exports seems to be relatively insensitive to changes in the real exchange rate. The movement of the dollar is therefore almost completely passed through to foreign prices. In contrast, foreign manufacturers (German, Japanese and UK exporters) often 'price to market' by revising export prices in their home currencies. The degree of stability of local-currency prices appears to vary widely by industry, however, and even within a given exporting country in the case of the US and the UK but not in the case of Germany and Japan. Industry effects hence appear to be more important than source-country effects in explaining differences in 'pricing-to-market' behaviour across trading relationships. For Japanese exports, for example, pooling over industries shows that destination-specific export price adjustments offset 48% of the impact of exchange rate changes on price in the buyer's currency. In other words, when the yen appreciates by 10%, the price of Japanese exports in the destination market when expressed in local currency only increases by 5.2%, as Japanese exporters (or local importers) absorb some of the exchange rate appreciation by squeezing profit margins. For Germany and the UK, the degree of the offset is 36% and for the US, it is close to zero.

These empirical results thus suggest that, in the case of exchange rate fluctuations, local-currency price stability is a relatively pervasive phenomenon, especially in the case of Germany, but also in a country like the UK.

Other authors also point to the fact that the prices of consumer goods may be sticky in terms of the currency of the country in which the good is sold. They do this through another approach showing that there is a connection between geographic market segmentation and price stickiness. On the one hand, it is easier to maintain a fixed nominal price if it is difficult for consumers or potential competitors to import: market segmentation thus reinforces price stickiness. On the other hand, the price of final goods – and in particular of goods sold to consumers – reflects not only the price of the actual products that are sold but also (and increasingly) the price of the service that brings the products to the market (distribution, advertising). This service component of prices to consumers varies a lot across countries[19] as it has a high labour content. This can further reinforce the tendency for prices to be sticky within national markets, even in cases of devaluation and high import penetration. All of this indicates that Cases C and D – characterized by an undetermined impact of exchange rate variations on price convergence patterns when price disparities are measured in ECU – are likely to concern only a limited number of product categories.

5.3. National price indices relative to the minimum price index

This section investigates the consistency of price structures across country groupings, and attempts to identify groups of countries in which price patterns have evolved in a consistent way over time. This analysis is mainly descriptive and concentrates on the groupings of countries with low price dispersion (referred to as the 'low discrepancy cases'). A similar analysis could, however, easily be made to identify groupings of countries with very dissimilar price structures ('high discrepancy' cases). This analysis of country groupings with low price discrepancy is structured in a way similar to that of the EU car price differentials survey, to make it possible to compare our findings with those of the car prices studies. The latter note that in November 1994 more than half of the car models had price differences across countries that are outside (higher than) the 20% margin above the lowest national price, a higher share than previously. The increased price dispersion is largely related to changes in

[19] In 'How wide is the border' (*NBER Working Paper*, 1994), Engel and Rogers develop a model which tests price disparities between the US and Canada. The authors indicate that it is possible that much of the inter-regional variations in prices reflect variations in the costs of the marketing service. When testing the significance of distance and the existence of the border in explaining price disparities, they find a significant impact of the 'distance' variable in most cases, with the notable exception of medical care and some textiles and apparel products.

exchange rates: if monetary fluctuations related to the devaluations of the peseta and escudo are excluded, one finds that manufacturers have actually tended to reduce price differentials for most of their models.

Table 5.3.1 sorts by country and product category the number of cases for which a given country/product has a price level which is within 30% of the lowest price level for that product category. The 30% threshold was chosen rather than the 20% figure used in the car prices studies, for two reasons:

(a) the analysis which is made here is based on prices inclusive of taxes;

(b) the products/services categories considered here are more heterogeneous than in the car price differentials study.

Based on the numbers in Table 5.3.1, one can constitute a grouping of countries/products with comparable prices. A key overall result is that low price discrepancy is observed in a growing number of cases over time: 25% of the cases in 1980, 37% in 1985, 33% in 1990 and 34% in 1993.

Looking at the results in more detail, by sub-product category, we find that there are two categories which show a significant increase in the number of low discrepancy cases over time: these are consumer durable goods (77 cases in 1980, or 27% of all potential cases for this sub-category; 147 cases (51%) in 1985; 133 cases (46%) in 1990 and 135 cases (47%) in 1993) and equipment goods (75 cases (30%) in 1980; 135 cases (54%) in 1985; 156 cases (62%) in 1990 and 124 cases (49%) in 1993).

For food products also, we find an increase in the number of low discrepancy cases, but mainly over the 1980–85 period (from 122 cases in 1980 – of which Italy, Greece, Spain and Portugal account for 70% – to 202 cases in 1993). This increase in the number of low price discrepancy cases is attributable to Germany, France, the Netherlands, Belgium, Luxembourg and the UK (whose number of low discrepancy cases jumps from 9 in 1980 to 29 in 1985).

Between 1985 and 1990, however, the number of low discrepancy cases in the food products category drops to 165 (or 33% of the total). Italy, Greece, Spain and Portugal only account for 46% of these, due to a decrease in the number of low discrepancy cases observed in Italy and Spain. Between 1990 and 1993, the number of low discrepancy cases increases to 177 (or 35% of the total), mainly due to an increase in the number of cases observed in Italy, Spain and Luxembourg.

The product categories where low discrepancy cases represent less than 20% of the total are, as expected, the two product categories where labour costs play a prevalent role: services – with 68 cases in 1980 and 1990; 76 cases in 1985; 93 cases in 1993 – and construction (see Table 5.3.1).

Concerning services, Portugal and Greece together account for 62% of the low discrepancy cases in this category in 1980; 58% in 1985, 59% in 1990 and 47% in 1993. In the case of construction, Portugal, Spain and Greece together account for more than 60% of the cases over the whole period.

Table 5.3.1. Number of low price discrepancy cases

	D	F	I	NL	B	L	UK	IRL	DK	GR	E	P	Total	%[1]
All categories														
1980	16	14	65	16	18	23	25	32	14	71	90	129	513	24.6
1985	61	45	57	74	53	72	81	50	18	79	70	107	767	36.7
1990	53	40	34	63	45	51	75	67	21	92	36	119	696	33.3
1993	38	30	67	50	50	54	85	73	23	93	68	83	714	34.2
Total all years	168	129	223	203	166	200	266	222	76	335	264	438	2,690	32.2
1980														
Food products	2	3	13	5	3	3	9	10	2	16	21	35	122	24.2
Beverages	0	2	4	2	2	3	2	1	0	4	5	8	33	30.6
Tobacco prod.	1	1	1	1	1	1	0	0	1	1	2	0	10	41.7
Cloth. & footwear	0	0	4	0	0	0	2	2	2	3	5	7	25	26.0
Durable cons. goods	6	2	10	4	3	3	5	4	2	6	19	13	77	26.7
Other manuf. goods	2	2	8	2	2	4	3	2	0	9	11	16	61	28.2
Energy	0	1	2	0	0	0	0	0	1	3	1	4	12	20.0
Services	0	0	9	0	0	2	1	8	2	17	4	25	68	15.3
Equipment goods	5	3	7	2	7	7	3	3	4	5	14	15	75	29.8
Construction	0	0	7	0	0	0	0	2	0	7	8	6	30	31.3
1985														
Food products	18	14	7	21	15	21	29	14	3	20	14	26	202	40.1
Beverages	2	1	4	4	3	3	2	1	1	4	6	3	34	31.5
Tobacco prod.	0	0	0	0	1	1	0	0	0	1	2	1	6	25.0
Cloth. & footwear	3	4	4	7	0	1	7	6	0	6	5	7	50	52.1
Durable cons. goods	18	11	18	16	9	17	17	10	3	7	12	9	147	51.0
Other manuf. goods	6	3	9	7	5	8	7	2	1	11	10	10	79	36.6
Energy	1	0	0	2	1	2	2	1	0	4	3	4	20	33.3
Services	1	0	3	6	3	2	5	3	2	17	7	27	76	17.1
Equipment goods	11	11	12	11	14	16	12	11	8	8	9	12	135	53.6
Construction	1	1	0	0	2	1	0	2	0	1	2	8	18	18.8
1990														
Food products	14	10	4	18	13	8	23	18	5	19	6	27	165	32.7
Beverages	2	3	4	3	1	2	2	1	0	4	4	6	32	29.6
Tobacco prod.	0	0	0	0	1	2	0	0	0	1	1	2	7	29.2
Cloth. & footwear	0	0	0	3	0	1	6	6	0	5	2	5	28	29.2
Durable cons. goods	14	8	11	15	9	8	19	12	3	11	4	19	133	46.2
Other manuf. goods	6	3	3	6	3	8	7	4	2	12	4	14	72	33.3
Energy	1	1	1	1	1	2	1	1	0	4	1	3	17	28.3
Services	1	1	2	1	4	5	5	5	1	17	3	23	68	15.3
Equipment goods	15	13	9	16	12	15	12	18	10	16	8	12	156	61.9
Construction	0	1	0	0	1	0	0	2	0	3	3	8	18	18.8
1993														
Food products	10	7	10	18	13	14	24	22	6	20	13	20	177	35.1
Beverages	3	0	5	4	2	5	3	1	1	4	5	5	38	35.2
Tobacco prod.	0	0	1	1	1	1	0	0	0	1	2	1	8	33.3
Cloth. & footwear	0	0	1	2	1	0	8	4	1	3	3	3	26	27.1
Durable cons. goods	9	9	19	10	10	9	17	14	2	11	13	12	135	46.9
Other manuf. goods	3	7	8	5	6	6	9	7	1	13	8	8	81	37.5
Energy	0	0	1	1	1	1	1	1	0	2	1	3	12	20.0
Services	2	0	8	3	6	7	8	8	0	23	7	21	93	20.9
Equipment goods	11	6	13	6	10	11	14	12	12	12	13	4	124	49.2
Construction	0	1	1	0	0	0	1	4	0	4	3	6	20	20.8

Source: DRI *et al.*

[1]As a percentage of the total cases.

Looking at the results by country and comparing 1980 with 1993, three types of trends are observed:

(a) In nine countries out of 12, the number of low discrepancy cases increases between 1980 and 1993. These nine countries are Germany, France, the Netherlands, Belgium, Luxembourg, the UK, Ireland, Denmark and Greece. In Ireland, Greece and Denmark, there has actually been a steady increase in the number of low discrepancy cases over the four years considered, whilst in all the other countries the number of low discrepancy cases has first increased, then fallen. Exchange rate variations cannot be the main explanation for this pattern as this last group of countries includes both countries whose currency has appreciated against the ECU and countries whose currency has depreciated against the ECU.

(b) In two countries the number of low discrepancy cases decreases between 1980 and 1993. These two countries are Spain and Portugal. The decrease is mainly observed in the food category for both countries, in the consumer durable goods category for Spain and in other manufacturing goods for Portugal.

(c) Finally, in Italy the number of low discrepancy cases has remained stable between 1980 and 1993, though it was reduced by half between 1980 and 1990 and then increased again to 67 in 1993. This U-shaped pattern in the number of low discrepancy cases in Italy over time might reflect the over-valuation of the Italian lira in 1990.

5.4. Correlation between national price indices

To identify groupings of countries for which prices have tended to behave in a similar way over time, correlations between pairs of countries have been calculated using national price indices for all products/services categories. The results are presented in Table 5.4.1, which displays only the correlation coefficients between pairs of countries that are statistically significant. Table 5.4.1 reveals that significant and positive price correlations are observed:

(a) between Germany, the Netherlands, Belgium, Luxembourg and Denmark from 1980 to 1993; these countries are geographically close;

(b) between Italy, Portugal and Greece from 1985 onwards, and Spain from 1990 onwards;

(c) between the United Kingdom and Ireland (though this correlation is decreasing over time);

(d) between the United Kingdom and Denmark, and between the United Kingdom and the Netherlands.

On the other hand, it can be observed that Italy shows negative price correlations with Germany, the United Kingdom, the Netherlands and Belgium, an interesting finding for a country which was the core of the EU-6. As for the United Kingdom, from 1985 onwards it displays negative correlations with Portugal, Spain and Greece. Finally, France has a less definite position, except that it always shows positive price correlations with Belgium.

Thus, by identifying a North–South divide in the correlations of national price indices, these results seem to confirm the general notion already expressed in Section 5.3, that geographical proximity is a crucial factor in explaining similarities (or dissimilarities) in the behaviour of prices between EU countries.

Table 5.4.1. Significant price correlations across country pairs

1980	D	NL	B	L	DK	F	I	E	P	GR	UK
NL	0.37	...	...	...	...	...	...	...	...	...	...
B	0.20	0.17	...	...	...	...	...	...	...	...	...
L	0.34	0.23	0.60	...	...	...	...	...	...	...	...
DK	0.45	0.24	...	...	...	...	...	...	...	...	...
F	...	...	0.31	0.19	...	...	...	...	...	...	...
I	...	-0.20	...	...	...	...	...	...	...	...	...
E	0.16	...	0.24	0.23	...	...	...	...	...	...	...
P	...	...	-0.16	...	...	...	...	-0.20	...	...	...
GR	...	...	...	...	...	...	0.36	-0.22	0.15	...	...
UK	...	...	...	-0.16	0.15	-0.27	0.19	...	...	...	...
IRL	...	...	...	...	0.35	...	...	...	...	...	0.59
1985											
NL	0.32	...	...	...	...	...	...	...	...	...	...
B	...	0.37	...	...	...	...	...	...	...	...	...
L	0.37	0.25	0.39	...	...	...	...	...	...	...	...
DK	0.43	0.49	0.17	0.25	...	...	...	...	...	...	...
F	0.16	...	0.25	0.24	0.18	...	...	...	...	...	...
I	-0.21	-0.24	-0.28	...	...	...	...	...	...	...	...
E	...	...	...	0.18	...	0.25	...	...	...	...	...
P	-0.22	-0.17	...	...	...	...	0.16	0.37	...	...	...
GR	...	...	-0.16	0.19	...	...	0.26	0.38	0.54	...	...
UK	...	0.23	...	-0.20	...	...	-0.41	-0.30	-0.22	-0.30	...
IRL	...	0.18	...	...	0.47	...	-0.24	-0.18	...	...	0.59
1990											
NL	0.30	...	...	...	...	...	...	...	...	...	...
B	0.17	0.27	...	...	...	...	...	...	...	...	...
L	0.31	0.19	0.35	...	...	...	...	...	...	...	...
DK	0.23	0.44		...	...	...	...	...	...	...	...
F	...	...	0.18	...	...	...	...	...	...	...	...
I	-0.17	-0.30	-0.27	...	...	...	...	...	...	...	...
E	-0.31	-0.22	...	...	...	...	0.37	...	...	...	...
P	...	...	...	...	...	...	0.26	0.43	...	...	...
GR	-0.19	...	...	...	...	...	0.27	0.45	0.40	...	...
UK	...	0.25	...	...	0.26	...	-0.37	-0.25	-0.18	-0.20	...
IRL	...	0.23	...	...	0.45	...	...	...	...	0.17	0.41
1993											
NL	0.32	...	...	...	...	...	...	...	...	...	...
B	0.24	0.30	...	...	...	...	...	...	...	...	...
L	0.22	0.31	0.45	...	...	...	...	...	...	...	...
DK	0.40	0.34	...	...	...	...	...	...	...	...	...
F	...	...	0.22	0.20	...	...	...	...	...	...	...
I	-0.18	-0.28	-0.25	...	...	...	...	...	...	...	...
E	...	-0.26	...	0.15	...	...	0.44	...	...	...	...
P	...	...	...	...	...	...	0.15	0.44	...	...	...
GR	...	...	...	...	...	...	0.44	0.39	0.34	...	...
UK	...	0.21	...	-0.23	0.29	...	-0.33	-0.23	-0.21	-0.29	...
IRL	...	...	...	...	0.26	...	...	...	...	0.17	0.38

Source: DRI *et al.*

These findings also confirm that similarities in structural factors (e.g. in industrial structure, consumer habits, etc.) are also important factors as they are likely to explain the positive correlations between the price structures of Greece and the other southern countries (Portugal, Spain and Italy) even though Greece is not geographically close to these three countries. The positive correlations of Italy with the other southern countries can be interpreted in the same way.

6. Price convergence and the SMP: theoretical impact

6.1. Definition of pan-European markets

If pan-European markets are markets where arbitraging is not prevented by firms or governments, the aim of the 1992 programme can be redefined as fostering the emergence of pan-European markets. This does not imply that price convergence will necessarily be observed, as:

(a) price homogeneity across different geographic markets is neither a necessary nor a sufficient condition for markets to be pan-European. The absence of price convergence (or the persistence of price disparities) following the inception of the SMP thus does not necessarily indicate that the SMP has not reached the desired objectives;

(b) there are a number of markets which were already largely pan-European before 1986, in which there was hence no reason to expect price convergence after 1986.

In theory, one says that two geographic areas form part of the same market if the 'law of one price' applies, i.e. if the prices of identical products are similar. The price of the same product at the same horizontal stage in two places will, however, be equal only if the two following conditions apply:

(a) consumers are willing to transfer demand between suppliers on the basis of prices net of transport costs (i.e. the cross-price elasticity of demand is high); and,

(b) consumers are able to transfer demand between suppliers.

The first condition is not necessarily always fulfilled in the EU, as there can be:

(a) high transport costs (these indeed vary between products and between the EU-6, EU-9, EU-12 and EU-15);

(b) language barriers;

(c) national preference bias (which can lead to vertical differentiation and market segmentation into branded/own label products, implying differences in packaging, quality, etc.);

(d) non-price based competition (reputation, after sales service, etc.).

However, for the second condition to be fulfilled, i.e. for customers to be able to transfer demand between suppliers implies that there is no market-sharing cartel, and that the distribution systems are organized in such a way that customers have access to suppliers from different or distant geographic markets. Exclusive distribution systems (as in the fine fragrances market) or stringent access-to-market regulations (as in the pharmaceutical products market) hinder the arbitraging process. Typical markets in which the 'law of one price' does not apply because consumers are not able to transfer demand across countries, are non-tradeable services.

The above conditions thus explain that price homogeneity is not a necessary condition for markets to be pan-European.

Price homogeneity is also not a sufficient condition for a market to be pan-European, as uniformity of prices could result from co-operation between firms. To discriminate between cases where price convergence results from increased competition and cases where it results from behaviours that are contrary to the single market philosophy, an analysis of the changes in market structure (number of companies, degree of concentration, trend in profitability) is needed. Hence, the fact that one observes price convergence in some markets after the inception of the SMP does not necessarily imply that the market has become more pan-European.

There are a number of factors which can explain price disparities for the same product at the same horizontal stage of development. As indicated above, this can be the case when there are structural characteristics on the demand or on the supply side which prevent the arbitrage process from taking place. These are referred to below as the **structural factors,** and include differences in consumer preferences or vertical differentiation of products.

Price disparities can, however, also result from strategies of companies aimed at segmenting markets or raising barriers to entry to reduce competition (see Table 6.1.1). These factors are referred to in the remainder of this report as the **behavioural factors** which can explain the failure of prices to converge in some markets. Table 6.1.1 provides some examples of typical company strategies depending on market conditions, and illustrates the many ways companies try to keep some control of their market by limiting the degree of competition in the market.

Table 6.1.1. Companies' strategic responses to certain market conditions, aimed at limiting the extent of competition

Market condition	Companies' response is to:
Many firms are too small to have an individual impact on prices	Increase scale, size
Entry and exit into industry is costless	Create/raise barriers to entry
Products are homogeneous	Aim for product differentiation, branding
There is perfect knowledge among buyers and sellers of prices and costs	Control/limit information
All firms have the same technology and production economics	Emphasize technological innovation, market share and the control of supply sources
Buyers have equal access to output of all suppliers	Control distribution

Source: DRI.

Finally, government policies can limit or constrain the arbitrage process (protective regulatory environment, existence of barriers to entry,...). These policies are referred to as the policy factors restraining price convergence in the remainder of the analysis.

For all the products/services markets in which price disparities are being observed, to assess the degree of pan-Europeanization of the market it is necessary to identify whether it is structural, behavioural or policy factors which explain the observed price differences.

6.2. European integration and price convergence

Whereas the creation of the single EU market was expected to have overall beneficial effects on the EU economy thanks to increases in competition, better exploitation of economies of scale and improved economic efficiency, the expected benefits (and the expectations in terms of price convergence) vary across sectors based on the extent of non-tariff barriers at the start of the period (some sectors were indeed already largely pan-European in 1986), and the potential for increased integration through the arbitrage process.

The greatest benefits from the SMP were thus expected to be seen:

(a) in markets where there were high non-tarrif barriers (NTBs) which have since been removed;

(b) in markets where there are no structural barriers to integration;

(c) in markets where there were high inefficiencies due to unfair competition, due to the particular behaviour of companies to maintain or increase market fragmentation, and where this behaviour is no longer possible.

The above implies that, in order to assess those markets in which the SMP has not achieved the desired effects, one needs:

(a) to identify those markets in which the SMP was expected to result in increased pan-Europeanization (i.e. those where NTBs were high and those which were not yet pan-European);

(b) among the product/services categories identified in (a) above, identify those in which this should have translated into price convergence (i.e. those in which 'structural' factors are not prevalent);

(c) among those product/services categories in which price convergence was expected but has not materialized, identify whether this is due to behavioural or to policy factors.

This is illustrated in Figure 6.2.1. Note that for products/services in the upper half of Figure 6.2.1, the fact that price convergence was not expected does not mean that the effects of the SMP in these markets were expected to be small, but rather that they would work through other variables than prices, for instance improvements in quality, technological intensity or product innovation.

Figure 6.2.1. Identification of the markets in which the SMP has not had the desired effects

Expected effect of the IMP	Price convergence	No price convergence
No price convergence	Suspicion of monopoly Analyse whether the observed convergence reflects – policy factors, or – behavioural factors	Expected impact of IMP not exerted through prices
Price convergence	Suspicion that IMP reached desired objectives but test for existence of behavioural factors which may explain an artificial convergence of prices (to a high rather than low level)	IMP has not reached objectives Need to identify cause for non-convergence; this can reflect either – behavioural factors – policy factors

Observed trend in price disparity

Source: DRI.
Note: IMP/SMP (internal/single market programme).

6.3. Theoretical discussion of the impact of European integration on prices based on certain market characteristics

6.3.1. Introduction

The previous section clarifies the link between the SMP and the pan-Europeanization process, and defines the limits within which price convergence was to be one of the expected results of integration. This section goes deeper into this analysis by focusing on the structural features of the markets which condition the extent to which the removal of NTBs (hence the easier access to a larger geographic market) was to result in lower (and more homogeneous) prices.

Clearly, the expectations from increased European integration in terms of price convergence vary based on whether products or services are tradeable or not. For non-tradeable goods or services, price convergence was not expected to be a result of the SMP as the non-tradeability of the products/services is itself a structural barrier to arbitrage. Examples of non-tradeable services are restaurants, beauty care, or hairdressers. Table 6.3.1 lists those products and services which are non-tradeable and for which the SMP was not expected to lead to price convergence.

Note that there is a set of services which are not strictly tradeable but for which price convergence might have been (and, as reported in Chapter 4, has been) a result of the SMP due to market liberalization, as these services are highly exposed to international competition. These services have thus been excluded from Table 6.3.1. These are all the (non-local) transport services (railway and road transport services, other transport services,...) along with the postal services, telephone, telegraph and telex services, and insurance, banking and other financial services. For all of these service categories, it has indeed been possible for consumers to engage in arbitrage across countries. In the case of postal services, for example, a practice which has developed is that of re-mail, on the basis of which companies send all their mail to another country with lower tariffs for postal services, and distribute it at world level from this other country.

Table 6.3.1. List of non-tradeables

Code	Description
1121021	Repairs to clothing
1122021	Repairs to footwear
1131013	General household maintenance costs
1131021	Water distribution charges
1141021	Repairs to furniture, furnishings, floorings
1142021	Repairs to household textiles
1143021	Repairs to heating, washing, kitchen appliances
1144021	Repairs to glassware, tableware, household utensils
1145021	Laundry and dry cleaning services
1145022	Other household services
1146011	Domestic services
1153011	General practitioner medical services
1153021	Specialist medical services
1153031	Dental services
1153041	Nurse services
1153051	Other medical and paramedical services
1162012	Vehicle maintenance costs
1162031	Other expenses related to personal transport
1163011	Local transport services
1171041	Repairs to recreational goods
1172011	Expenses related to cultural events and activities
1172021	Expenses for sporting events and activities
1172022	Charges for radio, television use
1172023	Other services nec
1174011	Tuition costs
1181011	Hairdressers, beauticians and other similar services
1183011	Expenditures in restaurants
1183012	Expenditures in cafes, bars
1183013	Expenditures in canteens
1183021	Hotels and other lodging expenses
1186011	Legal services
1321011	Housing – one family
1321021	Housing – multi-family
1322011	Agricultural buildings
1322021	Industrial buildings
1322031	Commercial buildings
1322041	Non-commercial buildings
1323011	Roads, bridges, tunnels
1323021	Other communication works, other than roads, bridges, tunnels

Source: DRI.

Among the tradeable goods and services, a second major distinction which conditions the extent to which economic integration is expected to lead to price convergence is the distinction between homogeneous and differentiated products. Below, we consider each of these cases in turn.

6.3.2. The case of homogeneous product markets

In homogeneous product markets, competition is by definition solely based on prices. For homogeneous products, one would expect the removal of all tariff and non-tariff barriers to trade to lead to price convergence provided that consumers are able to transfer demand across markets. (If the goods are homogeneous, there is indeed no reason, except for transport costs, why consumers would not be willing to transfer demand across markets.)

Figure 6.3.1 illustrates the expected trend in prices in homogeneous product markets when non-tariff barriers are removed, hence when the geographic end-market for given firms is enlarged.

Figure 6.3.1. Impact of market enlargement on price convergence in homogeneous product markets

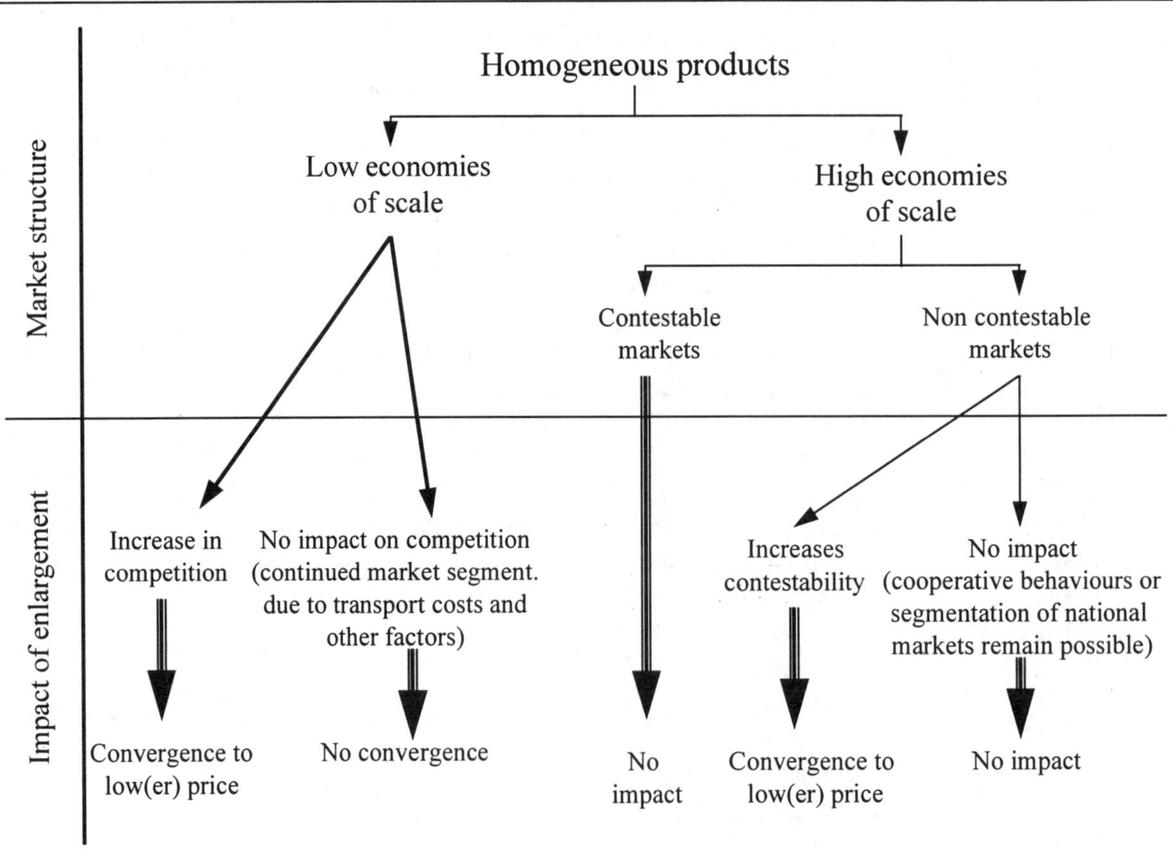

Source: DRI, E. de Ghellinck.

The interpretation of Figure 6.3.1 starts from the observation that in homogeneous markets competition is solely price based. Different situations arise, however, depending on the relative importance of economies of scale. In markets characterized by homogeneous products and where minimum efficient technical size (METS) is sufficiently low for scale not to represent a barrier to entry, the removal of non-tariff barriers (NTBs) to trade will lead to an increase in competition due to the arrival of new producers in the market. This will lead to price convergence towards a lower price (taking into account transport costs). Examples of homogeneous products with low METS are milk, flour, bread, or rice. When the degree of competition does not increase when NTBs are removed in such markets, it means that the market remains segmented, i.e. that transport costs or other factors prevent prices from converging towards the lower price. The specific organization of distribution in certain countries can explain persisting price disparities. In Germany, for example, the particular structure of distribution networks, with a concentrated distribution structure for flour in the north of Germany, and a much less concentrated structure in the south, explains persisting price disparities across regions for bread and bakery products.

In homogeneous markets characterized by high economies of scale (see the right hand side of Figure 6.3.1), 'structural' barriers to entry can limit the degree of competition in the market. Examples of markets where METS is high are the salt and the sugar markets. In the latter case, the organization of the common agricultural policy (CAP) (based on quotas allocated on the basis of past production) has tended to freeze the existing structure in each national market and hence to limit the realization of a truly integrated internal market.

In homogeneous product markets with high economies of scale, the trend in prices in different geographic markets when NTBs are removed will thus vary depending both on the degree of competition in the market before the removal of barriers and on the degree of market liberalization this entails.

The first thing to look at to assess the impact that market enlargement will have on prices in homogeneous markets with high economies of scale is the degree of competition in the market before enlargement. In markets in which the degree of competition within national markets was already high before NTBs were removed, i.e. in contestable markets, market integration will either have no impact or will lead to convergence to a lower price as competition further increases.

In homogeneous markets where economies of scale are high and markets were non-contestable before enlargement, two situations can arise when NTBs are removed. Either the factors which justified the non-contestability of markets still hold after market unification, and in this case there is no reason to expect price convergence (this is the case of energy markets as long as third-party access (TPA) is not granted), or market integration challenges the non-contestability of the market, and in this case a convergence of prices towards a low(er) level may be a consequence of integration. Examples of markets in which deregulation has increased contestability over the period are postal services, telecommunication services and air transport services, three markets for which we have indeed noted strong price convergence in Chapter 4.

When NTBs are removed, the possibility for governments or companies to continue to adopt behaviour that artificially fragments markets mainly depends on the degree of openness of the market (i.e. on the degree of tradeability of products/services). In sectors/markets which are open to competition from third-country suppliers, market segmentation strategies of companies or governments will typically be difficult to pursue.

6.3.3. The case of horizontally differentiated product markets

The second major classification of products/services in which the theoretical effect of the SMP may not be price convergence, is the differentiated products category.

There are two main types of differentiated products: each of these is likely to be affected in a different way by increased EU integration. Differentiated products can, indeed, be either horizontally or vertically differentiated. Horizontally differentiated products/services are products with no intrinsic difference in product quality across different suppliers/brand names. Examples of horizontally differentiated products are sugar confectionery, washing powders, cheese, detergents, or dairy products. Vertically differentiated products/services are products whose perceived quality by the buyers differs between suppliers/brand names. Examples of vertically differentiated products are cola beverages, electrical appliances, televisions, audio-visual equipment, and cars.

Figure 6.3.2. Effects of market enlargement on price convergence in horizontally differentiated product markets

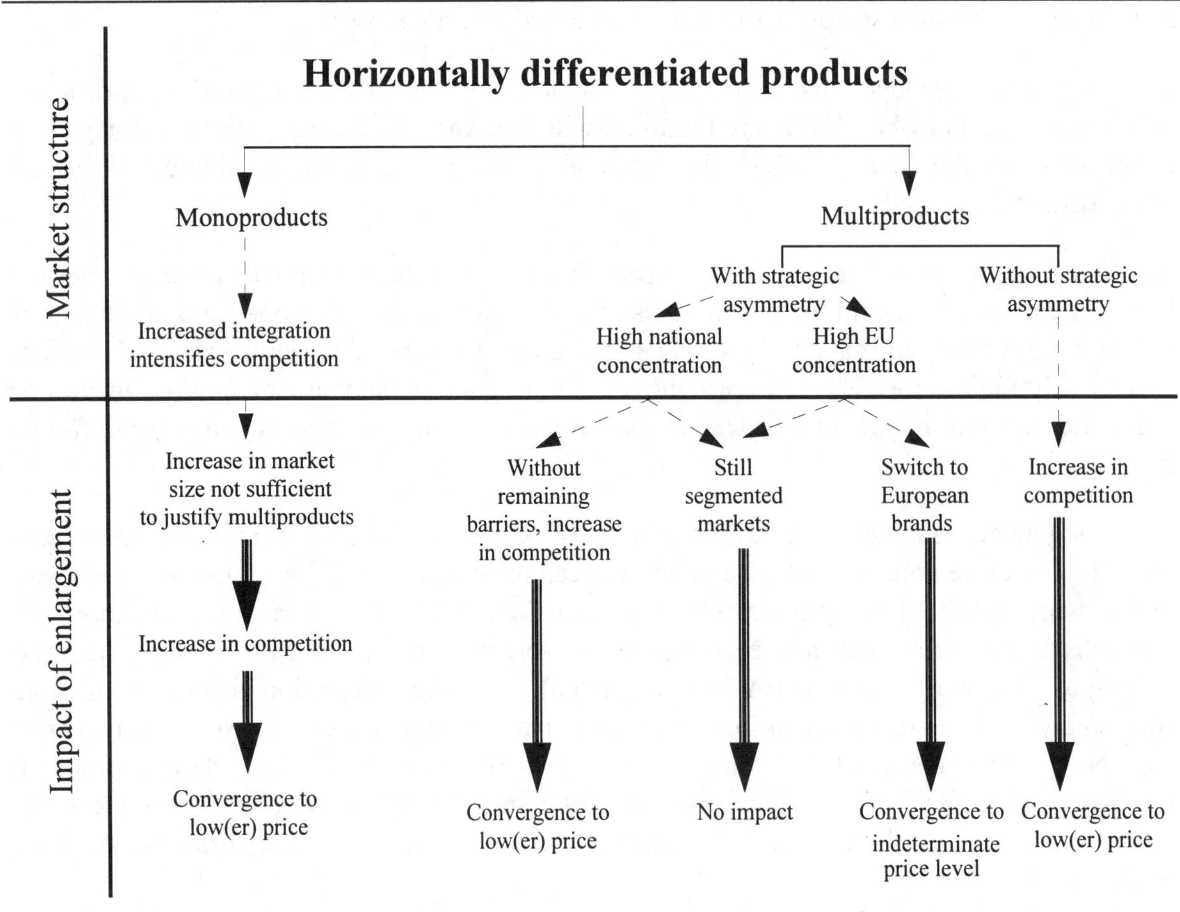

Source: DRI, E. de Ghellinck.

In the case of horizontally differentiated products, competition is based on price and on the choice of varieties. The removal of NTBs will have different effects on prices depending on whether companies in the market offer multiproducts or monoproducts (Figure 6.3.2). If companies in horizontally differentiated product markets offer only one or very few products on average, it means that before integration there were already a number of producers competing in each market (otherwise it would not be a horizontally differentiated product market), and hence that the environment was already fairly competitive. The removal of barriers to trade across different geographic markets will then lead to a further increase in competition, due to the entrance on a given geographic market of companies previously focused on another geographic market. The increase in competition will lead to a need for increased efficiency of the producers in the market, as well as to more varieties being offered to buyers in each market and to price convergence towards a lower price. Convergence of prices at the EU level should thus be observed when national segmented markets characterized by different sizes (and hence different numbers of producers) are replaced by a unique internal market.

In markets where firms offer multiproducts (i.e. several varieties of products, as in the case of washing powders, detergents or breakfast cereals), market enlargement through the removal of NTBs can, again, lead to different situations:

(a) either the degree of concentration in (segmented) national markets at the start of the period was such that the companies present did enjoy some market power; in this case, market enlargement or the removal of NTBs is likely either to increase competition (hence lead to downward convergence of prices and margins) or to confirm the dominance of a few operators who will take advantage of the enlarged markets to further enhance the number and variety of products offered (=> proliferation of products in the hands of a few operators), and hence further establish their market dominance (in raising the number of products offered, the producers typically raise entry costs and decrease the profitability for a new entrant due to the control they exert on distribution);

(b) or, the degree of concentration in fragmented markets at the start of the period was low, in which case the removal of NTBs reinforces the degree of competition and again leads to convergence to lower prices.

Price dispersion in markets with horizontally differentiated products can result from the existence of important economies of scope (multiproduct firms), first-mover advantages (strategic asymmetries between early and later entrants) and institutional or other factors affecting the toughness of price competition. If one firm has a first-mover advantage in a new market and is free to enter with many products, it may be optimal for this firm to fill up the line with an array of products, leaving the gap between adjacent products small enough to render entry by a new producer unprofitable. Sutton [1991], for example, notes that in the US market Campbell had a clear first-mover advantage and has retained its leadership in the soup market, while Heinz, its main rival, remains only a weak second. In the UK market, however, Heinz entered first, so that when Campbell entered, Heinz's position in this market was already well established. The UK market today is, as a result, a mirror image of the US market, with Heinz playing the leading role and Campbell a weak second in the canned soup category. Another example is the RTE cereals industry, in which Kellogg's enjoyed a first-mover advantage. The dynamics of competition in this market are primarily based on a constant flow of new offerings, most of which have a fairly short lifetime. Once one or a few firms dominate different national markets through first-mover advantages, price dispersion can still be observed, even after NTBs are removed.

6.3.4. The case of vertically differentiated product markets

The last category of products/services to be analysed is the vertically differentiated product category. Vertically differentiated markets include, as indicated above, products for which competition is based both on prices and on quality, the latter being in fact a key factor differentiating products in this market. Some vertically differentiated markets are characterized by dual structures (with a low price unbranded segment and a high price/high quality branded segment), but market dualization is not always present in vertically differentiated markets. For example, the market for VCRs is not (yet) really considered to be a dual market, whereas this is clearly the case for diapers, canned fruits and vegetables and car radios.

Vertical differentiation can be explained by regulatory (policy) factors (existence of certain norms for different qualities of products, e.g. environmental norms for packaging or energy efficiency standards) or by structural factors. Structural factors leading to vertical differentiation are linked with endogenous sunk costs, i.e. costs incurred with a view to enhancing consumers' willingness to pay for the firm's product. Competition in such markets is indeed essentially based on the perceived quality of the product. Advertising expenditures are typical endogenous sunk costs, and increasing expenditures on advertising has definitely been a strategy adopted by several companies in the soft drinks or personal care products (toothpaste, shampoos) sectors to protect or expand their market share.

As soon as the size of the market allows firms to invest profitably in outlays such as advertising or research and development, which allows them to differentiate their products vertically, increases in market size are associated with escalating levels of these fixed outlays by a limited number of firms. If consumers differ in their preference for quality, different levels of quality will be offered. In many consumer goods markets, there is a clear dichotomy between retail markets, where buyers are more or less sensitive to advertising outlays, and non-retail markets, where it is widely assumed that buyers choose their suppliers largely on the basis of price (and the physical characteristics of the good) alone and are relatively insensitive to the advertising-based brand image. In the audio equipment market, for example, a whole range of products are offered at a low price for mass consumers, whereas selective consumers with a willingness to pay for high quality products will nurture a high quality segment of the market, permitting innovation and technological improvements to take place.

If some consumers are sensitive to advertising or innovation whilst the remaining group simply choose the lowest priced product, then a dual structure emerges. Above a critical value of the market size, the market splits into two groups of firms. The first group sells in the retail segment, and the evolution of the number of firms and of quality is as above. The non-retail segment, where consumers buy on the basis of price, evolves as in the horizontally differentiated case (Figure 6.3.2). Once the size of the market is sufficiently large, all consumers in the retail segment strictly prefer the products of the advertising group, and vice versa, so that the two segments behave independently. For values of the market size intermediate between the splitting value and the switch point at which the two sub-markets become independent, the price of advertising products is constrained by that of the low price offerings of the competitive fringe, in that, at equilibrium, purchasers of advertised products are indifferent between these products and the low price non-advertised products. Increasing the size of the market will then lead to a change in the nature of competition from price competition to brand and product diversity competition.

As a consequence, in vertically differentiated markets both the disparity and the average level of prices can increase within a specific country when the size of the market increases, if this increase induces some firms to push up their investments in advertising or research (and hence the level of quality and the price of their product). This indeed widens the difference between the branded (or patent) products price and the own label products price.

Disparity in prices between countries can then be linked either to differences in the distribution of consumers' preferences or to strategic asymmetries (the first mover can monopolize the market by setting a value of quality so high that no later entrant will find it profitable to enter at any quality level). Differences in the ability of firms to increase the consumers' willingness to pay (linked to differences in the distribution of consumers' preferences) for their products explain why the mineral water market is classified as vertically differentiated in France but remains horizontally differentiated in Germany.[20]

Figure 6.3.3. Effects of market enlargement on price convergence in vertically differentiated product markets

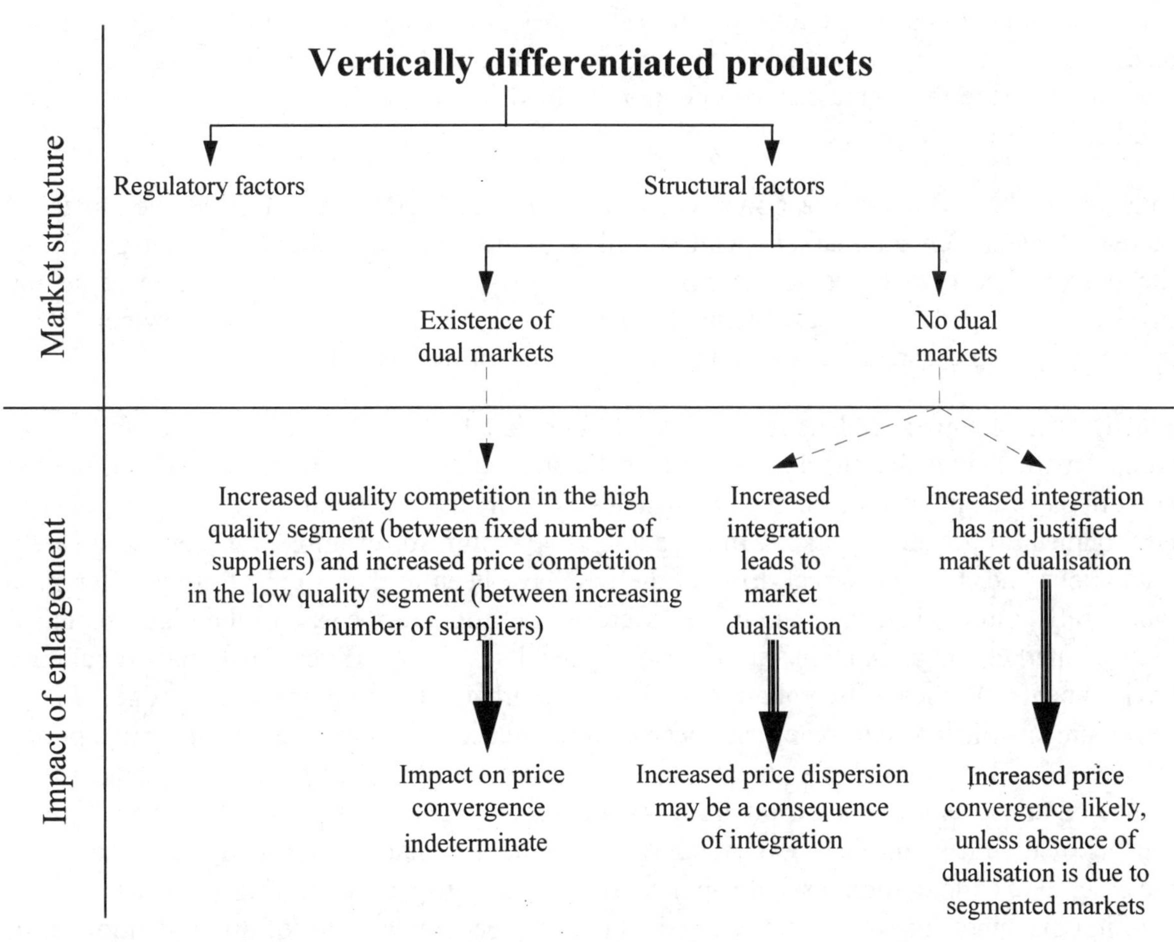

Source: DRI, E. de Ghellinck.

20 The case study on mineral waters shows, however, that the process of dualization of the German market is under way. 90 brands of mineral water are advertised in Germany, among which the 10 big players spend 50% of the total spent on advertising in this sector. The remaining 150 brands which are not advertised compete on price. Imports, which represent only a small share of domestic consumption, established their position as premium brands.

In small vertically differentiated markets, the absence of critical size may make market dualization a non-viable strategy: there may not be a sufficient number of consumers at the top of the market willing to pay for higher quality products to justify the investment by firms in research or advertising. In this case, price disparities across national markets reflect disparities in the nature of competition in the national markets: price competition can still be dominant in the smaller non-dualized markets, whereas competition is taking place on both price and quality in markets which are dualized. When NTBs are removed and companies have an easier access to a broader market, this widening of market access may give them the critical mass for making investments in quality financially viable (and successful) as it allows them to spread costs over a wider base. Diaper producers, for example, appear to have developed their competitive advantage by undertaking major R&D efforts to improve quality, while still maintaining a 'mass low quality' market segment for critical size.

In markets which were not dual before the SMP was launched, market dualization becomes possible as a result of enlargement only when transport costs or other factors (such as differences in packaging regulations and product definitions)[21] do not hinder trade. If dualization is the consequence of (geographic) market integration, price disparities in each market may increase as a new market develops in which it is quality and not price which is the basis for competition. If the removal of NTBs does not create a market of sufficient size to lead to dualization, increased price convergence is likely (but not certain) to be a result of integration due to the increase in competition in the different vertical segments of the market, and between segments of the market.

In larger markets where dualization already existed before NTBs were removed, the impact of increased integration and market openness will be to increase competition in both segments of the market, hence to decrease the price in the low-quality segment and to increase the investments in research and advertising by the firms active in the high-quality segment. This increases the price disparity between the two segments of the markets.

Finally, there are markets that are vertically differentiated mainly because of policy factors, as well as markets in which the degree of vertical differentiation partly reflects structural market conditions but is reinforced by companies which use differences in the regulatory environment to fragment markets. In the automotive sector, for example, differences in safety regulations and the right wheel drive in the UK have been at the origin of price differences which reflect more than the underlying difference in production costs. In the pharmaceutical sector, market fragmentation at EU level results from different national regulatory environments. Vertical differentiation has been exacerbated by the development of generics, a development which has in some cases been explicitly encouraged by a set of supportive policy measures. Increased emphasis on environmental protection and the tightening of standards in some countries has also been capitalized upon by companies which have emphasized 'green' aspects of products and thereby progressively fragmented markets vertically. This has been the case, for example, for household appliances, such as refrigerators or cookers and stoves, or washing machines for which energy consumption has become a factor of differentiation (and, in the case of washing machines, water consumption and noise).

21 See soft drinks and mineral water case study in Chapter 10.

6.4. Breakdown of the product categories between homogeneous and differentiated markets

The above theoretical analysis of the likely trends in price convergence as a result of market integration illustrates the complexity of the process and the multiplicity of factors at play. To apply this analysis to the whole sample of products considered in this study requires a huge amount of information at a very detailed level of disaggregation. To assess the nature of structural factors only, information on the importance of economies of scale, on the variety of products, on advertising intensity, on the importance of research and development expenditures and of economies of scope is required. Information on behavioural and policy factors is only available from case studies.

To go as far as possible in the analysis, however, we have tried to distinguish between markets where price competition is prevalent, and vertically differentiated markets where competition is mainly driven by outlays on fixed endogenous costs aimed at increasing consumers' willingness to pay for higher quality products. The distinction between these two markets was done on the basis of two proxies: advertising intensity and research and development intensity.

In advertising-intensive markets, the difficulty is to disentangle fixed and variable costs among advertising outlays: advertising outlays are considered as part of fixed costs when they benefit the whole product range rather than a specific brand and when advertising outlays contribute to the firm's stock of goodwill, i.e. when the firm's image created by advertising outlays carries over to successive generations of product offerings. Otherwise, advertising outlays are a variable cost.

In the case of R&D outlays, the main issue is whether R&D outlays incurred on a given technology can be carried over to the next technology. If the degree of carry-over is strong, industry leaders once established tend to retain their leadership. When the carry-over effect is weak, it may induce a switch from persistence of the dominance mode to one of leap-frogging, as industry leadership changes with every generation of technology. Patent protection also plays an important role in influencing the pattern of technical change and hence the evolution of market structure.

Such information on the type of advertising or on the effects of R&D on future generations of products is, however, not available for the sample of products considered in this study. Information on advertising intensity is available on a systematic basis[22] only for France, whilst R&D intensity is published at a very aggregated level in all countries. We then had to rely, first, on the detailed analysis realized by Sutton [1991] for a limited number of food and drink markets, and, second, on the classification made by Davies and Lyons [1996] at the NACE three-digit level between industries intensive in advertising, industries intensive in research, industries intensive in research and in advertising, and other industries. We have thus allocated all product groups of our sample belonging to one NACE three-digit industry to the same category, even if, according to Sutton's analysis, markets could include segments

[22] For France along the NAP600 classification, see Services des Statistiques Industrielles (SESSI) du Ministère de l'Industrie [1994], 'La dispersion des performances des entreprises en 1993'.

that differ widely in respect of the level of set-up costs incurred by entrants.[23] Services and energy products are not included as data on advertising and research expenditures are not available.

Estimates of the importance of exogenous sunk costs are based on a proxy for the importance of economies of scale relative to the size of the market. This proxy has been calculated on the basis of UK data as the share of the minimum efficient size in the value of production. The minimum efficient size is defined as the average size of the largest plants accounting for 50% of the value of production. This proxy is available at the NACE three-digit level for the manufacturing sector. This means that services are not included.

Table 6.4.1. Mean and standard deviation of the different variables

	All	RD&ADV=0	RD&ADV>0	RD or ADV	RD and ADV
	(n=77)	(n=27)	n=50)	(n=32)	(n=18)
CVAR	19.9 9.1	19.1 7.8	20.5 9.5	22.3 10.3	17.0 7.1
CVAT	66.3 36.9	67.7 37.6	67.4 36.2	84.5 28.7	36.6 26.3
CWEIGHT	54.5 25.9	50.6 25.5	56.6 26.6	62.8 27.7	46.3 20.3
ASHDV	34.5 17	38.7 19.8	33.2 15.1	26.6 11.8	42.8 14.2
MESSIZE	4.4 3.6	2.9 4.4	5.2 2.9	4.9 3.2	5.7 2.4
ADV	3.5 3.4	2.3 2.0	4.1 3.8	4.1 3.2	3.7 3.7
EU Herfindal	0.024 0.030	0.004 0.004	0.035 0.033	0.018 0.014	0.064 0.036
C4FR	43.6 25.1	22.8 10.7	55.8 23.6	52.2 22.3	60.5 23.8
extra-EU import rate	13.6 14.9	13.8 11	14.1 16.6	10.2 12.3	20.9 20.6
intra-EU import rate	19.6 11.5	18.1 7.7	20.8 12.9	16.4 8.2	28.7 15.9
mul	0.36 0.18	0.17 0.12	0.47 0.14	0.46 0.119	0.50 0.14
Source: DRI *et al.*					

[23] Examples of such cases are: roast and ground coffee, sugar and chocolate confectionery, chewing gum (very high set-up cost) and other sugar confectionery (extremely low set-up cost), mainstream products of the cornflakes kind (high set-up cost) and muesli-type (low set-up cost) in the ready-to-eat cereals market.

An alternative proxy for measuring the degree of vertical differentiation is based on the share of two-way trade in vertically differentiated products in intra-EU imports. Trade is considered to be 'two-way' when the value of the minority flow (e.g. imports) represents at least 10% of the majority flow (exports in this case). Traded products are considered to be vertically differentiated when the export and import unit values in bilateral trade differ by more than 15%.[24]

Table 6.4.1 compares the main descriptive statistics between the product markets for which information on the different variables is available, classified according to the intensity of research and/or advertising. It is once more important to recall that, despite the very extensive work of collecting data at the most detailed level, several variables are measured only at the NACE three-digit level, whilst most of our product groups are defined at the four- or five-digit level (the sample considers six categories of electric domestic appliances belonging to NACE 346 from the NACE 70 classification) or regroup products belonging to different NACE three-digit classes such as jewellery and watches, or musical instruments, pleasure boats, personal computers and software.

Products that are not intensive in research or advertising (RD&ADV=0) are characterized by a lower average efficient size (MESSIZE), advertising intensity (ADV), degree of concentration at the European (HEU) or national level (C4FR) and degree of multinationality (M) than products intensive in research and/or advertising (RD&ADV>0). This sub-sample includes both homogeneous products and horizontally differentiated products (having no information on product variety, we are not able to distinguish between these two types of markets). However, the share of two-way trade in vertically differentiated products is higher for products that are not intensive in research and advertising than for products that are intensive in research and/or advertising. Looking at the values taken by this variable (ASHCDV) in the different product groups classified as not intensive in either research or advertising reveals that high shares of two-way trade in vertically differentiated products are observed for clothing, footwear, furniture, floor coverings, glassware and tableware, cutlery, books, newspapers, articles for travelling, and paper and drawing supplies. In some of these markets, control of the distribution system by the producers[25] may explain differences between export and import unit values in bilateral trade and hence high levels for the variable ASHCDV. These products, however, do not appear to be characterized by high endogenous costs and hence should still be considered as horizontally differentiated markets.

The list of products included in this sample is shown in Table 6.4.2. This table shows the diversity of situations observed in this sample of markets. Note that, in the last column, a negative sign means a reduction in the coefficient of variation of prices in the EU-9 between 1985 and 1993.

---

[24] For more details on the construction of this variable, see CEPII [1996], 'The development of intra- versus inter-industry trade flows inside the EU due to the internal market programme', report prepared for the European Commission (DG II/DG XV).

[25] According to the study on price differentials by the DIW, furniture and cutlery products selected in their sample were characterized by a uniform national price due to fixed resale prices.

Table 6.4.2. List of products non-intensive in R&D and advertising (homogeneous and horizontally differentiated products)

Code	Product description	Economies of scale	National concentration	CVAR in 1985	Variation in CVAR (85–93)
1111011	Rice	0	0	16.5	2.6
1111012	Flour, other cereals	0	1	13.8	8.4
1111013	Bread	0	0	18.5	0.5
1111015	Pasta, noodles	1	1	17.8	3.9
1111016	Other cereal based products	0	1	19.1	0.5
1111021	Beef	0	0	18.4	-0.1
1111022	Veal	0	0	20.3	4.5
1111023	Pork	0	0	12.6	5.7
1111024	Mutton, lamb and goat meat	0	0	20.3	4.5
1111025	Poultry	0	0	6.5	2
1111026	Delicatessen	0	0	15.9	5.9
1111027	Meat prep. and other meat products	0	0	17.2	-2
1111028	Other fresh or frozen meat	0	0	23.6	10.7
1111031	Fresh, frozen fish	1	0	17.6	2.2
1111032	Dried or smoked fish	1	0	20.6	-15.9
1111033	Other seafood	1	0	27.9	-17.9
1111034	Preserved & prep. fish and seafood	1	0	15.0	3.2
1111081	Sugar	0	1	30.0	-7.8
1121011	Men's clothing	0	0	17.2	4.9
1121012	Women's clothing	0	0	16.7	3.6
1121013	Children's clothing (age 3–13 years)	0	0	37.4	3.4
1121014	Babies' clothing (age 0–2 years)	0	0	27.5	-5.9
1121015	Clothing accessories	0	0	21.3	-3.4
1122011	Men's footwear	0	0	16.1	4
1122012	Women's footwear	0	0	16.3	3.4
1122013	Children's and babies' footwear	0	0	22.5	8
1141011	Furniture and furnishing accessories	0	0	14.1	-2.3
1141012	Floor coverings	1	0	8.3	1.4
1144011	Glassware and tableware	0	0	21.9	3.4
1144012	Cutlery	0	0	13.7	-4.2
1173011	Books, brochures, & other	0	0	62.3	-40.4
1173012	Periodicals, newspapers	0	0	17.9	-0.2
1182021	Articles for travelling and luggage	0	0	15.2	-1.8
1182031	Paper and drawing supplies	0	0	23.6	2
1311011	Structural metal products	0	0	11.7	8.8
1311012	Products of boilermaking	0	0	23.4	7.7
1311021	Tools and finished metal articles	0	0	16.5	12.8
1311051	Machinery equip. for mining, metallurgy, building and civil eng.	0	0	6.7	8.2
1311062	Machinery for food, chemicals, rubber, packaging	0	0	8.3	-0.9
1313021	Ships	1	0	27.2	-14.6

Source: DRI.

Products characterized by relatively high economies of scale are pasta and noodles, fish products, sugar and floor coverings among the consumer goods, and ships among the equipment goods. High national concentration levels are observed in flour and other cereals, pasta and noodles, other cereal based products and sugar. The only market which is also concentrated at the EU level is sugar.

This market is particularly interesting as it is one of the markets belonging to this sample where the SMP had no effect. It is, indeed, the CAP (and particularly the mechanism of production quota allocation) which shapes the structures and behaviours in this market. The strong observed convergence in prices between 1985 and 1993 (with the coefficient of variation falling from 30.0 to 22.2) has nothing to do with the implementation of the SMP. This convergence has furthermore taken place despite major differences in prices of raw material and energy prices between the national markets.[26] Other markets belonging to this sample where it is the CAP and not the SMP which plays a significant role are the flour, the meat and the fish markets. Indirect effects of the CAP also affect the organization of production in downstream markets for these products (e.g. bread, sugar confectionery, meat preparations).

In the case of the flour market, transport costs and the CAP lead to a market fundamentally restricted within national borders. The high and increasing concentration in this market reflects the desire to exploit the potential economies of scale in production. The same tendency towards a greater concentration is observed in the processing of fishery products, driven by the scale economies at both the production and distribution levels. The relatively high level of price disparity observed in this market confirms the observation made by the Trade Association according to which prices do not converge at the EU level.[26]

Products characterized by relatively low economies of scale where convergence is observed between 1980 and 1993 in the EU-9 are furniture, glassware and tableware, books, articles for travelling and personal luggage, and paper and drawing supplies. These are markets of horizontally differentiated goods, for which increased price convergence was an expected effect of the SMP. Cutlery, on the other hand, shows a high and persistent level of price disparity. As mentioned already, control of the distribution system might be the main explanatory factor. Among the equipment goods, products of boilermaking and tools and finished metal articles show a huge increase in price dispersion. In the former case, customization of products and the persistence of internal barriers (through national testing bodies) are explanations provided by the Trade Association.

Among the products intensive in research and/or advertising – products which can either be horizontally or vertically differentiated – substantial differences appear between the products which are intensive in both research and advertising (RD&ADV) and products which are intensive either in research or in advertising (RDORADV). The former are characterized by a higher average efficient size, degree of concentration at the European (but not national) level, higher import penetration from both intra-EU and extra-EU countries and higher shares of vertically differentiated two-way trade than the latter. Furthermore, average disparity in preferences (CWEIGHT) and in fiscal policies (CVAT) appear to be lower in their case than in the case of products intensive in research or advertising. This suggests that this sub-sample regroups products which, due to the importance of both endogenous and exogenous costs, are

[26] See DRI [1995], 'Survey of the trade associations' perception of the effects of the single market', report prepared for the Commission of the European Communities (DG III).

mainly supplied by multinational firms acting on a pan-European basis. Products which are intensive both in research and in advertising are listed in Table 6.4.3.

Table 6.4.3. List of products intensive in R&D and advertising

Code	Product description	Economies of scale	National concentration	CVAR in 1985	Variation in CVAR (85–93)
1143011	Refrigerators, freezers	1	1	11.8	0.2
1143012	Washing machines, tumble dryers	1	1	13.5	-9.1
1143013	Cookers and stoves	0	1	15.8	-15.7
1143014	Heating and air conditioning appliances	0	0	19.4	-8.9
1143015	Cleaning equipment	0	0	22.5	-11.4
1143016	Other household appliances	0	0	8.4	0.4
1145011	Cleaning and maintenance products	0	0	16.7	-4.4
1151011	Medicines	0	0	30.1	2.8
1151021	Other pharmaceutical products	0	0	35.9	8.4
1152011	Lenses and glasses	1	0	35.1	-1.7
1161011	Motor vehicles	1	1	20.7	-9
1171011	Radios	0	0	20.4	-16.3
1171012	Televisions	0	0	15.0	-14.5
1171013	Record players, tape and cassette recorders	0	0	15.0	-18.9
1171021	Photographic and cinematographic equipment	1	0	9.1	-9.5
1171031	Records, cassettes, tapes	0	0	12.8	-0.2
1171034	Film and other photographic supplies	0	0	10.8	-0.2
1181022	Non-durable personal care products	0	1	14.7	-6.4
1182011	Jewellery, watches, precious stones	1	0	23.1	-2.9
1311031	Agricultural machinery and tractors	1	0	11.3	2
1311092	Optical instruments, photographic material	0	0	15.7	5.9
1312022	Electronic equipment, radios and televisions	0	0	24.9	1.3
1313011	Motor vehicles and engines	0	0	13.9	-11.3

Source: DRI.

Products with relative high economies of scale are refrigerators and freezers, washing machines and dryers, watches, products belonging to the optical instruments and photographic material industry, motor vehicles and agricultural machinery. Products with high relative national concentration are refrigerators and freezers, washing machines and dryers, cookers and stoves, motor vehicles and non-durable personal care products.

Once more, and in line with the theoretical approach, no systematic relation between structural characteristics and price convergence is observed. Among the four markets which show a stability of the price dispersion at a relatively high level, we find the two markets of medicine products (low concentration, low production economies of scale) where marketing regulations still hinder the arbitraging process, and the car market (high relative economies of scale, national concentration and degree of multinationalization) where protection against extra-EU imports and exclusive dealership systems maintain the segmentation of markets (the studies of car price differentials across the EU indeed indicate that price disparities in this market partly reflect the commercial policies of the car manufacturers, in addition to being influenced by exchange rate variations). No significant change in price disparity is observed in the refrigerator market and in the other household appliances market. In the former, increasing demand for variety, as consumers move from first time buying to replacement in the most mature markets of the EU, could explain this tendency, after considerable consolidation and restructuring during the 1980s. In contrast, strong price convergence is observed for cookers and stoves, cleaning and maintenance equipment, radios, televisions and other audio equipment, photographic and cinematographic equipment, non-durable personal care products (at least after 1985) and lenses and glasses (between 1980 and 1985; price dispersion then increased between 1990 and 1993). Strong price convergence is also observed for motor vehicles and engines bought as investment goods, i.e. mainly trucks and buses. Several of these markets are dominated by multinational companies, and we do not know to which level these prices did converge. Increasing power of the distribution market or extra-EU import competition suggests that they converged to a low(er) level.

The low average value of the share of two-way trade in vertically differentiated products observed for the markets which are either intensive in research or in advertising suggests that some of these markets could be classified as being horizontally differentiated markets.

The econometric analysis in Chapter 7 confirms that the structural factors identified above can explain at least some of the resistance of prices to converge. In Chapter 7, we test econometrically the relative significance of a number of structural and policy factors in explaining the observed trends in price disparities. This analysis will allow us to constitute a list of those products/services for which 'objective' factors (importance of economies of scale, degree of concentration, presence of multinationals, etc.) do not explain the persisting price disparities in 1993. The products/services in this list are thus in markets in which one may suspect either that policy factors remain which prevent the benefits of integration from materializing, or that companies are adopting behaviours that slow the integration process.

7. Factors underlying price convergence: descriptive analysis

7.1. Key results

Based on a comparison of the levels of and trends in price dispersion across the EU-15 between 1980(85) and 1993, this chapter shows that:

(a) Price dispersion is lowest the more traded products/services there are within the EU.

(b) The product categories which have seen the greatest convergence in prices following the launch of the SMP are the highly traded sectors and, more specifically, the sectors that are most open to competition from other EU producers. The reduction in price disparities for sectors classified as having been subject to high non-tariff barriers before the launch of the SMP is disappointing.

(c) The convergence of the EU-15 prices towards the EU-12 level is only notable after 1990, but it applies to all products/services categories, whether traded or non-traded.

(d) As expected, based on the theoretical framework presented in Chapter 6, the coefficients of price variation are higher and tend to converge less rapidly in markets characterized by a high advertising to sales ratio and by a high R&D intensity, i.e. markets in which high endogenous sunk costs can create barriers to entry or can be used by companies to fragment markets vertically and thereby limit competition in their market segment.

7.2. Price convergence patterns for traded versus non-traded products/services categories

On the basis of the analysis in Chapter 6, different types of product groupings can be done to understand the differences in the coefficients of price variation (and in the price convergence patterns) for selected types of goods and services. Here, five types of product groupings were constituted to compare price dispersion patterns:

(a) traded versus non-traded goods categories;

(b) products with a high rate of intra-EU trade versus products that are not highly traded within the EU;

(c) products with a high degree of extra-EU import penetration, as opposed to products with a low extra-EU import penetration ratio;

(d) markets subject to relatively high non-tariff barriers (NTBs) before the launch of the SMP, as compared to markets with moderate or low NTBs at the start of the period;

(e) markets subject to a high advertising to sales ratio and/or a high R&D intensity, to measure the impact of endogenous and exogenous sunk costs in explaining price disparities across different geographic markets.

The first of these aggregations (traded versus non-traded goods) was done to test the hypothesis that the price of traded goods in different EU countries will be more similar than those of non-traded goods. Here, tradeable goods are defined as all manufactured products as well as energy, whereas the non-tradeable goods category includes all the service sectors as well as construction.

The second and third groupings classify products based on the relative trade intensity of each market segment, considering intra-EU and extra-EU import penetration separately. In both cases the idea is that in markets in which there are no barriers to entry, the difference in the price of traded goods across countries/regions should mainly reflect differences in transport costs. Hence, should prices of highly traded goods really be dissimilar across different countries/regions, this would indicate that companies are discriminating across markets and/or that there are barriers to arbitrage so that parallel trade cannot take place to push prices towards convergence.

Making a distinction between highly and not highly traded products based on both intra-EU and extra-EU import penetration shows whether the competitive pressure exerted by extra-EU imports is greater than that associated with intra-EU imports.[27] Intra-firm trade represents a higher share of intra-EU trade than of extra-EU trade.

The distinction between highly traded and not highly traded products was made based on the average rate of extra- and intra-EU import penetration respectively (measured by imports as a share of apparent consumption) over the period 1980–93. Products with a rate of import penetration higher than average were classified as 'highly traded' products, and those with a rate of penetration lower than average were classified as 'not highly traded' products.

The next product grouping (d) was done to see the extent to which price disparities have been reduced comparatively more (or faster) following the launch of the SMP in markets initially subject to important NTBs than in other markets. The list of sectors subject to high NTBs before the launch of the SMP is that identified by P. Buigues *et al.* [1990]. The list was drawn based on the results of a questionnaire completed by 11,000 European enterprises [Nerb, 1988], on sectoral studies carried out for the Commission as part of its assessment of the cost of non-Europe [EC, 1988] and on a horizontal study of technical barriers in six industries [MAC, 1988]. The information was used to classify all the industrial sectors (NACE 3-digit) into three groups according to the overall impact of NTBs: slight impact, moderate impact or major impact. The sectors for which the impact of NTBs was deemed to be moderate are relatively varied and include a number of sectors in which the principal obstacles to market integration were differences in standards or administrative and technical controls. The sectors in which NTBs were deemed to have a major impact included those in which the public sector is the main purchaser (the public procurement sectors) and those in which differences in standards present a considerable obstacle to intra-Community trade. Among the 113 traded goods, 18 belong to a high NTB industry and 35 to a medium NTB industry.

Finally, different groupings were made to compare the coefficients of variation of prices for products characterized by a high advertising to sales ratio, a high R&D intensity, both or neither. The rationale for this product grouping was outlined in Chapter 6, and reflects the fact

[27] Jacquemin and Sapir [1991] show that the negative impact on price-cost margins is much more significant for extra-EU imports than for intra-EU imports.

that price convergence patterns following market enlargement will depend on a set of fundamental characteristics of the markets, among which the importance of endogenous sunk costs, and METS.

The mapping of the 174 product categories into each of these different types of groupings (tradeables or non-tradeables; highly traded or not; subject to high, moderate or low NTBs) is presented in Appendix C.

The results of the analysis of the coefficients of price variation of the more traded versus non-traded goods respectively are presented in Table 7.2.1. They confirm the expectation that price dispersion is lowest the more traded the products. For tradeable goods, the decrease in price dispersion appears to have occurred mainly between 1980 and 1985 in all three geographical groupings.

Table 7.2.1. Coefficients of variation for tradeable and non-tradeable products/services (based on prices including taxes)

	1980	1985	1990	1993
EU-6				
Tradeables	15.1	13.2	13.4	13.1
Non-tradeables	19.4	19.0	17.5	20.4
EU-9				
Tradeables	18.8	17.6	18.9	17.8
Non-tradeables	23.0	21.5	21.5	23.0
EU-12				
Tradeables	24.8	20.8	21.0	19.3
Non-tradeables	29.3	29.6	28.6	28.1
EU-15				
Tradeables	..	24.5	23.5	19.6
Non-tradeables	..	30.4	31.1	27.7

Source: DRI.

Within the EU-6 region, where countries have a longer history of market integration, one finds that the coefficient of variation for tradeable products was, at 15.1, already fairly low in 1980; even though it decreased further between then and 1985, it remained broadly stable at around 13.2 thereafter.

For the non-tradeable goods, although there was some reduction in price disparities between 1980 and 1990, the long-term trend shows no particular convergence.

Looking at the broader aggregate for the EU-9 shows two things. First, the coefficients of variation for both tradeable and non-tradeable goods are higher than for the EU-6, and remain so throughout the period. Second, although there does not seem to have been a tendency for non-tradeable category prices to converge, the same is not true for tradeable products. For this latter category, increased integration and possibly the implementation of the SMP do seem to have led to a greater homogeneity of prices across the EU-9.

Taking the whole of the EU-12 shows yet a different pattern, with some convergence taking place both for tradeables and for non-tradeable goods and services. Convergence has admittedly been faster for the tradeable goods than for non-tradeables, but it is important to note the reduction in overall price dispersion in the non-tradeable goods/services category, both over time and between the EU-12 and the EU-9. Whereas in 1980 the coefficient of variation of prices in the non-tradeable goods category in the EU-12 was 51% higher than in the EU-6, this difference had shrunk to 37.7% in 1993.

Table 7.2.2 presents similar information for product groups based on the rate of intra-EU import penetration.

Table 7.2.2. Coefficients of variation based on the rate of intra-EU import penetration (based on prices including taxes)

	1980	1985	1990	1993
EU-6				
Low	16.8	14.3	14.5	14.3
High	12.0	10.9	10.9	11.3
EU-9				
Low	21.0	18.4	20.2	19.3
High	15.4	15.8	16.0	15.8
EU-12				
Low	26.5	21.4	22.8	20.8
High	22.3	19.5	17.8	17.0
EU-15				
Low	..	26.0	26.2	21.1
High	..	20.9	18.6	17.0

Source: DRI.

As expected, the coefficient of variation of prices is lowest the higher the rate of (intra-EU) import penetration. Price disparities are particularly low in the highly traded sectors within the EU-6, which have a longer history of economic integration, and have thus shown no tendency to converge further between 1980 and 1993. If anything, there has been a slight increase in price disparities in the EU-6 between 1985 and 1993. The same holds for the EU-9 region.

In the EU-12, however, price disparities have been reduced progressively over time, such that the difference in the coefficient of variation of highly traded products between the EU-12 and the EU-6 has come down from 86% in 1980 to 79% in 1985, 63.3% in 1990 and 50% in 1993. The coefficient of variation of prices for non-highly-traded products has also decreased in the

EU-12 thanks to increased integration of the Greek, Spanish and Portuguese economies within the rest of Europe, but has not changed significantly in either the EU-6 or the EU-9.

In the EU-15, again, price convergence towards the EU-12 level has been observed for all product groupings, i.e. both for highly traded and for less traded products, the trend having been most pronounced between 1990 and 1993.

Looking at a similar table for product groups based on the relative rate of penetration of extra-EU imports, one finds a slightly different pattern. Although price disparities remain lower in the EU-6 than in the EU-9, lower in the EU-9 than in the EU-12, and lower in the EU-12 than in the EU-15, whatever the relative importance of extra-EU import penetration, one finds a continuous reduction in price disparities of highly traded goods even in the EU-6 between 1980 and 1993 (Table 7.2.3).

Table 7.2.3. Coefficients of variation based on the rate of extra-EU import penetration (based on prices including taxes)

	1980	1985	1990	1993
EU-6				
Low	15.4	13.5	13.5	13.9
High	14.4	12.3	12.2	11.7
EU-9				
Low	19.6	18.8	19.7	18.8
High	17.6	14.7	16.4	16.3
EU-12				
Low	26.1	22.2	21.9	20.1
High	22.7	17.6	18.7	17.9
EU-15				
Low	..	25.9	25.0	20.4
High	..	21.0	19.8	17.8

Source: DRI.

Whereas in 1980 the coefficient of price variation of products with a high rate of penetration of extra-EU imports was already fairly low in the EU-6 at 14.4, it decreased further to 11.7 by 1993. A similar decrease was observed within the EU-12, and to a lesser extent in the EU-9 but only over the 1980–85 period. Even in sectors with a relatively low rate of extra-EU import penetration, there was a downward trend in the coefficients of variation between 1980 and 1993 in the EU-12, whilst in the EU-6 it occurred between 1980 and 1985 and remained stable afterwards. This seems to indicate that globalization trends and increased competition at world level affected all tradeable products during the 1980–85 period.

Table 7.2.4 shows the trend in price disparities based on the level of NTBs before the launch of the SMP. The idea is to test whether the SMP has indeed succeeded in reducing price disparities (through the removal of NTBs and increases in competition) in the markets which were more regulated (or in which there were comparatively high NTBs) at the start of the period.

Table 7.2.4. Coefficients of variation based on the level of NTBs (based on prices including taxes)

	1980	1985	1990	1993
EU-6				
Low	15.0	13.0	12.8	11.0
High	19.6	18.3	20.2	19.0
Medium	12.6	11.1	10.0	11.5
EU-9				
Low	19.1	17.7	18.4	15.6
High	22.8	22.0	22.5	20.3
Medium	16.0	15.5	16.9	17.7
EU-12				
Low	24.8	21.0	20.7	17.4
High	26.9	25.0	24.9	23.9
Medium	23.0	18.3	18.6	17.9
EU-15				
Low	..	26.5	24.7	18.4
High	..	26.8	27.9	23.5
Medium	..	20.3	19.0	17.2

Source: DRI.

The results indicate that price disparities at the beginning of the period (in 1980 and 1985) were indeed lower in the market segments in which NTBs were low than in the market segments in which NTBs were comparatively high. Market segments characterized by medium NTBs are mainly equipment goods markets which show a lower dispersion of prices due to their highly traded nature. The econometric results (see Chapter 8) confirm that not only do NTBs increase the dispersion of prices, but also that variables affecting price disparity behave differently in markets characterized by NTBs. The trend towards price convergence remains more pronounced in the low NTB markets than in the high NTB markets, indicating that all NTBs to intra-EU trade have not yet been removed.[28] Within the EU-12, however, the trend towards price convergence for both high and low NTB markets has been relatively pronounced – a situation which contrasts with developments in either the EU-6 or the EU-9, and which may reflect the consequences of EU membership of these three countries more than the result of the SMP.

[28] Several of these remaining trade barriers are mentioned by the trade associations in DRI [1995], 'Survey of the trade associations' perception of the effects of the single market', report prepared for the European Commission (DG III).

Still, it is notable that after having increased in both the EU-6 and the EU-9 between 1985 and 1990, price disparities in markets characterized by high NTBs before the launch of the SMP have started to come down. This may reflect the late implementation of some of the measures in the SMP, the effects of which on prices started to be observed after 1990.

The last product grouping (Table 7.2.5) distinguishes the convergence patterns between markets which are non-intensive in either research or advertising (NotRD/ADV), markets intensive in advertising only (ADV), markets intensive in research only (RD), and markets intensive in both research and advertising (RD/ADV). Markets not intensive in research and advertising (i.e. homogeneous or horizontally differentiated product markets) show a relatively low price dispersion in all three regional groupings, with convergence occurring between 1980 and 1985. The highest level of price disparity is observed in markets intensive in advertising only (except for the EU-6 in 1993). This reflects the consumer inertia created by brand loyalty based on high advertising expenditures. Some convergence is observed between 1990 and 1993 in both the EU-6 and the EU-9, suggesting a switch to pan-European brands. In the EU-12, the convergence pattern occurs over the whole period, as in all market groupings, reflecting once more the consequences of EU membership.

Table 7.2.5. Coefficients of variation based on the intensity of R&D expenditure and/or advertising expenditure (based on prices including taxes)

	1980	1985	1990	1993
EU-6				
NotRD/ADV	14.3	11.6	10.6	11.1
ADV	17.6	16.0	16.8	11.9
RD	10.3	10.0	12.8	11.8
RD/ADV	15.2	15.0	13.2	15.6
EU-9				
NotRD/ADV	17.3	14.3	15.9	15.7
ADV	24.4	23.8	24.1	20.5
RD	11.9	11.7	14.0	13.4
RD/ADV	19.1	20.7	19.6	19.0
EU-12				
NotRD/ADV	22.2	16.4	18.3	16.7
ADV	31.5	28.3	26.9	23.2
RD	16.0	12.4	15.0	15.3
RD/ADV	26.4	25.3	21.8	19.8

Source: DRI.

In markets intensive in both research and advertising, the price disparity is relatively high and stable over time in both the EU-6 and the EU-9. This confirms that vertical differentiation and barriers to entry based on the high levels of endogenous costs effectively hinder the arbitraging process in these markets. On the contrary, markets intensive in research only show the lowest average price disparity in all regional groupings. This suggests that huge investments in research and development not coupled with advertising investments compels firms to adopt a European (or even global) marketing strategy in order to recoup these investments.

8. Factors underlying price convergence: econometric analysis

8.1. Key results

Chapter 6 showed that the impact on prices of the completion of the SMP is very complex to analyse as multiple factors are at play. The econometric analysis in this chapter assesses the relative importance of a number of structural and behavioural factors in explaining the observed patterns of price convergence across the EU-9 over the period 1980–93. The key results are the following:

(a) Objective factors, such as structural factors hindering the arbitraging process or leading to a competitive process based more on quality than on price, explain a significant part of the variation in price disparity across product categories.

(b) Disparities in fiscal policies and in consumer preferences across countries have a significant positive impact on price disparity across the EU.

(c) A high degree of concentration in national markets also favours price disparity, whereas a high degree of internationalization of the market, either through import penetration or through the presence of multinational companies in national markets, tends to decrease price disparity.

(d) The existence of high or moderate NTBs also explains part of the observed price disparities.

(e) Where there are no NTBs, or where these are ineffective, national structures (measured by high degree of concentration in national markets) and national regulations (in particular, differences in taxation) lose their effectiveness. In markets with low NTBs, thus, behavioural and policy factors are less effective in keeping markets fragmented, and it is mainly structural factors which explain price disparities, where these are still observed.

(f) The effects of the SMP have either not been strong enough or have been too concentrated over the later part of the period to have induced a major shift in the estimated parameters over the period considered.

(g) Overall, about 30% of the observed variance of the dependent variable (the coefficients of price variation including taxes in the EU-9) is explained by structural and quantifiable policy factors. The remainder is due to other factors, among which are behavioural responses of firms to the rise in competition in the market, or remaining policy barriers.

(h) Among the markets in which price dispersion is least explained by the set of explanatory variables used in the regression (mainly reflecting structural factors and fiscal policy) are:

(i) fresh and frozen fish,
(ii) other seafood,
(iii) books,

(iv) preserved milk,
(v) cocoa,
(vi) condiments and sauces,
(vii) mineral waters,
(viii) alcoholic beverages,
(ix) orthopaedic and therapeutic appliances and products.

Some of these are diversified products for which differences in product quality can explain price disparities. The different organization of distribution channels for these products across Member States can also explain some of the resistance of prices to converge. In the case of books, however, a category for which rapid price convergence has been observed since 1985 at EU-9 level, the poor fit of the regression indicates that there are more than structural factors which account for the rapid convergence in prices after the inception of the SMP.

8.2. Approach

Chapter 6 has shown that the impact of EU integration on price dispersion across countries is very complex. Not only structural but also behavioural and policy factors interact in determining the degree of price disparity at the EU level.

The objective of this econometric analysis is to shed some light on the relative importance of various factors in explaining the observed dispersion of prices across product categories.

Several hypotheses have been tested:

(a) To what extent are the effects of the SMP already strong enough and sufficiently diffused as to induce a shift in the estimated parameters over the period 1980–93?

(b) To what extent is the distinction made in Chapter 6 between, on the one hand, markets characterized by exogenous sunk costs (homogeneous or horizontally differentiated product markets) and, on the other hand, markets characterized by endogenous sunk costs (vertically differentiated product markets) validated by the empirical estimation?

(c) To what extent do markets characterized by moderate or high NTBs behave differently from markets characterized by low NTBs?

(d) What is the respective role of barriers to the arbitrage process, the nature of competition in the market, and the intensity of competition, in explaining the observed dispersion of prices?

The dependent variable in the econometric regressions is the coefficient of variation of the price indices inclusive of taxes at the EU-9 level.

Three groups of explanatory variables are considered.

The first one includes the **structural and quantifiable policy factors** affecting the arbitraging process:

(a) The disparity in fiscal policy across the EU countries (**CVAT**) is measured by the coefficient of variation of the VAT rates applied in each country.

(b) The disparity of demand across EU countries (**CWEIGHT**) is measured by the coefficient of variation of the shares of national consumption of the product considered in total national consumption.

(c) The existence of non-tariff barriers (**NTB**) is measured by a variable which takes the value 0 if NTBs are low, the value 1 if NTBs are moderate and the value 2 if NTBs are high. This information is available at the NACE three-digit level.[29]

These three variables are expected to exert a positive impact on the price dispersion across countries.

The second group of variables includes variables describing the **nature of competition** in each market. These variables, which are supposed to describe structural characteristics of the market, do not vary over time. This means that we do not take into account changes in these structural characteristics resulting from strategic adaptation to a new competitive environment. Furthermore, due to lack of data, we had to rely on national data for some variables. The hypothesis we have then to make is that the variation across product categories at the EU-9 level is the same as the variation observed at national level.

This second group of variables includes:

(a) The importance of exogenous sunk costs (**MESSIZE**), measured by the extent of economies of scale relative to the size of the market. This proxy has been calculated, on the basis of UK data, as the share of the minimum efficient size in the value of production. The minimum efficient size is the average size of the largest plants accounting for 50% of the value of production.

(b) The importance of endogenous sunk costs (**ADV**), measured by the ratio of advertising to sales in France in 1990.

(c) The extent of vertical differentiation (**ASHCDV**), measured for each product category by the EU-9 average in 1993 of the shares of vertically differentiated trade in intra-EU imports.[30]

The expected impact of economies of scale is ambiguous, as discussed in Chapter 6. High economies of scale limit the number of firms active in a market. They can induce firms to standardize their production and increase the geographic market in which they sell in order to better exploit these economies of scale. However, when cooperative behaviour is sustained by high transport costs or by a protective regulatory environment, dispersion of prices between markets will persist over time.

The expected impact of ADV is positive, as it measures the extent of brand competition and hence consumer inertia between suppliers.

The extent of vertically differentiated intra-industry trade (ASHCDV) is also expected to increase price dispersion across countries, as it reveals competition based on quality rather than price alone.

---

[29] This variable comes from Buigues *et al.* [1988].

[30] This variable has been kindly supplied by CEPII.

The third group of variables includes variables describing the **extent of competition** in each product category:

(a) Intra-EU import penetration (**INTRA**) is the share of intra-EU imports in total EU apparent consumption (sales minus exports plus imports) at the NACE three-digit level.

(b) Extra-EU import penetration (**EXTRA**) is the share of extra-EU imports in total apparent consumption. Measures of import penetration at the level of our product classification have been calculated as the ratio of imports for the relevant products divided by total consumption expenditures on these products (TMINTRA and TMEXTRA). However, without information on the share of imports which goes to final consumption, these ratios exceed the true penetration level in several cases, such as sugar, dried vegetables or fruits, fats, tyres, etc. These ratios even take values higher than 100 for some products.

(c) **C4FR** is the share in total sales of the four largest firms in France in 1990 at the NAP600 level.

(d) **C5UK** is the share of the five leading firms in total sales in the UK in 1990 at the NACE three-digit level.

(e) **HEU** is a proxy for concentration at the EU level[31] measured by the Herfindhal index at the NACE three-digit level.

(f) A proxy for multinationalization in a given industry,[31] is measured as the weighted average of the degrees of multinationality for constituent firms in each NACE three-digit industry.

INTRA and EXTRA are expected to decrease price disparity across EU countries, as they reveal the extent of competitive pressure associated with the presence of foreign suppliers.

The expected impact of national degrees of concentration is difficult to predict. Ideally, one should have introduced a variable measuring the disparity in national concentration degrees. Differences in the published indices at the national level (C4 in France, C3 or C6 in Germany, C5 in the UK) and in the classification used (NAP600 for France, SYPRO 4-digit for Germany and NACE 3-digit for the UK), however, prevented the construction of such a variable.

The correlation coefficient between C4FR and C5UK is equal to .73, revealing that the ranking of product categories according to the degree of concentration is quite similar between these two countries. We tried both variables as C4FR is available at a more detailed level than C5UK.

High degrees of concentration reveal the existence of potential market power in the national market and hence ability to price discriminate. However, when preferences are biased towards national production, high degrees of concentration might also increase the cost of entry for foreign suppliers.

[31] See Davies, S. and Lyons, B. [1996], *Industrial Organization in the European Union*, Oxford University Press.

Concentration at the European level, on the other hand, suggests high mutual recognition between the players. As these concentration variables are measured in one specific year, we do not take into account consolidation processes which may have been under way in some markets, partly in anticipation of the single market. One example of such market restructuring is detailed in the white goods case study.[32]

The extent of multinationality in a given sector reveals the ability of firms to organize themselves on a pan-European basis. The impact on price disparity can be positive or negative depending on whether firms choose to exploit the differences among markets (by selling the same product under different brand names) or to exploit the economies of scale by adopting a uniform marketing approach across the EU. Furthermore, an extensive presence of multinationals also questions the competitive pressure associated with the rate of import penetration, as these imports could be mainly intra-firm trade.

Tests of the stability of the coefficients over time allow us to pool the data.[33] This indicates that the completion of the single market has not had the effect of leading to coefficients significantly different in the more recent years as compared with the beginning of the period. Depending on the set of explanatory variables, the sample covers between 253 and 316 observations concerning only consumer goods products.[34] About one third of the observed variance of the dependent variable is explained by the independent variables.

8.3. Results of the econometric analysis

Table 8.3.1 presents the results for the whole sample. Disparity in fiscal policies (CVAT) and in consumer preferences (CWEIGHT) as well as the existence of non-tariff barriers (NTB) exert, as expected, a significant positive impact on price disparity across EU countries. The importance of disparity in consumer preferences is approximately twice as high as the importance of disparity in fiscal policies.[35]

Among the variables describing the nature of competition, vertical differentiation (ASHCDV) exerts a significant positive impact on price disparity, whose importance is similar to that of the disparity in preferences variable.

32 Whilst 150 white goods producers supplied 75% of the market in 1985, 15 international groups controlled 80% by 1990 and seven groups had 86% by 1995. This consolidation, which occurred essentially through acquisitions, is driven by economies of scale, just-in-time logistics and consolidation of component supply.

33 According to the specification, the F test takes a value which varies between 1.04 and 1.11. This value is well below the significance level, indicating that allowing the coefficients to vary over time does not improve significantly the results of the estimation. Distinguishing between 1980 and 1985, on the one hand, and 1990 and 1993, on the other hand, also leads to the conclusion that the coefficients do not differ significantly between these two periods (F=1.33 or 1.35). This is not really surprising as the speed of adjustments to the single market situation varies between markets.

34 Price indices for equipment goods and construction goods are net of VAT. Furthermore, competition in these markets obeys different rules than those observed in consumer goods markets, due to differences in the buying side of the market and in the importance of regulatory policies.

35 Except when TMINTRA and TMEXTRA are used as indicators of foreign competitive pressure.

Table 8.3.1. Regression analysis of price disparity across the EU-9

	(1)	(2)	(3)	(4)	(5)	(6)	(7)	(8)	(9)	(10)
constant	2.0	2.8	5.9	5.1	1.9	2.4	6.3	5.3	0.73	1.07
	(0.8)	(1.1)	(1.9)*	(1.9)*	(0.8)	(1.0)	(2.2)*	(2.1)*	(0.3)	(0.4)
CVAT	0.058	0.065	0.053	0.052	0.080	0.080	0.080	0.076	0.096	0.097
	(3.8)**	(4.4)**	(3.4)**	(3.4)**	(4.7)**	(5.0)**	(4.4)**	(4.4)**	(5.7)**	(5.8)**
CWEIGHT	0.130	0.129	0.135	0.135	0.120	0.121	0.125	0.124	0.104	0.102
	(7.2)**	(7.1)**	(7.4)**	(7.4)**	(6.5)**	(6.5)**	(6.7)**	(6.7)**	(5.1)**	(5.1)**
ASHDV	0.139	0.131	0.112	0.117	0.135	0.129	0.125	0.108	0.117	0.116
	(4.4)**	(4.2)**	(3.5)**	(3.8)**	(4.3)**	(4.1)**	(3.2)**	(3.5)**	(3.5)**	(3.5)**
MESSIZE	0.367	0.329	0.136	0.163	0.389	0.313	0.136	0.185	0.103	0.117
	(2.0)*	(1.8)	(0.8)	(1.1)	(2.2)*	(1.8)	(0.8)	(1.2)	(0.6)	(0.7)
ADV	0.217	0.218	0.138	0.155	0.179	0.194	0.123	0.146	0.463	0.445
	(1.5)	(1.5)	(0.9)	(1.0)	(1.1)	(1.2)	(0.7)	(0.9)	(3.1)**	(3.0)**
EXTRA	-0.097	-0.115			-0.116	-0.126				
	(-2.3)*	(-2.9)**			(-3.0)**	(-3.3)**				
INTRA			-0.203	-0.180			-0.221	-0.189		
			(3.1)**	(-3.9)**			(-3.4)**	(-3.9)**		
TMEXTRA									-0.009	
									(-.23)	
TMINTRA										-0.032
										(-0.73)
M	-0.048	-0.061	-0.054	-0.049	-0.069	-0.082	-0.073	-0.065	-0.095	-0.095
	(-1.7)	(-2.3)**	(-1.9)*	(-1.8)	(-2.2)*	(-2.7)**	(-2.3)**	(-2.2)*	(-2.8)**	(-2.7)**
HEU	-0.301		0.148		-0.280		0.208			
	(-1.4)		(0.5)		(-1.3)		(0.7)			
C4FR					0.067	0.060	0.066	0.069	0.065	0.066
					(2.7)**	(2.5)**	(2.6)**	(2.8)**	(2.5)**	(2.6)**
C5UK	0.066	0.05	0.075	0.080						
	(1.8)	(1.4)	(2.2)*	(2.5)**						
NTB	1.62	1.40	1.18	1.29	1.79	1.59	1.34	1.51	2.11	2.13
	(2.3)**	(2.1)*	(0.5)	(1.9)*	(2.5)**	(2.3)**	(1.8)	(2.2)*	(2.9)**	(2.9)**
n	310	310	308	308	298	298	296	296	253	253
F	14.5	15.8	15.0	16.7	13.9	15.2	14.2	15.7	12	12.1
adj R2	0.30	0.30	0.31	0.31	0.30	0.30	0.31	0.31	0.28	0.28

Source: DRI.

The coefficient of the economies of scale variable (MESSIZE) is also positive but not always significant. The importance of the advertising to sales ratio leads to significantly increased price dispersion across EU countries only when the import penetration variables are not included in the specification.[36]

Among the variables describing the extent of competition, there are two which tend to decrease significantly the price disparity across the EU. These are the rate of import penetration, either from other EU countries (INTRA) or from countries outside the EU (EXTRA), as well as the extent of multinationalization (M). On the other hand, the degree of national concentration, measured by either C4FR or C5UK, exerts a significant positive impact on price disparity (implying that high degrees of national concentration are associated with high price disparities across the EU).

In a second step, the sample has been split into two groups of markets. The first one includes the markets where NTBs have been estimated to be low (NTB=0), whilst the second group covers the markets where NTBs have been estimated to be moderate or high (NTB>0).

F tests of homogeneity of the coefficients between the two sub-samples show that these coefficients are significantly different between the two sub-samples.[37] The results of the estimations in this case are presented in Table 8.3.2.

The main differences between the two types of sectors are the following: in markets in which NTBs are low, disparity in preferences and the share of vertically differentiated intra-industry trade in the EU exert a positive impact on price dispersion, whilst disparity in fiscal policies has a very low impact and national concentration no significant impact at all. On the other hand, in markets characterized by moderate or high NTBs, disparity in fiscal policies and national concentration both exert a significant positive impact on price disparity, whilst the coefficient of the disparity in preferences variable is not significant.

This confirms that when NTBs are ineffective, national structures and regulations lose their effectiveness. Objective factors such as disparity in preferences or vertical differentiation are then the driving factors explaining the observed price disparity.

A third step has been to split the sample between homogeneous and horizontally differentiated goods and goods differentiated on the basis of intensity of R&D and advertising expenditures (as a proxy for vertically differentiated goods) (Table 8.3.3).

F tests of homogeneity of the coefficients between the two sub-samples show that the coefficients are significantly different between the two sub-samples.[38]

In this case, disparities in fiscal policy and in preferences exert the same positive effect on price dispersion in the two sub-samples. ASHCDV, on the other hand, exerts a positive and significant impact only in markets that are not intensive in research or advertising. Markets

---

[36] Or when TMINTRA or TMEXTRA are used as indicators of import penetration ratios.

[37] These tests take values between 3.03 and 3.97, depending on the variables introduced in the specification, values which are largely above the significance level at 1%.

[38] These tests take values between 1.85 and 2.55, depending on the variables introduced in the specification, values which are above the significance level at 1% for the specifications including C5UK, and above the 5% significance level for the specifications including C4FR.

which show a discrepancy between the observed and the estimated dispersion of prices greater than .10 in two years or more are the following : fresh and frozen fish, other seafood, books.

Table 8.3.2. Regression analysis of price disparity across the EU-9

	NTB=0				NTB>0			
	(1)	(2)	(3)	(4)	(5)	(6)	(7)	(8)
constant	1.7	4.5	3.3	7.0	3.0	10.2	-0.01	2.9
	(0.5)	(1.0)	(1.0)	(1.8)	(0.7)	(1.9)*	(-0.02)	(0.5)
CVAT	0.039	0.035	0.046	0.042	0.134	0.120	0.189	0.183
	(1.8)*	(1.6)	(2.0)*	(1.8)*	(4.4)**	(3.9)**	(5.9)**	(5.6)**
CWEIGHT	0.154	0.159	0.142	0.147	0.018	0.036	0.004	0.007
	(6.9)**	(7.1)**	(6.4)**	(6.5)**	(0.5)	(1.0)	(0.1)	(0.2)
ASHDV	0.151	0.128	0.140	0.109	0.087	0.059	0.152	0.133
	(3.6)**	(2.8)**	(3.3)**	(2.5)**	(1.5)	(0.8)	(2.4)**	(1.9)*
MESSIZE	0.332	0.107	0.473	0.201	-0.275	0.168	-0.237	-0.358
	(1.4)	(0.6)	(2.3)*	(1.1)	(-0.5)	(0.3)	(-0.5))	(-0.6)
ADV	0.036	0.006	-0.015	-0.046	0.517	-0.017	0.983	0.817
	(0.2)	(0.1)	(-0.1)	(-0.2)	(1.2)	(-0.1)	(2.4)**	(1.8)
EXTRA	-0.101		-0.140		0.021		-0.015	
	(-1.3)		(-1.9)*		(0.3)		(-0.3)	
INTRA		-0.161		-0.203		-0.179		-0.096
		(-1.6)		(-2.0)*		(-1.7)		(-0.9)
M	-0.049	-0.050	-0.045	-0.036	-0.007	-0.036	-0.071	-0.077
	(-1.1)	(-1.1)	(-0.9)	(-0.8)	(-0.1)	(-0.8)	(-1.7)	(-1.7)
HEU	0.487	0.775	0.586	0.909	-0.794	-0.436	-0.511	-0.205
	(1.3)	(1.7)	(1.5)	(1.9)*	(-2.1)*	(-0.9)	(-1.6)	(-0.5)
C4FR			0.033	0.033			0.148	0.143
			(1.0)	(1.0)			(4.1)**	(3.7)**
C5UK	0.070	0.070			0.194	0.152		
	(1.4)	(1.6)			(2.7)**	(2.5)**		
n	184	184	176	176	126	124	122	120
F	8.6	8.8	7.6	7.7	12.3	12.7	13.4	13.7
adj R2	0.27	0.28	0.25	0.26	0.45	0.46	0.48	0.49

Source: DRI.

Table 8.3.3. Regression analysis of price disparity across the EU-9

	Non-intensive in R&D or adv				Intensive in adv and/or R&D			
	(1)	(2)	(3)	(4)	(5)	(6)	(7)	(8)
constant	-11.9	-10.4	-5.7	-8.7	1.58	8.36	5.0	11.7
	(-1.4)	(-1.5)	(-1.1)	(-1.4)	(0.3)	(1.5)	(1.3)	(2.7)**
CVAT	0.075	0.081	0.089	0.107	0.057	0.061	0.075	0.079
	(2.5)**	(2.2)*	(2.4)**	(2.5)**	(2.9)**	(3.1)**	(3.4)**	(3.6)**
CWEIGHT	0.060	0.064	0.069	0.063	0.133	0.138	0.126	0.132
	(2.0)*	(1.9)*	(2.1)*	(1.8)	(5.5)**	(5.7)**	(5.1)**	(5.3)**
ASHDV	0.409	0.400	0.336	0.369	0.031	0.004	0.036	0.001
	(3.8)**	(4.0)**	(3.9)**	(3.8)**	(0.7)	(0.1)	(0.8)	(0.1)
MESSIZE	1.269	1.336	1.309	1.464	0.558	0.273	0.710	0.237
	(1.9)*	(1.9)*	(1.9)	(2.0)*	(2.0)*	(1.1)	(2.4)**	(0.8)
ADV	-0.951	-0.892	-0.490	-0.650	0.271	0.125	0.165	0.027
	(-0.95)	(-0.92)	(-0.49)	(-0.65)	(1.58)	(0.69)	(0.94)	(0.14)
EXTRA	0.039		-0.0020		-0.082		-0.145	
	(0.37)		(-0.02)		(-1.36)		(-3.20)**	
INTRA		0.044		0.099		-0.258		-0.336
		(0.31)		(0.69)		(-2.5)**		(-3.9)**
M	0.196	0.148	0.062	0.038	-3.780	-0.055	-0.062	-0.073
	(1.2)	(1.0)	(0.5)	(0.3)	(-0.8)	(-1.2)	(-1.4)	(-1.7)
HEU	-7.600	-7.140	-6.650	-8.180	-0.325	0.426	-0.192	0.703
	(-1.3)	(-1.3)	(-1.0)	(-1.2)	(-1.3)	(1.0)	(-0.8)	(1.9)*
C4FR			0.056	0.073			0.059	0.036
			(0.5)	(0.6)			(1.9)*	(1.2)
C5UK	0.159	0.110			0.103	0.075		
	(0.9)	(0.7)			(1.7)	(1.4)		
NTB	1.500	1.110	0.870	-0.436	2.010	1.180	1.890	0.950
	(0.6)	(0.4)	(0.3)	(-0.1)	(2.4)**	(1.3)	(2.2)*	(1.0)
n	108	108	104	104	202	200	194	192
F	5.9	5.9	5.2	5.3	11.8	12.4	10.7	11.5
adj R2	0.31	0.31	0.29	0.29	0.35	0.36	0.34	0.35

Source: DRI.

Differentiating further among the markets of differentiated products by considering separately the markets which are both research and advertising intensive,[39] confirms the differences between these two types of markets (Table 8.3.4).

[39] The F tests on the splitting in three groups take values between 3.1 and 3.9, above the significance level at 1%.

Table 8.3.4. Regression analysis of price disparity across the EU-9

	intensive in R&D or in adv				intensive in adv and R&D			
	(1)	(2)	(3)	(4)	(5)	(6)	(7)	(8)
constant	-3.8	-3.8	13.7	16.8	18.2	35.9	18.2	8.1
	(-0.4)	(-0.4)	(2.3)*	(2.6)**	(0.6)	(1.1)	(2.7)**	(1.3)
CVAT	-0.019	-0.016	0.030	0.052	0.202	0.219	0.217	0.235
	(-0.4)	(-0.3)	(0.6)	(1.2)	(8.4)**	(9.0)**	(10.8)**	(11.3)*
CWEIGHT	0.176	0.175	0.162	0.158	0.032	0.032	0.058	0.054
	(5.8)**	(5.8)**	(5.0)**	(5.0)**	(1.0)	(1.1)	(1.8)	(1.7)
ASHDV	0.046	0.040	-0.068	-0.117	0.010	-0.023	0.076	0.036
	(0.5)	(0.4)	(-0.9)	(-1.5)	(0.2)	(-0.5)	(1.6)	(0.6)
MESSIZE	0.357	0.179	1.222	0.448	-2.340	-5.68	-2.23	-3.200
	(0.8)	(0.6)	(2.7)**	(1.1)	(-1.3)	(-2.5)**	(-2.8)**	(-2.9)**
ADV	0.600	0.582	0.188	0.076	0.038	0.979	0.233	0.316
	(2.0)*	(1.9)*	(0.7)	(0.3)	(0.5)	(1.2)	(0.9)	(1.1)
EXTRA	-0.0680		-0.258		0.153		0.125	
	(-0.6)		(-2.7)**		(2.3)*		(1.9)*	
INTRA		-0.071		-0.369		0.057		0.090
		(-0.4)		(-2.9)**		(0.6)		(1.0)
M	0.002	0.016	-0.168	-0.147	-0.1510	-0.239	-0.242	-0.076
	(0.1)	(0.1)	(-1.5)	(-1.3)	(-0.5)	(-0.8)	(-4.5)**	(-1.0)
HEU	0.239	5.170	-0.559	1.990	0.186	3.460	0.075	1.168
	(0.3)	(0.5)	(0.6)	(2.2)*	(0.1)	(1.8)	(.21)	(1.3)
C4FR			0.007	0.032			0.083	0.059
			(0.1)	(0.7)			(2.3)*	(1.5)
C5UK	0.228	0.235			0.098	-0.290		
	(2.6)**	(2.5)**			(0.3)	(-0.8)		
NTB	-0.420	-0.680	-0.090	-1.100	0.950	4.050	0.706	3.680
	(-0.3)	(-0.5)	(-0.1)	(-0.8)	(0.4)	(1.6)	(0.4)	(1.5)
n	128	128	120	120	74	72	74	72
F	8.1	8.0	6.2	6.4	18.1	20.5	20.2	21.2
adj R2	0.36	0.35	0.31	0.31	0.70	0.73	0.72	0.74

Source: DRI.

In markets which are both research and advertising intensive, more than 70% of the variance of the dependent variable is explained by the explanatory variables. However, severe multicollinearity problems[40] affect the standard errors of the estimates and hence the significance level of several coefficients.

Disparity of fiscal policies and the rate of imports coming from extra-EU countries exert a significant positive impact on the price dispersion whilst economies of scale have a negative impact. On the other hand, disparity of preferences has no significant impact. The positive impact of imports coming from outside the EU suggests that, in these types of markets, imports being essentially of an intra-firm type, they do not increase the competitive pressure. The negative impact of economies of scale might reflect the incentive to adopt pan-European marketing strategies in order better to exploit these economies of scale.[41]

In markets which are either research or advertising intensive, disparity of fiscal policies is not significant but disparity of preferences exerts a positive and significant impact, in line with the suggestion that some of these markets are horizontally differentiated markets. The coefficients of the import penetration variables, when significant, are negative. Among these markets, the following show a discrepancy between the observed and the estimated dispersion of prices greater than .10 in two years or more: preserved milk, cocoa, condiments and sauces, mineral waters, alcoholic beverages, orthopaedic and therapeutic appliances and products.

In conclusion, the results of the regressions suggest that:

(a) objective factors, such as structural factors hindering the arbitraging process or leading to a competitive process based more on quality than on price, explain a significant part of the variation in price disparity in the EU-9 across product categories. Concentration in national markets favours price disparity whilst internationalization of the markets either through import penetration or through the presence of multinational firms tends to decrease price disparity. Finally, the existence of high or moderate NTBs leads to a higher dispersion of prices across countries;

(b) the effects of the single market have either not been strong enough or have been too concentrated over a short period (or have not been realized yet) to translate into a significant shift in the estimated parameters over the period considered;

(c) the theoretical distinction between markets characterized by endogenous sunk costs and the other types of markets is validated by the data;

(d) markets characterized by moderate or high NTBs behave differently than markets where these NTBs are considered to be low. National concentration significantly increases price dispersion only in the former.

The completion of the single market, following the elimination of NTBs between EU countries, will hence lead to a higher degree of price convergence between countries as far as it promotes the competitive pressure by imports and decreases the disparity in consumers' preferences between countries.

There are a number of remaining potentially important explanatory factors which could not be included in the estimation. With the exception of transport costs, the factors which could not

40 The correlation between INTRA and MESSIZE, INTRA and HEU and HEU and MESSIZE is higher than .90.

41 See the white goods case study (Chapter 10).

be included are mainly behavioural and policy factors. Among the factors mentioned in the theoretical approach developed in Chapter 6 and in the case studies, the following could play a significant role in explaining observed price disparities: asymmetries between firms, mergers and acquisitions, nature and evolution of the distribution structure and disparity in policy regulations. Some of these have been examined in more detail through the case studies presented in Chapters 10 to 13.

Asymmetries between firms based on historical events (such as in the European cola beverages market) or on strategic behaviour (such as in the ready-to-eat cereals market) may prevent arbitraging from taking place. Strategic reactions, driven by the anticipation of the completion of the single market and leading to the consolidation of market structures through mergers and acquisitions and the dominance by a few big players, could also decrease the ability of buyers to engage in arbitraging. Changes in the structure of distribution (mainly through the creation of buying networks at the EU level) could, on the other hand, increase the power of retailers and allow them profitably to engage in arbitraging.

The case studies suggest that there are remaining policy factors which segment the markets, either because of differences in regulations (e.g. the product definition in the mineral waters market varies between countries) or because of different degrees of stringency in their application (e.g. environmental regulation). Further harmonization of EU regulations and a stricter monitoring of implementation could help reduce such segmentation and favour the pan-Europeanization of markets.

9. Selection criteria for the case studies

The last part of the study analyses the factors underlying price convergence in the EU in more detail in four market segments: soft drinks and mineral waters, white goods, construction and chocolate confectionery. As indicated below, the choice of the case studies was done in such way that they would both cover sufficiently different but representative markets, and provide useful indications of the types of factors, whether structural, behavioural or policy factors, which influenced price developments in the EU after the launch of the SMP.

9.1. Soft drinks and mineral water

Soft drinks and mineral water are two products for which rapid price convergence has been observed at the EU-12 level between 1980 and 1986. The trend in prices for these two product categories has not been identical, however, and the price disparities for mineral water remain high, with a coefficient of variation of 26.3 in 1993, compared with a figure of 18.9 for other soft drinks.

With reference to the theoretical framework presented in Chapter 6, both products are differentiated products. In the case of mineral water, one could speak, at least at the start of the period, of horizontally differentiated products. However, with the enlargement of the market, a shift seems to have taken place in some countries towards vertically differentiated products along with a dualization of the market. In small national markets, dualization strategies were not viable before the launch of the SMP, but have become so as markets have become more integrated and as exports have developed.

In the case of 'other soft drinks', in contrast, the market has always been characterized by vertically differentiated products. The objectives of the case study on soft drinks and mineral waters which is presented in Chapter 10 are to explain the different price dispersion patterns observed for soft drinks and for mineral waters, and to try to identify the specific contribution of the SMP to the change in the structural nature of the market, as well as the implications for price convergence patterns and the degree of competition. The case study also identifies the remaining barriers to the creation of a single market in this sector, distinguishing structural, behavioural and policy barriers to integration.

9.2. White goods

The white goods market was and still is a vertically differentiated market. The question, however, is whether increased European integration has led to the creation of a dual market, and whether it is structural, behavioural or policy changes which explain the observed convergence of prices at the EU level, both for equipment and for (after-sales) services. In theory, in vertically differentiated markets in which market size is not sufficient to justify a dualization of markets, when market size increases and dualization occurs, there is a tendency for prices to diverge. This not being the case in the white goods market in general, further analysis of the changes both in the organization of that sector and in the organization of distribution seems appropriate to assess the relative impact of the structural, behavioural and policy factors in explaining the changes. The results of this analysis are presented in Chapter 11.

9.3. Construction

The choice of the construction and contracting sector was dictated more by the analysis of the trends in the coefficients of variation of prices done in Chapters 3 and 4 than by the theoretical framework of Chapter 6. The main reasons influencing the choice were that:

(a) this is a service market, thereby influenced by (and responding to) different forces than the manufactured products covered by the other case studies;
(b) the observed increased divergence in construction prices across the EU after 1986 was counter-intuitive, given that this is a sector in which a number of measures (such as the liberalization of public procurement markets or the free movement of persons) were taken as part of the SMP to remove intra-EU barriers;
(c) the validity of the underlying data is questionable, given the difficulties in measuring the price of 'identical' projects across countries.

The construction case study presented in Chapter 12 addresses the above issues, and provides a number of explanations for the observed trends.

9.4. Chocolate confectionery

The confectionery market is a market characterized by horizontally differentiated products with high sunk costs. Based on the theoretical framework outlined in Chapter 6, different price convergence patterns following market enlargement will be observed whether companies respond to the increase in market size by increasing the number of products on the market or not. If, as seems to be the case with chocolate confectionery, an increase in market size results in an increase in the number of products offered by the different producers (and in the advertising to sales ratio of the leading producers), this tends to raise barriers to entry. In this case, where price convergence is observed, this could indicate a reduction in the degree of competition as opposed to a rise in competition with prices tending towards a lower level.

The chocolate confectionery market is, on the other hand, one in which the SMP has given rise to intensive ownership restructuring, with the larger producers expanding their presence in all EU Member States through acquisition, and non-EU producers seeking to strengthen their presence in the EU. These can be considered as 'pan-European' strategies of companies. To expand their market share in new markets, companies adopted aggressive marketing strategies which directly influenced demand. In this market segment, thus, both demand and the organization of supply are likely to have been affected by the SMP.

The objectives of the case study for chocolate confectionery are firstly to assess the extent to which the structural changes in supply and in demand that have been observed can be attributed to the SMP, and secondly to analyse whether or not the observed changes in price disparities after 1986 reflect an increase in the degree of competition with convergence to lower price levels. This market is, indeed, one in which the theoretical framework in Chapter 6 provides no clear-cut answer.

10. The soft drinks and mineral water sector

10.1. Single market indicators

As outlined in Chapter 4, the beverages category is one in which price dispersion has been quite high in the past. The data show that the coefficient of price variation for mineral water remains high in 1993, but there has been a significant reduction in disparities between 1980 and 1993 compared to the situation in the early 1980s. Other soft drinks tended to have below average coefficients of variation which also diminished over time (see Figure 10.1.1).

Figure 10.1.1. Coefficient of variation of mineral water and soft drinks, EU-9, price excluding taxes

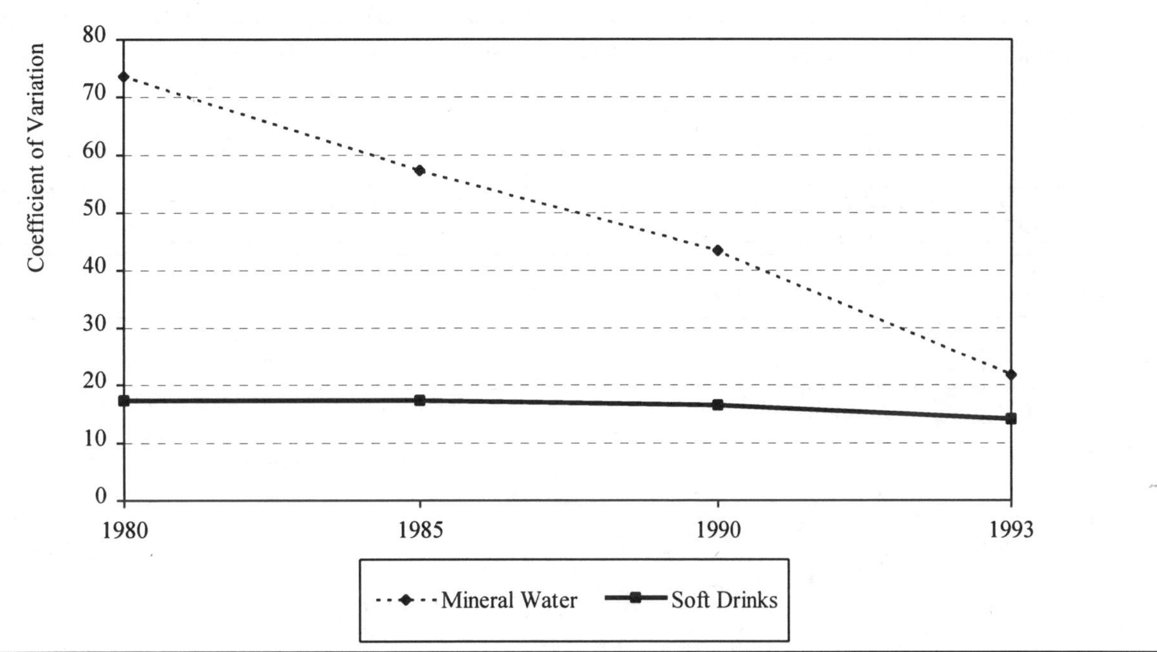

Source: DRI.

In the major EU markets, sales of both mineral water and soft drinks have been growing rapidly in the last three to five years. In fact, volume of mineral water and soft drink sales has grown faster than constant value of sales which suggests that real prices (i.e. excluding inflation) have been falling. In Figures 10.1.2 to 10.1.6 we have calculated the implied price index per litre of sales in France, Italy, Germany, Spain and the UK between 1984 and 1993 in current and constant prices for both mineral water and soft drinks. In every case, the constant unit price has declined.

These data show that on average the real prices of the products in question are falling, not rising, and that therefore the price convergence we noted above is not, on average, to a higher level. Two of the main reasons for this are: (a) the general trend to the use of larger pack sizes which are usually cheaper unit for unit; and (b) the growth of low price retailer own-brands. In the next section of this report we shall comment on additional factors which may contribute to this trend.

Figure 10.1.2. Price of soft drinks and mineral water – France

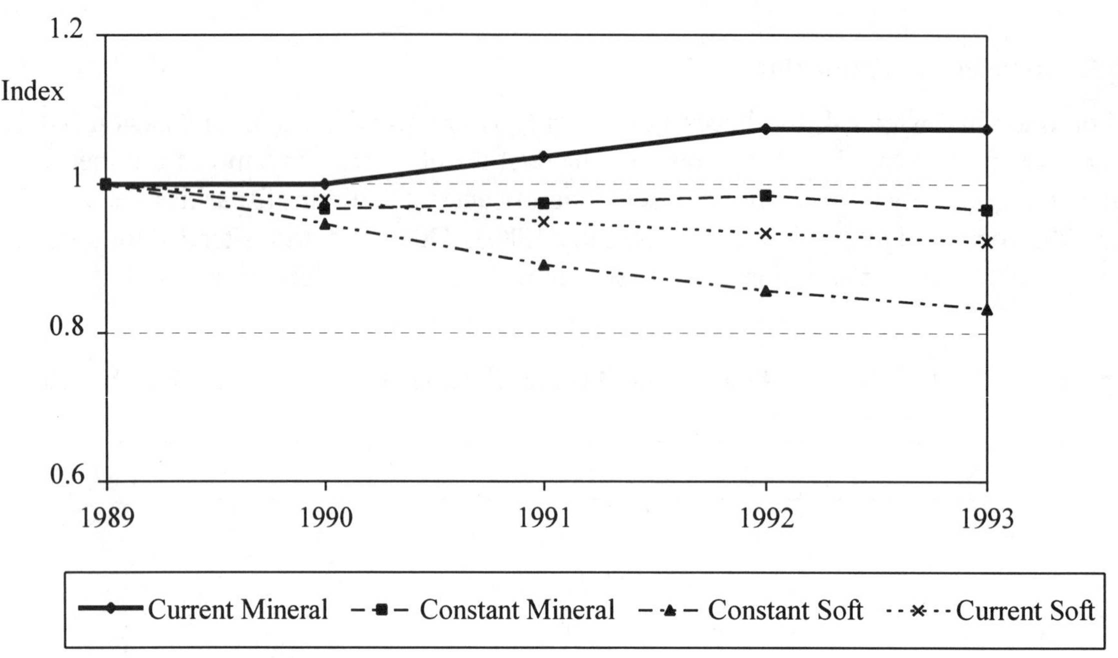

Source: Euromonitor.

Figure 10.1.3. Price of soft drinks and mineral water – Italy

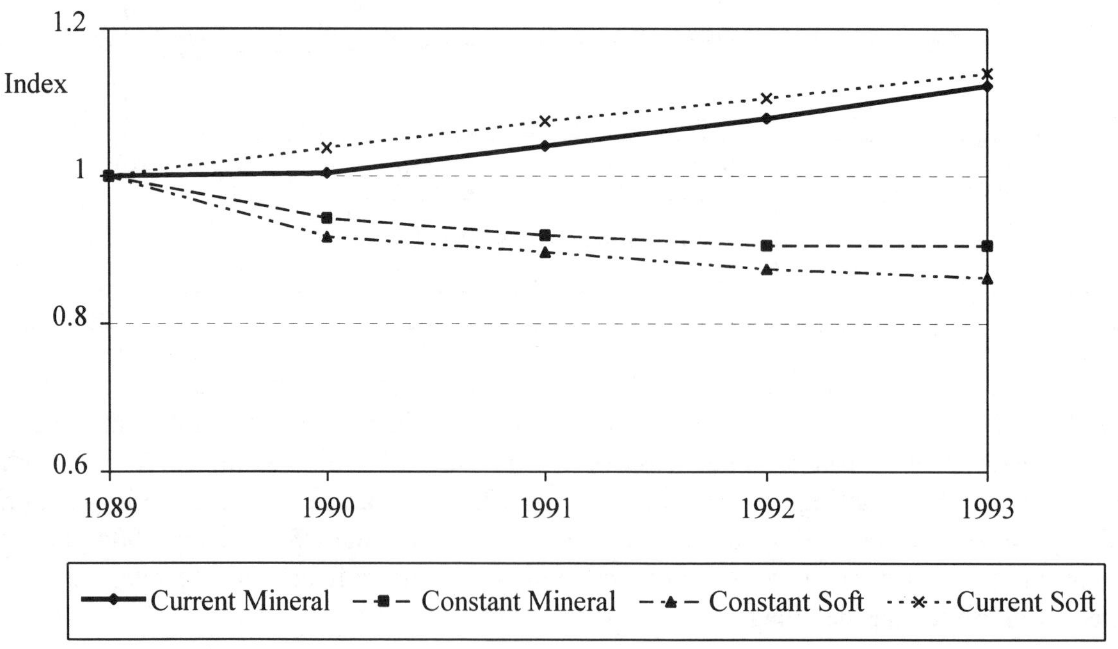

Source: Euromonitor.

The markets for soft drinks and for mineral waters are highly competitive in all EU countries, and price cutting is widespread. In fact, price cutting is less prevalent in Germany where discount grocery chains do not have facilities for handling returns and therefore are less significant in the market.

Figure 10.1.4. Price of soft drinks and mineral water – Germany

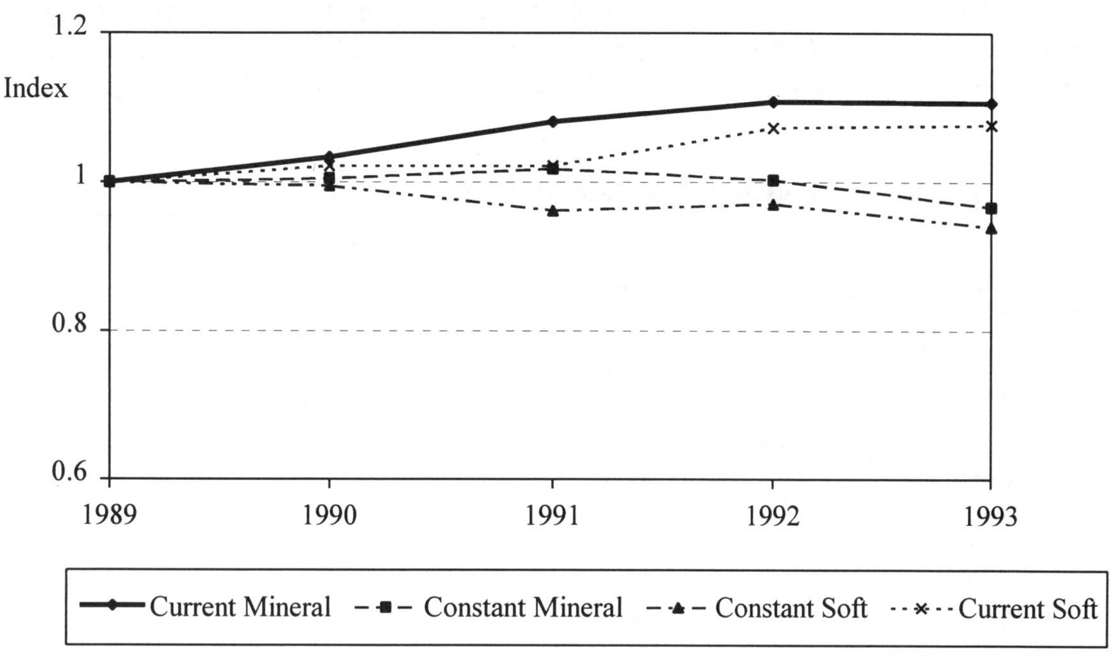

Source: Euromonitor.

Figure 10.1.5. Price of soft drinks and mineral water – Spain

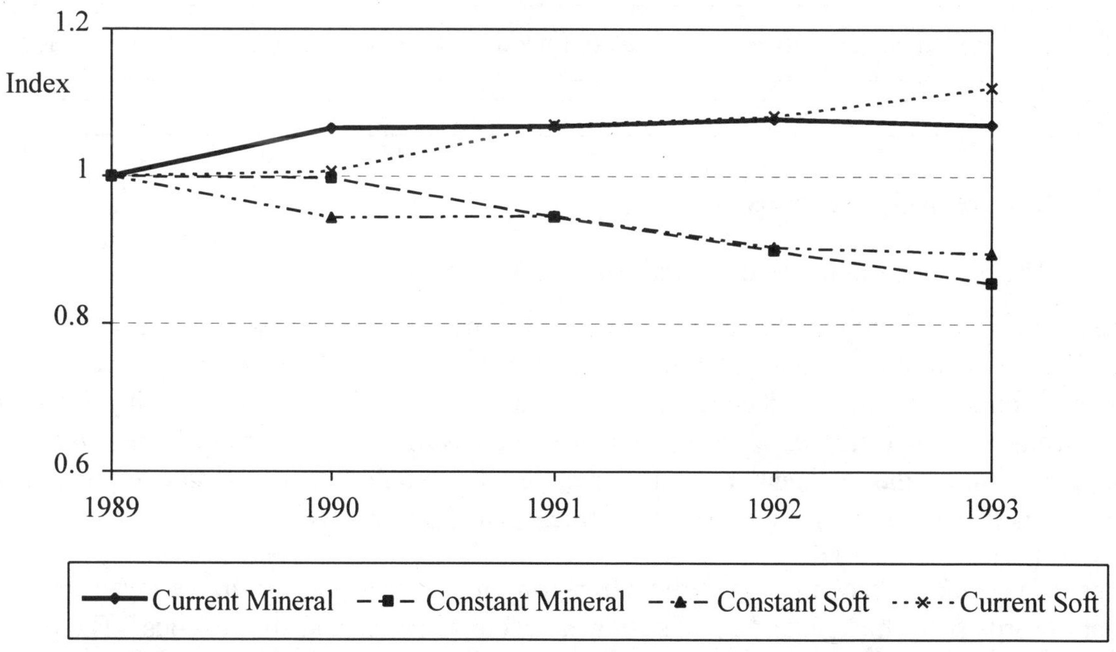

Source: Euromonitor.

This may in part account for the less pronounced decline in real unit prices in Germany than elsewhere in the EU.[42] However, retail prices (and hence retail margins) vary widely according to the product, the type of outlet, the package size, and the packaging itself.[43]

42 Source: Interviews and Horack, Adler & Associates analysis.
43 The Economist Intelligence Unit.

As it happens, the variation in price between outlets, unit size and packaging inside a country is at least as great as any variation between countries. According to the Economist Intelligence Unit, in a recent price check in Madrid, a 33cl can of 'Sprite' varied from PTA 2 in a hypermarket to PTA 75.5 in a smaller self-service retailer, while in France, the price per litre of 'Orangina Light' was FF 6.60 in a 1½ litre plastic bottle and FF 9.84 in a 33cl can.

Figure 10.1.6. Price of soft drinks and mineral water – UK

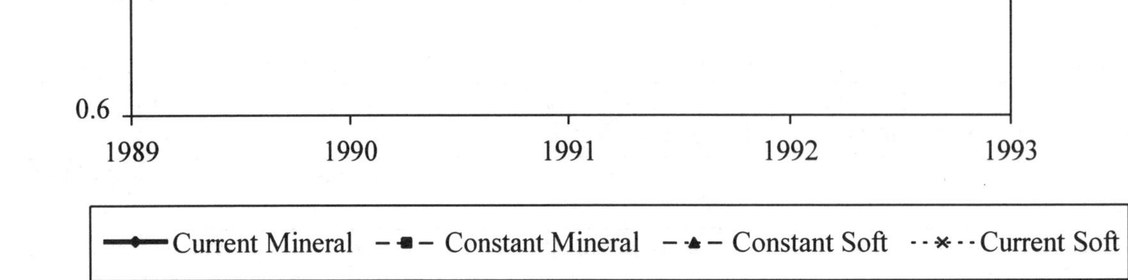

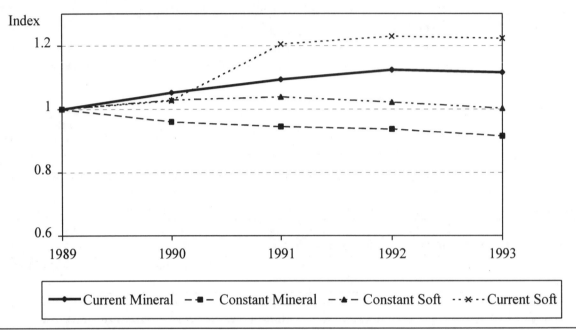

Source: Euromonitor.

10.2. Main trends in the industry

10.2.1. The European food and drink industries: the context

The population of Europe is forecast to grow only slowly – about 1.5% in the next five years. The largest increases are anticipated in the older age groups. The trend in most countries is for expenditure on food to decline as a proportion of total household spending. Equally significant, the proportion of working women is increasing. This results in larger disposable incomes among the affluent but also smaller households, and greater emphasis on convenience and technology, e.g. the use of freezers and microwaves.[44]

Consumers are also becoming more nutrition-conscious, resulting in a move away from red meat towards fish, chicken, and cereals, as well as convenience and snack foods. The growth in more convenient, ready-prepared meals is associated with increasing numbers of working women and single person households.[45] Consumers are also turning more and more to fresh products, such as fruits and vegetables, and so there are resulting shifts in preference towards higher quality and higher variety.

[44] Bates Dorland Advertising.

[45] Frost & Sullivan.

These shifts in demography and socio-economics are having a major impact on the food and beverage companies who believe that failure to respond accordingly will leave them behind in the race for market share. As a consequence, the strategy for new products and brands is changing fast. There is growing emphasis on appearance of freshness in packaged goods. The amount of processing may actually decline in some cases as the use of chiller cabinets, glass packaging and generally superior quality are stressed. New processes, such as biotechnological development of superior strains and use of techniques like irradiation, may contribute to this trend. Consumers are looking towards 'authenticity' in food quality or regional/ethnic appearance, while sensory gratification in terms of taste, texture or aroma are put to the fore.[46]

Figure 10.2.1. Growth in European food and drink markets 1989–93

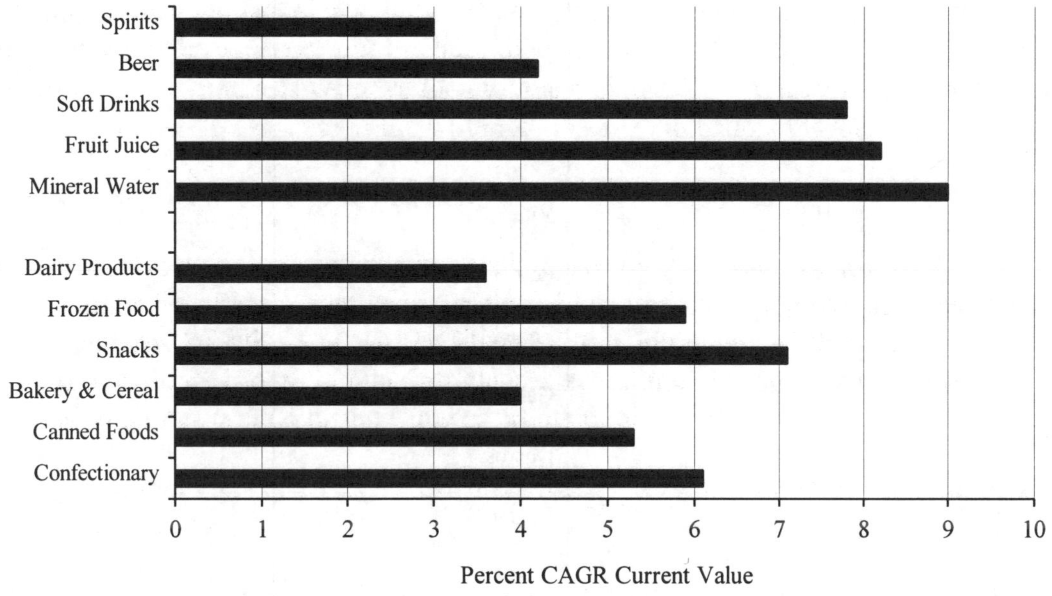

Source: Various.

The most important feature of the food and drink market is that its overall maturity conceals immense variations in growth rates for different segments. The major players' main objective is to 'ride' these patterns of growth and decline and above all to try to 'lead' the market by defining and shaping how different categories develop.[47]

The mineral water and soft drinks market has been one of the high growth sectors in the food and drink industry in Europe (see Figure 10.2.1). As such, this sector has attracted tremendous attention from the major industry players, as well as prompting a significant number of new entrants. Although growth rates have varied from country to country and from product to product, the overall picture is one of dynamism and significant changes in market structure.

---

[46] Nestlé.

[47] BSB Dorland.

10.2.2. Impact of the single market

The report on 'The Cost of Non-Europe'[48] highlighted over 200 types of NTBs in the European food market[49] and suggested that the benefit of removing trade barriers represented 1–2% of total food sales.

Table 10.2.1. Major food and drinks acquisitions, 1990–93

Bidder	Country	Target	Country
Cadbury Schweppes	UK	Bouquet d'Or	F
Cadbury Schweppes	UK	A & W Brands	USA
Guinness	UK	Moet Hennessy	F
Albert Fisher	UK	Fresh Western	USA
Unilever	UK/NL	Unit of Kraft	USA
Nestlé	CH	Vittel	F
Nestlé	CH	Perrier	F
Philip Morris	USA	Freia Marabou	N
BSN	F	Galbani	I
Ferruzzi	I	Ducros	F
Ferruzzi	I	Beghin Say	F
Besnier	F	Bridel	F
Besnier	F	Jean Jacques	F
Besnier	F	Valmont	F
MD Foods	DK	Ass. Fresh Foods	UK
ABF	UK	British Sugar	UK
Northern Foods	UK	Express Dairy	UK
Booker	UK	Fitch Lovell	UK

Source: Horack, Adler & Associates.

Although the food and drink market remains fragmented, the harmonization effect has generally been seen by the main industry participants as quite significant.[50] The marketing function is cited as being the most important area to be altered by single market changes.

48 European Commission [1988], Vol. 12, Parts A and B.

49 'The cost of non-Europe', European Commission, 1988.

50 Results of a survey by Frost & Sullivan 'European food & drink strategies'.

Companies anticipated benefits from greater pan-European co-ordination of brands, product development, advertising, and standardization of the marketing mix.

At the same time, a major restructuring of the industry via mergers and acquisitions has taken place. Much of this was in anticipation of the single market, and was designed to create multinational brands in confectionery, pet food and beverages. Table 10.2.1 summarizes a number of recent deals.

Despite this frenzy of activity, trade in soft drinks and mineral water remains small in relation to total consumption. Figure 10.2.2 shows that intra-EU trade has grown much faster than EU consumption as a whole, but nevertheless remains at only 6% of the total market. Import penetration remains low on average, with soft drinks having greater 'tradeability' than mineral water (Table 10.2.2). This is because the water market is fragmented by the localized nature of production (from a 'source'), while soft drinks can be manufactured to some extent in larger production lines. Nevertheless, the high cost of transport dictates that local markets are most economically served by local products.

Manufacturer shares of soft drinks versus mineral water show that most national markets are dominated by national manufacturers. Only Coca Cola and Pepsi Cola in soft drinks, and Nestlé Source International and BSN in mineral water, operate on a truly multinational basis. However, in the latter category, the brands tend to remain local, even if the ownership is non-national (Tables 10.2.3a and 10.2.3b).

Figure 10.2.2. Trade and consumption in soft drinks and mineral water

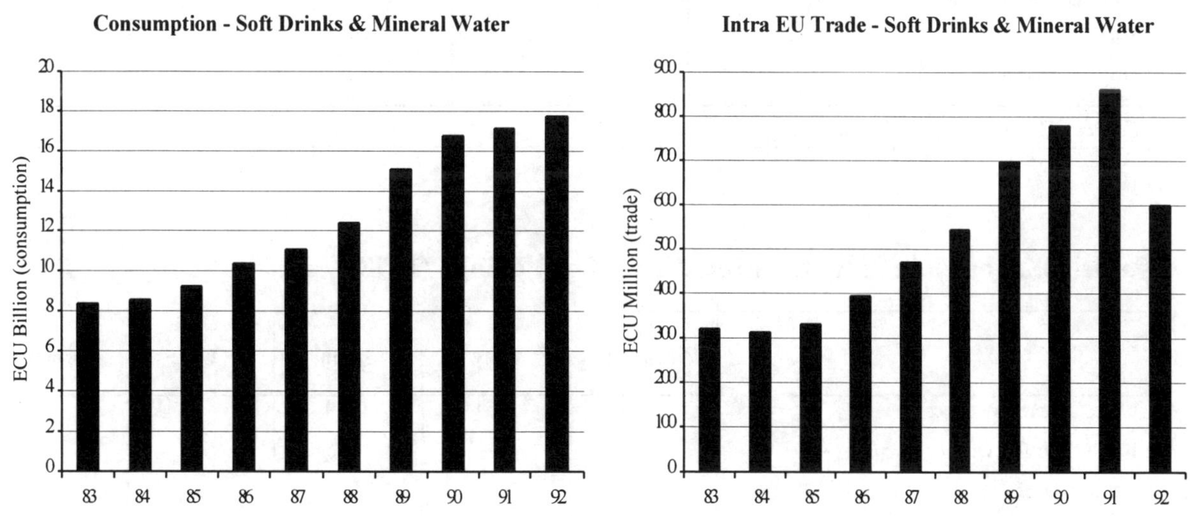

Source: DEBA.

Table 10.2.2. Import penetration (1991/1992)

	Soft drinks (%)	Mineral water (%)
Italy	2.3	0.6
Germany	5.9	2.8
Spain	1.2	0.6
UK	1.1	--
France	--	1.2

Source: Horack, Adler & Associates.

In general, the industry sees the growth of the mineral water market as having been 'driven' by a number of factors which overshadow the impact of the SMP. For example, growth has been equally, if not more, rapid in non-EU markets like the USA and Japan than in the EU.[51]

Table 10.2.3a. Main manufacturer share of mineral water (1993)

	France	Italy	Spain	UK
Nestlé	37	14	--	17
BSN	32	17	19	18
Castel	20	--	--	--
San Pellegrino	--	26	--	--
San Benedetto	--	12	--	--
Vichy Catalan	--	--	9	--
Highland Spring	--	--	--	6

Source: Horack, Adler & Associates.

Table 10.2.3b. Main manufacturer share of soft drinks (1993)

	France	Italy	Spain	UK	Germany
Coca Cola/ Schweppes	53	51	39	38	30
Pepsi Cola/Britvic	4	--	15	20	3
Pernod Ricard	11	--	--	--	--
San Benedetto	--	12	--	--	--
La Cusera	--	--	14	--	--

Source: Horack, Adler & Associates.

[51] Source: Interviews with industry participants.

The impact of the single market on the development of this business is seen in three principal ways:

(a) Psychologically, the run-up to the single market focused the major players on the possibilities of developing Eurobrands. Considerable industry restructuring and jockeying for position took place (e.g. Nestlé's and BSN's acquisition strategies).

(b) Labelling regulations have enabled producers to operate more easily between countries and the harmonization has stimulated cross-border activity. National differences remain, however. For example, as one industry participant put it, 'In France carbonation cannot be added to water which came from the source without it. But in the UK, that is allowed, and the water can still be called "natural mineral water"'.

(c) The use of recyclable and returnable containers has been stimulated by EU regulations, and uniform standards are important. Again, the measures have gone some way to creating the proverbial 'level playing field', but clear national differences with consequences for trade still remain.

The majority of those who were interviewed, however, took the view that these effects were secondary to the broader sweep of market trends which are global and not just European (Table 10.2.4).

Table 10.2.4. Key trends in the soft drink and mineral water market

	Mineral water	Soft drinks
DEMAND	Rapid growth	Less rapid, but buoyant pressure to innovate on 'sports/health' drinks
	Home consumption	
	Consumer trend to 'healthy' lifestyles	
	Growth of niche 'flavoured water' market	
PACKAGING	PET containers and pack variety proliferation	Ditto : search for differentiation through packaging
	Recyclability important	
INDUSTRY	Few 'global' players	Greater consolidation
		Truly global brands (e.g. Coca Cola, Pepsi,...)
RETAILING	Key to rapid growth	Ditto
	Own label products driving prices down but expanding market	

Source: Horack, Adler & Associates.

10.3. Remaining barriers to the establishment of a single market

Below we discuss the remaining barriers to the single market according to whether they may be considered structural, policy or behavioural.[52]

10.3.1. Structural barriers

The most important structural obstacle to a single market for mineral water is the existence of the source. This is a fundamental difference compared to the rest of the soft drinks market, since the location of bottling plants is determined by accidents of nature, not logistics. As a result, there is a 'local' character to mineral water which is fixed by geography.

In contrast, sparkling water or table water (which is not tied to a source) is more like the soft drinks business where manufacturing and bottling can be located anywhere. However, in both cases the scale of production is limited by transportation costs. As a result, there is relatively little cross-border trade compared to total consumption. Major soft drink brands have bottling plants in all national markets, while purely local brands can still compete effectively, since significant economies of scale in production are negated by transport costs.

The second main structural barrier has to do with national consumer preferences and habits of consumption. Figure 10.3.1 shows the per capita consumption of mineral water versus soft drinks in different European countries. It is clear that in some countries (e.g. Italy, France) mineral water is preferred to other soft drinks, while in others (e.g. UK, Norway, Ireland) mineral water consumption is low compared to other beverages. These patterns may converge over time, but consumer preferences remain widely different. This results in very different production and distribution economics for the suppliers.

Figure 10.3.1. Per capita consumption 1991 – soft drinks vs mineral water

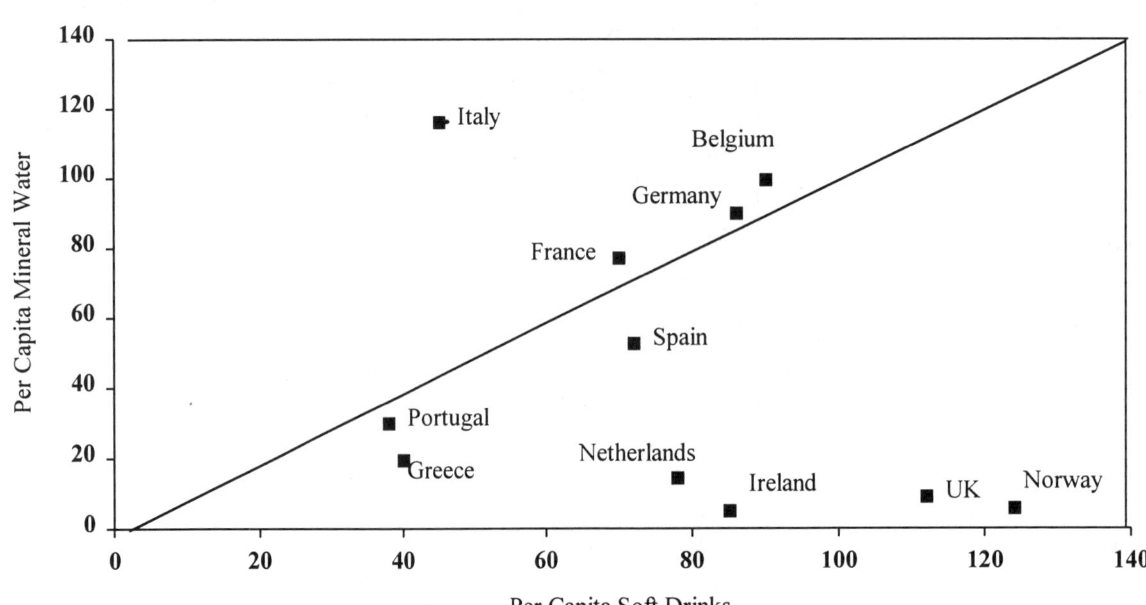

Source: LFRA estimates.

[52] For definitions, see Chapter 6.

In addition, there are differences in consumer preferences within the mineral water category. Still water is preferred in France, while sparkling water dominates in Italy and Germany. As one industry participant said: 'Germans want sparkle in their water...still water is the norm in France and the UK...and you still get very strong regional preferences and patterns. In France, we are very loyal to our own regional waters.'

Finally, there are structural features of the market which actually stimulate its growth and development. Industry experts agree that the most significant of these is a 'cultural' shift in tastes which makes people increasingly ready to buy a substitute for tap water. Despite EU norms on quality, much of the growth in mineral water consumption has been stimulated by dissatisfaction with tap water taste and safety.

10.3.2. Behavioural barriers

In terms of company behaviour, the overwhelming evidence is that the industry participants have geared up to take advantage of the single market whenever possible, and to jump on the bandwagon of rapid growth in the sector.

Two large groups, Nestlé and Danone, have systematically consolidated and absorbed others to create European, indeed global brands. This trend sufficiently alarmed the European Commission recently to enforce a dilution of Nestlé's brand share.[53]

In addition, the growth of the PET container has enabled a proliferation of packaging, especially in large sizes, without falling foul of regulations or provoking customer resistance on the grounds of environmental concerns. Larger bottle sizes mean lower unit costs and exercise downward pressure on prices.

Finally, the role of the distributor has been central. Retailer own brands have stimulated market growth and caused intense price competition. This has fuelled consumption and consumer awareness, while enforcing price discipline on the main manufacturers' brands.

In this context, there has been a variety of competitive responses. Established local players in various national markets have entrenched positions which have often been successfully maintained or developed. Brands have proliferated as a means of differentiation often supported by high advertising budgets and other positioning strategies around premium pricing and packaging.[54]

The key development has been the growth of a two-tier market. At one extreme, there exists a 'commodity no frills' segment typified by own labels which has led prices sharply downwards. In parallel, an 'up market' segment, typified by brands like Perrier and sold in glass, not plastic bottles, has premium prices. The most important differentiators here include bottling and advertising. In the words of one commentator, 'We think the market is going to polarize increasingly between high cost premium brands and lower cost supermarket brands'.

---

[53] European Commission [1994], *Panorama of EU Industry*, Chapter 13.

[54] Interviews, various other sources.

10.3.3. Policy barriers

The most significant barriers to the single market remain those that persist at a policy level. There is still a wide diversity in national regulations which have a major impact on soft drinks in general and on mineral waters in particular.

First, the question of packaging remains unresolved. Directive 85/339/EEC[55] on disposable containers has been applied in different ways by Member States.[53] Thus, obstacles to free movement of products remain within the context of large differences in national practices with regard to returnability, recyclability, deposits on bottles and the like.

Second, and more specifically related to mineral water, there are national differences in product definition and product benefits claimed. Differences persist on what can and cannot be called 'mineral water' and what can and cannot be added or subtracted at source. Consumer confusion persists about the differences between mineral water, spring water and table water. In the UK, for example, spring water is cheaper, because it can be bottled away from source, can contain water from several sources, and can be treated.

There is some concern that proposed new EU standards will actually result in higher prices. As one distributor argued: 'As we see it, these new standards...will bring the price of spring water up as production costs come into line with what are now called natural mineral waters...In order to qualify, spring water will have to have a devoted production line. In other words, you will not be able to mix soft drink production and mineral water production, and this means companies will have to invest in new production facilities.'

These aspects of harmonization are yet to be resolved fully at EU or national levels. They represent the most significant barriers to single market developments.

The analysis in this chapter is summarized in Table 10.3.1.

Table 10.3.1. Main barriers to the single market in mineral waters

Structural	Policy	Behavioural
Economic	Lack of standardization in	Brand proliferation
High transport costs	(a) product definition	Development of two-tier market and product differentiation
Bottling at source	(b) product benefits claimed and labelling	
Culture	(c) recycling vs. returnability in containers	Product development, e.g. 'flavoured waters'
National preferences and drinking habits	(d) product treatment and adulteration	Retailers' own brands may 'crowd out' non-national products
Local brand loyalty		
Perceptions of tap water quality		

Source: Horack, Adler & Associates.

[55] Council Directive 85/339/EEC of 27 June 1985 on containers of liquids for human consumption (OJ L 176, 6.7.1985, p. 18).

11. The white goods sector

11.1. Single market indicators

The study of price disparities in the EU demonstrates that in the white goods market, price disparities were quite low at the start of the period and continued to diminish over time. In the case of repairs and services to electrical appliances, price disparities remain high, but show a pattern of convergence (Figure 11.1.1).

Figure 11.1.1. Coefficient of variation for white goods in the EU-12

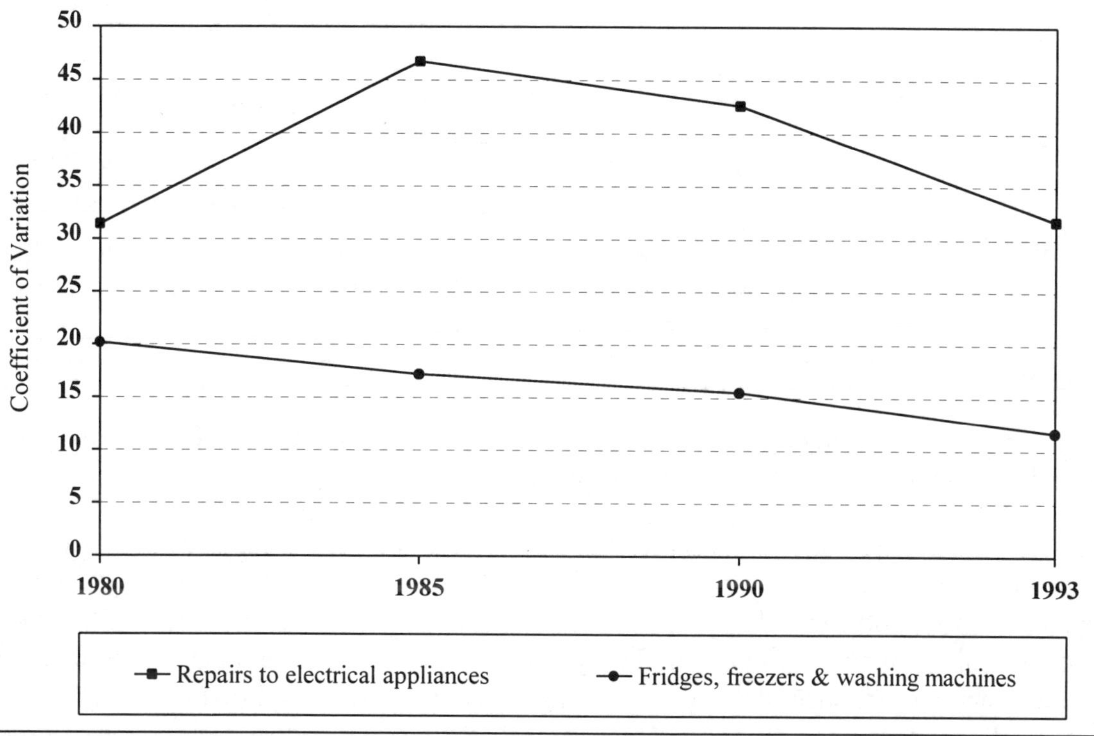

Source: DRI.

The white goods sector is, in fact, one of the most international both inside and outside Europe. There are relatively few large international producers who dominate the market, trade flows are significant and there is multi-location manufacturing by the major players. Brand names are increasingly global, and the biggest suppliers have tended more and more towards business strategies that are geared to the internationalization of the market.[56]

In addition to the price data analysed in Chapter 4, there are a variety of other indicators which demonstrate the extent to which white goods markets in Europe are apparently converging.

First, trade between EU Member States is high and accounts for a growing proportion of consumption. Figure 11.1.2 shows that intra-EU trade accounted for about 35% of apparent consumption in 1992, and over the period 1983–92 intra-EU trade grew by a factor of 2.5, while consumption in the same period grew by only 1.6. Figure 11.1.2 also shows trade flows

[56] Interviews by Horack, Adler & Associates with main suppliers.

with non-EU members. In the same period, extra-EU exports grew by a factor of 2.3, and extra-EU imports by a factor of more than 3.

Figure 11.1.2. Trade patterns in white goods (1983–92)

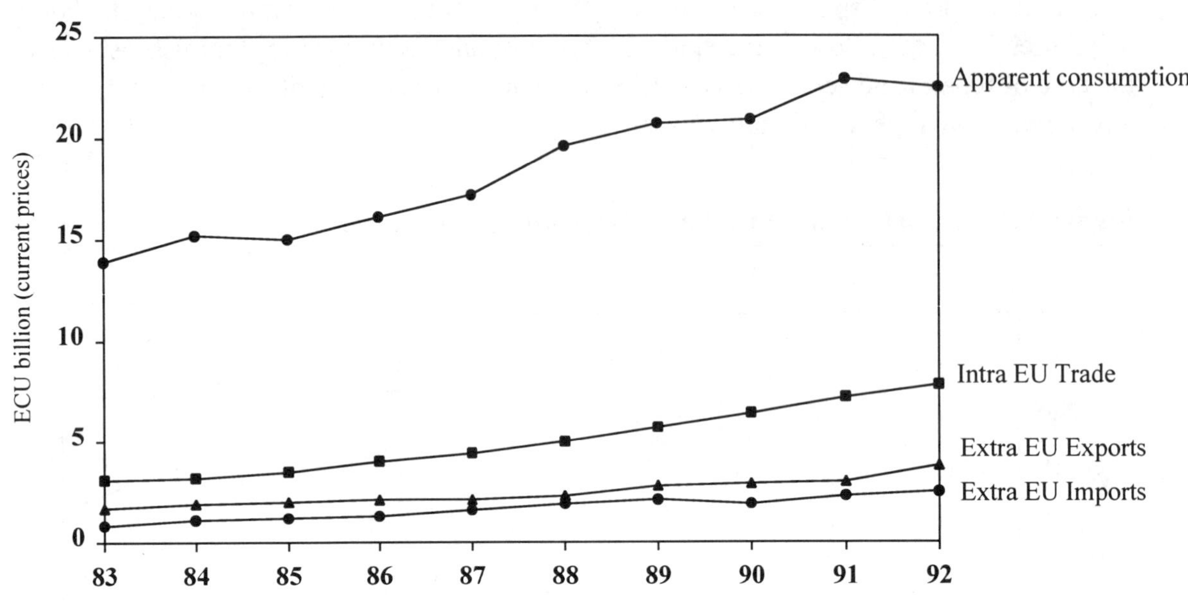

Source: DEBA.

In this latter case, it is important to note that about one third of the extra-EU imports came from the EFTA region, and in particular Sweden, the home base of Electrolux.

If extra-EU imports are taken as an indication of the international competitiveness of the EU white goods industry, then it is worth noting that extra-EU imports have risen from about 6% of apparent consumption in 1983 to about 11% by 1992. Apart from the role of Electrolux, the bulk of this growth is accounted for by the microwave oven market rather than the 'traditional' appliances, such as fridges, washing machines, ovens and dishwashers.[57] Other indicators of the existence of a single market include the trend towards rationalization of production facilities which would not have been possible if significant barriers to trade continued to exist.

Thus, the European white goods industry has undergone considerable consolidation and restructuring during the 1980s, partly in anticipation of the single market and partly in response to the problem of overcapacity and manufacturing attempts to build economies of scale.[58] In 1985, 150 companies supplied three quarters of the market. By 1990, 15 international groups controlled 80% of the market, and by 1995 seven groups had a market share of 86%.[59] Table 11.1.1 summarizes some of the recent M&A activity in the sector.

Perhaps a more significant development, and more revealing of a sort of 'subterranean' single market, emerges from a more detailed analysis of the manufacturing strategies of the main white goods suppliers.

[57] *Source*: Euromonitor.
[58] *Source*: Interviews with industry participants.
[59] *Source*: *Financial Times*, May–June 1995.

Table 11.1.1. Major acquisitions in the white goods sector in Europe

Purchaser	Company acquired	Date
Electrolux	Zanussi	1984
Electrolux	Zanker	1985
Candy	Rosières	1987
Electrolux	Thorn EMI appliances	1987
LEC	Creda	1987
Electrolux	Corbero / Domar	1988
Merloni	Indesit	1988
SEB	Rowenta	1988
Whirlpool	Philips Appliances	1988
Bosch-Siemens	Balay / Safel	1989
Merloni	Scholtes	1989
Maytag	Hoover	1989
Moulinex	Krups	1990
Electrolux	Lehel	1991
Candy	Otsein	1991
Electrolux	AEG White Goods	1993
Candy	Hoover Europe	1995

Source: Horack, Adler & Associates.

Although we cannot precisely 'quantify' the following analysis, our interviews suggest an even more pronounced consolidation of the components industry for white goods, which could in part also explain the convergence in the price of repairs and services to electrical appliances. As one industry participant said: 'Component suppliers are increasingly common to all manufacturers. In some strategic sectors like ceramic hobs, there are only two or three suppliers in all Europe.' (Head of Strategy, major European brand.)

The most commonly sourced components, such as compressors for fridges, motors for washing machines and electronic controls for ovens, are supplied by only a few manufacturers and are in fact common to many of the major brands. This consolidation is more and more driven by three main 'facts of life' for the manufacturer:

(a) economies of scale in production;

(b) just-in-time logistics both at the factory gate and in delivery to the distribution system;

(c) the reorganization of component supply to reflect 'first tier' suppliers of systems and sub-assemblies as opposed to 'second tier' suppliers of individual parts.[60]

In effect, the absence of significant trade barriers inside Europe appears to be reflected by an even more pronounced 'single market effect' in components and sub-assemblies. This permits the larger manufacturers to have final assembly plants located closer to national markets, while the 'hidden' components can be sourced more centrally.

11.2. Remaining barriers to the establishment of a single market

As in other case studies, we discuss below the remaining barriers to the establishment of a single market according to whether they relate to structural, behavioural or policy factors.

11.2.1. Policy barriers

There are few, if any, significant policy barriers to the free movement of white goods in Europe,[61] and two EC Directives[62] on Low Voltage Equipment and Electromagnetic Compatibility have directly affected the free movement of goods. More recently, regulations concerning the environment, especially the phasing out of CFCs in fridges, and measures to economize on energy and water use, are more likely to stimulate product innovation or product replacement than to increase trade flows or the further development of the single market.[63]

A more pressing concern for the industry in this regard is the possible impact of environmental regulations in reducing the free circulation of products because of differential impacts or differential degrees of stringency in their application. Two examples illustrate the point:

First, EU regulations on fridges/freezers require the use of a sticker on the appliance's door indicating the 'EC Guide to Efficiency and Economy' of the product. Some retailers are concerned that consumers do not fully understand the categorization system and also that the programme is not uniformly enforced in different EU Member States.[64] The variation in degree of enforcement represents in effect a new non-tariff barrier.

Second, the need to comply with standards may impact more heavily on smaller, marginal producers, thus potentially adding to the factors leading to industry consolidation and perhaps reducing consumer choice.

On balance, however, it is widely acknowledged that policy barriers are of minor importance to the development of the market.

---

60 Interviews with industry experts and industry participants.

61 CECED.

62 Council Directive 89/336/EEC of 3 May 1989 on the approximation of the laws of Member States relating to electromagnetic compatibility (OJ L 139, 23.5.1989, p. 19) and Council Directive 73/23/EEC of 19 February 1973 on the harmonization of the laws of Member States relating to electrical equipment designed for use within certain voltage limits (OJ L 77, 26.3.1973, p. 29).

63 European Commission [1994], *Panorama of EU industry*, 'Domestic Electronic Appliances'.

64 Interviews with retailers.

11.2.2. Structural barriers

Market maturity variations

Whether or not demand is homogeneous across countries has an important impact on how far integration can be developed. This, in turn, is influenced in part by the maturity of demand, and in particular the fact that demand for variety grows as consumers move from first-time buying to replacement.[65] Although saturation rates in white goods are on average high and demand is increasingly for replacement, this varies a great deal by product and between countries. Table 11.2.1 shows that household penetration rates for the main white goods products vary significantly between countries. This implies not only that markets are at varying phases of maturity, but also that demand for variety is also likely to be significantly different.

Table 11.2.1. Approximate household penetration ratios for domestic appliances (1993–94)

Country	Washing machines	Fridges	Dishwashers	Microwave ovens
W. Germany	93	96	42	46
E. Germany	92	96	3	15
Italy	98	-	25	-
Spain	96	99	18	22
Netherlands	89	97	11	22
France	90	93	34	40

Source: Euromonitor, EW, Horack, Adler & Associates.

Consumer preferences

It is widely accepted in the industry that national markets exhibit wide differences in preference for product features, which militates against standardization of production. For example, top-loading washing machines are more popular in France and the Netherlands than in other countries. Spin speeds tend to be higher in northern Europe, and fridges and freezers tend to be larger.

The French prefer their ovens to have higher maximum cooking temperatures, whereas the Germans like their dishwashers to be built-in rather than free-standing. The British and Spanish are more likely to be price-sensitive, while the French and Italians prefer more features and options. In yet another contrast, the German or Dutch consumer is more environment conscious, and looks for water and energy saving devices. [66]

Distribution

Increased trade has not acted to remove these differences completely, partly because there are few, if any, large pan-European retailers of domestic appliances, and partly because purchasing patterns vary significantly from country to country (Table 11.2.2). As a result,

[65] Stepford, John and Baden Fuller, Charles, 'Globalization Frustrated: The Case of White Goods', *SMJ*, Vol. 12, 1991.
[66] Interviews.

there is little pressure from distributors to enforce standardization or to 'lead' consumer preferences.[67]

Some market analysts detect a growing trend towards homogenization of product features. This is partly because structural differences are gradually eroding. For example, the French preference for top-loading machines is sometimes attributed to the need to economize space in typically smaller French kitchens. Yet this 'historical' explanation is no longer strictly speaking valid. Indeed, front-loading machines are now at about 75% of the European market and growing.[68]

Furthermore, the distribution systems in different countries are converging even if multinational retailers are thin on the ground. Thus the share of hypermarkets in total white goods sales is growing rapidly in most EU Member States, and this has resulted in significant pressure to reduce product prices.[69]

Table 11.2.2. Distribution patterns of white goods[1]

Distribution	Italy	Germany	France	Spain	Netherlands
Hypermarkets	5	10	19	22	10
Department stores	37	5	8	6	11
Specialists	50	60	45	40	60
Other	8	25	28	12	19

1 Estimated.
Source: Horack, Adler & Associates.

The recent referral by the Office of Fair Trading to the Monopolies and Mergers Commission in the UK of the alleged refusal of some manufacturers to supply out-of-town discount warehouses is, at its heart, a battle for power between retailers and manufacturers over control of the market. The same issues exist in other European markets.[70]

To allow control to pass to the retailer, as has happened to some extent in other consumer products, may reinforce the trend to own-label brands and to greater product standardization at lower prices. This would in turn reinforce the single market by accentuating the trend to pan-European manufacturing strategies. It might also result in further consolidation of supply, and accelerate the shift to lower cost production facilities outside the EU.

11.2.3. Behavioural barriers

The existence of the single market does not necessarily mean that the players in the market behave in similar ways as a result. The main behavioural factors influencing the market are the strategic responses of the players.

---

67 In contrast to parts of the furniture market (e.g. IKEA) or the automobile market.
68 Interview with major manufacturer.
69 *Les Echos*, June 1994.
70 *The Observer*, April 1995; Horack, Adler & Associates.

Table 11.2.3. Import penetration[1] by product (1993–94) (%)

Country	Washing machines	Fridges	Dishwashers	Microwave ovens
Italy	12	13	39	68
France	36	57	65	22
West Germany	44	69	11	~ 100
Netherlands	~ 100	~ 100	~ 100	~ 100

[1] Defined as imports / apparent consumption.
Source: EIU, Euromonitor, National Accounts.

Table 11.2.3 shows the import penetration ratios for several European countries by major product, whereas Table 11.2.4 shows which manufacturer brands dominate the market in different countries.

Table 11.2.4. Leading white goods brands and brand shares (1993–94) (%)

	White goods		*Washing machines*	*Dishwashers*
Sweden		**Italy**		
Electrolux	68	Electrolux/Zanussi	22	18
Bosch-Siemens	14	Candy	18	12
		Merloni	17	13
		Whirlpool	12	11
Netherlands		**Germany**		
Whirlpool (Philips)	25	Bosch-Siemens	30	35
Bosch-Siemens	24	Quelle	18	8
Electrolux	16	AEG (Electrolux)	16	15
ATAG	6	Miele	13	16
Spain		**France**		
BYSE (Bosch-Siemens)	20	Thomson	-	31
Fagor	20	Whirlpool	-	22
Albilux (Electrolux)	14	Bosch-Siemens	-	15
Whirlpool	7	Electrolux	-	8

Source: Horack, Adler & Associates.

These essentially national differences help explain why firms developed different strategies based on different starting points: about ten years ago, it was possible to distinguish three broad strategic responses from the major manufacturers, based often on their starting points in relation to their domestic (national) markets and hence their local strengths.

For example, firms like Thomson or Hotpoint were overwhelmingly national players concentrating on their domestic markets. In contrast, firms like Bosch-Siemens, Candy or Merloni tended to use a strong domestic position as a springboard to export in large volumes to other European countries. Finally, firms like Electrolux or Philips (now Whirlpool) with small domestic markets saw themselves as global players and had widely distributed manufacturing facilities and local subsidiaries from which they attacked other European (or international) markets.

In recent years, this pattern has changed, and the creation of the single market is one of the reasons for the change. Many of the purely national players have disappeared via acquisitions by the exporters or global players. Exporters are increasingly close to the global players, as firms like Candy, Merloni and Bosch-Siemens have acquired brands and production facilities in other countries.

By 1995, the key differences have become, on the one hand, market positioning, and, on the other, the extent to which integrated production and distribution across the European Union has been used as a vehicle for generating lower costs and cutting time to market.

Figure 11.2.1 is a simple analysis of 'positioning' which shows the leading manufacturers according to whether they are mainly up-market, more expensive and feature-led, versus whether they are less expensive and more standardized, and comparing this to whether they are broad-range or more specialized. Figure 11.2.2 shows the approximate operating configuration of several of the major European suppliers.

Figure 11.2.1. Broad market positioning of main white goods brands

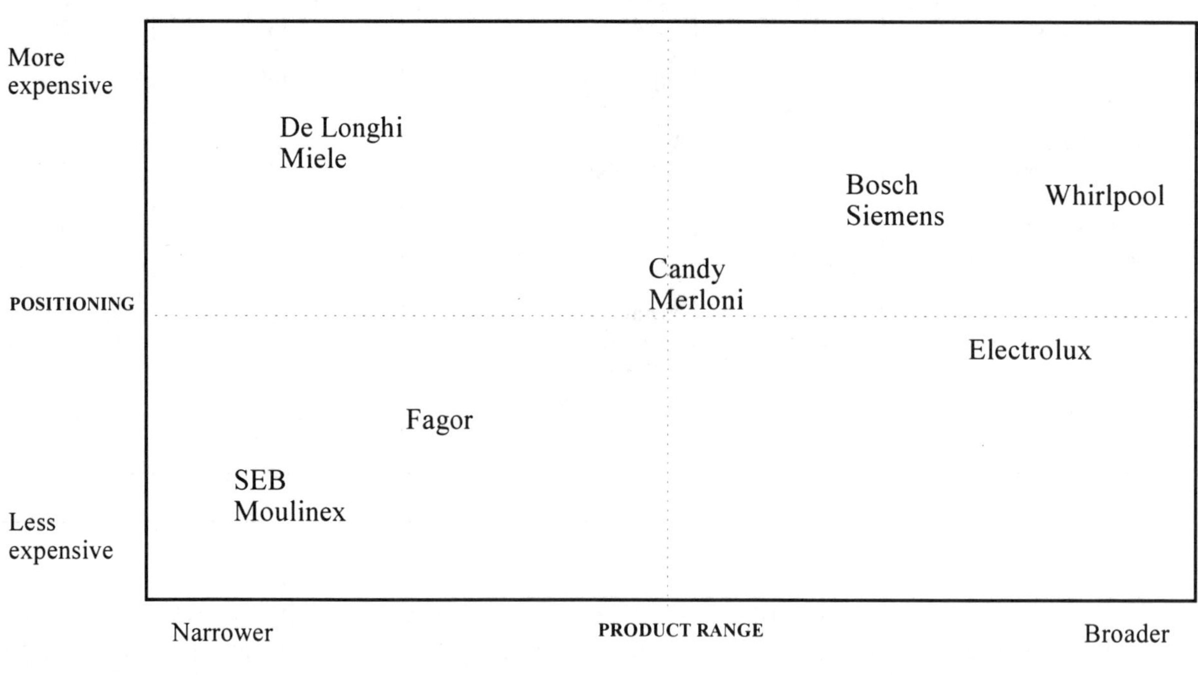

Source: Horack, Adler & Associates.

Figure 11.2.2. Estimated operating configuration of main white goods manufacturers in Europe

	Bosch Siemens		Whirlpool Philips		Candy		Merloni		Electrolux[1]		Miele	
Production sites	Germany	5	France	1	Italy	6	Italy	6	Italy		Germany	8
	Spain	4	Germany	3	France	1	France	1	Nordic countries		Austria	1
	Greece	1	Italy	6	UK	3	Portugal	1	Germany			
			Spain	1	Spain	1	UK	1	Spain			
			Sweden	1					UK			
									Hungary			
% sales in domestic market	50 %		n/a		30 %		35 %		12 %		50 %	

[1] Exact data unavailable.
Source: Horack, Adler & Associates.

The contrast between the players is quite striking, and their strategic responses to the European market are self-evident. To some extent the 'response' is governed by the starting point. Electrolux and Whirlpool (Philips) were early global players because of the small size of their domestic markets. Companies like Merloni and Candy have only recently begun to install significant manufacturing capacity outside their home base, while firms like Miele and Fagor remain more oriented both to supplying, and manufacturing, in their home markets.

Probably the most 'European' company is, paradoxically, the US-owned Whirlpool which has publicly announced an ambitious revamping of its logistics, production and distribution. For Whirlpool, Europe is divided into four commercial zones – 'one factory, one product, one region' in the slogan adopted by the firm.[71] In the early 1990s, in the words of Whirlpool's CEO 'the washing machines made in the Italian and German facilities didn't have one screw in common. Today products are being designed to ensure that a wide variety of models can be built on the same basic platform'.

[71] *Le Nouvel Economiste*, August 1995; and 'The Right Way to Go Global', HBR, April 1994.

The analysis of this section is summarized in Table 11.2.5.

Table 11.2.5. Remaining barriers to the single market in white goods

Structural	Behavioural	Policy
(a) Differentiated consumer preferences in national markets (b) Different phases of market maturity by product and by country (c) Retail and distribution systems	(a) National brands shares and dominance of local markets increase cost of entry for outsiders (b) Manufacturing strategies not yet entirely pan-European (c) Product positioning creates entry barriers (d) Balance of power between retailers and manufacturers	(a) Environmental regulations may increase manufacturing costs and hurt 'marginal' players (b) Consumer awareness of EU regulations probably low

Source: Horack, Adler & Associates.

12. The construction services sector

12.1. Single market indicators

The study of price disparities in Chapter 4 highlighted the construction sector as one in which the coefficient of variation of prices in the periods 1980, 1985, 1990 and 1993 has tended to increase (Figure 12.1.1). This is not totally surprising, since construction work as such is non-tradeable, or at least only tradeable in part. Ultimately, structures must be constructed at a fixed location. Nevertheless, international competition, especially in larger projects, does take place, and therefore persistent price differentials between countries might be an indicator of either a lack of international competition or an absence of a 'single market' effect.

Figure 12.1.1. Coefficient of price variation for construction in the EU-12

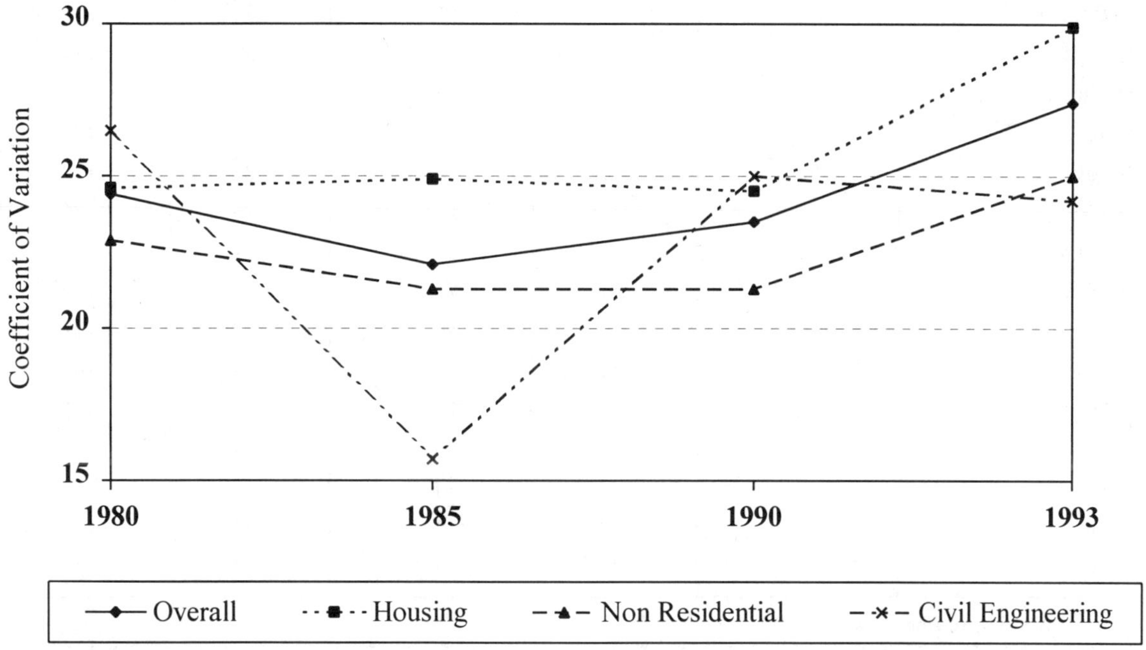

Coefficient of Variation
30
25
20
15
1980 1985 1990 1993
Overall · Housing · Non Residential · Civil Engineering

Source: DRI.

There are some additional data on price differentials which tend to support the thesis that the construction sector has not yet reached the level of some other sectors in terms of pan-European integration.

A recent report by WS Atkins for the European Commission, 'Strategies for the European Construction Sector'[72] examined a series of construction cost indicators across the EU. There were three main conclusions:

(a) **Regarding projects**: There was a very large range in average project costs which are particularly marked in public sector works, and which cannot be attributed solely to differences in average price levels and exchange rates.

[72] Office for Official Publications of the EC and Construction Europe, 1994.

(b) **Regarding products**: There were again large differences which the authors suggest are due to high trade barriers in addition to high transport costs.

(c) **Regarding labour**: There were large, expected differences in and no apparent relationship between labour costs and overall project costs. Low labour costs thus do not 'explain' differences in overall project costs. (Table 12.1.1 presents part of the WS Atkins data on construction costs.)

Table 12.1.1. Construction cost indicators, 1990

Country	Buildings		Public works		Total at PPP
	Market rate	At PPP	Market rate	At PPP	
UK	100	100	100	100	200
Netherlands	105	105	87	86	191
Italy	84	97	79	92	189
Denmark	117	107	79	72	181
Spain	73	94	65	84	178
Ireland	82	96	70	81	177
Greece	70	100	53	76	176
Belgium	82	96	68	79	175
Germany	97	96	75	74	170
France	81	101	54	67	168
Portugal	53	98	34	63	161
EC median	82	98	75	79	177
Turkey	35	na	20	na	na
Japan	86	77	98	88	165
USA	73	108	76	112	220

Source: WS Atkins, from OECD.

Another recent study, by Bernard Williams Associates[73] looked at overall building efficiency in the EU. The study concludes that there were large differences in typical building costs and large differences in construction efficiency (Figures 12.1.2 and 12.1.3). In addition, other information suggests large and persistent differences in labour productivity in construction between European countries (Figure 12.1.4).

A major conclusion of the Bernard Williams study was that differences in output efficiency relate to 'all the issues such as efficient design, clear instructions, buildability...use of plant and industrialized methods...' and are accounted for by the efficiency of the whole management process. This 'management efficiency' varies significantly from country to country in the EU.

[73] 'Building and development economics in the EC' paper given by B. Williams FRICS to DEBA Seminar, Brussels, November 1994.

Therefore, the evidence on the persistence of significant price differentials (even in the public sector and in large 'international' type buildings) tends to confirm that the original price disparities data analysed in Chapter 4 were not merely a statistical aberration.

Figure 12.1.2. The development budget: international offices – 5,000m^2 NIA

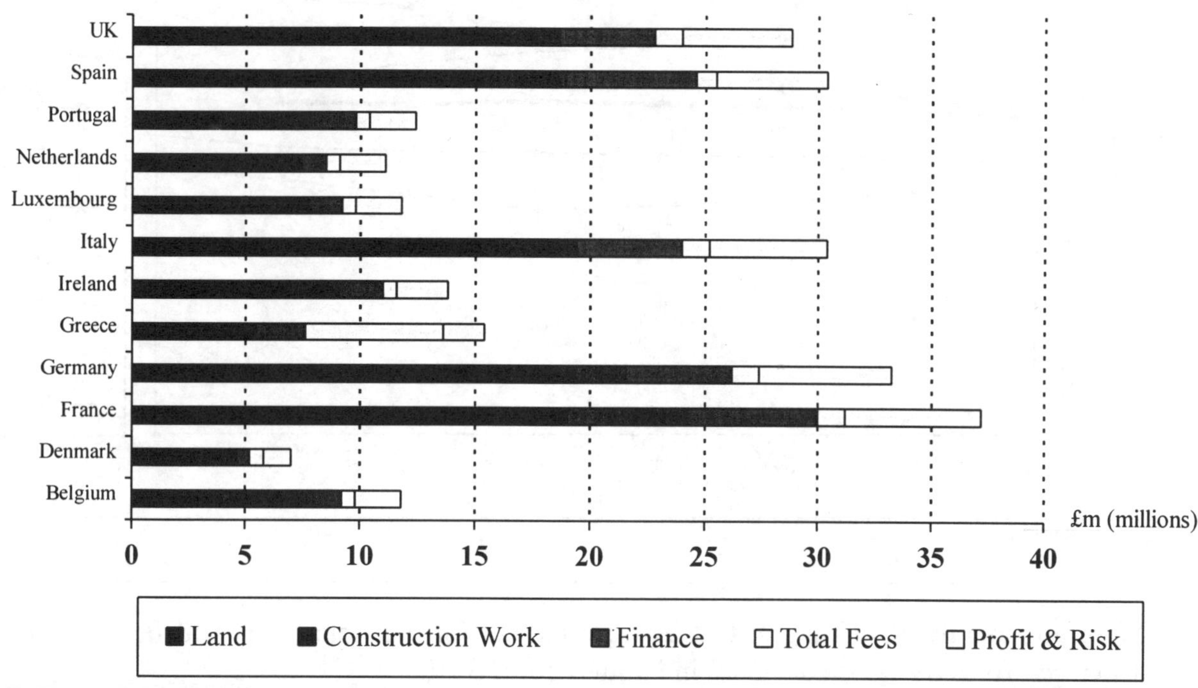

Source: Bernard Williams Associates (BWA).

Figure 12.1.3. Index of construction efficiency: international standard office buildings

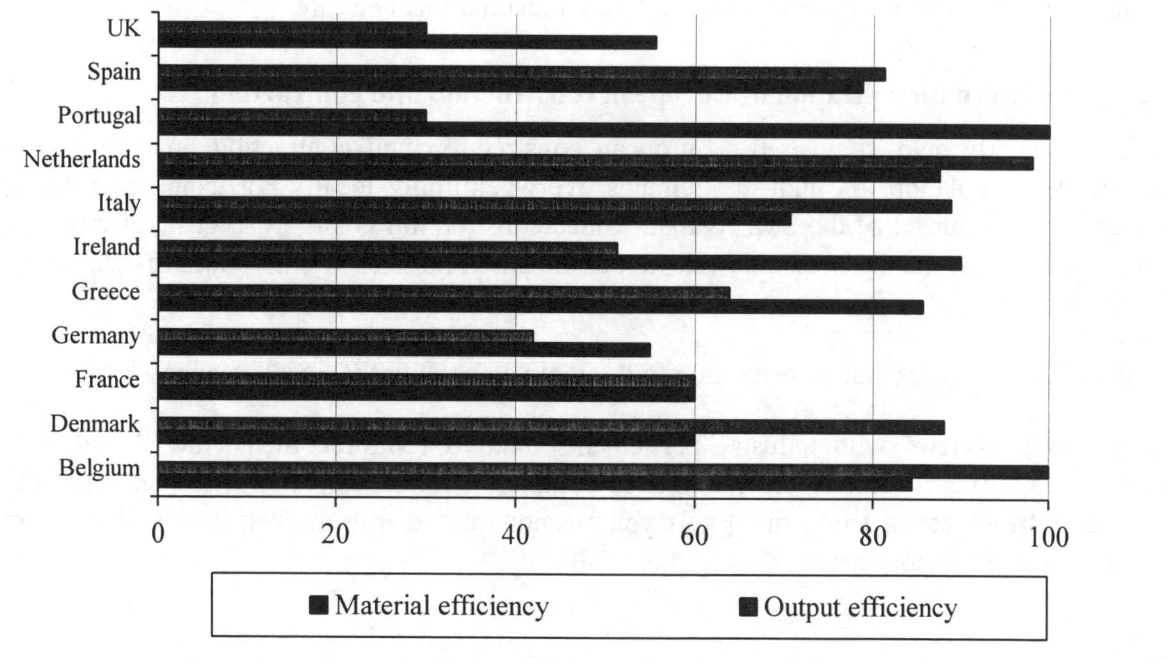

Source: BWA.

Figure 12.1.4. Efficiency of the EU construction industry (total EU construction output / total EU employment)

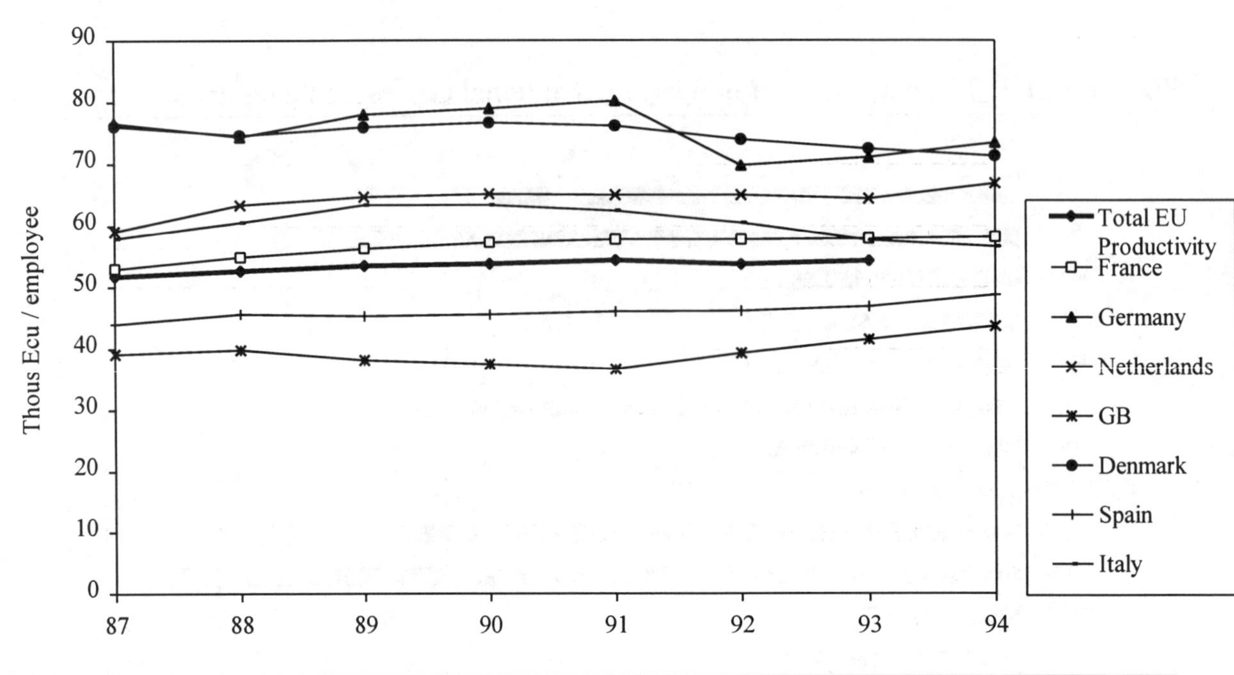

Source: DEBA.
GB = UK

More importantly, they suggest that a single market for construction is still far from being achieved. As WS Atkins concludes in its study for DG III:

'The EC construction market is heterogeneous in almost every important respect...The creation of the single market seeks to remove regulatory or procedural differences where they restrict trade. However, at present the EC construction industry consists of many very different local industries, each of which reflects a distinct local culture'.

12.2. The internationalization of European construction and contracting

The dominantly held view of the European construction and contracting business is that despite EU regulation, the industry remains overwhelmingly local. For example, FIEC's[74] analysis of the impact of the SMP is that: 'Since construction is largely a local activity...the single market has mostly been only relevant to the small number of enterprises that engage in large projects.'

Another expert writes that 'construction will remain an essentially "local" business'.[75]

Our own interviews with industry participants tend to reinforce their view: 'Traditional practices survive...' (Italian project finance company); 'EU legislation has had very little impact' (British construction firm); 'If you are not wanted in a market, they will stop you anyway' (Swedish contractor).

74 Fédération de l'industrie européenne de construction, DRI survey for DG III.

75 Goodall, John, 'The Role of the Construction Economist is Raising the Relative Efficiency of the National Construction Industry in Europe', Brussels, May 1995.

There has been relatively little research carried out on the actual impact of measures such as the Public Works Directive[76] in stimulating cross-border bids for significant projects. What work exists on the subject tends to be sceptical, as do the comments of industry participants.

For example, in the UK, the National Economic Development Council[77] carried out a Europe-wide survey which concluded that 'the Public Works Directive has had little effect on the public sector construction market'. The research suggested that, in the EU as a whole, the directive only captured 26% of the contracts by value in 1991, compared to the 80% that was originally intended, and less than 1% by number compared to the 20% planned. In a three-year period (1989–91) only six contracts out of 6,315 were in fact awarded to non-national bidders, and only 21% of the contracting authorities noticed any increase in non-national bidders (79% detected no increase).

Our own interviews tend to some extent to confirm this. Comments such as…'EU intervention has had minimal impact'; 'Collusion, known as "clubbing" survives to keep out foreigners…Even if you win a contract, you will soon wish you hadn't'; and, 'Habit, emotional ties and language-based attitudes are still powerful forces…' were typical of the views expressed.

Despite this, we have tried to look at statistical and other data relevant to the issue. This evidence suggests that quite a large amount of international business does in fact occur inside Europe, and perhaps more interestingly, the trends appear to be moving towards a greater degree of internationalization.

The statistical data are, frankly, not very comprehensive, and we believe them to be suggestive, not conclusive.

However, there are three main trends we would draw from these data:

(a) International construction and contracting business in Europe as a whole is growing much faster than domestic construction activity as a whole (Figure 12.2.1).

(b) International business in Europe which is won by European companies is growing faster than these same companies' total international business elsewhere in the world (Figure 12.2.2).

(c) European companies are getting a larger share of European international business, i.e. non-European companies' share of the international market inside Europe is diminishing (Figure 12.2.3).

Taken together, these trends suggest that the European construction industry's European international business is growing quite fast, albeit from a small base.

[76] Council Directive 93/37/EEC of 14 June 1993 concerning the co-ordination of procedures for the award of public works contracts (OJ L 199, 9.8.1993, p. 54).

[77] NEDC European Public Purchasing Working Party, 'European Community Public Works Directive: A Study of the Application in Practice', 1992.

Figure 12.2.1. Growth of European international contracts compared to the growth of the total EU construction output (base year 1988)

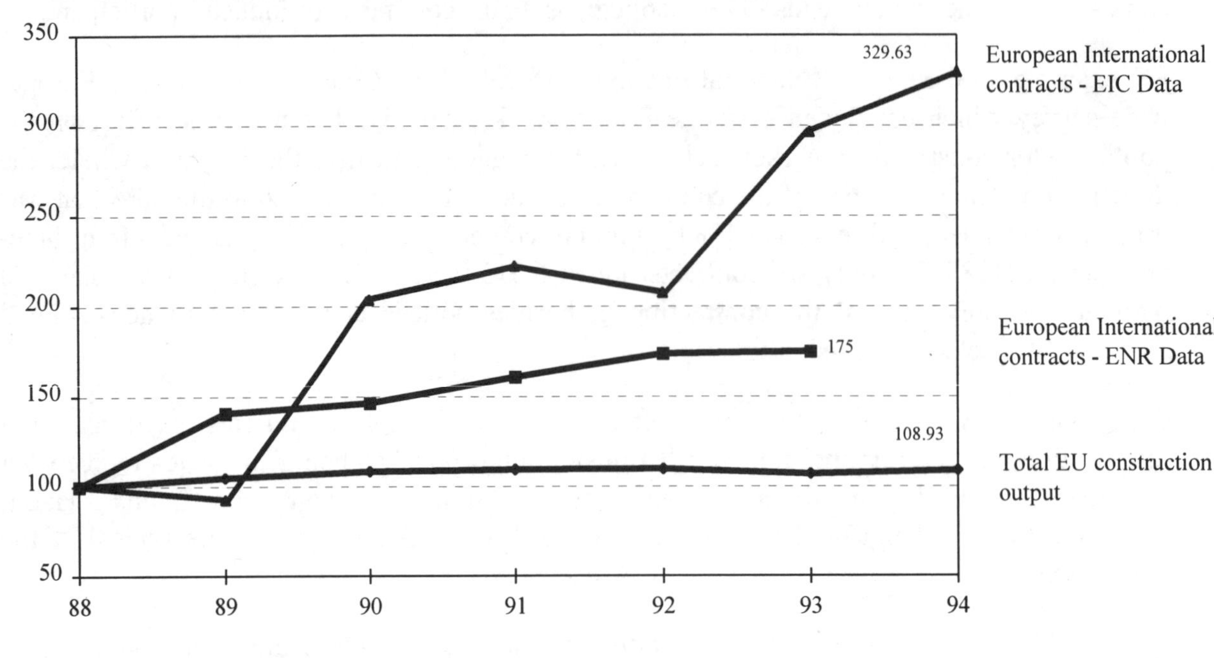

Source: Horack, Adler & Associates.

Figure 12.2.2. European international business won by European companies as a percentage of their total international business

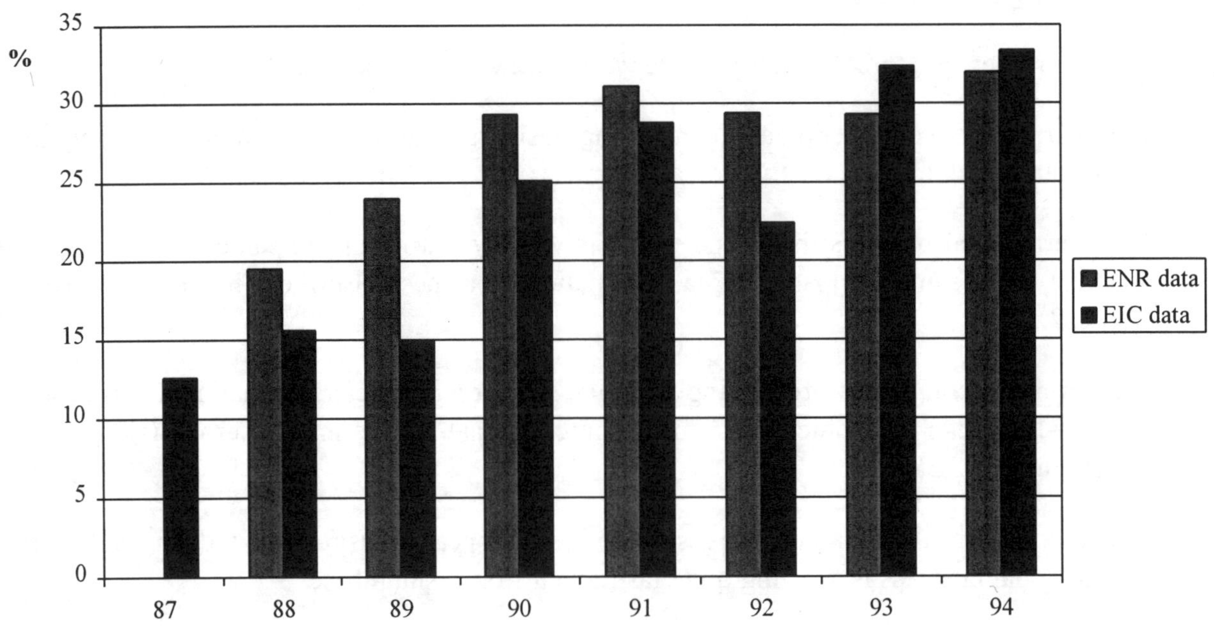

Source: Horack, Adler & Associates.

Figure 12.2.3. The share of total European international contracts won by European companies (1987–94)

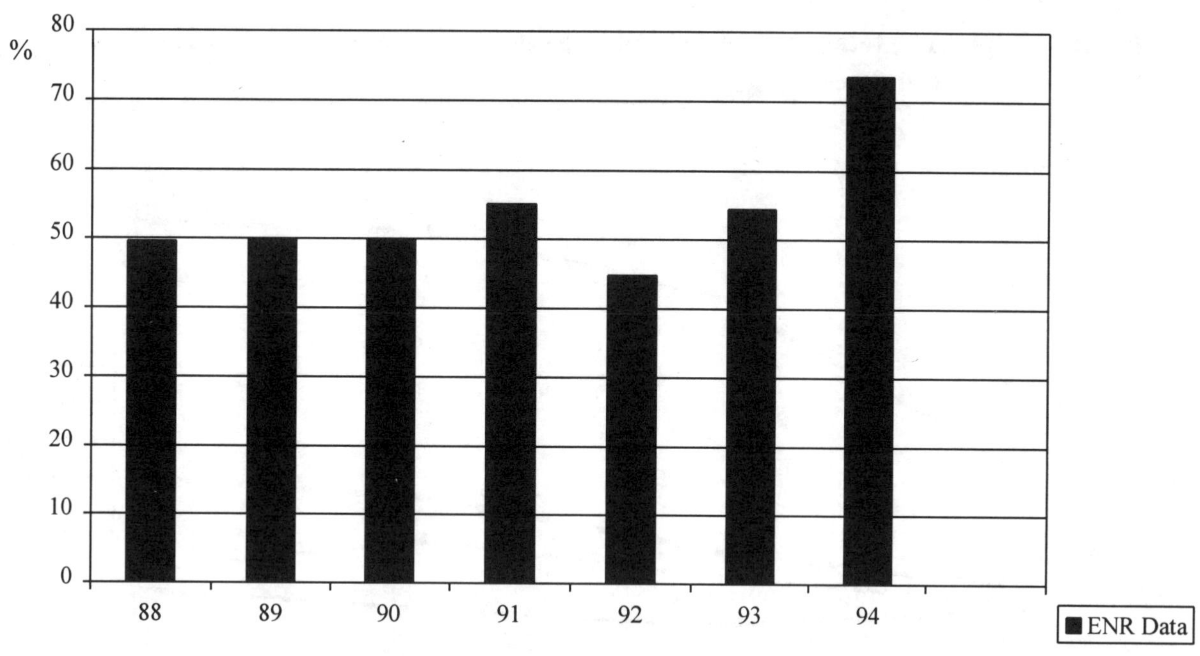

Source: Horack, Adler & Associates.

It is also likely to be true that only a small proportion of total construction activity is susceptible to any 'international' competition. Conventional wisdom in the industry suggests that contract sizes of less than about ECU 10–15 million are unlikely to be worthwhile for a non-domestic competitor.

This limitation is also suggested by experience in other markets. For example, in the United States one industry expert reports that only about 6% of construction activity is done by out-of-state companies.[78]

We estimate that between 3 and 5% of construction activity in the EU is won by non-domestic firms (including local subsidiaries of non-national businesses). If 'large' contracts over ECU 15 million represent no more than 15% of total construction output, then 20–30% of eligible contracts are probably won by international firms.

The second main feature of international business is that the construction industry's key tactic in winning non-domestic business has been the establishment of local subsidiaries, local joint ventures and local alliances. In fact, most international contractors are really 'multi-local' rather than 'multinational'. This pattern is also common outside Europe, where in the Far East or elsewhere, the international contractors have established local subsidiaries.

Figure 12.2.4 shows the rapid growth in Europe of locally owned subsidiaries or international equity participation in local companies. In practice, almost all contractors see local knowledge and the 'appearance' of being a domestic supplier as key success factors. Bidding from the outside is seen as being far less likely to succeed:

[78] Goodall, J. [1995].

'Traditionally, foreign firms have bought domestic ones' (a French construction company); 'The cost efficiency of local supply and local labour and awareness of local design and contracting processes are major home market advantages' (a British contractor).

Figure 12.2.4. The total of recorded holdings in other countries by five European countries

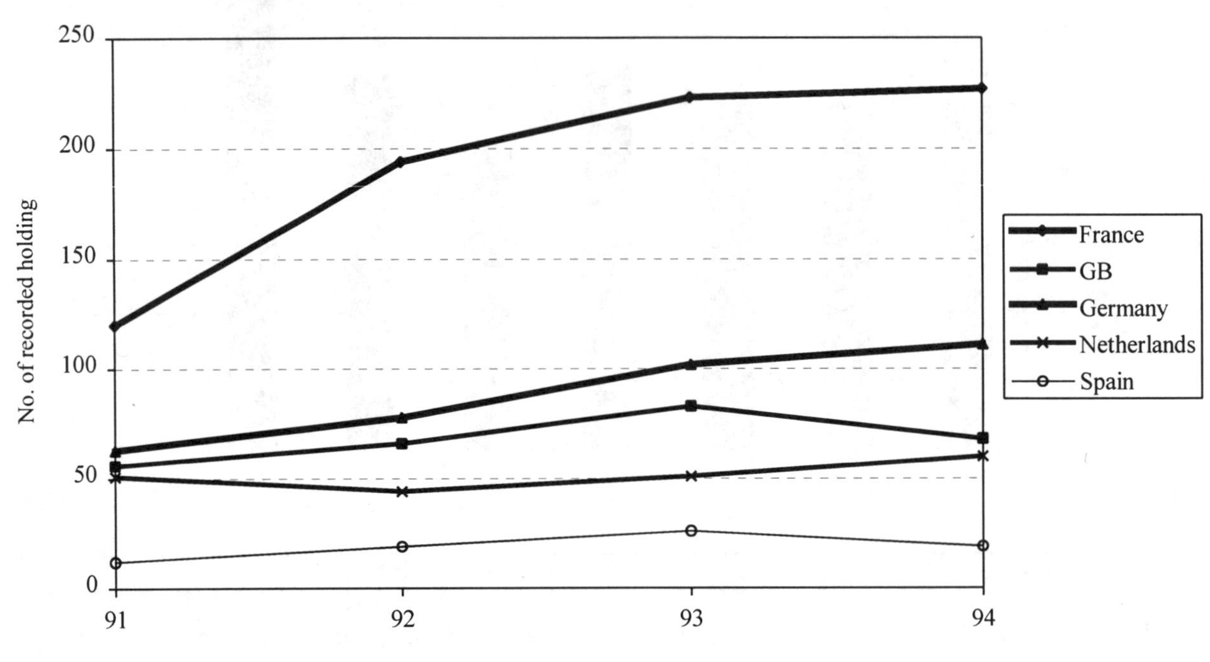

Source: EIC.
GB = UK.

In sum, therefore, we disagree with the profoundly pessimistic analyses which dominate discussion of the impact of EU regulations on construction. Although price differentials persist, there is evidence that European construction is undergoing an internationalization process of some importance at the 'top' end of the market.

Equally interesting, there is at least some evidence to suggest that an efficient domestic industry is related to success in international markets. Figure 12.2.5 shows the relationship between productivity (output/person employed) in national construction industries and success in European international business (measured as European international contracts as a percentage of domestic construction output). Generally, countries with higher productivity tend to do better in other European markets, relative to the size of their domestic construction industry.

This suggests that 'efficiency' is in some sense exportable, i.e. that superior management expertise can be translated into international success, even when non-domestic markets are targeted primarily by being multi-local. If management and contracting techniques are 'exportable' as this evidence suggests, then the persistence of wide efficiency differentials should not be seen as a permanent and inevitable feature of the European construction industry.

Table 12.2.1. The top 20 European companies in terms of number of recorded holdings in other countries

Company	No. of holdings	Nationality
EIFFAGE (merger between former Fougerolle & SAE)	54	French
Bouygues SA	38	French
Skanska AB	38	Swedish
Campenon-Bernard	28	French
Cogefar-Impresit SpA	24	Italian
Strabag Bau AG	23	German
Maculan Holding	23	Austrian
Lyonnaise des Eaux-Dumez	23	French
Royal Boskalis Westminster NV	19	Dutch
Société Générale d'Entreprises (SGE)	18	French
John Mowlem & Co. Plc	15	British
Philipp Holzmann AG	15	German
Royal Volker Stevin	14	Dutch
Ballast Nedam Construction Ltd	14	Dutch
Brochier Holding GmbH & Co.	14	German
Hojgaard & Schultz AS	13	Danish
Dyckerhoff & Widmann AG (Dywidag)	13	German
Cochery Bourdin Chaussée	11	French
Zschokke Holding SA	11	Swiss
Porr	11	Austrian

Source: EIC.

Taking into account that under any reasonable scenario only a small percentage of construction activity would be the subject of international competition anyway, the levelling of the playing field has therefore probably had some impact, mainly via the growth in local subsidiaries of international firms. We would certainly recommend that more research than we have been able to carry out in this overview, would help to clarify the picture further.

Figure 12.2.5. Relationship between productivity and success in Europe international markets

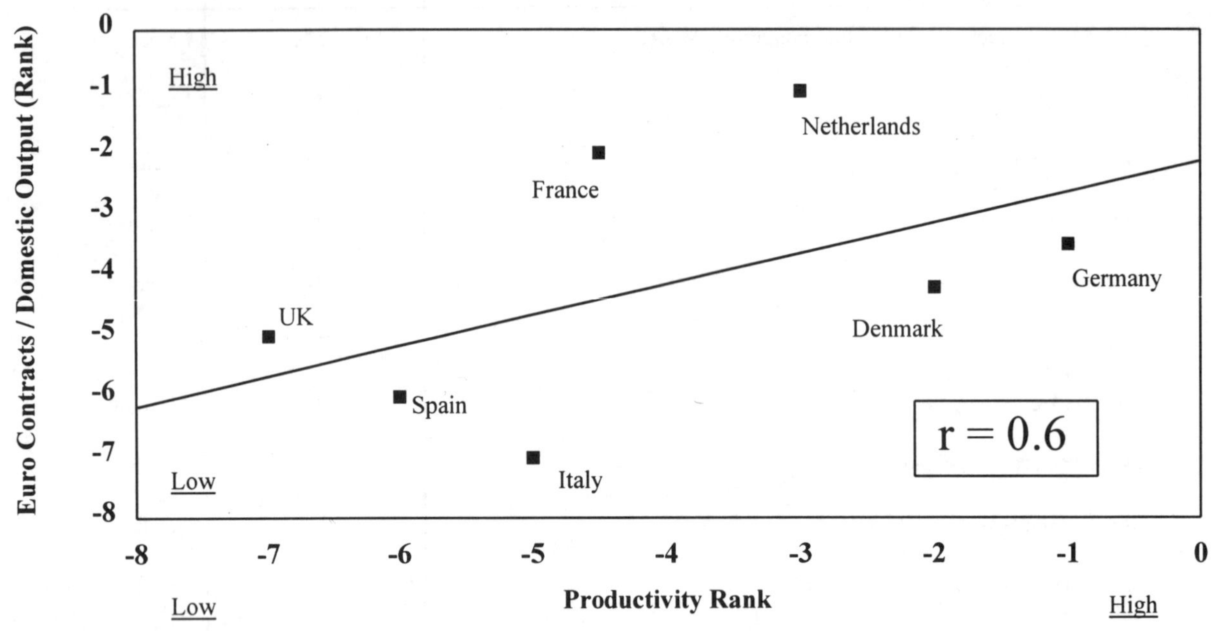

Source: EIC, FIEC, EuroConstruct, Horack, Adler & Associates.

Nevertheless, we would also point to the persistence of a considerable number of 'barriers' to the single market for construction. We analyse these continuing barriers in the next section of this report.

12.3. Remaining barriers to the establishment of a single market

Barriers to the single market are categorized according to whether they can be considered as 'behavioural', 'policy' or 'structural'. Behavioural barriers are taken to include the activities or behaviour of companies which may themselves be reactions to EU regulations or directives, and which may have the effect of limiting or reducing the effect of single market policies.

Policy barriers are typically legal or official statutes, codes or laws which in some sense run counter to single market policies. This may include non-compliance with European legislation or the simple persistence of legal or industry norms which have the effect of maintaining barriers.

Structural barriers are taken to mean features of markets, customer behaviour or culture which may be the result of historical differences, tastes, habits, or simple 'facts of life'. In a different context, national preferences for, say, beer over wine, may be considered structural.

12.3.1. Behavioural barriers

Interviews with industry participants and experts suggest that behavioural barriers do persist to some extent. These barriers are not, however, confined to 'domestic' firms. Potential 'exporters'[79] have often been slow to exploit the opportunities offered by the single market. Companies frequently cite their perceived fear of failure, or inability to identify any clear competitive advantage, compared to better opportunities in non-EU foreign markets (e.g. other parts of the world) where there is more rapid economic growth and where local domestic industry is seen as less competitive. High costs of tendering in other EU countries, combined with lower chances of success (low 'hit rate') are potent arguments for looking at opportunities elsewhere in the world.

As has been mentioned, the main strategy for construction firms seeking to enter other EU markets has been to overcome these barriers by appearing to be 'local', i.e. by establishing a local presence.

From the point of view of the domestic firms, there have been several changes in business practice which are in part a response to single market competitive challenges. So-called 'collusive tendering' or 'clubbing' is frequently mentioned as a tactic, but by definition is almost impossible to quantify.

More strategically, firms are seeking to increase their competitive advantage by exploiting their links to domestic sources of finance to fund projects. This constitutes a major attraction for customers which is much harder for non-domestic companies to match, given their lack of close ties to financial institutions in foreign countries.

In addition, many construction firms are seeking to enhance their 'design and build' capabilities and to create more enduring and long-term relationships with sub-contractors and suppliers. This strategy is aimed at persuading customers of the value of an integrated approach and the attraction of working with established teams over time. This may be seen as a countermeasure to EU norms which are viewed as favouring the disaggregation of projects into sub-components, each of which may be tendered for separately.[80]

12.3.2. Policy barriers

There is widespread acknowledgement that EU regulations relating to construction have had an impact in reducing the barriers to international activity, especially in the field of public procurement, trade in construction products, and the development of common construction codes and practices.[81]

Despite this, industry experts still point to several areas where policies at government and industry levels continue to create barriers. Detailed analysis of these policies country-by-country is beyond the scope of this study. However, it is common knowledge that qualifications and norms for entry into construction-related professions are still significantly different and not always mutually recognized.

Equally important, contracting policies in terms of management practices, methods of aggregating and disaggregating the functional specialities of the construction process, and the like, are also widely different. Some of these practices are the result of custom and habit, but others are enshrined in industry codes, the structure of calls for tender, and also in legal

79 'Exporters' in the sense of non-domestic suppliers.

80 Sources for the above include interviews with industry participants, articles and books in industry journals, and comment by industry experts. For a full list of sources, see Appendix L.

81 For a summary of measures, see European Commission [1994 and 1995], *Panorama of EU Industry*, 'Construction'.

practice. Industry observers have also highlighted differences in legal requirements for such critical areas as insurance, performance bonds and guarantees, which may have the effect of discriminating against non-domestic firms.

Lastly, poor compliance with existing regulations is sometimes mentioned as being significant in some places.

12.3.3. Structural barriers

We have divided structural barriers into four types: economic, information, risk and culture. Economic barriers include the on-site nature of projects and the average size of contracts. The vast majority of construction projects are of small size and are fundamentally uneconomic for non-local firms. Industry participants suggest that contracts of less than ECU 10–15 million are unattractive to international bidders. In addition, tender costs are usually proportionately smaller the larger the project size;[82] smaller projects thus have a double economic disincentive.

Equally important, construction projects are typically carried out by a variety of independent sub-contractors and suppliers, from the architect to the project manager to the site-crews and more. The ability to manage this complexity is a key factor in cost competitiveness in which non-local players may be severely disadvantaged.

Table 12.3.1. Main barriers to the single market in construction/contracting

Structural	Policy	Behavioural
Economic On-site nature of work Small average project size Cost of tendering Inefficiency of sub-contractor/supplier management	 Professional and industry qualifications Contracting practices and definition of functional skills and specialization	'Foreign' firms Fear of failure High tender costs Low 'hit rates' No competitive advantage
Information Knowledge of sub-contractor/supplier market Management contracting practices	 Insurance, performance bonds, guarantees	'Domestic' firms Links to local sources of project finance Move to 'design and build' Move to 'enduring partnerships'
Risk Project complexity Likelihood of legal action Financial fragility of contractor	Poor compliance with EU regulations	Collusive tendering/clubbing
Culture Language Customer preference for local suppliers		

Source: DRI.

Information is another critical structural hurdle to the non-local firm. Knowing the supplier and sub-contractor market and knowing how and where to source efficiently are in themselves

[82] Latham, Sir Michael [1994], 'Constructing the Team', HMSO, July.

key success factors which favour local contractors against non-local ones. Contracting and management contracting practices (e.g. 'main contracting' versus 'trades contracting' or the functions normally carried out by designers versus contractors) vary significantly based on custom and tradition. These differences represent significant knowledge barriers.

Closely related to information is risk, and assessment of risk is important for both suppliers and customers. The likelihood of legal action in construction and contracting is very great.[83] Construction projects are inherently complex and require co-ordination of several participants. From the point of view of both sides, risk of underperformance, risk of legal action and risk of financial fragility strongly favour the local or national firm. If legal action is a likely scenario, few people prefer an international case.

Last, but according to some, far from least, are cultural barriers. Language differences are always seen as an obstacle, but in addition many sources cite simple customer preference for the familiar rather than the foreign. 'Better the devil you know' is seen as a potent force for favouring the national supplier, even if he is more expensive and less reliable!

[83] One interview we carried out suggested that as many as 75% of all large contracts involved some form of legal process to resolve them.

13. The chocolate confectionery sector

13.1. Price data and convergence

The study of prices in the EU shows that for chocolate and confectionery, price disparities have remained roughly constant and higher than the average for food products over the period 1980–95 (Figure 13.1.1). In addition, when comparing the EU-6 to the EU-12, chocolate and confectionery products showed a further tendency towards greater price disparities.

Figure 13.1.1. Chocolate and confectionery (EU-12)

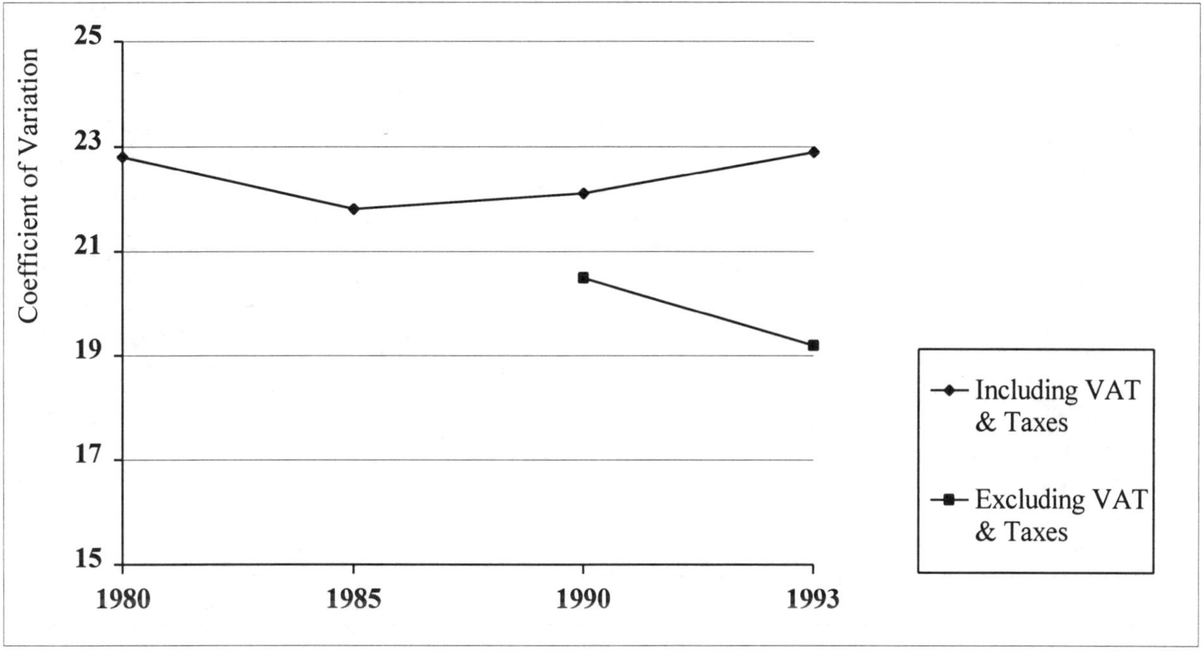

Source: DRI.

In many ways, this is a surprising finding given that chocolate confectionery in particular is a highly traded product, that the sector is served by some of the largest multinational food companies, and that there is a high degree of industrial concentration in this market segment.

On closer examination of the price data, further indications of the underlying reasons for price dispersion become apparent. Figure 13.1.1 also compares the coefficient of price dispersion for the chocolate and confectionery sector based on prices with and without VAT and other taxes. Since the VAT and tax rates on these products were not totally uniform in all EU Member States in the period, it is not surprising that price dispersion is lower for prices excluding taxes.

However, far bigger differences are observed when comparing the data for the EU-6 with the EU-12 (see Figure 13.1.2). In fact, the successive enlargements of the Community in 1973, and again in 1981 and 1986 added some very distinct groupings to the Union. Price dispersion is lowest in the EU-6, higher in Greece, Spain and Portugal, and higher still in the UK, Ireland and Denmark. How can this be explained? First, as shown in Figure 13.1.3, Spain, Greece and Portugal are all economies with very low per capita consumption of chocolate compared to the rest of the EU (Italy excepted). As well as this structural difference, the distributors of chocolate and confectionery products tend to be less concentrated in larger supermarkets or grocery chains in the three southern Member States than in the EU-9. Supermarkets and large grocery chains are less significant in the three southern Member States than smaller outlets, confectionery specialists, cafés and bars (see Table 13.1.1). As a result prices tend to be less uniform, and higher retail margins are more common.[84]

Figure 13.1.2. Chocolate and confectionery[1]

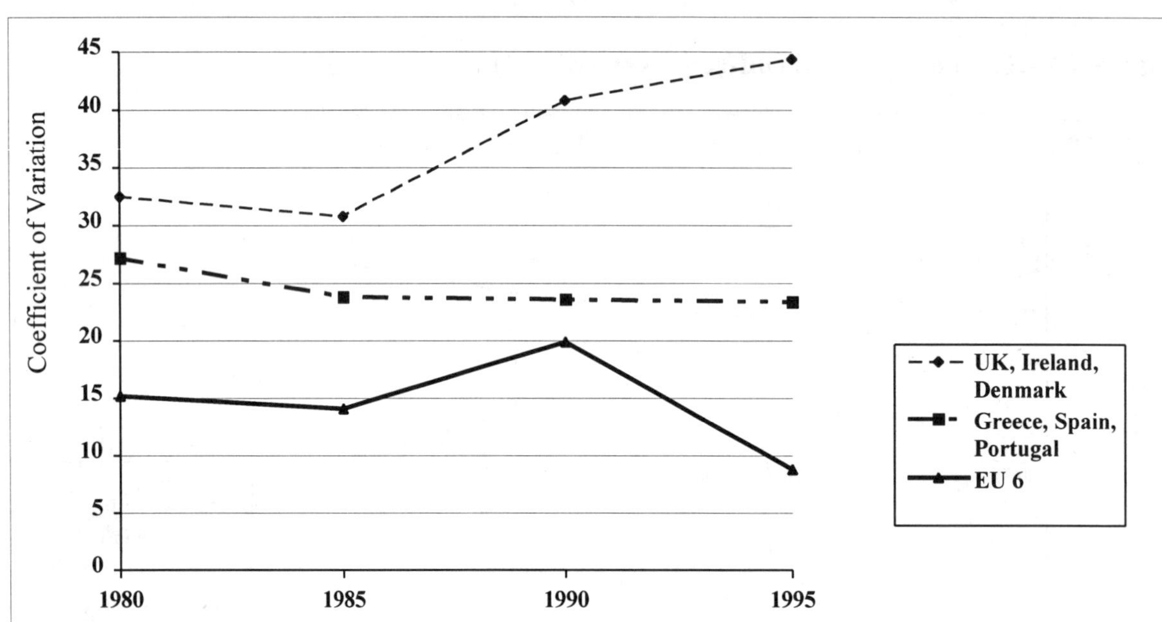

[1] Including VAT and excise duties.
NB: Data for 1990 for Greece, Spain and Portugal not available (chart shows extrapolated calculation).
Source: DRI.

Finally, the UK and Ireland have tended to remain, in trading terms, very closely linked in the chocolate sector, as well as sharing distinctively different consumption patterns which emphasize a preference for dairy milk chocolate and higher cocoa butter substitute (CBS) content.[85] Ireland is the UK's largest export market for chocolate confectionery, accounting for more than one-third of total exports.[86] On a per capita basis, Denmark is the second biggest consumer of 'UK style' chocolate in the EU, after Ireland.[87]

It is therefore likely that the initial statistical finding of approximately constant price disparities camouflages the existence of three significant sub-economies for chocolate confectionery within the EU:

(a) markets where there remains a higher level of CBSs permitted in chocolate (Sweden, Finland, Austria, Portugal, UK, Ireland and Denmark);

(b) markets with historically low per capita chocolate consumption and/or fragmented distribution (Italy, Greece, Spain, Portugal, Ireland, UK);

84 Euromonitor, Horack, Adler & Associates.
85 Interviews with industry experts.
86 BCCCA UK, 1994.
87 Horack, Adler & Associates estimate.

(c) markets which historically have high per capita chocolate consumption of the traditional 'European' variety, and which are also original signatories to the Treaty of Rome (France, Germany, Belgium, the Netherlands and Luxembourg).

Figure 13.1.3. Per capita consumption of chocolate (1994)

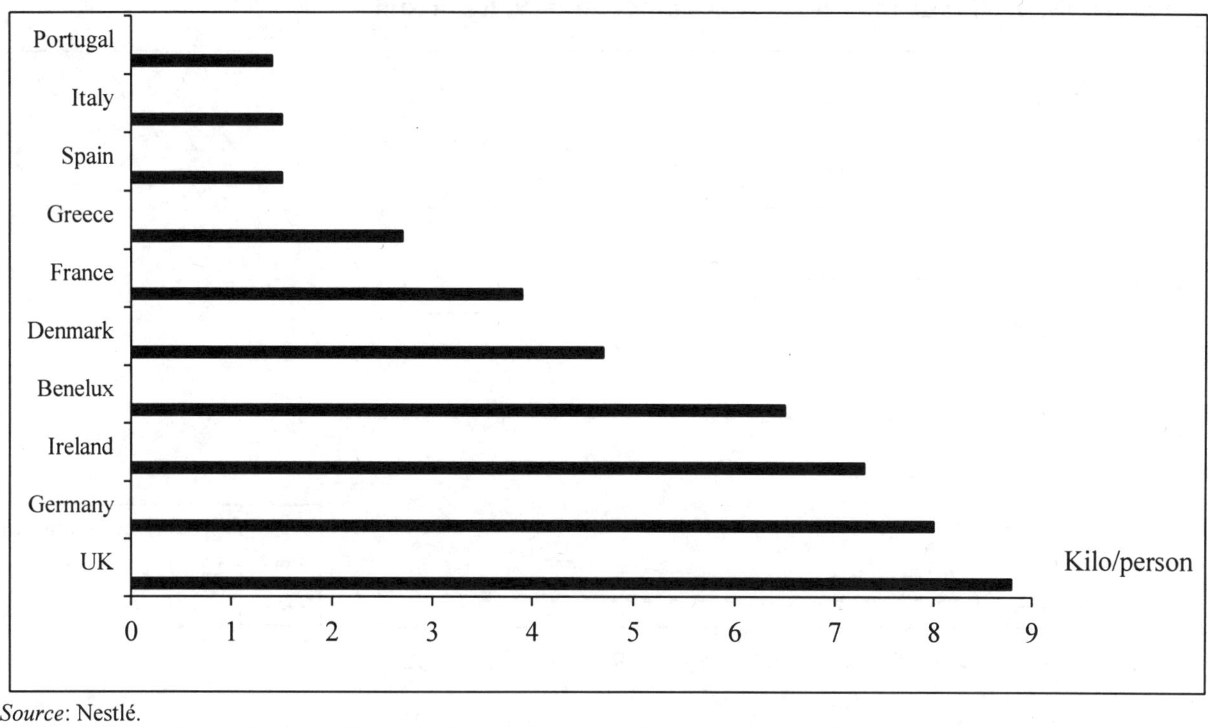

Source: Nestlé.

Table 13.1.1. Estimated distribution of chocolate confectionery (1994) (%)

	France	Germany	Italy	Spain	UK
Hyper-super market	80	75	55	45	40
CTNs[1]	5	5	25	30	25
Cafés / bars	-	-	10	15	-
Specialists	15	10	10	-	20
Other	-	10	-	10	15

[1] Coffee, tobacco, newsagents.
Source: Horack, Adler & Associates and estimates.

Although it is clear that in some cases this segmentation can overlap, these broad categories indicate why price disparities for chocolate confectionery have increased, in contrast to the trend observed in some other sectors. With the successive enlargements of the EU, the degree of heterogeneity in taste, consumption habits, and patterns of distribution has increased.

13.2. Single market indicators

Apart from the price data discussed in the previous section, there are a number of other indicators which demonstrate whether chocolate confectionery markets in Europe are converging and to what extent.

Figure 13.2.1. Trade in cocoa, sugar confectionery, ice cream

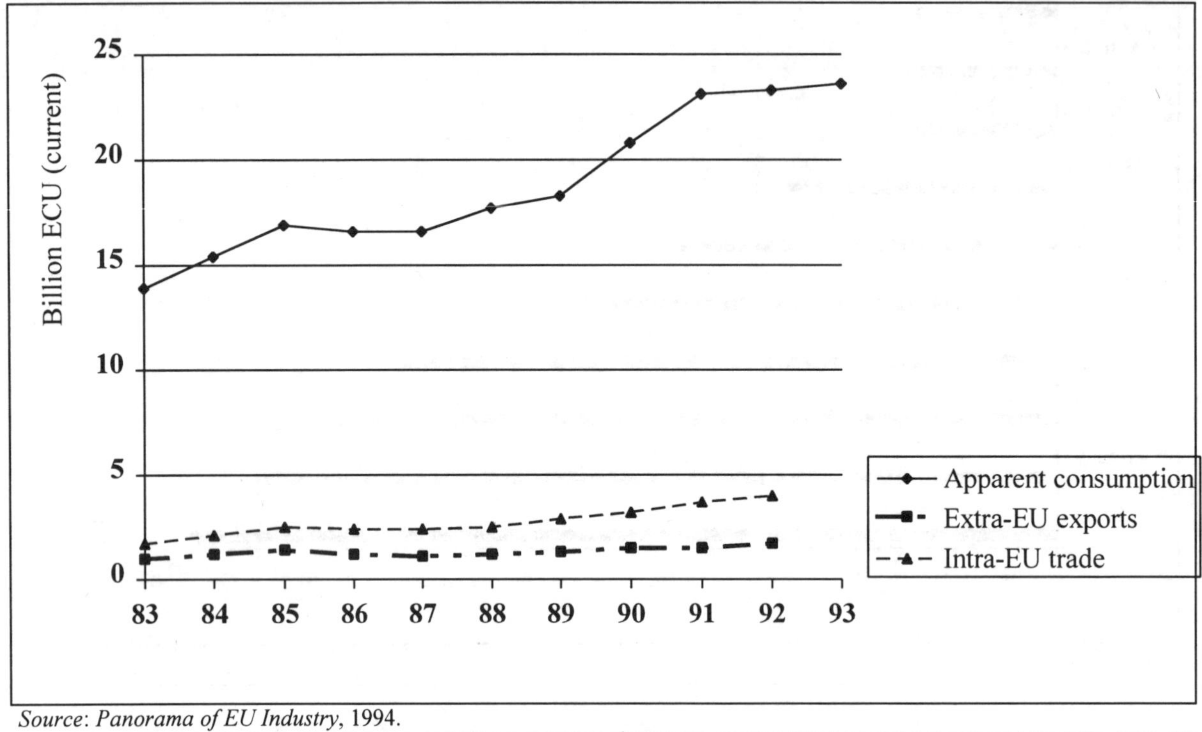

Source: *Panorama of EU Industry*, 1994.

Figure 13.2.2. Volume of national chocolate consumption represented by imports (%)

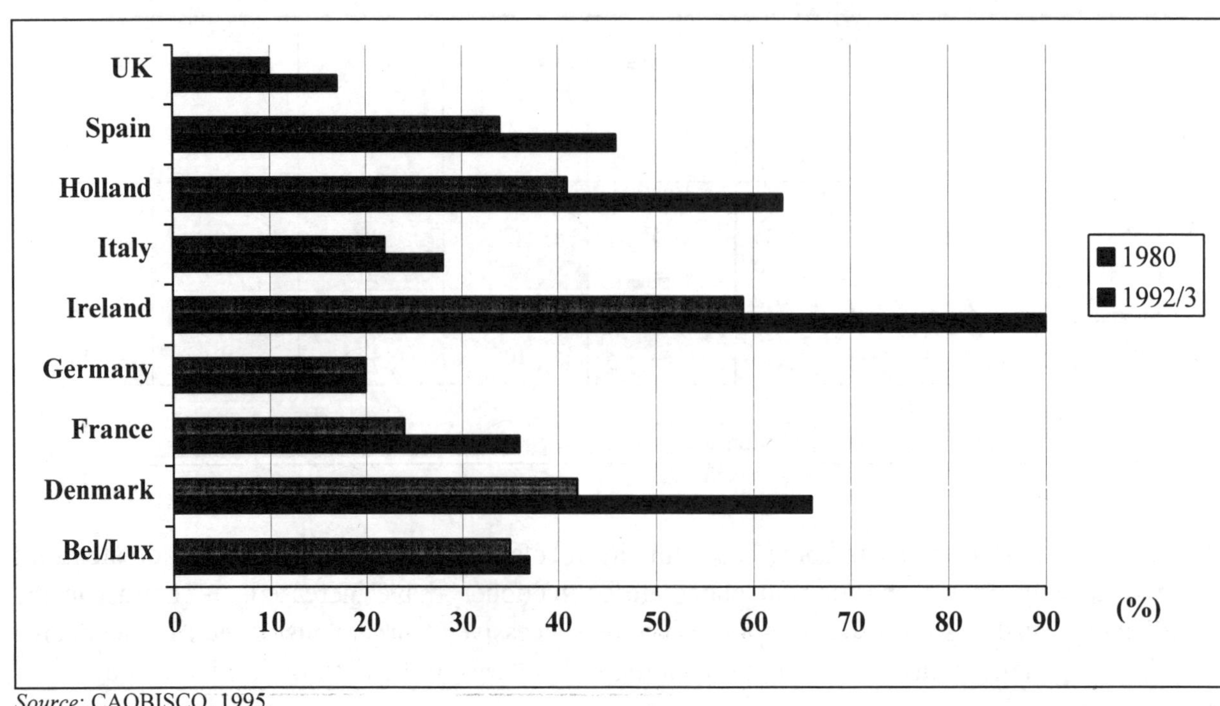

Source: CAOBISCO, 1995.

First, trade between EU Member States accounts for a high and growing proportion of consumption. Figure 13.2.1 shows that intra-EU trade as a proportion of consumption has grown from about 12% in 1983 to 17% by 1992. In that period, intra-EU trade has grown by a factor of 2.4, while consumption grew by a factor of 1.7. Figure 13.2.2 shows that in all individual Member States, imports represent a high and growing proportion of consumption.

Figure 13.2.3 shows that exports from EU members are also growing rapidly, suggesting a higher degree of international competitiveness.

Second, in common with several other sectors of the economy, the European chocolate industry has undergone considerable consolidation and restructuring during the 1980s. Much of this was in anticipation of the single market.[88] 'We all began to think about it well in advance of its happening...most of what we did happened before 1992.' (Head of Strategy, international chocolate company.)

Figure 13.2.3. Percentage of chocolate production represented by exports (%)

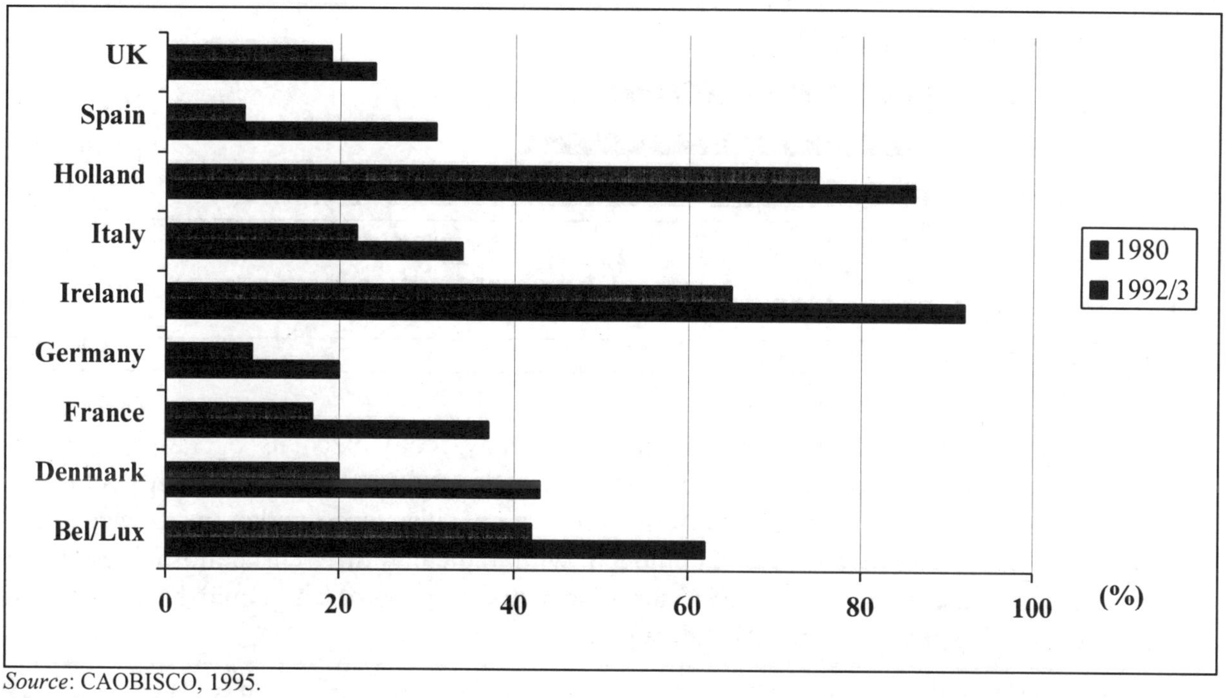

UK
Spain
Holland
Italy
Ireland
Germany
France
Denmark
Bel/Lux
0 20 40 60 80 100 (%)
1980
1992/3

Source: CAOBISCO, 1995.
NB: Bel/Lux = Benelux.

Industry globalization and concentration were major trends. Hershey acquired the US business of Cadbury-Schweppes in 1988, while Nestlé and Philip Morris also had ambitious acquisition programmes globally. Europe is now concentrated around a small number of large groupings. In 1989 Nestlé acquired Rowntree, while Kraft (Philip Morris) acquired Jacobs Suchard in 1990 and Terrys (UK) in 1993. Figure 13.2.4 shows the extent of this phenomenon. One recent study[89] counted 295 changes of ownership in Europe in the period 1990–95 and concluded that 53% of these involved a cross-border transaction. Five suppliers (Nestlé, Kraft/Jacobs Suchard, Mars, Cadbury and Ferrero) control 81% of the European market for chocolate confectionery. Several case studies of the European confectionery market also strongly suggest that this spate of activity was influenced by the prospect of a

88 HAA interviews with industry participants.
89 de Reuver, T. [1996], 'Concentration of the European Snack and Confectionery Industry', *The Manufacturing Confectioner*, January.

single market, although the consensus is that this accelerated a trend already in place rather than caused it to occur in the first place.[90]

Figure 13.2.4. Acquisitions, mergers, joint ventures and MBOs in the European snacks and confectionery industry (1990–95)

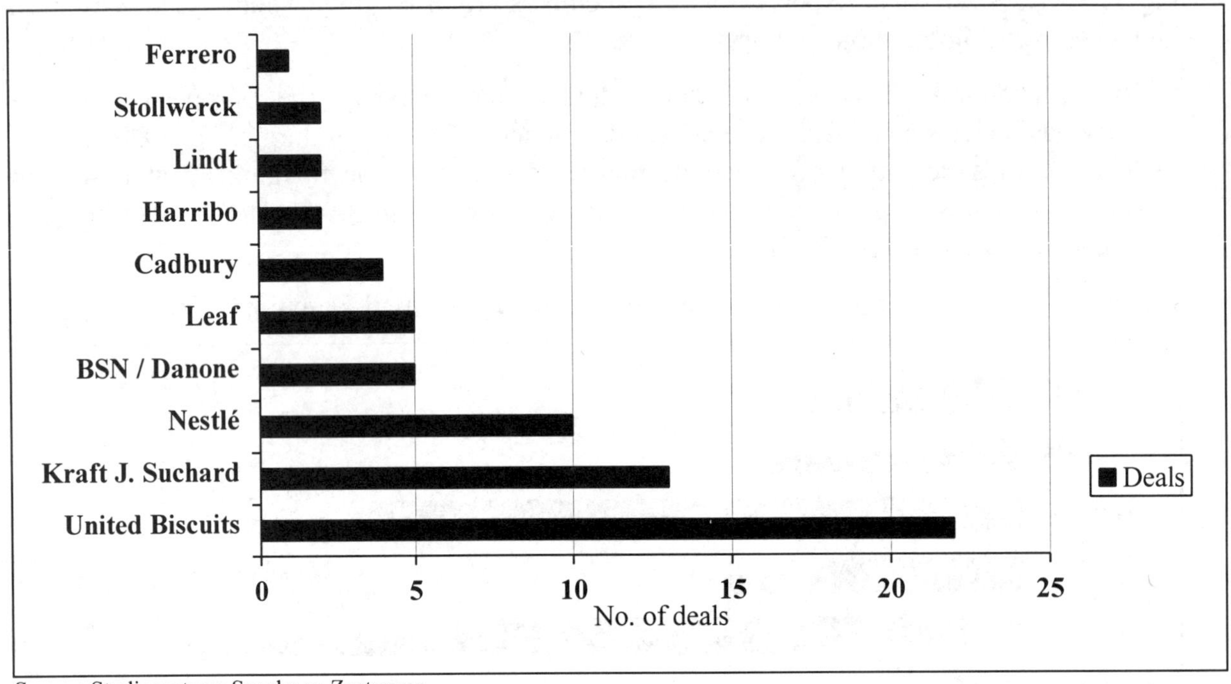

Source: Studiecentrum Snacks en Zoetwaren.

Nevertheless, Jacobs Suchard, for example, completely reorganized its operating structure from a number of autonomous national units to a more unified structure which could take advantage of larger scale, eliminate some production sites, and market its brands more globally.[91] Both Nestlé and Mars, although with radically different philosophies about globalization,[92] also took advantage of the ease with which products could be transported within the EU to streamline and rationalize production.

Last but not least, the recent growth in the chocolate and confectionery market is attributed by some industry observers[93] to a more pan-European trend to snacking and a breakdown of traditional meal-taking structures. Especially among the young, this trend is encouraged by the manufacturers through advertising and promotion. It is industry 'lore' that global or pan-European branding is more effective with younger consumers than older ones, and that '…you must "educate" the younger generation to newer habits of consumption' (Head of Exports, international confectionery manufacturer).

Rates of per capita chocolate consumption over time (Figure 13.2.5) show that there is some degree of convergence between the markets. The lower per capita consumption countries of southern Europe are now eating relatively more chocolate, and projections of these trends show much more rapid market growth in southern than in northern Europe (Figure 13.2.6).

90 HAA interviews.
91 Harvard Business School.
92 See below.
93 Euromonitor, HAA interviews.

Figure 13.2.5. Per capita chocolate consumption

Northern Europe
Average* Growth = 23 %

UK
NL
IRL
GER
FR
DK
BL/LX
0 1 2 3 4 5 6 7 8

Southern Europe
Average* Growth = 58 %

Portugal **
Spain
Italy
0 0.5 1 1.5 2 2.5
kilo /pc /pa

1980 1993

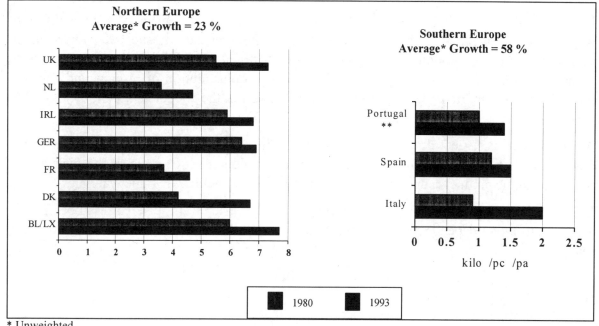

* Unweighted.
** HAA estimates.
Source: CAOBISCO, 1995.

Figure 13.2.6. Index of forecast sales value (1994–97)

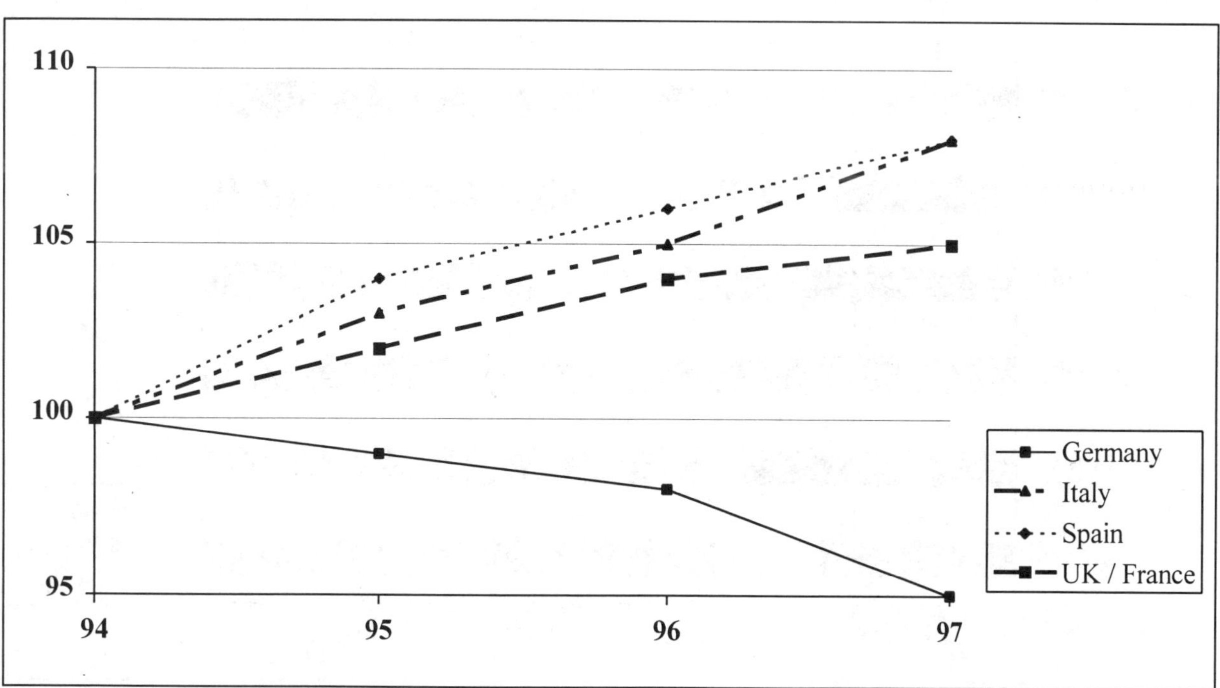

Source: Market Research Europe, HAA estimates.

13.3. Remaining barriers to the establishment of a single market

13.3.1. Structural barriers

There are two principal kinds of structural barriers in the chocolate confectionery market which we have already touched upon in earlier sections of this chapter. The first barrier relates to variations in national or local consumption habits and patterns of behaviour; the second relates to distribution channels.

Figures 13.1.3 and 13.2.5 show that chocolate confectionery is consumed in very different ways on a per capita basis in EU Member States. For instance, in the UK people eat on average six times the amount of chocolate eaten in Portugal. In addition, chocolate competes with other kinds of confectionery: in southern Europe consumption of biscuits and cakes is relatively more important (see Figure 13.3.1). Even within the chocolate sector, there are big variations by type of chocolate consumed (Table 13.3.1).

As a consequence, and despite the convergence in taste patterns, the economics of the business are likely to be different. There are fewer economies of scale in the distribution process, and the product cannot be marketed or positioned in quite the same way.

It is also the case that distribution structures tend to be different in different Member States. When distribution depends more on smaller outlets than large grocery chains there are three major consequences:

(a) prices charged to the customers are less uniform;
(b) retail margins tend to be higher;
(c) impulse purchases tend to be greater;
(d) consumers' ability or desire for comparative shopping is lower.[94]

Figure 13.3.1. Per capita consumption of confectionery items

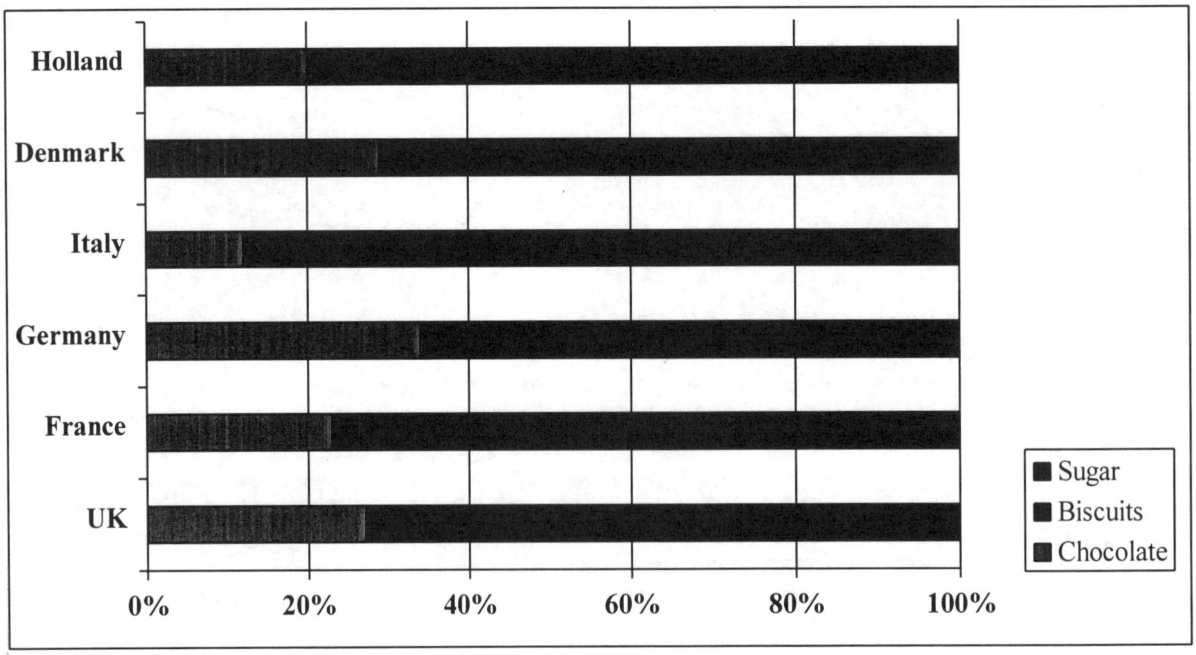

Source: BISCOFA, 1992.

[94] Interviews with industry participants.

Table 13.3.1. Market shares of chocolate by type (1993) (%)

	UK	Germany	France	Italy	EU12
Countlines	68	31	35	36	44
Blocks / Bars	14	40	46	24	31
Boxes / Bags	13	17	17	29	17
Other	6	13	3	11	8

Source: Nestlé, Brillat-Savarin; Horack, Adler & Associates.

13.3.2. Behavioural barriers

The major behavioural challenge to the single market derives from the different strategies adopted by the major manufacturers. Table 13.3.2 summarizes the operating configuration of some of the major players in the business. Firms like Mars and Ferrero have strategies which emphasize global or pan-European brands. Their marketing and advertising tend to be consistent across countries and their production and manufacturing strategies are more homogeneous. In contrast, Nestlé has formed a 'multi-country' approach which allows local managers far more autonomy in decisions about branding, positioning and even manufacturing.[95]

Table 13.3.2. Operating configuration of major chocolate companies operating in Europe

	Cadbury	Ferrero	Lindt & Sprungli	Mars	Kraft Jacobs Suchard	Nestlé
Business outside home market	46%	65%	30%	~ 100%	~ 95%	~95%
Production facilities	UK, IRL, F, E, NL, D	I, D, B	CH, D, F	UK, NL, D, F, A	CH, B, D, F, UK, I, E	CH, D, F, B, E, GR, I, NL, P, IRL, UK
% Confectionery of sales	45%	95%	100%	50%	10%	15%
Share of EU chocolate market	8%	13%	-	11%	12%	15%
World-wide rank in chocolate	5	4	~7	3	2	1
Some major brands	Dairy Milk Fruit & Nut Wispa Crunchie Flake	Ferrero Rocher Kinder	Lindt	M & M Mars Snickers Twix Milky Way	Milka Suchard Toblerone Terry's Freia Marabou	Rowntree Kit-Kat Perugina Bouquet d'Or Smarties

Source: Horack, Adler & Associates.

95 Interviews with industry participants.

A further consideration relates to pricing policy. In general, the greater the penetration of the larger multi-national brands, the more price discipline is imposed on local manufacturers who need to position their products taking competition into account. As one industry participant said: 'Consumers still look at value...price per kilo of chocolate. If we cost more than a Mars Bar, we suffer' (large international confectionery company).

In addition, the manufacturers are conscious of the arbitrage opportunities open to distributors if prices for the same product vary too much country by country.

As a result, there is greater price regularity in markets with concentrated distribution and high penetration of major international brands, and less regularity in the opposite case. The manufacturers also have more freedom to price differently in these less structured markets.

Inter-company pricing strategy also plays a role. If products are manufactured in one location and transported to another, and if the company requires all local subsidiaries to generate similar margins, then smaller, more distant markets will have higher prices. This accounts for a large part of the price disparities for some otherwise globally marketed brands.[96]

Figure 13.3.2. Confectionery cost structure (% of selling price)

10 %	**Trading Profit**
20 %	**Marketing & Sales** (of which Advertising, 5% - 8%)
5 %	**Distribution**
20 %	**Production**
10 %	**Packaging**
35 %	**Raw Materials**

Source: 'Nestlé Takes over Rowntree' (EMJ March 1991) Horack, Adler & Associates.

Advertising and marketing expenses are a significant factor in positioning brands and protecting brand shares. On average, marketing and sales costs are thought to be about 20% of costs (Figure 13.3.2) and advertising accounts for 5–8% of this.[97] Industry sources do not see the advertising costs increasing dramatically since the inception of the single market, but refer to them instead as 'creeping up slowly'.

More significant, perhaps, is the effort expended on research and development: 'The impact has not been that we necessarily spend more on R&D, but the focus has changed. For example, we used to invest a lot in trying to make cheaper products. More recently, we spent

96 Industry interviews.
97 Interviews.

money on quality. Now, it is all about innovation and new products' (Product Manager, international confectionery company).

As a consequence, there is a simultaneous tendency towards producer concentration and brand fragmentation as the majors seek to develop new categories and create new niches. This, in turn, leads to greater price dispersion.

13.3.3. Policy barriers

The most significant barrier to the single market at a policy level remains the distinction between Member States on the use of cocoa butter substitutes. Completely free trade is impeded by the fact that, over the period considered, in seven out of 15 Member States, substitutes were permitted, and in the remaining they were prohibited. The question of the reform of the 1973 Directive[98] has long remained a political 'hot potato'.

According to industry sources, the existence of two quite distinct regimes for chocolate manufacturers has three consequences:

(a) manufacturing costs are increased because production lines cannot be fully rationalized;

(b) other costs also increase because of labelling on wrappers which show recipes are different;

(c) consumers in some countries pay more for essentially the same product because ingredient costs differ (vegetable substitutes are less expensive than chocolate).

Table 13.3.3. Continuing barriers to the single market in chocolate confectionery

Structural	Behavioural	Policy
National consumption, habits and preferences	Company strategy not always pan-European	CBS variations in national markets
Per capita consumption	Local market strengths	Advertising and promotion rules different, especially for children
Type of chocolate preferred	Branding / advertising	VAT rates not uniform
Social 'role' of snacks in diet	Product positioning	
Distribution and retail systems	Innovation and product development	
Climate	Uniform profit targets imply local price variations	

Source: Horack, Adler & Associates.

The second major policy barrier revolves around advertising and promotion. This is seen as particularly acute for products which are frequently aimed at children and where national regulations are extremely variable.

98 Council Directive 73/241/EEC of 24 July 1973 on the approximation of the laws of the Member States relating to cocoa and chocolate products intended for human consumption (OJ L 228, 16.8.1973, p. 23).

'This is a serious barrier, because we cannot have unified advertising and promotion across countries. Everywhere it is different and this causes significant costs in time, legal fees, production of commercials and promotional materials, and management effort' (Product Manager, confectionery company).

The arguments in this section of the report are summarized in Table 13.3.3.

The consequence of this array of structural, behavioural and policy barriers, together with the countervailing forces produced by the Single European Act and a number of global trends in the industry, seems to have resulted in the 'triple market' structure we outlined in the first part of this chapter.

APPENDIX A

About the data

A.1. General description

The analysis of price convergence across regions and over time is done using price indices for 174 goods and services categories provided by Eurostat.

Among the 174 goods and services categories, are:

(a) consumer goods, of which:
  (i) 51 food and drink products,
  (ii) 2 tobacco products,
  (iii) 8 clothing and footwear products,
  (iv) 24 durable goods,
  (v) 18 other manufactured goods;

(b) services;

(c) energy products;

(d) equipment goods;

(e) construction categories.

A detailed list of all these products and services is presented in Appendix C. The price indices data supplied to DRI by Eurostat covers the years 1980, 1985, 1990 and 1993. The price indices database provided to DRI is put together by Eurostat based on the survey of price levels for a wide variety of goods and services (identified as basic headings) conducted at regular intervals with the help of the EU Member States' statistical institutes. Eurostat has devised a method to ensure the greatest degree of comparability between headings across countries when performing the surveys. For each EU Member State, the prices collected are representative of the whole of the national territory and correspond to an annual average.[99]

Two important features of the price indices supplied by Eurostat must be underlined: [100]

(a) The series consist of national price indices as compared to the EU-12 average, and not price levels. Detailed price levels could not be made available to DRI for confidentiality reasons. For each Member State, each product/service and each year considered, the price index is calculated in such a way as to be equal to 100 if the observed price is equal to the EU-12 average. This means that it is possible to compare changes in price dispersion between years but it is impossible to compare changes in price levels over time (in other words, it is possible to say whether prices have converged over time but impossible to say whether they have converged towards a

[99] The price levels collected in the surveys also form the basis for calculating purchasing power parities.

[100] For a detailed description of the methods employed by Eurostat in collecting prices data, see Eurostat [1995], *Comparison in real terms of the aggregates of ESA, results for 1992 and 1993.*

higher or a lower average level). DRI did not receive the weights which were used to calculate the average EU-12 price for each product category.

(b) The indices are based on prices inclusive of taxes (both VAT and excise duties) for consumption goods and services and net of deductible VAT in the case of equipment goods and construction. It is to be noted that, in a few cases, price indices for equipment goods could be distorted by other indirect taxes, but the problem ought to be relatively inconsequential so that Eurostat data have been used without further manipulations. This is also the decision that was made in the 1988 European Commission study on price convergence.[101] For consumer goods, DRI calculated price indices net of taxes using a special procedure which is outlined in Appendix B. Given that the integration of European economies translated into both the removal of trade and competition hindering barriers and the harmonization of indirect taxation, dispersion in prices inclusive of taxes as well as in prices net of taxes are worth investigating.

The availability of price levels would have made it possible to calculate prices net of taxes and net of excise duties in a more appropriate way, whereas the availability of the weights would have made it possible to calculate EU-6 and EU-9 average price levels. To calculate the price dispersion within the EU-6 and EU-9 countries, it would indeed have been preferable to recalculate all the price indices based on the EU-6 and EU-9 average price levels respectively, as opposed to the price indices in relation to the average EU-12 price level as has been done in this report.[102] The same holds for the EU-15.

The following describes the price collection methods used by Eurostat for the type of products and services analysed in our report.

A.1.1. Household consumer goods and services

For the purposes of the Eurostat comparison, the prices are collected by the national statistical institutes (NSIs) under the co-ordination of Eurostat. Responsibility for the work is assumed by a working party comprising representatives of the NSIs, which lays down the methodology to be followed, discusses the definitions of the products which make up the survey sample, and adopts the results after analysis of the surveys.

The sample is constructed in accordance with the principle of graduality, taking account of the following three criteria:

(a) representativeness;

(b) strict definitions in order to avoid distortions due to differences in quality;

(c) equi-characteristicity.

---

[101] See Commission of the European Communities [1988], 'The Economics of 1992', in *European Economy*, No 35, March 1988, Part D (The effects of market integration, p.118).

[102] In Commission of the European Communities [1988], 'The Economics of 1992', in *European Economy*, No 35, March 1988, Part D (The effects of market integration, p.118), the authors do not specify which weights have been used to calculate the average price figure for the EU-9. Weiss [1994], in his article 'Price differentials in Western Europe', in *EFTA Economic Affairs Department* (March), uses OECD data weighted by GDP in order to calculate an average EU-12 price figure of 100. He does not recalculate the indices at the EU-6 or EU-9 level, however, to compare the trend in price dispersion across broader geographical areas.

The products are defined on the basis of very strict equivalence criteria. Whenever possible, branded products are used for easy identification. In the other cases, the definitions are exhaustive and include all the factors that might influence prices and enable the product to be identified.

In order to guarantee the equi-characteristicity of the sample, each country must, when drawing up the list, propose at least one product characteristic of its own consumption for each elementary heading. At the end of the survey, when the country supplies the prices recorded, it also provides indications of characteristicity for the various products. This information is used in the calculation of the parities for the basic headings so as to guarantee equi-characteristicity.

The size of the sample is roughly 2,600 products. Each country does not have to record prices for the whole of the sample, and the number of products for which a price is given varies from one country to another. The surveys are carried out in the countries' capitals. As the target average price is that for the whole of the national territory, some countries supply spatial coefficients by group of products that can be used to convert the price in the capital to the national average price. For other countries, the average price in the capital is deemed to represent the national average. The Netherlands carries out the surveys in four major cities, thereby obtaining directly an average price representative of the whole of the national territory.

As the target average prices are the annual average prices for any reference year, the countries supply detailed monthly consumer price indices covering the 214 basic headings of consumption. On the basis of these indices, temporal coefficients are calculated in order to convert the average prices at the time of the survey to the annual average prices for the reference year.

The outlets where the prices are to be collected are selected by the national statistical institutes. However, this choice must be in keeping with the structure of national consumption at the various outlets, depending on the group of products in question. Accordingly, the prices recorded are automatically weighted in order to arrive at an average price representative of the country's consumption.

The outlets are divided into the following categories:

(a) department stores,

(b) supermarkets and hypermarkets,

(c) wholesale self-service (discount stores),

(d) specialized shops,

(e) open-air markets,

(f) service enterprises in the private sector,

(g) service enterprises in the public sector.

For each product, it is difficult to give precise instructions regarding the number of price quotations to be recorded, owing to the characteristics specific to the various countries and the product itself. General guidelines are, however, drawn up. Accordingly, for products with a unique price, one price quotation is sufficient. For the others, the degree of price dispersion and the degree of availability of the product should have an effect on the number of price quotations.

A.1.2. Specific area: health

The comparison of health expenditure calls for special attention as regards the concepts used and price collection.

The problem in this case is closely linked to the concepts used in the national accounts, particularly the distinction between household final consumption expenditure, government final consumption expenditure or private non-profit institutions. It is merely pointed out that, for calculating purchasing power parities in accordance with the ICP classification, all health expenditure is lumped together and transferred to the actual individual final consumption.

At present, the following information is collected for calculating the parities:

(a) Market prices are collected for medical and pharmaceutical products, therapeutic appliances and equipment, and the services of physicians, nurses and related practitioners. In most of the countries, the prices are those actually charged; in others, they are estimated. These estimates are fairly reasonable for two groups (medical products and therapeutic equipment), but very difficult for certain parts of a third group when there is no payment for services rendered.

(b) In the case of hospital care, the approach adopted is based on the prices of the 'inputs'. Even in those countries where the hospitals have scales of charges, the prices are often heavily subsidized by government. Purely private clinics are of limited importance in all the countries. Expenditure in hospitals has been subdivided into three large groups: compensation of employees, intermediate consumption and depreciation. For the first of these, data on wage costs for twelve different types of jobs (doctors, paramedical staff, administrative staff) have been collected.

The input price approach is based on the assumption that services not sold at market prices have a value equal to the value of production estimated on the basis of the costs incurred. It is implicitly assumed that productivity is identical in all the countries – an assumption that shows the limitations of this approach. In actual fact, productivity depends not only on factors such as the quality of the staff but also on the whole equipment infrastructure placed at their disposal.

For comparing these services, Eurostat has considered using an approach based on indicators of physical output. A preliminary study has shown the advantages of such an approach, but has not given rise to an operational definition of a methodology that can replace the one currently used. The search for such a solution is still one of Eurostat's objectives.

A.1.3. Equipment goods

For equipment goods the detailed description of the technical characteristics is absolutely essential to ensure precise identification of each product. For almost every product there is a more or less wide range of different versions on the market, from the very simple to the highly sophisticated machine, and the description of each product on the basis of a number of characteristics prevents any risk of confusion between the different versions of a product or between the products themselves.

The technical characteristics must refer above all to performance data (capacity, speed, power, size, output, etc.), operating data (hydraulic controls, number of speeds, power source used, etc.) and data relating to the quality of the machine (steel quality, weight of the machine, precision of work). The performance data are the most important and are absolutely binding, i.e. they should be the same in all countries, whereas the others may be interpreted with some flexibility.

For a large number of products it is also necessary to define additional characteristics, such as details of accessories to be included in the price, as well as the terms of payment, any installation costs, after-sales service and the number of products purchased. In the case of equipment goods, 150 products are included in the list.

The prices supplied must tally with the prices which form the basis for the values that make up gross fixed capital formation in the national accounts, i.e. the purchase prices actually paid by the purchaser of a fixed capital good. This price includes distribution costs, any installation costs and the amount of non-deductible VAT, but excludes any rebates given.

The price must also reflect the level of average prices in the whole of the national territory; this condition is fairly easy to meet since, for most products, the market is dominated by a large national producer or a large international firm which sells its product on the same terms throughout the country or which can provide information on any differences in prices which it applies.

As it would be too costly to record prices at several dates during the year, the work of obtaining annual average prices is carried out on the assumption that variations in prices are spread uniformly throughout the year, and is limited to a single recording of prices in the middle of the year. Since there are no monthly indices covering the whole range of capital goods, this method cannot be checked or corrected.

The products are chosen according to the same criteria, namely representativeness of the products chosen within the group, characteristicity of the products chosen for the participating countries, strict definitions in order to ensure comparability between countries.

A.1.4. Construction and civil engineering

The major difficulty in this area stems from the fact that identical or comparable buildings do not exist, either within a country or, to an even lesser extent, in different countries. For the same type of building, there may be substantial differences as regards shape, size, location, finishing, materials used, etc.

For the purposes of international comparisons, a method has therefore been devised which involves defining a standard object and estimating the price as though it had actually been built. This method, known as the 'standard construction projects method', comprises the establishment, on the basis of a construction plan, of a detailed bill of quantities giving rise to the definition of a 'standard' construction, which forms the basis for the comparison.

First of all, a bill of quantities is usually broken down into a number of major components, such as earthworks, foundations, masonry, joinery, painting, etc. Each of these major components comprises a number of elementary components defining the construction work or operations specific to a given item by means of a precise description of the work to be carried out and the materials to be used. In accordance with this method, a wall, for example, is defined by the type of bricks (concrete, sand-lime, baked), their size, the finishing (joining, plastering, mortaring, number of coats of paint, wallpaper).

The description of each element on the basis of the materials/labour ratio leads to the determination of a quantity (m, m^2, m^3, kg), to which a unit price valid for this type of operation must be applied.

It is acknowledged that, as construction standards, regulations, materials and methods vary from country to country, a certain latitude of interpretation is necessary if the countries are to supply characteristic prices for the various projects. The general rule is that if the effect of complying to the letter with the specifications is that a material cannot be readily used or a special price study is necessary, the price of a more common material must be supplied, since the object of the exercise is to avoid non-representative prices.

The bills of quantities have been designed to be representative of actual constructions in the countries with regard to their shape and size, their finishing, their internal fittings and, to a lesser extent, to the construction materials and methods used. Since there is a close link between the construction methods adopted, and since both materials and methods vary between countries, variants for a number of components are included in the bills of quantities. When pricing components with variants, experts should attempt to price all the alternatives and indicate which of them corresponds best to the materials and methods most widely used in their respective countries.

The information on the characteristicity of each variant in the different countries is taken into account in the calculation of the parities for the basic headings.

As an example, the list for the 1993 Eurostat comparison comprises the following works:

(a) Residential buildings
One-family house – Detached house – Flat in an eight-storey block

(b) Non-residential buildings
Agricultural shed – Factory building – Office building – Primary school

(c) Civil engineering
Construction of a road – Construction of a concrete road – Main sewer – Sports field – Construction of a bridge.

The prices supplied must be the market prices actually paid by the principal. The price of a building includes such things as architect's fees, the rate of non-deductible VAT and a whole series of preliminary costs or building related costs, such as lawyer's fees, patent fees, special local taxes and installations for storing materials.

The unit prices used in the evaluation of buildings and works are derived from a large number of existing bills of quantities, submitted by construction enterprises when tendering for work;

they therefore constitute a good representative average. However, considerable divergences are generally observed in the invitations to tender and, instead of taking the invitations to tender, use is made of the average of the lowest prices which can still be regarded as realistic and enable the work to be carried out under normal conditions. This solution is, moreover, in keeping with standard practice on the construction market, where the extreme valuations, at either end of the scale, are discarded by the principals.

As in the case of equipment goods, the prices are recorded in the middle of the year (July), the assumption being that the prices at that date correspond to the annual average level of prices throughout the national territory and take regional differences into account.

A.2. Calculation of price dispersion coefficients

Price dispersion measures, defined as coefficients of variation of prices (standard deviation divided by the average), were calculated for each of the 174 product/service categories contained in the price indices database and for various subsets of products/services depending on the main characteristics of the market (see Chapter 6).

For each of the four years considered (1980, 1985, 1990, 1993), we have calculated:

(a) the coefficient of variation of prices based on price indices inclusive of taxes for the six founding EU Member States;

(b) the coefficient of variation of prices based on price indices inclusive of taxes for the nine EU Member States (the EU-6 plus Denmark, Ireland and the United Kingdom);

(c) the coefficient of variation of prices based on price indices inclusive of taxes for the 12 EU Member States (the EU-9 plus Greece, Portugal and Spain);

(d) the coefficient of variation of prices based on price indices inclusive of taxes for the 15 EU Member States (the EU-12 plus Austria, Finland and Sweden), but only for 1985, 1990 and 1993 as Sweden and Finland are not included in the price database in 1980;

(e) same as (a) with price indices net of VAT;

(f) same as (b) with price indices net of VAT;

(g) same as (c) with price indices net of VAT, but only for the last two years of data;

(h) same as (d) with price indices net of VAT, but only for the last two years of data;

(i) for the key products on which excise duties are applied, same as (e) based on prices net of VAT and net of excise duties;

(j) for the key products on which excise duties are applied, same as (f) based on prices net of VAT and net of excise duties.

Note that the calculation of coefficient of variation based on prices net of taxes was only done in all four years for the EU-9. For the EU-12 and EU-15, the prices net of taxes could only be estimated for the two latter years, 1990 and 1993. The indirect tax system in Spain, Portugal and Greece was indeed fairly complex before the adoption of the VAT system, as it was based on a number of sales taxes. In the absence of actual price levels and total sales figures for the same product categories, it was not possible to calculate precise price indices net of taxes for these three countries before 1990.

Note that the entry of Spain and Portugal into the EU in 1986 means that observed price convergence between these two countries and the rest of Europe may be a consequence of entry as much as a result of the single market programme. To a lesser extent, this also applies to Greece, at least over the period 1985–90.

A.3. Questionable data points

DRI has observed a few questionable data points in the price indices database provided by Eurostat. A suspicious data point is defined as a price index for a single product/service category in a specific country which shows in one of the four years covered in the database (1980, 1985, 1990 and 1993), an 'abnormal' behaviour relative to the preceding or following price index for the same category and country. Anomalous data points were identified using the following criteria:

(a) for 1980: a price index which precedes an increase or decrease of 150%, or an increase or decrease of 125 in absolute terms;

(b) for 1985, 1990 and 1993: a price index which represents an increase or decrease of 150% from the preceding price index, or an increase or decrease of 125 in absolute terms from the preceding price index.

In addition, if a price index for a product/service met the above criteria in a country, it was verified if the data point in question changed the trend observed from 1980 to 1993 for that product/service in that specific country. If it was found that it altered the trend, it was considered as a dubious data point.

17 products/services satisfy these quantitative and qualitative criteria and, thus, are considered as questionable price indices. They are the following:

(a) children's clothing in Denmark in 1980 (13.6);
(b) town gas and natural gas in Greece in 1980 (1.7);
(c) cigarettes in Portugal in 1980 (316.4);
(d) other tobacco products in Portugal in 1980 (544.3);
(e) cleaning equipment in Portugal in 1980 (331.8);
(f) other paramedical services in Germany (246.4), Greece (235.9) and Portugal (117.1) in 1985;
(g) legal services in Germany (209.8) and Denmark (244.7) in 1985;
(h) trains and railway equipment in Luxembourg in 1985 (18.1);
(i) repairs to heating, washing and kitchen appliances in Ireland in 1985 (260.7);
(j) books, brochures and similar printed matters in Denmark in 1985 (255.9);
(k) cookers and stoves in Portugal in 1985 (211.2);
(l) nurses services in Portugal in 1985 (187.6);
(m) repairs to furniture, furnishings and floorings in Ireland in 1993 (143.1);
(n) tea in Spain in 1993 (282.6).

A request was sent to Eurostat to verify these data points, but Eurostat has reported that it is not in a position to change these data points which come from the surveys.

In order to verify if these dubious price indices have an impact on the results of the price convergence analysis presented in this report, a correction was applied to these data points and new coefficients of price variation were calculated using the 'corrected' price indices. The method used to correct the 17 questionable price indices consisted in replacing them by the weighted average price index of their product/service category (excluding the suspect price index) in the year considered. For instance, the price index for children's clothing in Denmark in 1980 was replaced by the average price index for the clothing and footwear products category in Denmark in 1980, calculated excluding children's clothing.

The new coefficients of price dispersion resulting from the correction procedure were found not to affect the results presented in the report. These coefficients of variation are available from DRI upon request. The inclusion of the corrected price dispersion coefficients in the analytical framework of Chapter 3 does not alter the trends in price dispersion across regions (EU-6, EU-9, EU-12) and over time (from 1980 to 1993) for broad product and service categories. The corrected coefficients of price variation also do not change conclusions reached in Chapter 4 about price convergence/divergence patterns for detailed products and services. For these reasons, it was decided to use the original Eurostat price indices for the above mentioned 17 products/services in the analysis without correcting them.

APPENDIX B

Methodology for the calculation of price dispersion indices net of taxes

The calculation of prices net of VAT is, in theory, relatively simple. Given the *ad valorem* nature of VAT, the only information required is the VAT rate in each of the years considered. The problem is, however, somewhat more complicated as some of the consumption items listed in Appendix C cover elementary products subject to different VAT rates. Normally, the procedure should be to deduct VAT from the prices at the most disaggregated level (i.e. basic products) and then to recalculate price dispersion indices net of VAT for each consumption item. For confidentiality reasons, however, DRI could not receive the necessary detailed price level data, nor has Eurostat calculated the dispersion indices net of taxes themselves, as had been the case in 1988 when the Commission did the first study of price dispersion. To solve the problem, DRI proceeded in the following way.

First of all, DRI has collected all the information on VAT rates and structure in each of the years considered (1980, 1985, 1990 and 1993) directly from the national tax authorities, at the greatest possible level of detail. Using this information and the description of the 174 product/service categories listed in Appendix C, DRI was then able to recalculate a set of price indices net of VAT by deducting the VAT rate from the price index of each product/service.

The calculation of prices net of excise duties has been substantially more complicated. For excise duties based on an *ad valorem* basis the method used for VAT has been applied. However, excise duties are frequently expressed on a non *ad valorem* basis (for instance, as a function of alcoholic strength, weight or any other physical unit). Ideally, information on both price levels and consumption value for very detailed product types should have been available to calculate the prices net of excise duty. This, again, was not possible. DRI has therefore collected information on tax revenue from excises at the greatest possible level of detail from the national tax authorities, and has collected information on consumer expenditure for the same items in order to calculate an implicit (ex post) *ad valorem* excise rate. This has then made it possible to calculate prices net of excise for selected consumer items (notably tobacco products, energy products and alcoholic beverages) in a similar way to that for VAT.

APPENDIX C

List of the 174 product/service categories and summary of aggregations

Code	Description	Basic	Second level	NTB	Tradeability	Intra-EC rate	Extra-EC rate	RD and ADV intensity
1111011	Rice	Cons. goods	Food	Low	Tradeables	Low	High	NotRD/ADV
1111012	Flour, other cereals	Cons. goods	Food	Low	Tradeables	Low	Low	NotRD/ADV
1111013	Bread	Cons. goods	Food	Low	Tradeables	Low	Low	NotRD/ADV
1111014	Cakes, biscuits	Cons. goods	Food	Low	Tradeables	Low	Low	NotRD/ADV
1111015	Pasta, noodles	Cons. goods	Food	High	Tradeables	Low	Low	NotRD/ADV
1111016	Other cereal based products	Cons. goods	Food	Low	Tradeables	Low	Low	NotRD/ADV
1111021	Beef	Cons. goods	Food	Low	Tradeables	Low	Low	NotRD/ADV
1111022	Veal	Cons. goods	Food	Low	Tradeables	Low	Low	NotRD/ADV
1111023	Pork	Cons. goods	Food	Low	Tradeables	Low	Low	NotRD/ADV
1111024	Mutton, lamb and goat meat	Cons. goods	Food	Low	Tradeables	Low	Low	NotRD/ADV
1111025	Poultry	Cons. goods	Food	Low	Tradeables	Low	Low	ADV
1111026	Delicatessen	Cons. goods	Food	Low	Tradeables	Low	Low	NotRD/ADV
1111027	Meat preparations, other meat products	Cons. goods	Food	Low	Tradeables	Low	Low	NotRD/ADV
1111028	Other fresh or frozen meat	Cons. goods	Food	Low	Tradeables	Low	Low	NotRD/ADV
1111031	Fresh, frozen fish	Cons. goods	Food	Low	Tradeables	Low	High	NotRD/ADV
1111032	Dried or smoked fish	Cons. goods	Food	Low	Tradeables	Low	High	NotRD/ADV
1111033	Other seafood	Cons. goods	Food	Low	Tradeables	Low	High	NotRD/ADV
1111034	Preserved, prepared fish and other seafood	Cons. goods	Food	Low	Tradeables	Low	High	NotRD/ADV
1111041	Fresh milk	Cons. goods	Food	Low	Tradeables	Low	Low	ADV
1111042	Preserved milk	Cons. goods	Food	Low	Tradeables	Low	Low	ADV
1111043	Other milk products, except cheese	Cons. goods	Food	Low	Tradeables	Low	Low	ADV
1111044	Cheese	Cons. goods	Food	Low	Tradeables	Low	Low	ADV
1111045	Eggs	Cons. goods	Food	Low	Tradeables	Low	Low	ADV
1111051	Butter	Cons. goods	Food	Low	Tradeables	Low	Low	ADV
1111052	Margarine	Cons. goods	Food	Low	Tradeables	Low	High	ADV
1111053	Edible oils	Cons. goods	Food	Low	Tradeables	Low	High	ADV
1111054	Other animal or vegetable fats	Cons. goods	Food	Low	Tradeables	Low	High	ADV
1111061	Fresh fruits	Cons. goods	Food	Low	Tradeables	High	High	ADV
1111062	Dried fruits	Cons. goods	Food	Low	Tradeables	High	High	ADV
1111063	Fruits frozen, preserved, and as juice	Cons. goods	Food	Low	Tradeables	High	High	ADV
1111064	Fresh vegetables	Cons. goods	Food	Low	Tradeables	High	High	ADV
1111065	Dried vegetables	Cons. goods	Food	Low	Tradeables	High	High	ADV
1111066	Frozen vegetables	Cons. goods	Food	Low	Tradeables	High	High	ADV
1111067	Vegetables preserved, prepared, soups	Cons. goods	Food	Low	Tradeables	Low	Low	ADV
1111071	Potatoes	Cons. goods	Food	Low	Tradeables	High	High	ADV
1111072	Products derived from potatoes	Cons. goods	Food	Low	Tradeables	High	High	ADV
1111081	Sugar	Cons. goods	Food	Low	Tradeables	Low	Low	NotRD/ADV
1111091	Coffee	Cons. goods	Beverages	Low	Tradeables	Low	Low	ADV
1111092	Tea	Cons. goods	Beverages	Low	Tradeables	Low	Low	ADV
1111093	Cocoa	Cons. goods	Beverages	High	Tradeables	Low	Low	ADV
1111101	Jams, marmalades, honey, syrups	Cons. goods	Food	Low	Tradeables	Low	Low	ADV
1111102	Chocolate	Cons. goods	Food	High	Tradeables	Low	Low	ADV
1111103	Confectionery	Cons. goods	Food	High	Tradeables	Low	Low	ADV
1111104	Ice cream	Cons. goods	Food	Low	Tradeables	Low	Low	ADV
1111105	Condiments, sauces, spices,salt	Cons. goods	Food	Low	Tradeables	Low	Low	ADV
1112011	Mineral water	Cons. goods	Beverages	High	Tradeables	Low	Low	ADV
1112012	Other soft drinks	Cons. goods	Beverages	High	Tradeables	Low	Low	ADV
1113011	Alcohol	Cons. goods	Beverages	Low	Tradeables	Low	Low	ADV
1113012	Wine	Cons. goods	Beverages	High	Tradeables	Low	Low	ADV
1113013	Beer	Cons. goods	Beverages	High	Tradeables	Low	Low	ADV
1113014	Other alcoholic drinks	Cons. goods	Beverages	Low	Tradeables	Low	Low	NA
1114011	Cigarettes	Cons. goods	Tobacco	Low	Tradeables	Low	Low	ADV
1114021	Other tobacco products	Cons. goods	Tobacco	Low	Tradeables	Low	Low	ADV
1121011	Men's clothing	Cons. goods	Clothing and footwear	Medium	Tradeables	Low	High	NotRD/ADV

Code	Description	Basic	Second level	NTB	Tradeability	Intra-EC rate	Extra-EC rate	RD and ADV intensity
1121012	Women's clothing	Cons. goods	Clothing and footwear	Medium	Tradeables	Low	High	NotRD/ADV
1121013	Children's clothing (age 3 to 13 years)	Cons. goods	Clothing and footwear	Medium	Tradeables	Low	High	NotRD/ADV
1121014	Babies' clothing (age 0 to 2 years)	Cons. goods	Clothing and footwear	Medium	Tradeables	Low	High	NotRD/ADV
1121015	Clothing accessories	Cons. goods	Clothing and footwear	Medium	Tradeables	Low	High	NotRD/ADV
1121021	Repairs to clothing	Services	Services	NA	Non Tradeables	NA	NA	NA
1122011	Men's footwear	Cons. goods	Clothing and footwear	Medium	Tradeables	High	High	NotRD/ADV
1122012	Women's footwear	Cons. goods	Clothing and footwear	Medium	Tradeables	High	High	NotRD/ADV
1122013	Children's and babies' footwear	Cons. goods	Clothing and footwear	Medium	Tradeables	High	High	NotRD/ADV
1122021	Repairs to footwear	Services	Services	NA	Non Tradeables	NA	NA	NA
1131013	General household maintenance costs	Services	Services	NA	Non Tradeables	NA	NA	NA
1131021	Water distribution charges	Services	Services	NA	Non Tradeables	NA	NA	NA
1132011	Electricity	Energy	Energy	NA	Tradeables	Low	Low	NA
1132021	Town gas and natural gas	Energy	Energy	NA	Tradeables	Low	Low	NA
1132022	Liquefied gas	Energy	Energy	NA	Tradeables	Low	Low	NA
1132031	Heating oil and other heating fuels	Energy	Energy	NA	Tradeables	Low	Low	NA
1132041	Coal, coke and other solid combustibles	Energy	Energy	NA	Tradeables	Low	Low	NA
1141011	Furniture and furnishing accessories	Cons. goods	Durable goods	Low	Tradeables	Low	Low	NotRD/ADV
1141012	Floor coverings	Cons. goods	Durable goods	Medium	Tradeables	High	High	NotRD/ADV
1141021	Repairs to furniture, furnishings, floorings	Services	Services	NA	Non Tradeables	NA	NA	NA
1142011	Household textiles	Cons. goods	Durable goods	Medium	Tradeables	NA	NA	NA
1142021	Repairs to household textiles	Services	Services	NA	Non Tradeables	NA	NA	NA
1143011	Refrigerators, freezers	Cons. goods	Durable goods	Medium	Tradeables	High	Low	RD/ADV
1143012	Washing machines, tumble dryers	Cons. goods	Durable goods	Medium	Tradeables	High	Low	RD/ADV
1143013	Cookers and stoves	Cons. goods	Durable goods	Medium	Tradeables	High	Low	RD/ADV
1143014	Heating and air conditioning appliances	Cons. goods	Durable goods	Medium	Tradeables	High	Low	RD/ADV
1143015	Cleaning equipment	Cons. goods	Durable goods	Medium	Tradeables	High	Low	RD/ADV
1143016	Other household appliances	Cons. goods	Durable goods	Medium	Tradeables	High	Low	RD/ADV
1143021	Repairs to heating, washing, kitchen appliances	Services	Services	NA	Non Tradeables	NA	NA	NA
1144011	Glassware and tableware	Cons. goods	Durable goods	Low	Tradeables	High	Low	NotRD/ADV
1144012	Cutlery	Cons. goods	Durable goods	Low	Tradeables	Low	Low	NotRD/ADV
1144013	Non-electrical kitchen and household utensils	Cons. goods	Durable goods	Low	Tradeables	NA	NA	NA
1144014	Gardening equipment	Cons. goods	Durable goods	Low	Tradeables	NA	NA	NA
1144015	Light bulbs and electrical accessories	Cons. goods	Other manufact.	High	Tradeables	NA	NA	RD
1144021	Repairs to glassware, tableware, household utensils	Services	Services	NA	Non Tradeables	NA	NA	NA
1145011	Cleaning and maintenance products	Cons. goods	Other manufact.	Low	Tradeables	Low	Low	RD/ADV
1145012	Other non-durable household articles	Cons. goods	Other manufact.	Low	Tradeables	NA	NA	NA
1145021	Laundry and dry cleaning services	Services	Services	NA	Non Tradeables	NA	NA	NA
1145022	Other household services	Services	Services	NA	Non Tradeables	NA	NA	NA
1146011	Domestic services	Services	Services	NA	Non Tradeables	NA	NA	NA
1151011	Medicines	Cons. goods	Other manufact.	High	Tradeables	Low	Low	RD/ADV
1151021	Other pharmaceutical products	Cons. goods	Other manufact.	High	Tradeables	Low	Low	RD/ADV

1152011	Lenses and glasses	Cons. goods	Other manufact.	Low	Tradeables	High	High	RD/ADV
1152021	Orthopaedic, therapeutic appliances and products	Cons. goods	Other manufact.	High	Tradeables	High	High	RD
1153011	General practitioner medical services	Services	Services	NA	Non Tradeables	NA	NA	NA
1153021	Specialist medical services	Services	Services	NA	Non Tradeables	NA	NA	NA
1153031	Dental services	Services	Services	NA	Non Tradeables	NA	NA	NA
1153041	Nurse services	Services	Services	NA	Non Tradeables	NA	NA	NA
1153051	Other medical and paramedical services	Services	Services	NA	Non Tradeables	NA	NA	NA
1161011	Motor vehicles	Cons. goods	Durable goods	Medium	Tradeables	High	Low	RD/ADV
1161021	Other modes of personal transport	Cons. goods	Durable goods	Low	Tradeables	High	High	RD
1162011	Tyres, inner tubes, replacement parts for motor vehicles	Cons. goods	Other manufact.	Low	Tradeables	High	Low	RD
1162012	Vehicle maintenance costs	Services	Services	NA	Non Tradeables	NA	NA	NA
1162021	Fuels and lubricants for motor vehicles	Cons. goods	Other manufact.	Low	Tradeables	Low	Low	NotRD/ADV
1162031	Other exp. related to personal transport	Services	Services	NA	Non Tradeables	NA	NA	NA
1163011	Local transport services	Services	Services	NA	Non Tradeables	NA	NA	NA
1163021	Railway and road transport services	Services	Services	NA	Non Tradeables	NA	NA	NA
1163022	Other transport services	Services	Services	NA	Non Tradeables	NA	NA	NA
1163031	Other expenses related to transport services	Services	Services	NA	Non Tradeables	NA	NA	NA
1164011	Postal services	Services	Services	NA	Non Tradeables	NA	NA	NA
1164021	Telephone, telegraph and telex services	Services	Services	NA	Non Tradeables	NA	NA	NA
1171011	Radio equipment	Cons. goods	Durable goods	Medium	Tradeables	High	High	RD/ADV
1171012	Televisions	Cons. goods	Durable goods	Medium	Tradeables	High	High	RD/ADV
1171013	Record players, tape and cassette recorders	Cons. goods	Durable goods	Medium	Tradeables	High	High	RD/ADV
1171021	Photographic and cinematographic equipment	Cons. goods	Durable goods	Medium	Tradeables	High	High	RD/ADV
1171022	Other important leisure durable goods (including personal computers)	Cons. goods	Durable goods	Medium	Tradeables	High	High	ADV
1171031	Records, cassettes, magnetic tapes and accessories	Cons. goods	Durable goods	Medium	Tradeables	High	High	RD/ADV
1171032	Sports equipment	Cons. goods	Durable goods	Medium	Tradeables	High	High	ADV
1171033	Games and toys	Cons. goods	Durable goods	Medium	Tradeables	High	High	ADV
1171034	Film and other photographic supplies	Cons. goods	Durable goods	Medium	Tradeables	High	High	RD/ADV
1171035	Flowers, other recreational goods	Cons. goods	Other manufact.	Low	Tradeables	NA	NA	NA
1171041	Repairs to recreational goods	Services	Services	NA	Non Tradeables	NA	NA	NA
1172011	Expenses for cultural events and activities	Services	Services	NA	Non Tradeables	NA	NA	NA
1172021	Expenses for sporting events and activities	Services	Services	NA	Non Tradeables	NA	NA	NA
1172022	Charges for radio, television use	Services	Services	NA	Non Tradeables	NA	NA	NA
1172023	Other services nec	Services	Services	NA	Non Tradeables	NA	NA	NA
1173011	Books, brochures, other similar printed matter	Cons. goods	Other manufact.	Low	Tradeables	Low	Low	NotRD/ADV
1173012	Periodicals, newspapers	Cons. goods	Other manufact.	Low	Tradeables	Low	Low	NotRD/ADV
1174011	Tuition costs	Services	Services	NA	Non Tradeables	NA	NA	NA
1181011	Hairdressers, beauticians and other similar services	Services	Services	NA	Non Tradeables	NA	NA	NA
1181021	Durable and semi-durable personal care products	Cons. goods	Other manufact.	Low	Tradeables	NA	NA	NA
1181022	Non-durable personal care products	Cons. goods	Other manufact.	Low	Tradeables	Low	Low	RD/ADV
1182011	Jewellery, watches, precious stones	Cons. goods	Other manufact.	Medium	Tradeables	Low	High	RD/ADV
1182021	Articles for travelling and personal luggage	Cons. goods	Other manufact.	Low	Tradeables	High	High	NotRD/ADV

Code	Description	Basic	Second level	NTB	Tradeability	Intra-EC rate	Extra-EC rate	RD and ADV intensity
1182031	Paper and drawing supplies	Cons. goods	Other manufact.	Low	Tradeables	Low	Low	NotRD/ADV
1183011	Expenditures in restaurants	Services	Services	NA	Non Tradeables	NA	NA	NA
1183012	Expenditures in cafés, bars	Services	Services	NA	Non Tradeables	NA	NA	NA
1183013	Expenditures in canteens	Services	Services	NA	Non Tradeables	NA	NA	NA
1183021	Hotels and other lodging expenses	Services	Services	NA	Non Tradeables	NA	NA	NA
1185011	Insurance, banking and other financial services	Services	Services	NA	Non Tradeables	NA	NA	NA
1186011	Legal services	Services	Services	NA	Non Tradeables	NA	NA	NA
1311011	Structural metal products	Equip. goods	Equip. goods	Low	Tradeables	Low	Low	NotRD/ADV
1311012	Products of boilermaking	Equip. goods	Equip. goods	High	Tradeables	Low	Low	NotRD/ADV
1311021	Tools and finished metal articles	Equip. goods	Equip. goods	Low	Tradeables	Low	Low	NotRD/ADV
1311031	Agricultural machinery and tractors	Equip. goods	Equip. goods	Medium	Tradeables	High	Low	RD/ADV
1311041	Machine tools for metal working	Equip. goods	Equip. goods	Medium	Tradeables	High	High	RD
1311051	Machinery/equipment for mining, metallurgy, building and civil engineering	Equip. goods	Equip. goods	Medium	Tradeables	High	Low	NotRD/ADV
1311061	Textile machinery	Equip. goods	Equip. goods	Medium	Tradeables	High	High	RD
1311062	Machinery for food, chemicals, rubber, packaging	Equip. goods	Equip. goods	Medium	Tradeables	High	Low	NotRD/ADV
1311063	Machinery for working wood, paper	Equip. goods	Equip. goods	Medium	Tradeables	High	High	RD
1311071	Other machinery and mechanical equipment	Equip. goods	Equip. goods	Medium	Tradeables	High	High	RD
1311081	Office and data processing machines	Equip. goods	Equip. goods	High	Tradeables	High	High	RD
1311091	Precision instruments	Equip. goods	Equip. goods	High	Tradeables	High	High	RD
1311092	Optical instr., photographic material	Equip. goods	Equip. goods	Low	Tradeables	High	High	RD/ADV
1312011	Electrical equipment including lighting	Equip. goods	Equip. goods	High	Tradeables	High	Low	RD
1312021	Telecommunications equipment, meters	Equip. goods	Equip. goods	High	Tradeables	Low	High	RD
1312022	Electronic equipment, radio and television	Equip. goods	Equip. goods	Low	Tradeables	High	High	RD/ADV
1313011	Motor vehicles and engines	Equip. goods	Equip. goods	Low	Tradeables	High	Low	RD/ADV
1313021	Ships	Equip. goods	Equip. goods	High	Tradeables	Low	Low	NotRD/ADV
1313022	Trains, railway equipment	Equip. goods	Equip. goods	High	Tradeables	Low	Low	RD
1313023	Aircraft, helicopters, aeronautical equipment	Equip. goods	Equip. goods	Medium	Tradeables	High	High	RD
1313024	Other transport equipment (bicycles, motorcycles, etc.)	Equip. goods	Equip. goods	Low	Tradeables	High	High	RD
1321011	Housing – one family	Construction	Construction	NA	Non Tradeables	NA	NA	NA
1321021	Housing – multi-family	Construction	Construction	NA	Non Tradeables	NA	NA	NA
1322011	Agricultural buildings	Construction	Construction	NA	Non Tradeables	NA	NA	NA
1322021	Industrial buildings	Construction	Construction	NA	Non Tradeables	NA	NA	NA
1322031	Commercial buildings	Construction	Construction	NA	Non Tradeables	NA	NA	NA
1322041	Non-commercial buildings	Construction	Construction	NA	Non Tradeables	NA	NA	NA
1323011	Roads, bridges, tunnels	Construction	Construction	NA	Non Tradeables	NA	NA	NA
1323021	Other communication works (other than roads, bridges, tunnels)	Construction	Construction	NA	Non Tradeables	NA	NA	NA

Source: DRI.

APPENDIX D

Test for the equality of price variances over time

Let us define s^2 as the sample variance used as an unbiased point estimator of the population variance σ^2. If a random sample of size n is selected from a normal population with variance σ^2, then $(n-1)s^2/\sigma^2$ follows a χ^2 distribution with $(n-1)$ degrees of freedom.

A two-sided confidence interval for the population variance σ^2 with confidence coefficient $1-a$, when the population is normal or approximately so, is of the form

$L<= \sigma^2 <= U$, where

$L = ((n-1)s^2) / (\chi^2(1-a/2;n-1))$ $\qquad$ $U = ((n-1)s^2) / (\chi^2(a/2;n-1))$

With 12 countries, $(n-1)=11$. Hence, for a 95% confidence interval for σ^2:

$L = (11s^2) / (\chi^2(.975;11)) = (11s^2) / (21.92)$ $\quad$ $U = (11s^2) / (\chi^2(.025,11)) = (11s^2) / (3.82)$

$=> L<= \sigma^2 <= U$ $\qquad$ $=> 3.82<= (n-1)s^2/ \sigma^2 <= 21.92$

If we want to test if the observed variance in 1985 equals the true variance σ^2, where σ^2 is the observed variance in 1993, then we can write on that basis a statistical test for the equality of variances over time:

H_0 : $\qquad$ if $3.82<= (n-1)s^2/ \sigma^2 <= 21.92$

H_1 : $\qquad$ if $(n-1)s^2/ \sigma^2 < 3.82$ or > 21.92

where s^2 is the observed variance in 1985.

The way the tests have been constructed - namely considering the variance in the last period of the sample as being the true variance - works against accepting significant divergence cases. In presence of divergence, $s^2 < \sigma^2$ hence the ratio $(n-1)s^2/ \sigma^2$ tends to be included between the two benchmarks.

The following hypotheses have been tested in Chapter 5.

var80 = var93
var85 = var93
var90 = var93
var80 = var85

APPENDIX E

Analysis of the convergence in sectoral producer price indices

E.1. Approach

As indicated in *The geographical dimension of competition in the European single market*,[103] if two geographical areas form part of the same market, or if they are in two markets linked together by possible arbitrage, then prices of identical products will be similar.[103]

The prices of the same product at the same horizontal stage in two places will indeed be equal if:

(a) customers are willing to transfer demand between suppliers on the basis of the price net of transport costs; and,

(b) are able to do it.

The first of these two conditions stresses the importance of transport costs (which vary between the EU-6, EU-9 and EU-12), as well as that of norms and standards, language barriers or differences in consumer behaviour in influencing the choice of a product.

Technically, the conditions for price uniformity can be expressed as follows.[103]

(a) There are no barriers to (or costs involved in) the transfer of demand between two places A and B, so that for any one product the cross-price-elasticity of demand between them is infinite. This condition is sufficient to bring about price equality even if there are major differences in the level and elasticity of demand for the product between the two areas.

(b) Each of a large number of competing suppliers has equal access to A and B, with no cost differences. If the price in A exceeded that in B, then supply to A would rise relatively to supply to B, causing price equality.

(c) Given monopoly or collusive oligopoly across both A and B, the price-elasticity of demand at any single price is the same in each area.

As the main objective of the single market programme was to create 'pan-European' markets by removing both tariff and non-tariff barriers across national and regional markets, another important way of assessing the degree to which this has taken place is to test the above three conditions.

Neither this nor the analysis of the trend in the coefficient of variation of detailed final product prices is, however, a 'sufficient' condition to demonstrate that EU markets have

[103] See Fishwick, F. and Denison, T. [1993], The geographical dimension of competition in the European single market, European Commission, Office for Official Publications of the EC, Luxembourg.

effectively become pan-European. These two analyses are nevertheless complementary and provide some basis to draw useful conclusions.

One can, indeed, think of a number of cases whereby price uniformity does not imply that the products/services are part of the same market (e.g. collusive prices, fixed resale prices). Conversely, one can think of a number of cases whereby the absence of price homogeneity does not mean that there are barriers to trade or that the market is not pan-European. Price differences for the same product in different geographic markets can, for instance, result from differences in the mode of commercialization (chain stores versus specialized shops) or from different marketing strategies. It is important to stress that parallel imports imply a uniform price across markets only if consumers view parallel imports as perfect substitutes for the same product bought domestically. And, in many product segments, there are national differences in brand names, packaging size, quality of products, or other factors which reflect different 'average' consumer preferences.

The literature cites two tests of 'degree of market integration', only one of which is really applicable in our case.

The first test is the Horowitz test. Horowitz suggested that geographical areas could be grouped into the same market if differences in price between the same products were tending to zero over time. Given the effects of inflation and common time trend, the Horowitz test is presented in terms of difference of logarithms rather than based on levels, and requires estimating the following equation:

$$(\log P_x - \log P_y)_t = a + b\,(\log P_x - \log P_y)_{t-1} + W_t \qquad (1)$$

where t is time, P_x is the price of the product in one market, P_y the price of the product in another market and W_t is the random variation.

However useful this calculation, it has been questioned on the basis of the fact that it implies that prices will converge at a decreasing rate, which contradicts what one would expect, namely that demand and supply substitution would both have an accelerating effect on the establishment of a common price.

In our particular case, an additional difficulty arises from the fact that this test requires continuous time series of price levels, something which is not readily available.

Another test has been suggested by Stigler and Sherwin (1985), which focuses not on absolute price levels but on simultaneous changes in prices. Because of common time trends reflecting technological change or inflation, serial correlation may be expected in models comparing price levels. Stigler and Sherwin therefore propose that the test for grouping either geographical areas or product ranges into the same markets should be the correlation between percentage changes in their prices (first difference in logarithms). The equation is thus defined as follows:

$$\Delta \log P\mathrm{x} = a + b\,(\Delta \log P\mathrm{y}) \qquad (2)$$

If markets are identical, the equation would yield values of a and b that would not be significantly different from 0 and 1 respectively.

Again, there are a few pitfalls in using this approach which have to be kept in mind when interpreting the results. These are:

(a) the fact that there can be a common influence on prices from costs of inputs, which can not necessarily be removed by the use of multiple regression because of collinearity problems;

(b) the fact that if both *a* and *b* are significantly different from 0 and 1 respectively, the results cannot be easily interpreted;

(c) if changes in the two series are correlated but the price level is still significantly different, the test can provide a misleading message. What is tested is market interdependence rather than market integration.

This test nevertheless has the advantage that it can be applied to time series of price indices, for similar product or service categories.

DRI has collected price indices over time from a number of statistical organizations, and also has producer price indices by Member State at the NACE 3-digit level (for manufacturing and construction only) from the Data for European Business Analysis database (DEBA).

Following the analysis of the overall trend in price convergence over time and across regions based on final product prices, the next step in the study has thus consisted in investigating the degree to which different national markets have effectively become more integrated into a pan-European market. This was done by calculating the Stigler–Sherwin index for the NACE 3-digit sectors, comparing each Member State's producer price trend to the EU average, since a multiple comparison of bilateral countries/regional groupings would provide information which is very difficult to interpret.

The results are then compared to the analysis of convergence of final product prices over time to identify similarities/differences and give an idea of the extent to which the convergence (or absence of convergence) of final product prices in the EU is explained by underlying changes at the sectoral level. In many cases, the differences can be attributed to developments having taken place at the distribution level.

E.2. Analysis of the convergence in sectoral producer price indices

This section presents the results of the estimation of the equation suggested by Stigler–Sherwin in order to test the degree to which different markets have become integrated. The estimation was based on time trends of producer price indices across the 12 EU Member States, at the NACE 3-digit level over the period 1980–93. The price indices come from DEBA, done in co-ordination with Eurostat. An average price index for the EU-12 for each sector was calculated based on a weighted average of the producer price indices of the 12 Member States. Due to the large number of countries involved, the test was made by estimating the trend in convergence over time of the producer price index of a given country/sector against the EU average for that same sector. An overview of the results is presented in Table E.2.1.

The first column of Table E.2.1 shows the average value of the *a* coefficient in the equation below; the second column shows the number of cases for which the test of *a*=0 is significant; the third column shows the average value of the *b* coefficient in the equation, and the fourth column shows the number of cases for which the value of *b* is significantly equal to 1. The equation which was estimated is:

$$\Delta \log Px_i = a + b\,(\Delta \log Px_{12})$$

where Px_i is the producer price index for sector x in country i, and Px_{12} is the average producer price index of the same sector in the EU-12.

The sectors in Table E.2.1 are ranked according to the number of cases for which both *a* is significantly equal to zero and *b* is significantly equal to 1.

Table E.2.1. Summary table of Stigler–Sherwin country regressions

NACE category	Industry description	Value of coeff. *a*	Number of countries *a*=0	Value of coeff. *b*	Number of countries *b*=1	Total rank
3130	SEC.TRANSF.,TREATM.OF METAL	0.012	10	0.986	10	20
4280	SOFT DRINKS,NAT.SPA WATERS	0.030	8	0.892	10	18
2470	MANUFACT.OF GLASS & GLASSWARE	0.024	7	1.024	11	18
4140	PROC.OF FRUIT AND VEGETABLES	0.024	7	1.050	11	18
3200	MECHANICAL ENGINEERING	0.009	9	1.194	8	17
4630	CARPENTRY & JOINERY COMPONENTS	0.018	9	1.129	8	17
4190	BREAD AND FLOUR CONFECTIONERY	0.031	8	0.806	9	17
2400	NON-METALLIC MINERAL PRODUCTS	0.028	7	0.853	10	17
3700	INSTRUMENT ENGINEERING	0.018	7	0.962	10	17
3240	MACHINES FOR FOOD & CHEM.IND.	0.019	8	1.035	8	16
3520	MANUF.BODIES FOR MOTOR VEHIC.	0.016	8	1.200	8	16
3140	STRUCTURAL METAL PRODUCTS	0.015	7	0.942	9	16
4800	PROC. OF RUBBER AND PLASTICS	0.017	7	1.193	9	16
2220	MANUFACTURE OF STEEL TUBES	0.040	6	0.803	10	16
3500	MOTOR VEHICLES AND PARTS	0.000	9	1.584	6	15
2430	STRUCT.CONCRETE,CEMENT,PLASTER	0.028	8	0.918	7	15
3100	MANUFACTURE OF METAL ARTICLES	0.012	8	1.191	7	15
4670	MANUF. OF WOODEN FURNITURE	0.021	8	1.006	7	15
3280	OTHER MACHINERY & EQUIPMENT	0.016	7	1.067	8	15
4130	MANUFACTURE OF DAIRY PRODUCTS	0.023	7	1.203	8	15
4900	OTHER MANUFACTURING INDUSTRIES	0.017	7	1.224	8	15
4910	MANUF.ARTICLES OF JEWELLERY	0.010	7	1.167	8	15
4940	TOYS AND SPORT GOODS	0.016	7	1.301	8	15
2200	METALS (PROD.,PREL.PROC.)	0.025	6	0.945	9	15
4410	TANNING,DRESSING OF LEATHER	0.037	6	0.950	9	15
4150	PROC. AND PRESERVING OF FISH	0.031	5	0.721	10	15
3250	MACHINES FOR IRON & STEEL IND.	0.012	8	1.199	6	14
3720	MEDICAL & SURGICAL EQUIPMENT	0.005	8	1.359	6	14
2580	SOAP,DETERGENTS,PERFUME	0.019	7	1.188	7	14
4380	CARPETS,LINOLEUM,FLOOR COVER.	0.019	7	1.260	7	14
4600	TIMBER AND WOODEN FURNITURE	0.016	7	1.137	7	14
2210	IRON & STEEL INDUSTRY (ECSC)	0.029	6	1.051	8	14
4270	BREWING AND MALTING	0.029	6	0.940	8	14
5000	BUILDING AND CIVIL ENGINEERING	0.014	6	0.931	8	14
9001	MANUFACTURING INDUSTRY	0.020	5	1.069	9	14
3600	OTHER MEANS OF TRANSPORT	0.028	5	0.972	9	14
4400	LEATHER AND LEATHER GOODS	0.031	5	0.922	9	14
3220	MACHINE TOOLS WORKING METAL	0.017	7	0.906	6	13
3260	TRANSMISSION EQUIPMENT	0.078	7	-0.184	6	13
2410	CLAY PROD.FOR CONSTR.PURPOSES	0.036	6	0.446	7	13
2570	PHARMACEUTICAL PRODUCTS	0.027	6	0.967	7	13
2420	CEMENT,LIME,PLASTER	0.031	5	1.056	8	13
4420	LEATHER PRODUCTS,SUBSTITUTES	0.039	5	0.717	8	13
3730	OPTICAL INSTR.,PHOTO EQUIPMENT	0.022	7	0.910	5	12

NACE category	Industry description	Value of coeff. *a*	Number of countries *a*=0	Value of coeff. *b*	Number of countries *b*=1	Total rank
3110	FOUNDRIES	0.014	6	0.992	6	12
3150	BOILERS,RESERVOIRS,TANKS	0.010	6	1.286	6	12
3710	MEASURING & PRECISION INST.	0.029	6	0.838	6	12
4650	OTHER WOOD MANUF.(EXC.FURN.)	0.032	6	0.664	6	12
4360	KNITTING INDUSTRY	0.030	5	0.791	7	12
2601	CHEMICS AND MAN-MADE FIBRES	0.027	4	0.938	8	12
4100	FOOD,DRINK,TOBACCO INDUSTRY	0.025	4	0.981	8	12
4120	SLAUGHTERING,PREP.OF MEAT	0.024	4	0.911	8	12
4160	GRAIN MILLING	0.030	4	1.130	8	12
4220	ANIMAL AND POULTRY FOODS	0.029	3	0.913	9	12
3400	ELECTRICAL ENGINEERING	0.013	8	1.195	3	11
2230	DRAWING,COLD ROLLING OF STEEL	0.029	6	1.147	5	11
3510	MAN.,ASSEMBLY MOTOR VEHICLES	0.013	6	1.375	5	11
4830	PROCESSING OF PLASTICS	0.019	6	1.171	5	11
3270	EQUIPM.F.USE IN SPEC.BRANCHES	-0.016	5	1.858	6	11
4930	PHOTOGRAPH. AND CIN.LABORAT.	0.006	5	1.095	6	11
2590	MANUF.OF OTHER CHEM.PRODUCTS	0.014	4	1.233	7	11
3610	SHIPBUILDING	0.031	4	0.840	7	11
4500	FOOTWEAR AND CLOTHING IND.	0.035	4	0.734	7	11
4720	PROC. OF PAPER AND BOARD	0.033	4	0.863	7	11
4640	MANUF.OF WOODEN CONTAINERS	0.041	3	0.523	8	11
3210	AGRICULT.MACHINERY & TRACTORS	0.010	7	1.341	3	10
4110	MANUFACTURE OF OILS AND FATS	0.030	7	0.787	3	10
4210	COCOA AND SUGAR CONFECTIONERY	0.012	6	1.537	4	10
3160	TOOLS & FINISHED METAL GOODS	0.006	5	1.178	5	10
3230	TEXTILE MACHIN.,SEWING MACH.	0.017	5	0.934	5	10
3530	MANUF.OF PARTS OF MOT.VEHIC.	0.015	5	1.565	5	10
4330	SILK INDUSTRY	0.027	5	0.717	5	10
3120	FORGING,PRESSING,STAMPING	0.011	4	0.868	6	10
4230	MANUF. OF OTHER FOOD PROD.	0.026	4	1.434	6	10
4310	WOOL INDUSTRY	0.036	3	0.765	7	10
4620	SEMI-FINISHED WOOD PRODUCTS	0.038	3	0.884	7	10
1400	MINERAL OIL REFINING	0.022	5	1.018	4	9
3440	MANUF.OF TELECOM.EQUIPMENT	0.002	5	1.532	4	9
4320	COTTON INDUSTRY	0.029	5	1.086	4	9
2480	MANUFACTURE OF CERAMIC GOODS	0.038	4	0.635	5	9
3165	DOMESTIC HEATING APPLIANCES	0.006	4	1.076	5	9
4560	MANUF.OF FURS AND FUR GOODS	0.027	4	0.662	5	9
4710	MANUF.OF PULP,PAPER,BOARD	0.032	4	0.911	5	9
4510	FOOTWEAR	0.040	2	0.585	7	9
3166	MANUF. OF METAL FURNITURE	0.004	4	1.057	4	8
2460	GRINDSTONES,ABRASIVE PRODUCTS	0.024	3	1.042	5	8
2510	BASIC INDUSTR.CHEM.,PETROCHEM.	0.041	3	0.867	5	8
4370	TEXTILE FINISHING	0.025	3	0.819	5	8
2500	CHEMICAL INDUSTRY	0.041	2	0.869	6	8
4700	PAPER; PRINTING AND PUBLISH.	0.034	2	0.830	6	8
4920	MANUF. OF MUSICAL INSTRUMENTS	0.007	4	0.759	3	7
2240	NF-METALS (PROD.,PREL.PROC.)	0.040	3	0.734	4	7
2600	MAN-MADE FIBRES INDUSTRY	0.026	3	1.074	4	7
3450	MANUF.OF RADIOS & TV-REC.	0.020	3	0.948	4	7
4170	MANUF.OF SPAGHETTI,MACARONI	0.046	3	1.007	4	7
4530	MANUF.OF CLOTHING	0.032	3	0.763	4	7
4660	ART. OF CORK AND STRAW,BRUSHES	0.039	3	0.565	4	7
4950	MISCELLANEOUS MANUF.INDUSTRIES	0.043	3	0.192	4	7
2591	MAN. OF PHOTOGRAPHIC CHEM.MAT.	0.012	2	1.017	5	7
3300	OFFICE AND DP-MACHINERY	0.010	2	0.675	5	7
4240	ETHYL ALCOHOL,SPIRIT DIST.	0.053	2	0.730	5	7
4610	SAWING AND PROCES.OF WOOD	0.039	2	0.592	5	7
3740	MANUF.OF CLOCKS AND WATCHES	0.013	4	0.916	2	6
2436	MANUF. READY-MIXED CONCRETE	0.022	2	0.663	4	6
3620	MANUF.OF RAILWAY ROL.- STOCK	0.037	2	0.766	4	6
3470	MANUF.ELECTR.LAMPS & OTHERS	0.019	3	1.312	2	5
2440	MANUF.OF ART.OF ASBESTOS	0.025	2	0.319	2	4
3460	DOMESTIC TYPE ELECTR.APPL.	0.036	2	1.199	2	4

NACE category	Industry description	Value of coeff.	Number of countries	Value of coeff.	Number of countries	Total rank
		a	a=0	b	b=0	
4250	WINE OF FRESH GRAPES,CIDER	0.056	2	0.581	2	4
3630	MANUF.OF CYCLES,MOTOR CYCLES	0.041	1	0.430	3	4
3640	AEROSPACE EQUIPMENT MANUF.	0.025	1	0.594	3	4
2450	WORK.OF STONES & NON-MET.PROD.	0.058	0	0.439	2	2

Source: DRI.

The results are generally consistent with those of the analysis of price dispersion based on the surveys of final end-user prices which were presented in Chapter 3 and in the first part of Chapter 4, particularly for consumer products.

Sectors like soft drinks and spa waters, motor vehicles and parts, various specialty chemicals (soaps, detergents and perfumes) have all shown a trend towards increased pan-Europeanization of markets based on the Stigler–Sherwin index, whereas textile products have generally shown no or very low (intra-EU) integration patterns.

Interestingly, however, Table E.2.1 points to an increased integration of most mechanical engineering subsectors, including some for which we observed increased price disparities at both EU-6 and EU-12 levels. This raises the question of the reliability of the price dispersion data for the investment goods sectors, due to the wide mix of products in each category.

Appendix F.1: List of products/services ranked by EU-12 coefficient of price variation in 1993 (based on price including taxes)

	D	F	I	NL	B	L	UK	IRL	DK	GR	E	P	A	S	FIN	Coefficients of price variation EU6	EU9	EU12	EU15
Final consumption																			
1111071 Potatoes	139.8	148.4	92.9	78.6	41.7	50.3	143.1	128.2	241.8	44.4	85.3	58.6	98.9	88.6	88.6	44.2	48.8	**53.8**	49.6
1153051 Other medical and paramedical services	114.3	154.6	66.4	135.0	182.8	208.3	27.2	95.2	110.2	120.9	26.5	47.1	127.6	196.2	41.6	32.1	43.7	**52.1**	52.4
1131021 Water distribution charges	233.8	129.6	40.5	133.7	138.8	196.7	121.4	97.2	251.3	46.8	70.9	99.6	208.5	208.4	134.1	41.5	42.3	**49.9**	45.4
1153041 Nurse services	131.1	75.6	266.8	84.0	91.7	98.5	36.1	131.0	171.2	194.1	101.2	74.4	188.4	144.4	166.1	52.9	52.4	**49.9**	44.2
1132031 Heating oil and other heating fuels	73.7	100.8	213.9	104.6	60.7	66.0	70.9	89.3	176.9	124.9	99.4	51.3	100.5	139.0	86.9	50.5	47.5	**45.5**	41.4
1132021 Town gas and natural gas	101.5	103.3	101.6	89.6	95.6	71.4	97.1	134.4	240.7	24.9	104.7	114.9	102.4	161.2	118.0	11.8	40.9	**44.7**	40.5
1151011 Medicine	190.5	73.2	72.2	209.7	126.8	123.6	127.4	155.7	203.9	55.0	61.3	86.1	140.8	114.9	123.9	39.6	34.2	**43.4**	38.8
1186011 Legal services	108.3	148.7	72.4	114.7	70.7	53.2	123.4	101.0	141.1	40.4	44.1	63.3	107.7	121.4	107.8	34.2	29.8	**40.0**	35.5
1163021 Railway and road transport services	140.4	133.4	51.8	117.7	105.9	60.9	144.3	106.3	130.4	47.0	51.8	53.4	103.4	141.8	90.2	33.4	28.6	**39.4**	36.1
1153011 General practitioner medical services	95.9	97.4	245.1	89.5	74.9	138.8	107.8	117.5	177.9	143.5	239.2	132.5	140.0	276.3	208.5	46.7	39.8	**38.7**	39.9
1111092 Tea	215.7	172.5	159.7	73.8	133.7	158.4	58.5	109.3	178.7	149.9	282.6	139.9	218.4	125.3	160.0	28.1	34.5	**37.6**	35.0
1162012 Vehicle maintenance costs	149.2	91.5	77.9	95.3	75.4	86.1	104.0	75.1	160.2	53.4	67.5	40.5	113.3	142.6	89.5	25.9	29.4	**37.5**	35.0
1113011 Alcohol	96.6	105.1	75.7	113.3	97.7	86.9	138.8	132.4	220.8	73.8	66.2	86.2	116.8	178.8	242.2	12.6	34.4	**37.3**	42.1
1111053 Edible oils	219.0	133.4	87.6	196.6	165.0	146.5	118.4	121.3	266.7	105.8	85.0	101.2	223.0	409.2	409.3	27.0	33.0	**37.2**	54.8
1111065 Dried vegetables	81.7	102.9	101.0	103.3	142.3	84.8	100.5	131.3	231.2	90.6	110.3	62.0	136.5	151.5	160.5	19.2	36.3	**37.0**	33.7
1144012 Cutlery	146.1	105.9	66.5	161.5	117.5	94.9	141.2	97.2	185.8	91.3	68.4	47.6	135.8	172.9	109.6	27.3	28.5	**36.1**	33.8
1113012 Wine	139.7	95.6	100.4	132.2	93.2	110.4	156.3	229.2	172.3	134.9	62.2	69.7	159.7	208.2	187.4	16.0	30.7	**36.0**	34.9
1151021 Other pharmaceutical products	163.1	159.3	65.0	96.9	178.7	115.4	106.7	98.2	130.7	53.1	89.6	62.4	129.1	145.8	102.7	31.2	28.3	**35.9**	32.5
1146011 Domestic services	103.9	85.0	125.3	94.8	91.1	131.4	104.2	67.6	186.6	65.4	116.3	44.4	108.8	112.1	103.7	16.5	29.8	**35.0**	31.0
1172022 Charges for radio, television use	108.2	148.9	97.0	93.1	151.8	159.5	82.5	84.7	140.4	32.1	104.2	66.1	144.9	161.0	145.0	21.8	24.9	**34.9**	32.8
1183013 Expenditures in canteens	122.9	108.7	131.2	47.7	43.8	144.7	61.1	99.1	109.0	120.9	109.8	57.8	190.6	218.7	142.2	39.8	36.2	**34.4**	42.2
1132041 Coal, coke and other solid combustibles	176.4	131.6	85.9	124.7	96.5	106.0	60.4	82.0	129.1	98.8	69.1	50.5	87.1	113.5	78.1	24.6	29.4	**33.6**	31.5
1163031 Other expenses related to transport services	119.1	120.8	90.1	83.8	154.0	97.4	86.9	60.4	96.6	40.8	74.2	55.3	98.5	128.7	79.4	21.4	25.2	**33.3**	31.1
1122021 Repairs to footwear	128.1	142.4	99.8	126.0	130.0	151.9	77.8	134.7	191.8	66.0	77.9	56.8	166.1	154.2	171.1	12.5	22.9	**33.3**	31.7
1174011 Tuition costs	111.9	116.4	101.0	89.5	79.5	54.6	111.6	56.1	159.0	79.7	74.1	53.6	66.5	168.1	140.2	22.7	31.4	**33.0**	36.6
1181011 Hairdressers, beauticians and other similar services	107.9	126.7	92.5	124.2	91.0	128.5	85.6	72.3	178.6	65.3	104.2	47.9	146.8	122.8	107.3	14.0	26.9	**32.7**	30.1
1153021 Specialist medical services	110.5	100.6	95.5	79.8	50.5	46.0	61.7	139.1	130.5	135.3	125.1	132.9	98.8	157.9	172.5	30.5	35.0	**32.4**	33.6
1141021 Repairs to furniture, furnishings, floorings	124.1	86.7	74.4	136.2	113.3	89.8	138.7	143.1	110.8	57.4	78.0	40.9	143.1	142.1	96.4	21.1	20.8	**32.1**	30.7
1143021 Repairs to heating, washing, kitchen appliances	123.6	84.5	69.7	130.8	110.9	85.4	126.5	134.8	104.8	50.8	76.6	42.6	140.3	143.7	91.8	22.1	20.4	**31.7**	31.0
1163011 Local transport services	140.8	125.1	70.1	118.4	123.6	119.4	114.4	127.3	157.3	37.9	101.7	56.2	100.5	163.2	128.0	18.8	18.2	**31.5**	30.0
1164021 Telephone, telegraph and telex services	147.4	83.2	81.2	71.8	124.9	57.9	90.6	148.3	89.8	52.8	98.9	88.1	158.4	63.8	82.4	33.2	31.1	**31.4**	33.8
1114011 Cigarettes	114.0	99.4	82.4	99.1	104.3	80.1	128.8	136.4	176.9	64.1	65.5	71.6	104.5	142.6	134.1	12.3	25.2	**31.3**	29.1
1132022 Liquified gas	163.4	158.9	104.6	180.5	112.7	102.3	131.5	152.1	216.9	120.6	66.7	85.8	191.4	334.3	181.2	22.9	24.5	**30.8**	46.7
1145022 Other household services	91.3	101.0	71.5	141.3	168.2	123.6	92.7	76.6	111.1	59.7	111.0	63.3	173.2	165.7	138.8	27.8	27.2	**30.8**	32.8
1171041 Repairs of recreational goods	97.1	104.2	74.2	143.6	173.6	128.1	94.1	76.1	112.3	57.8	117.1	71.5	178.7	170.9	143.2	27.1	27.4	**30.7**	32.7
1162031 Other expenses related to personal transport	129.2	116.2	139.4	90.7	52.3	90.3	83.1	117.0	128.8	56.4	105.4	52.8	133.4	125.1	111.8	28.2	25.1	**30.6**	28.3
1153031 Dental services	131.9	74.9	89.1	76.6	162.6	124.5	80.0	134.7	155.1	52.0	134.5	133.5	118.4	151.4	97.0	29.3	28.6	**30.6**	28.5
1111028 Other fresh or frozen meat	121.2	138.1	97.6	121.1	102.4	130.9	83.7	58.9	106.0	55.2	60.7	62.1	101.7	110.0	108.0	12.2	21.9	**30.4**	27.0
1172011 Expenses related to cultural events and activities	95.3	126.1	117.9	77.5	79.6	47.5	90.5	52.2	79.6	74.2	104.6	48.0	81.3	84.0	60.3	29.1	29.0	**29.8**	28.0
1183012 Expenditures in cafes, bars	125.7	132.6	110.3	115.0	113.1	99.7	101.4	114.5	189.0	87.0	89.2	42.2	146.1	196.8	117.1	9.2	20.8	**29.7**	31.2
1142021 Repairs to household textiles	108.4	127.2	94.7	80.9	83.8	115.6	59.2	71.4	123.7	42.6	80.6	64.5	140.5	152.1	112.0	16.5	23.6	**29.2**	31.5
1111054 Other animal or vegetable fats	131.0	149.9	90.6	54.3	141.1	73.0	94.0	72.8	147.4	112.6	126.9	88.0	118.8	169.6	135.4	33.8	32.6	**29.0**	28.5
1172023 Other services nec	114.8	136.5	68.6	138.9	141.8	137.6	81.8	63.7	146.4	65.0	115.2	97.5	130.8	87.0	105.2	21.1	27.8	**28.4**	26.5
1111103 Confectionery	118.5	144.3	118.4	126.9	108.7	113.0	76.3	106.7	234.6	127.5	150.3	126.6	146.5	178.0	198.9	9.5	32.6	**28.3**	27.9
1142011 Household textiles	111.5	161.8	111.4	90.7	106.9	101.3	87.5	151.9	98.0	76.1	78.3	60.7	83.8	109.2	72.5	19.8	21.7	**27.4**	26.8
1111064 Fresh vegetables	124.6	110.5	104.2	111.3	99.4	89.4	99.8	140.1	170.8	57.2	85.6	78.2	122.7	170.2	181.1	10.2	20.4	**26.8**	29.9
1112011 Mineral water	109.7	106.3	71.5	90.9	93.4	85.4	105.5	131.6	172.5	133.5	92.6	67.8	72.2	162.9	145.7	13.8	26.1	**26.8**	29.2
1111022 Veal	125.2	137.2	113.5	151.9	109.4	122.2	80.7	105.9	172.9	83.8	75.2	76.9	122.8	140.1	98.8	11.4	20.5	**26.3**	24.3
1152011 Lenses and glasses	104.0	104.4	111.3	73.2	71.6	88.0	92.2	90.4	152.0	59.8	86.1	64.3	113.5	99.6	93.8	16.9	23.1	**26.2**	23.7
1111024 Mutton, lamb and goat meat	135.0	124.0	107.8	129.4	144.2	134.0	96.1	74.5	133.6	64.2	107.8	63.7	106.4	122.7	129.7	8.8	17.8	**25.3**	22.8
1111042 Preserved milk	103.9	111.3	181.2	94.9	103.4	102.6	79.8	86.0	83.4	84.0	128.6	121.5	123.1	105.8	94.7	25.3	27.3	**25.2**	23.0
1122013 Children's and babies' footwear	123.7	127.4	131.3	122.9	174.5	156.8	58.4	101.8	132.5	119.8	84.2	98.6	113.7	88.3	93.8	13.9	24.6	**24.8**	24.5

	D	F	I	NL	B	L	UK	IRL	DK	GR	E	P	A	S	FIN	Coefficients of price variation EU6	EU9	EU12	EU15
1182011 Jewellery, watches, precious stones	160.1	163.1	63.4	165.6	156.9	156.7	126.0	134.5	202.4	114.1	108.7	123.4	135.7	130.3	146.8	25.2	24.3	**24.5**	22.1
1111023 Pork	120.0	106.9	92.7	114.4	81.5	106.5	88.0	79.4	148.0	64.4	74.3	70.0	100.0	136.2	119.0	12.5	19.8	**24.5**	23.7
1111012 Flour, other cereals	102.5	129.8	73.7	94.2	84.0	91.0	117.8	98.7	152.9	131.6	123.5	60.2	149.5	127.4	151.5	18.3	22.1	**24.5**	24.8
1144014 Gardening equipment	86.4	128.3	116.9	112.8	118.5	102.1	155.2	117.1	156.3	94.2	82.7	60.9	97.2	117.0	105.3	12.1	17.6	**24.3**	22.2
1111034 Preserved, prepared fish and other seafood	142.0	113.7	118.4	82.9	88.5	99.0	56.7	55.2	104.7	98.9	107.7	101.2	77.5	99.8	98.6	18.6	28.0	**24.1**	22.4
1144021 Repairs to glassware, tableware, household utensils	104.8	97.0	77.6	115.5	103.8	100.2	98.4	117.0	118.2	56.6	77.3	47.5	129.2	140.9	109.6	11.5	11.6	**24.0**	24.8
1131013 General household maintenance costs	107.7	141.6	88.8	116.2	126.6	109.5	90.9	96.4	129.9	61.9	67.7	77.4	142.5	146.7	123.1	14.3	15.4	**23.8**	24.3
1172021 Expenses for sporting events and activities	106.4	113.6	112.5	101.4	85.0	81.9	65.5	86.6	106.4	117.8	166.9	90.5	117.3	144.6	80.4	12.5	16.2	**23.7**	24.0
1111032 Dried or smoked fish	99.1	125.3	140.7	133.7	102.1	97.0	113.7	75.6	149.8	63.0	87.7	95.1	114.2	90.1	67.2	15.1	19.7	**23.7**	24.2
1121021 Repairs to clothing	93.6	182.0	104.4	129.4	103.1	134.1	82.6	101.9	123.8	93.1	123.5	87.0	136.7	192.7	141.6	23.7	23.8	**23.3**	25.8
1161021 Other modes of personal transport	98.7	104.2	91.7	109.2	104.5	102.9	98.5	105.3	192.6	107.2	98.6	100.2	118.1	108.1	126.3	5.4	25.8	**23.3**	20.9
1171021 Photographic and cinematic equipment	101.1	121.1	103.4	112.7	117.1	94.2	84.2	121.7	111.3	183.1	83.8	149.8	119.2	100.0	122.2	8.7	11.2	**23.3**	21.2
1111025 Poultry	124.2	111.5	119.0	123.2	141.1	124.2	65.1	94.4	156.9	89.7	101.1	75.3	106.8	140.8	138.9	7.2	21.1	**23.0**	21.8
1111102 Chocolate	89.4	105.2	110.4	115.1	93.1	102.6	81.8	86.3	170.8	94.0	108.1	146.5	109.8	152.1	151.1	8.8	23.8	**22.9**	23.3
1111063 Fruits frozen, preserved, and as juice	114.4	112.3	110.5	98.1	120.1	132.4	71.9	70.2	154.3	124.5	115.4	162.5	107.3	132.3	118.3	9.0	23.1	**22.9**	20.8
1183021 Hotels and other lodging accommodations	91.5	113.5	85.6	85.1	83.6	84.3	125.9	93.2	132.2	59.6	99.0	63.4	88.4	68.5	65.8	11.7	18.2	**22.7**	23.3
1122012 Women's footwear	120.6	120.8	104.4	114.0	114.2	124.6	73.3	95.4	127.9	78.6	71.4	62.6	136.3	88.5	84.3	5.6	14.7	**22.3**	22.5
1152021 Orthopedic, therapeutic appliances and products	101.0	102.6	106.5	95.9	106.5	87.8	106.6	81.2	65.9	45.0	62.6	95.6	141.5	99.2	75.5	6.6	14.0	**22.1**	24.4
1111062 Dried fruits	84.6	138.0	97.8	102.6	142.7	134.2	87.3	110.0	180.1	107.0	135.8	111.5	97.3	195.0	138.3	19.2	24.7	**22.1**	25.1
1111013 Bread	124.1	107.0	97.6	82.2	89.2	100.6	72.3	83.2	133.1	85.7	94.9	53.8	118.8	129.7	140.1	13.3	19.1	**22.0**	23.5
1144015 Light bulbs and electrical accessories	105.9	110.2	77.3	108.5	97.4	92.7	105.9	97.0	135.4	50.4	93.2	71.6	104.9	115.8	99.0	11.5	14.4	**21.7**	19.8
1111016 Other cereal based products	105.3	102.6	148.7	91.1	84.3	106.9	90.7	95.0	154.3	138.5	109.2	82.6	113.9	121.7	127.7	19.3	22.0	**21.7**	19.6
1144011 Glassware and tableware	117.6	86.8	68.0	91.1	87.6	83.6	95.1	106.5	98.8	87.8	59.0	50.2	84.8	116.2	87.0	16.5	14.4	**21.3**	20.5
1163022 Other transport services	112.1	123.5	89.6	123.9	129.0	112.1	82.8	73.1	114.2	65.0	82.5	83.7	116.9	95.6	79.4	11.3	17.6	**21.3**	20.4
1111061 Fresh fruits	139.1	114.0	92.8	108.3	108.7	107.9	117.2	130.6	150.2	59.7	86.6	103.5	122.2	115.9	108.5	12.4	14.2	**21.0**	18.8
1111051 Butter	85.9	112.5	117.8	90.2	107.4	98.4	82.5	81.8	104.2	137.3	159.7	125.6	128.2	92.6	131.4	11.3	12.9	**20.9**	20.0
1111021 Beef	124.0	108.0	96.7	128.7	91.1	115.2	95.8	87.8	144.2	66.6	80.8	87.6	104.8	118.2	126.8	12.3	16.5	**20.9**	19.4
1161011 Motor vehicles	95.4	104.9	88.5	119.1	94.6	95.6	103.3	131.6	176.7	129.9	104.0	132.2	113.7	96.7	128.1	9.9	23.3	**20.8**	19.4
1132011 Electricity	118.8	112.7	65.7	85.3	129.5	103.8	90.3	77.3	115.1	67.9	116.7	113.1	106.3	69.8	57.3	20.9	20.1	**20.7**	23.5
1143014 Heating and air conditioning appliances	96.9	120.1	82.0	115.1	140.4	112.2	93.4	86.9	149.4	128.2	73.6	114.1	135.6	92.1	107.9	16.5	19.9	**20.5**	19.7
1111067 Vegetables preserved, prepared, soups	102.8	114.5	104.3	98.0	101.6	108.9	78.3	71.9	143.3	127.9	113.4	152.2	124.8	130.0	141.2	5.1	18.9	**20.4**	19.4
1113013 Beer	109.1	101.4	108.1	85.5	93.1	91.0	100.2	154.0	88.3	80.3	95.5	70.3	84.1	165.5	156.7	9.0	18.9	**20.4**	26.9
1111101 Jams, marmalades, honey, syrups	110.2	83.6	113.0	92.6	100.3	125.2	70.2	92.1	122.4	131.4	100.3	152.5	130.4	124.4	149.0	13.2	17.1	**20.2**	20.1
1121014 Babies' clothing (age 0 to 2 years)	108.1	111.3	127.1	75.8	111.4	100.0	66.3	82.4	66.7	119.7	102.0	112.2	91.9	72.8	101.8	14.7	22.1	**20.1**	19.6
1182031 Paper and drawing supplies	111.7	110.7	76.5	114.6	84.9	97.8	107.4	93.0	126.6	63.9	79.8	72.7	112.3	128.1	119.2	14.5	14.5	**19.7**	19.7
1114021 Other tobacco products	102.0	104.8	133.6	92.4	75.7	94.3	112.0	147.2	113.3	115.7	71.4	99.0	94.5	120.5	106.3	17.4	18.9	**19.7**	18.1
1122011 Men's footwear	120.0	125.4	106.6	116.4	104.8	129.6	82.3	93.7	131.3	88.1	75.9	71.7	119.9	110.3	95.7	7.8	14.1	**19.5**	17.9
1173012 Periodicals, newspapers	116.4	102.6	104.9	101.9	112.1	97.3	69.8	113.4	151.1	97.3	108.5	72.9	97.7	133.6	129.1	6.1	18.6	**19.2**	18.9
1112012 Other soft drinks	103.9	110.2	95.9	103.6	99.3	90.1	94.4	107.5	164.3	81.6	102.8	122.3	103.9	142.4	126.8	6.4	19.4	**18.9**	18.7
1111052 Margarine	93.5	153.4	110.9	80.9	100.8	113.9	97.9	94.6	83.5	105.3	136.1	117.2	135.4	128.9	154.5	20.9	19.8	**18.7**	19.9
1111091 Coffee	129.6	83.8	101.3	89.9	88.2	100.6	63.1	105.5	115.8	95.6	75.8	77.3	117.2	92.1	110.2	15.3	18.6	**18.7**	17.8
1121013 Children's clothing (age 3 to 13 years)	126.9	107.5	111.9	97.4	100.6	114.9	61.9	76.2	99.3	129.4	104.2	128.9	102.0	77.2	99.7	8.8	18.8	**18.7**	18.4
1111093 Cocoa	85.8	122.1	81.7	117.0	105.0	85.3	105.7	69.3	127.8	77.5	111.6	116.2	94.0	88.0	100.6	16.2	19.2	**18.6**	17.2
1111044 Cheese	112.4	111.5	88.9	114.3	115.0	98.8	84.0	115.6	155.2	89.9	97.0	142.6	139.1	133.6	133.4	9.1	17.5	**18.5**	18.1
1111014 Cakes, biscuits	116.3	113.9	110.7	97.6	106.5	100.0	66.6	86.0	148.7	91.4	106.2	102.3	111.1	143.2	156.4	6.4	20.2	**18.1**	20.8
1111043 Other milk products, except cheese	88.2	101.0	115.7	83.7	129.1	100.0	109.3	101.6	83.2	145.7	134.3	95.4	109.1	99.1	84.9	15.1	14.2	**18.1**	17.4
1145021 Laundry and dry cleaning	124.9	99.1	95.2	67.6	97.5	112.4	95.9	63.1	108.0	95.9	121.6	97.1	83.4	117.9	68.4	17.7	19.5	**18.0**	19.3
1113014 Other alcoholic drinks	95.2	114.8	89.3	108.7	99.5	91.0	119.0	147.7	141.5	115.3	89.4	88.2	120.1	162.1	214.9	9.3	17.9	**17.9**	28.1
1121015 Clothing accessories	110.8	135.5	88.8	76.0	97.4	108.7	86.1	86.4	103.7	75.1	87.9	79.2	108.2	88.3	80.8	18.2	16.9	**17.8**	16.9
1111104 Ice cream	107.3	115.8	107.2	95.7	83.7	94.4	63.5	75.2	127.9	103.1	96.0	116.5	136.6	114.9	90.1	10.5	19.8	**17.7**	18.5
1173011 Books, brochures, other similar printed matters	116.2	78.3	104.0	112.0	92.9	97.1	86.5	89.3	136.6	99.3	120.4	140.4	120.7	102.4	104.0	12.6	16.7	**17.6**	16.1
1144013 Non-electrical kitchen and household utensils	105.8	105.9	69.9	101.6	81.6	80.1	100.6	99.1	119.1	77.1	89.8	64.0	114.2	103.5	108.5	15.6	15.3	**17.6**	17.0
1164011 Postal services	127.6	110.2	81.4	105.4	99.6	74.5	80.2	110.6	118.0	84.0	77.0	91.1	83.8	123.4	114.6	17.8	17.2	**17.5**	17.7
1111026 Delicatessen	98.3	119.5	109.3	106.4	81.4	112.1	71.8	69.9	112.1	85.2	85.7	83.9	150.3	139.1	126.4	11.6	18.1	**17.2**	22.5
1111066 Frozen vegetables	115.1	102.4	130.3	91.0	95.7	106.9	76.2	83.7	134.1	83.5	101.0	91.8	136.2	108.8	160.4	12.2	18.0	**17.2**	21.1
1111045 Eggs	102.0	121.7	94.5	91.4	113.5	100.7	96.6	129.2	138.9	96.4	89.5	72.9	141.4	137.8	127.2	10.1	14.5	**17.1**	18.6

	D	F	I	NL	B	L	UK	IRL	DK	GR	E	P	A	S	FIN	Coefficients of price variation EU6	EU9	EU12	EU15
1111015 Pasta, noodles	104.6	149.9	90.4	88.9	88.2	95.1	88.2	100.6	124.1	96.1	117.1	106.0	146.1	139.2	176.5	21.2	19.1	**17.0**	23.2
1121011 Men's clothing	106.5	110.7	101.8	105.3	121.8	116.4	67.6	69.4	122.2	90.3	108.7	103.2	99.0	94.6	103.8	6.2	18.9	**16.8**	15.3
1121012 Women's clothing	114.2	124.0	103.1	88.8	109.2	130.9	65.2	92.5	107.7	108.0	95.5	89.3	107.7	89.3	99.2	12.3	18.0	**16.5**	15.3
1141012 Floor coverings	89.9	100.5	95.6	125.7	106.3	139.5	106.3	78.7	112.8	97.3	98.6	136.4	133.8	101.3	103.4	15.9	16.3	**16.4**	15.9
1185011 Insurance, banking and other financial services	113.7	107.5	87.8	103.7	101.2	96.2	88.2	89.9	131.6	77.4	86.2	72.4	109.1	119.6	106.7	8.1	13.1	**16.3**	15.7
1143016 Other household appliances	122.0	105.8	105.2	96.1	113.0	121.6	64.8	89.1	113.6	131.9	100.3	109.6	121.3	93.5	104.5	8.4	16.5	**15.9**	15.0
1111027 Meat preparations, other meat products	135.0	115.6	108.6	109.4	117.3	119.9	85.5	113.8	144.7	100.5	129.2	156.5	136.6	170.9	148.2	7.4	13.5	**15.5**	17.4
1171033 Games and toys	106.2	122.0	102.7	101.6	117.0	97.8	79.7	82.7	127.4	90.1	86.4	119.6	131.7	118.8	106.3	8.1	14.8	**15.0**	15.0
1111033 Other seafood	114.2	119.3	117.4	81.0	96.0	88.0	98.9	85.9	97.3	109.0	74.6	82.9	227.1	143.8	98.2	14.6	13.4	**14.9**	33.1
1162011 Tyres, inner tubes, replacement parts for motor vehicles	118.2	101.4	86.9	104.3	99.7	80.4	86.3	65.7	109.7	81.5	89.3	100.7	78.8	107.3	114.7	12.4	16.2	**14.9**	15.3
1111031 Fresh, frozen fish	104.4	114.9	111.9	93.2	128.9	108.0	91.6	90.6	125.9	88.4	88.2	79.8	130.0	100.4	81.9	9.8	12.5	**14.9**	15.9
1171034 Film and other photographic supplies	87.0	109.7	84.2	115.3	95.1	97.4	103.7	106.3	132.0	98.9	122.5	79.5	108.7	114.6	94.2	11.4	13.5	**14.6**	13.6
1143011 Refrigerators, freezers	107.2	110.3	78.5	97.7	121.1	137.6	95.7	81.9	109.6	114.1	108.5	107.7	130.2	113.6	111.6	16.9	16.7	**14.6**	14.0
1145012 Other non-durable household articles	97.6	117.0	90.2	87.8	108.8	99.1	108.7	96.8	102.9	60.2	92.3	86.2	78.8	119.5	102.4	10.1	8.8	**14.5**	15.1
1171035 Flowers, other recreational goods	113.5	113.2	116.0	107.5	102.3	110.9	68.7	100.0	98.0	121.4	123.8	126.4	135.1	145.1	176.8	4.1	13.2	**13.7**	19.9
1171011 Radios	102.8	105.6	97.2	111.3	104.7	124.7	82.9	91.8	123.6	130.4	110.5	130.5	133.6	87.2	110.1	8.0	12.3	**13.3**	14.2
1183011 Expenditures in restaurants	100.1	111.6	97.5	117.7	105.8	113.0	96.5	117.8	119.5	91.7	95.2	70.7	90.2	102.1	117.0	6.7	7.9	**13.1**	12.7
1111072 Products derived from potatoes	115.5	88.8	121.5	76.3	100.7	88.2	100.5	88.6	117.5	109.1	100.1	97.8	136.2	167.0	153.1	16.1	14.8	**13.0**	22.1
1111011 Rice	123.7	98.6	84.0	78.5	104.3	95.3	104.3	103.8	116.8	109.9	92.5	84.8	73.7	83.7	77.8	15.0	13.3	**13.0**	15.2
1182021 Articles for travelling and personal luggage	110.7	103.0	101.1	105.0	104.1	99.0	79.5	100.6	134.4	125.7	100.3	120.7	114.4	98.9	117.0	3.5	12.9	**12.9**	12.0
1143013 Cookers and stoves	105.7	115.2	98.9	97.8	117.5	111.7	78.3	82.6	108.1	114.9	107.6	125.9	121.1	85.5	109.3	7.1	12.8	**12.7**	13.0
1171031 Records, cassettes, magnetic tapes and accessories	106.0	118.2	93.7	99.9	90.5	81.1	79.2	91.7	117.8	109.5	109.5	106.9	128.5	84.6	98.4	12.0	13.7	**12.5**	13.8
1145011 Cleaning and maintenance products	112.8	97.6	95.6	115.8	113.0	109.5	98.3	82.9	121.2	85.4	91.2	86.4	127.9	145.1	139.6	7.3	11.0	**12.5**	17.4
1111105 Condiments, sauces,spices,salt	99.4	105.5	97.9	78.8	98.8	88.0	95.2	107.7	132.2	104.3	107.0	104.3	138.8	147.3	174.9	9.3	13.9	**12.1**	21.9
1111041 Fresh milk	84.2	111.4	120.3	86.3	89.1	98.0	99.2	111.9	102.1	113.6	94.7	85.5	120.1	102.9	94.2	13.7	11.7	**11.8**	11.7
1171013 Record players, tape and cassette recorders	108.2	119.8	90.7	104.6	115.9	115.1	76.2	99.8	112.4	119.0	114.9	105.3	144.0	107.7	122.3	8.8	12.6	**11.5**	13.3
1171032 Sports equipment	108.8	98.3	98.4	104.6	91.0	116.9	77.5	96.5	122.4	97.9	103.9	95.6	114.2	91.3	96.7	8.1	12.6	**11.1**	10.9
1182022 Other personal articles nec	114.8	117.6	90.7	103.8	113.3	130.8	112.1	120.6	130.7	121.9	107.1	139.1	136.0	103.9	121.7	11.0	10.3	**10.8**	10.9
1111081 Sugar	94.2	100.5	100.9	92.0	91.4	101.6	105.1	111.1	113.3	103.0	98.0	133.2	99.3	116.0	119.1	4.5	7.3	**10.6**	10.5
1181022 Non-durable personal care products	96.0	104.5	97.6	105.4	111.0	105.0	98.5	96.6	134.9	91.5	107.3	99.2	112.0	127.6	121.5	4.9	10.8	**10.3**	11.2
1171012 Televisions	112.5	111.0	93.6	97.8	108.6	117.1	82.8	97.4	124.6	107.5	106.4	107.6	130.3	97.6	104.7	7.8	11.7	**10.2**	10.9
1171022 Other important leisure durables (incl. computers)	101.3	97.9	105.5	102.8	94.0	105.4	84.2	101.3	110.4	103.6	88.8	126.6	121.6	101.0	94.6	4.1	7.2	**10.1**	10.4
1143015 Cleaning equipment	100.8	108.5	94.4	85.2	107.7	100.2	98.7	91.1	95.5	127.1	105.8	97.6	112.3	78.1	95.1	8.0	7.2	**10.1**	11.3
1143012 Washing machines, tumble dryers	114.2	109.2	91.1	96.7	112.6	116.3	84.9	90.9	111.5	95.3	102.8	101.8	133.5	98.2	96.4	8.8	11.0	**9.8**	11.7
1181021 Durable and semi-durable personal care products	114.8	102.3	94.2	100.6	99.7	107.4	84.4	83.6	113.7	104.7	102.3	90.5	132.0	100.3	108.5	6.3	10.6	**9.7**	11.6
1162021 Fuels and lubricants for motor vehicles	94.4	105.8	118.3	104.1	103.8	83.3	92.4	98.8	97.8	92.1	96.1	99.9	98.3	120.6	101.9	10.6	9.3	**8.4**	9.2
1141011 Furniture and furnishing accessories	105.9	105.2	88.6	96.1	103.3	109.9	102.1	94.9	101.5	83.0	93.2	92.8	101.4	91.3	103.4	7.0	6.1	**7.7**	7.3

Appendix F.2: List of products/services ranked by EU-9 coefficient of price variation in 1993 (based on price excluding VAT)

Final consumption	D	F	I	NL	B	L	UK	IRL	DK	GR	E	P	A	S	FIN	Coefficients of price variation			
																EU6	EU9	EU12	EU15
1153041 Nurse services	114.0	75.6	266.8	84.0	76.7	85.7	36.1	131.0	171.2	179.7	101.2	70.9	157.0	144.4	166.1	58.2	**55.8**	52.1	45.5
1132031 Heating oil and other heating fuels	64.1	85.0	196.2	98.7	54.2	58.9	70.9	79.4	141.5	105.8	86.4	48.9	91.4	111.2	71.2	52.5	**46.4**	44.2	40.3
1153011 General practitioner medical services	83.4	97.4	245.1	76.2	62.7	120.7	107.8	117.5	177.9	132.9	239.2	126.2	116.7	276.3	208.5	53.6	**44.6**	43.0	44.4
1111071 Potatoes	121.6	140.7	89.3	74.2	39.3	48.8	143.1	128.2	193.4	41.1	80.5	55.8	89.9	73.2	72.6	42.5	**43.2**	48.5	45.9
1131021 Water distribution charges	203.3	122.8	34.0	113.8	130.9	191.0	121.4	80.3	201.0	43.3	66.9	85.9	189.5	166.7	109.9	41.9	**40.4**	48.0	43.9
1153051 Other medical and paramedical services	99.4	154.6	66.4	135.0	153.0	181.1	27.2	95.2	110.2	111.9	26.5	44.9	106.3	196.2	41.6	29.0	**39.9**	48.7	50.8
1153021 Specialist medical services	96.1	100.6	95.5	67.9	42.3	40.0	61.7	139.1	130.5	125.3	125.1	126.6	82.3	157.9	172.5	34.4	**39.1**	35.2	37.2
1183013 Expenditures in canteens	106.9	103.0	126.2	45.0	36.7	125.8	52.0	88.1	87.2	111.9	103.6	55.0	158.8	180.7	142.2	40.1	**37.3**	35.1	40.2
1132021 Town gas and natural gas	88.3	87.1	93.2	84.5	80.0	67.4	97.1	119.5	192.6	21.1	91.0	109.4	93.1	129.0	96.7	9.8	**34.6**	39.9	36.0
1174011 Tuition costs	97.3	116.4	101.0	89.5	66.5	47.5	111.6	56.1	159.0	79.7	74.1	51.0	66.5	168.1	140.2	26.5	**34.6**	35.2	38.7
1111092 Tea	201.6	163.5	146.5	69.6	126.1	153.8	58.5	109.3	143.0	138.8	266.6	133.2	198.5	103.6	131.1	27.9	**32.8**	37.0	35.3
1151011 Medicine	178.0	71.7	66.2	197.8	119.6	120.0	127.4	128.7	163.1	50.9	59.5	82.0	117.3	91.9	101.6	39.1	**32.0**	41.0	37.7
1164021 Telephone, telegraph and telex services	128.2	70.2	81.2	71.8	104.5	50.3	77.1	148.3	89.8	44.7	98.9	83.9	158.4	51.0	82.4	30.0	**31.8**	32.5	36.6
1171041 Repairs of recreational goods	90.7	87.9	62.4	135.5	163.8	124.4	80.1	67.6	89.8	49.0	101.8	61.6	148.9	136.7	117.4	30.6	**31.7**	34.9	33.5
1151021 Other pharmaceutical products	152.4	151.0	59.6	91.4	168.6	112.0	90.8	81.2	104.6	49.2	87.0	59.4	107.6	116.6	84.2	31.4	**31.1**	37.1	33.6
1186011 Legal services	94.2	125.4	60.8	108.2	59.2	46.3	123.4	83.5	112.9	34.2	38.3	54.6	107.7	121.4	107.8	34.9	**30.8**	41.0	37.5
1113011 Alcohol	84.0	88.6	69.4	96.4	81.8	75.6	118.1	109.4	176.6	62.5	57.6	66.3	97.3	143.0	198.5	10.5	**30.8**	34.7	39.7
1145022 Other household services	79.4	85.2	65.6	120.3	158.7	107.5	78.9	68.1	88.9	50.6	104.7	54.6	144.3	132.6	113.8	30.0	**29.6**	33.1	32.6
1162012 Vehicle maintenance costs	129.7	77.2	65.5	81.1	63.1	74.9	88.5	62.1	128.2	45.3	58.7	34.9	94.4	142.6	73.4	27.2	**28.7**	36.5	37.0
1111065 Dried vegetables	76.4	97.5	97.1	97.5	134.2	82.3	100.5	131.3	185.0	83.9	107.1	59.0	124.1	125.2	131.6	18.9	**28.6**	30.3	27.3
1163021 Railway and road transport services	131.2	126.4	51.8	111.0	99.9	59.1	144.3	106.3	130.4	43.5	48.9	50.9	103.4	126.6	90.2	32.0	**28.5**	39.9	35.8
1113012 Wine	121.5	80.6	92.1	112.5	78.0	98.6	133.0	189.4	137.8	114.3	54.1	66.4	133.1	166.6	153.6	16.2	**28.4**	33.2	31.9
1111054 Other animal or vegetable fats	122.4	126.4	83.1	51.2	133.1	70.9	94.0	72.8	117.9	104.3	119.7	83.8	108.0	140.2	111.0	31.7	**28.4**	25.5	24.2
1144012 Cutlery	127.0	89.3	55.9	137.4	98.3	82.5	120.2	80.3	148.6	77.4	59.5	41.0	113.2	138.3	89.8	27.8	**27.6**	35.0	32.4
1172011 Expenses related to cultural events and activities	89.1	119.5	99.1	66.0	75.1	46.1	77.0	52.2	79.6	71.3	104.6	41.4	73.9	84.0	60.3	28.6	**27.4**	29.6	27.5
1111053 Edible oils	204.7	126.4	84.2	185.5	155.7	142.2	118.4	121.3	213.4	98.0	80.2	96.4	202.7	338.2	335.5	26.2	**27.2**	32.3	47.4
1111042 Preserved milk	97.1	105.5	166.2	89.5	97.5	99.6	79.8	86.0	66.7	77.8	121.3	115.7	111.9	87.4	77.6	23.7	**26.7**	24.9	23.7
1111034 Preserved, prepared fish and other seafood	132.7	107.8	108.6	78.2	83.5	96.1	56.7	55.2	83.8	91.6	101.6	96.4	70.5	82.5	80.8	17.9	**26.6**	22.9	22.1
1132041 Coal, coke and other solid combustibles	153.4	111.0	78.8	106.1	86.2	94.6	60.4	72.9	103.3	83.7	60.1	48.1	79.2	90.8	64.0	23.1	**26.5**	30.8	29.2
1146011 Domestic services	90.3	71.7	105.3	80.7	85.9	114.3	88.7	60.1	149.3	55.4	101.1	38.3	90.7	112.1	103.7	15.8	**26.4**	32.5	29.2
1172023 Other services nec	99.8	115.1	68.6	118.2	133.8	119.7	69.6	56.6	117.1	55.1	100.2	84.1	109.0	69.6	105.2	18.9	**26.2**	27.4	25.9
1153031 Dental services	123.3	74.9	89.1	76.6	136.1	108.3	80.0	134.7	155.1	48.1	134.5	127.1	98.7	151.4	97.0	22.8	**26.0**	29.2	27.9
1181011 Hairdressers, beauticians and other similar services	93.8	106.8	77.7	105.7	76.2	111.7	72.9	59.8	142.9	55.3	90.6	41.3	122.3	122.8	107.3	14.8	**25.5**	31.3	29.6
1182011 Jewellery, watches, precious stones	139.2	137.5	45.9	140.9	131.3	136.3	107.2	111.2	161.9	96.7	94.5	106.4	113.1	104.2	120.3	28.0	**25.4**	24.9	22.7
1122013 Children's and babies' footwear	107.6	107.4	110.3	104.6	146.0	152.2	49.7	101.8	106.0	101.5	73.2	85.0	94.8	70.6	76.9	16.3	**25.2**	25.5	26.1
1111103 Confectionery	110.7	121.7	108.6	119.7	102.5	109.7	76.3	94.8	187.7	118.1	141.8	120.6	133.2	147.1	163.0	5.9	**25.2**	22.2	21.7
1162031 Other expenses related to personal transport	112.3	98.0	117.1	77.2	43.8	78.5	70.7	96.7	103.0	47.8	91.7	45.5	111.2	100.1	91.6	28.3	**24.7**	30.1	27.5
1121021 Repairs to clothing	81.4	153.5	87.7	122.1	86.3	116.6	70.3	90.6	99.0	78.9	107.4	75.0	113.9	154.2	116.1	23.7	**24.0**	23.6	24.4
1172022 Charges for radio, television use	94.1	145.8	93.3	93.1	135.5	138.7	70.2	84.7	112.3	27.2	98.3	57.0	131.7	128.8	145.0	20.1	**23.5**	34.6	32.5
1163031 Other expenses related to transport services	111.3	114.5	90.1	79.1	145.3	94.6	86.9	60.4	96.6	37.8	70.0	52.7	98.5	114.9	79.4	20.2	**23.3**	32.6	29.8
1161021 Other modes of personal transport	85.8	87.9	77.1	92.9	87.4	89.5	83.8	87.0	154.1	90.8	85.7	86.4	98.4	86.5	103.5	5.6	**23.0**	20.5	18.6
1114011 Cigarettes	99.1	83.8	69.2	84.3	93.1	71.5	109.6	112.7	141.5	54.3	57.0	61.7	87.1	114.1	109.9	12.8	**22.4**	28.9	26.7
1111028 Other fresh or frozen meat	113.3	130.9	89.5	114.2	96.6	127.1	83.7	58.9	84.8	51.1	57.3	59.1	92.5	90.9	88.5	13.3	**22.1**	30.4	27.1
1141021 Repairs to furniture, furnishings, floorings	107.9	73.1	62.5	115.9	94.8	78.1	118.0	127.2	88.6	48.6	67.8	35.3	119.3	113.7	79.0	21.5	**22.0**	32.7	30.7
1142021 Repairs to household textiles	94.3	107.3	79.6	68.9	79.1	100.5	50.4	63.5	99.0	36.1	70.1	55.6	117.1	121.7	91.8	15.2	**21.9**	28.1	29.4
1112011 Mineral water	102.5	100.8	65.6	85.8	88.1	82.9	105.5	131.6	138.0	123.6	87.4	64.6	65.6	134.6	119.4	14.0	**21.8**	23.2	24.6
1132022 Liquified gas	142.1	134.0	96.0	170.3	94.3	96.5	131.5	135.2	173.5	102.2	58.0	74.0	174.0	307.4	148.5	23.6	**21.8**	29.6	42.3
1122021 Repairs to footwear	111.4	120.1	83.9	118.9	108.8	132.1	66.2	119.7	153.4	55.9	67.7	49.0	138.4	123.4	140.2	13.2	**21.3**	32.3	30.2
1142011 Household textiles	97.0	136.4	93.6	77.2	100.8	88.1	74.5	125.5	78.4	64.5	68.1	52.3	69.8	87.4	59.4	18.6	**21.0**	26.7	26.6
1161011 Motor vehicles	83.0	88.4	74.4	101.4	79.2	83.1	87.9	108.8	141.4	110.1	90.4	114.0	94.8	77.4	105.0	10.0	**20.7**	18.9	17.9
1143021 Repairs to heating, washing, kitchen appliances	107.5	71.2	63.9	111.3	104.6	74.3	107.7	119.8	83.8	43.1	72.3	36.7	116.9	115.0	75.2	21.8	**20.6**	31.6	30.1
1145021 Laundry and dry cleaning	108.6	83.6	80.0	57.5	81.6	97.7	81.6	52.1	86.4	81.3	105.7	83.7	69.5	97.4	56.1	18.7	**20.4**	19.0	20.3
1121014 Babies' clothing (age 0 to 2 years)	94.0	93.8	106.8	64.5	93.2	97.1	66.3	82.4	53.4	101.4	88.7	96.7	76.6	58.2	83.4	14.2	**20.4**	18.3	19.0

	D	F	I	NL	B	L	UK	IRL	DK	GR	E	P	A	S	FIN	Coefficients of price variation			
																EU6	EU9	EU12	EU15
1111062 Dried fruits	79.1	130.8	94.0	96.8	134.6	130.3	87.3	110.0	144.1	99.1	131.8	106.2	88.5	161.2	113.4	19.6	**19.9**	18.4	20.3
1111063 Fruits frozen, preserved, and as juice	106.9	106.4	106.3	92.5	113.3	128.5	71.9	70.2	123.4	115.3	112.0	154.8	97.5	109.3	97.0	9.8	**18.9**	20.5	18.9
1152011 Lenses and glasses	97.2	104.4	107.0	69.1	67.5	83.0	78.5	90.4	121.6	55.4	81.2	55.4	94.6	79.7	76.9	18.1	**18.9**	23.6	21.5
1111012 Flour, other cereals	95.8	123.0	67.6	88.9	79.2	88.3	117.8	98.7	122.3	121.9	116.5	57.3	135.9	105.3	124.2	18.8	**18.8**	22.1	21.7
1121011 Men's clothing	92.6	93.3	85.5	89.6	101.9	101.2	57.5	57.4	97.8	76.5	94.5	89.0	82.5	75.7	85.1	6.3	**18.8**	16.8	15.6
1121012 Women's clothing	99.3	104.6	86.6	75.6	91.4	113.8	55.5	76.4	86.2	91.5	83.0	77.0	89.8	71.4	81.3	13.0	**18.7**	16.9	16.0
1113013 Beer	94.9	85.5	99.2	72.8	77.9	79.1	85.3	127.3	70.6	68.1	83.0	67.0	70.1	132.4	128.4	11.1	**18.7**	19.2	24.5
1114021 Other tobacco products	88.7	88.4	122.6	78.6	67.6	84.2	95.3	121.7	90.6	98.1	62.1	85.3	85.9	96.4	87.1	19.1	**18.5**	19.3	17.4
1111052 Margarine	87.4	129.3	106.6	76.3	90.0	110.6	97.9	94.6	66.8	97.5	128.4	111.6	123.1	106.5	126.6	17.5	**18.4**	18.1	17.7
1163011 Local transport services	131.6	118.6	70.1	111.7	116.6	115.9	114.4	127.3	157.3	35.1	95.9	53.5	100.5	130.6	128.0	17.3	**18.2**	32.1	29.0
1164011 Postal services	119.3	92.9	81.4	99.4	94.0	64.8	80.2	110.6	118.0	71.2	67.0	86.8	83.8	123.4	114.6	18.1	**18.1**	19.9	20.3
1183012 Expenditures in cafes, bars	109.3	125.7	101.2	108.5	94.6	86.7	86.3	101.8	151.2	80.6	84.2	40.2	121.8	162.6	117.1	11.8	**18.0**	26.4	27.4
1132011 Electricity	103.3	95.0	60.3	72.6	108.4	97.9	90.3	68.7	92.1	57.5	101.5	107.7	96.6	55.8	47.0	19.3	**17.8**	20.0	24.3
1111015 Pasta, noodles	91.0	142.1	86.9	83.9	83.2	92.3	88.2	100.6	99.3	89.0	110.5	101.0	132.8	115.0	144.7	21.4	**17.8**	16.0	19.3
1143011 Refrigerators, freezers	93.2	93.0	66.0	83.1	101.3	119.7	81.4	67.7	87.7	96.7	94.3	92.8	108.5	90.9	91.5	17.7	**17.7**	15.4	14.5
1111102 Chocolate	83.6	99.7	101.3	108.6	87.8	99.6	81.8	76.7	136.6	87.0	102.0	139.5	99.8	125.7	123.9	8.8	**17.6**	19.2	18.5
1143014 Heating and air conditioning appliances	84.3	101.3	75.2	98.0	117.5	97.6	79.5	71.8	119.5	108.6	64.0	98.4	113.0	73.7	88.4	13.9	**17.5**	18.5	18.4
1121015 Clothing accessories	96.3	114.2	74.6	64.7	81.5	94.5	73.3	71.4	83.0	63.6	76.4	68.3	90.2	70.6	66.2	18.4	**17.4**	17.9	17.3
1152021 Orthopaedic, therapeutic appliances and products	94.4	102.6	102.4	90.5	100.5	82.8	106.6	81.2	52.7	41.7	59.1	91.0	117.9	79.4	61.9	7.5	**17.4**	24.5	25.1
1111025 Poultry	116.1	105.7	109.2	116.2	133.1	120.6	65.1	94.4	125.5	83.1	95.4	71.7	97.1	116.4	113.9	7.5	**17.3**	19.9	18.2
1141012 Floor coverings	78.2	84.7	80.3	107.0	89.0	121.3	90.5	65.0	90.2	82.5	85.7	117.6	111.5	81.0	84.8	16.7	**17.3**	17.3	16.8
1143016 Other household appliances	106.1	89.2	88.4	81.8	94.6	105.7	55.1	73.6	90.9	111.8	87.2	94.5	101.1	74.8	85.7	9.6	**17.1**	16.3	15.7
1121013 Children's clothing (age 3 to 13 years)	110.3	90.6	94.0	82.9	84.2	111.6	61.9	76.2	79.4	109.7	90.6	111.1	85.0	61.8	81.7	12.0	**17.1**	16.8	17.9
1111091 Coffee	121.1	79.4	92.9	84.8	83.2	97.7	63.1	105.5	92.6	88.5	71.5	73.6	106.5	76.1	90.3	14.9	**17.1**	17.2	16.6
1171035 Flowers, other recreational goods	106.1	107.3	97.5	101.4	85.6	104.6	58.5	82.6	78.4	112.4	107.7	109.0	122.8	116.1	144.9	7.3	**16.9**	16.2	19.3
1111016 Other cereal based products	98.4	97.3	136.4	85.9	79.5	103.8	90.7	95.0	123.4	128.2	103.0	78.7	103.5	100.6	104.7	18.1	**16.9**	17.6	15.8
1111043 Other milk products, except cheese	82.4	95.7	106.1	79.0	121.8	97.1	109.3	101.6	66.6	134.9	126.7	90.9	99.2	81.9	69.6	14.8	**16.8**	19.2	19.9
1122012 Women's footwear	104.9	101.9	87.7	97.0	95.6	121.0	62.4	78.8	102.3	66.6	62.1	54.0	113.6	70.8	69.1	10.2	**16.7**	23.4	23.6
1111104 Ice cream	93.3	109.8	98.3	90.3	79.0	91.7	63.5	66.8	102.3	95.5	90.6	111.0	124.2	95.0	73.9	9.9	**16.7**	15.7	17.3
1111024 Mutton, lamb and goat meat	126.2	117.5	98.9	122.1	136.0	130.1	96.1	74.5	106.9	59.4	101.7	60.7	96.7	101.4	106.3	9.7	**16.6**	24.4	22.0
1122011 Men's footwear	104.3	105.7	89.6	99.1	87.7	125.8	70.0	77.4	105.0	74.7	66.0	61.8	99.9	88.2	78.4	12.4	**16.5**	21.0	19.3
1131013 General household maintenance costs	93.7	119.4	74.6	98.9	119.4	95.2	77.4	79.7	103.9	52.5	58.9	66.7	118.8	117.4	100.9	15.6	**16.5**	24.3	23.7
1162011 Tyres, inner tubes, replacement parts for motor vehicles	102.8	85.5	73.0	88.8	83.4	69.9	73.4	54.3	87.8	69.1	77.7	86.8	65.7	85.8	94.0	12.8	**16.4**	15.1	15.0
1111026 Delicatessen	91.9	113.3	100.3	100.4	76.8	108.8	71.8	69.9	89.7	78.9	80.8	79.9	136.6	115.0	103.6	12.1	**16.3**	15.7	19.3
1144014 Gardening equipment	75.1	108.2	98.2	96.0	99.2	88.8	132.1	96.8	125.0	79.8	71.9	52.5	81.0	93.6	86.3	10.9	**16.2**	22.8	21.0
1111032 Dried or smoked fish	92.6	118.8	129.1	126.1	96.3	94.2	113.7	75.6	119.8	58.3	82.7	90.6	103.8	74.5	55.1	14.1	**16.0**	21.0	23.7
1111022 Veal	117.0	130.0	104.1	143.3	103.2	118.6	80.7	105.9	138.3	77.6	70.9	73.2	111.6	115.8	81.0	11.8	**16.0**	23.0	21.7
1111064 Fresh vegetables	116.4	104.7	100.2	105.0	93.8	86.8	99.8	140.1	136.6	53.0	83.1	74.5	111.5	140.7	148.4	9.2	**15.9**	23.6	24.5
1163022 Other transport services	104.8	117.1	89.6	116.9	121.7	108.8	82.8	73.1	114.2	60.2	77.8	79.7	116.9	85.4	79.4	9.7	**15.8**	20.8	20.2
1172021 Expenses for sporting events and activities	92.5	95.8	94.5	86.3	80.2	79.5	55.7	86.6	106.4	109.1	166.9	78.0	97.8	144.6	80.4	7.5	**15.5**	27.3	27.4
1111093 Cocoa	80.2	103.0	75.0	110.4	99.1	82.8	105.7	69.3	102.2	71.8	105.3	110.7	85.5	72.7	82.5	14.2	**15.5**	16.3	16.2
1111101 Jams, marmalades, honey, syrups	95.8	79.2	103.7	87.4	94.6	121.6	70.2	81.9	97.9	121.7	94.6	145.2	118.5	102.8	122.1	13.7	**15.4**	20.3	18.9
1113014 Other alcoholic drinks	82.8	96.8	81.9	92.5	83.3	79.1	101.3	122.1	113.2	97.7	77.7	67.8	100.1	129.7	176.1	7.4	**15.0**	16.4	26.1
1185011 Insurance, banking and other financial services	98.9	90.6	87.8	103.7	84.7	83.7	88.2	89.9	131.6	65.6	86.2	69.0	109.1	119.6	106.7	8.0	**14.8**	17.9	18.1
1144011 Glassware and tableware	102.3	73.2	57.1	77.5	73.3	72.7	80.9	88.0	79.0	74.4	51.3	43.3	70.7	93.0	71.3	17.6	**14.8**	21.0	19.8
1111014 Cakes, biscuits	108.7	108.0	106.4	92.1	100.5	97.1	66.6	86.0	119.0	84.6	100.2	97.4	101.0	118.3	128.2	6.0	**14.8**	13.5	14.7
1111066 Frozen vegetables	107.6	97.1	125.3	85.8	90.3	103.8	76.2	83.7	107.3	77.3	98.1	87.4	123.8	89.9	131.5	12.7	**14.7**	14.5	16.9
1111023 Pork	112.1	101.3	85.0	107.9	76.9	103.4	88.0	79.4	118.4	59.6	70.1	66.7	90.9	112.6	97.5	12.9	**14.6**	20.7	19.3
1111072 Products derived from potatoes	107.9	84.2	116.8	72.0	95.0	85.6	100.5	78.8	94.0	101.0	94.4	93.1	123.8	138.0	125.5	16.1	**14.5**	12.7	17.8
1144013 Non-electrical kitchen and household utensils	92.0	89.3	58.7	86.5	68.3	69.7	85.6	81.9	95.3	65.3	78.1	55.2	95.2	82.8	88.9	16.1	**14.5**	16.6	15.9
1182031 Paper and drawing supplies	97.1	93.3	64.3	97.5	71.0	85.0	91.4	76.9	101.3	54.2	69.4	62.7	93.6	102.5	97.7	15.2	**14.2**	19.0	18.4
1183021 Hotels and other lodging accommodations	79.6	107.6	78.5	80.3	78.9	81.8	107.1	82.8	105.8	55.2	93.4	60.4	73.7	54.8	65.8	12.3	**14.1**	19.2	20.9
1112012 Other soft drinks	97.1	104.5	88.0	97.7	83.1	87.5	94.4	88.8	131.4	75.6	89.4	105.4	86.6	117.7	103.9	7.9	**14.1**	14.3	14.3
1111041 Fresh milk	78.7	105.6	115.7	81.4	84.1	95.1	99.2	111.9	81.7	105.2	91.9	81.4	109.2	85.0	77.2	14.5	**14.0**	13.3	13.7
1171033 Games and toys	92.3	102.9	86.3	86.5	97.9	85.0	67.8	68.3	101.9	76.4	75.1	103.1	109.8	95.0	87.1	7.2	**13.9**	14.3	14.1
1173012 Periodicals, newspapers	108.8	86.5	100.9	96.1	105.8	94.5	69.8	100.8	120.9	93.6	105.3	69.4	88.8	133.6	129.1	7.5	**13.8**	15.0	17.8

	D	F	N	NL	B	L	UK	IRL	DK	GR	E	P	A	S	FIN	Coefficients of price variations EU6	EU9	EU12	EU15
1111067 Vegetables preserved, prepared, soups	96.1	108.5	100.3	92.5	95.8	105.7	78.3	71.9	114.6	118.4	110.1	145.0	113.5	107.4	115.7	5.7	**13.6**	17.7	16.0
1111051 Butter	74.7	106.6	113.3	85.1	101.3	95.5	82.5	81.8	83.4	127.1	150.7	119.6	116.5	76.5	107.7	13.5	**13.5**	21.3	20.6
1111033 Other seafood	106.7	113.1	104.8	76.4	90.6	85.4	98.9	85.9	77.8	100.9	70.4	79.0	206.5	118.8	80.5	13.5	**13.3**	14.6	31.9
1111013 Bread	107.9	101.4	93.8	77.5	84.2	97.7	72.3	83.2	106.5	79.4	89.5	51.2	108.0	107.2	114.8	10.9	**13.2**	17.7	18.2
1143013 Cookers and stoves	91.9	97.1	83.1	83.2	98.3	97.1	66.6	68.3	86.5	97.4	93.6	108.5	100.9	68.4	89.6	7.0	**13.1**	13.3	13.9
1144015 Light bulbs and electrical accessories	92.1	92.9	65.0	92.3	81.5	80.6	90.1	80.2	108.3	42.7	81.0	61.7	87.4	92.6	81.1	11.8	**13.0**	20.6	18.6
1111011 Rice	115.6	93.5	77.1	74.1	98.4	92.5	104.3	103.8	93.4	101.8	87.3	80.8	67.0	69.2	63.8	15.0	**13.0**	12.6	17.1
1111045 Eggs	95.3	115.4	86.7	86.2	107.1	97.8	96.6	129.2	111.1	89.3	86.9	69.4	128.5	113.9	104.3	10.7	**13.0**	15.7	15.9
1171013 Record players, tape and cassette recorders	94.1	101.0	76.2	89.0	97.0	100.1	64.9	82.5	89.9	100.8	99.9	90.8	120.0	86.2	100.2	9.1	**12.8**	11.9	13.3
1171031 Records, cassettes, magnetic tapes and accessories	92.2	99.7	83.7	85.0	75.7	70.5	67.4	75.8	94.2	92.8	95.2	92.2	107.1	67.7	80.7	11.5	**12.7**	12.0	13.8
1111021 Beef	115.9	102.4	88.7	121.4	85.9	111.8	95.8	87.8	115.4	61.7	76.2	83.4	95.3	97.7	103.9	12.8	**12.6**	18.3	16.4
1171032 Sports equipment	94.6	82.9	82.7	89.0	76.2	101.7	66.0	79.8	97.9	83.0	90.3	82.4	95.2	73.0	79.3	9.6	**12.5**	11.0	11.2
1171011 Radios	89.4	89.0	81.7	94.7	87.6	108.4	70.6	75.9	98.9	110.5	96.1	112.5	111.3	69.8	90.2	9.1	**12.3**	13.7	14.9
1171034 Film and other photographic supplies	75.7	92.5	70.8	98.1	79.6	84.7	88.3	94.5	105.6	83.8	106.5	68.5	90.6	91.7	77.2	11.3	**12.0**	13.8	12.8
1111044 Cheese	105.0	105.7	85.5	107.8	108.5	95.9	84.0	115.6	124.2	83.2	91.5	135.8	126.5	110.4	109.3	8.1	**12.0**	15.2	14.4
1144021 Repairs to glassware, tableware, household utensils	91.1	81.8	65.2	98.3	86.9	87.1	83.7	104.0	94.6	48.0	67.2	40.9	107.7	112.7	89.8	12.0	**11.9**	23.9	23.8
1173011 Books, brochures, other similar printed matters	108.6	74.2	100.0	105.7	87.6	94.3	86.5	89.3	109.3	95.5	116.9	133.7	109.7	81.9	85.2	12.2	**11.7**	15.2	15.3
1111061 Fresh fruits	130.0	108.1	89.2	102.2	102.5	104.8	117.2	130.6	120.2	55.3	84.1	98.6	111.1	95.8	88.9	11.5	**11.7**	19.4	18.1
1143012 Washing machines, tumble dryers	99.3	92.1	76.6	82.3	94.2	101.1	72.3	75.1	89.2	80.8	89.4	87.8	111.3	78.6	79.0	9.7	**11.7**	10.4	12.2
1171012 Televisions	97.8	93.6	78.7	83.2	90.9	101.8	70.5	80.5	99.7	91.1	92.5	92.8	108.6	78.1	85.8	8.8	**11.5**	10.0	11.0
1182021 Articles for travelling and personal luggage	96.3	86.8	85.0	89.4	87.1	86.1	67.7	83.1	107.5	106.5	87.2	104.1	95.3	79.1	95.9	4.2	**11.4**	12.0	11.4
1145011 Cleaning and maintenance products	98.1	82.3	80.3	98.6	94.6	97.8	83.7	68.5	97.0	72.4	79.3	74.5	106.6	116.1	114.4	8.3	**11.3**	12.4	15.9
1181021 Durable and semi-durable personal care products	99.8	86.3	86.4	85.6	83.4	93.4	71.8	69.1	91.0	88.7	89.0	78.0	110.0	80.2	88.9	6.4	**10.8**	9.8	11.3
1111105 Condiments, sauces,spices,salt	92.9	100.0	89.8	74.3	93.2	85.4	95.2	107.7	105.8	96.6	100.9	99.3	126.2	121.7	143.4	8.9	**10.3**	9.2	16.3
1171021 Photographic and cinematic equipment	87.9	102.1	86.9	95.9	98.0	81.9	71.7	100.6	89.0	155.2	72.9	129.1	99.3	80.0	100.2	7.6	**10.2**	23.2	21.5
1182022 Other personal articles nec	99.8	99.2	76.2	88.3	94.8	113.7	95.4	99.7	104.6	103.3	93.1	119.9	113.3	83.1	99.8	12.0	**10.2**	10.9	11.3
1111027 Meat preparations, other meat products	126.2	109.6	99.6	103.2	110.7	116.4	85.5	113.8	115.8	93.1	121.9	149.0	124.2	141.2	121.5	7.8	**10.1**	14.1	14.0
1111031 Fresh, frozen fish	97.6	108.9	102.7	87.9	121.6	104.9	91.6	90.6	100.7	81.9	83.2	76.0	118.2	83.0	67.1	9.9	**9.8**	13.0	15.7
1183011 Expenditures in restaurants	87.0	105.8	89.4	111.0	88.5	98.3	82.1	104.7	95.6	84.9	89.8	67.3	75.2	84.4	117.0	9.5	**9.7**	12.4	14.1
1162021 Fuels and lubricants for motor vehicles	82.1	89.2	99.4	98.2	86.9	78.6	78.6	81.7	78.2	78.1	83.6	95.1	89.4	96.5	101.9	8.6	**9.0**	8.9	9.4
1145012 Other non-durable household articles	84.9	98.7	75.8	74.7	91.0	86.2	92.5	80.0	82.3	51.0	80.3	74.3	65.7	95.6	83.9	9.8	**8.8**	14.3	14.4
1111081 Sugar	88.0	95.3	92.6	86.8	86.2	98.6	105.1	111.1	90.6	95.4	92.5	126.9	90.3	95.9	97.6	5.1	**8.5**	11.6	10.6
1181022 Non-durable personal care products	83.5	88.1	89.5	89.7	92.9	91.3	83.8	79.8	107.9	77.5	93.3	85.5	93.3	102.1	99.6	3.3	**8.5**	8.5	8.8
1143015 Cleaning equipment	87.7	91.5	79.3	72.5	90.1	87.1	84.0	75.3	76.4	107.7	92.0	84.1	93.6	62.5	78.0	7.9	**7.9**	10.6	12.4
1141011 Furniture and furnishing accessories	92.1	88.7	74.5	81.8	86.4	95.6	86.9	78.4	81.2	70.3	81.0	80.0	84.5	73.0	84.8	8.0	**7.4**	8.3	8.1
1171022 Other important leisure durables (incl. computers)	88.1	82.5	88.7	87.5	78.7	91.7	71.7	83.7	88.3	87.8	77.2	109.1	101.3	80.8	77.5	5.0	**6.9**	10.3	10.7

Appendix G.1: List of products/services ranked by EU-12 coefficient of price variation in 1980 (based on price including taxes)

	D	F	I	NL	B	L	UK	IRL	DK	GR	E	P	Coefficients of price variation EU6	EU9	EU12
Final consumption															
1114021 Other tobacco products	85.1	80.4	155.3	93.2	77.7	76.1	182.0	139.3	94.1	147.1	74.1	544.3	29.3	33.9	**86.0**
1112011 Mineral water	141.1	94.1	62.4	124.3	103.2	89.2	258.5	466.8	203.4	79.1	72.7	68.2	24.6	69.6	**76.1**
1173011 Books, brochures, other similar printed matters	145.7	103.9	68.9	338.1	82.2	145.5	67.5	102.8	91.5	70.7	80.3	42.7	61.1	62.3	**66.5**
1114011 Cigarettes	144.1	105.1	59.4	88.1	91.2	79.2	119.4	93.5	210.2	58.9	69.2	316.4	27.6	38.2	**60.0**
1174011 Tuition costs	145.5	170.0	92.2	129.1	106.8	57.5	98.9	27.0	264.9	34.3	77.8	98.8	31.3	53.7	**57.1**
1172021 Expenses for sporting events and activities	90.5	114.2	125.2	104.9	250.1	158.1	81.9	42.8	83.5	79.2	85.6	10.3	37.9	47.9	**56.0**
1143015 Cleaning equipment	84.8	160.2	81.8	123.6	106.6	109.9	83.2	96.1	127.2	86.5	75.4	331.8	23.6	22.5	**55.1**
1113012 Wine	141.3	85.7	80.5	158.2	142.0	105.5	320.1	300.6	249.9	162.2	77.6	67.8	25.1	48.9	**53.1**
1132021 Town gas and natural gas	141.8	123.6	114.4	81.7	130.1	117.1	75.0	189.4	231.2	1.7	77.8	51.6	15.7	34.9	**52.4**
1144021 Repairs to glassware, tableware, household utensils	131.6	117.7	41.0	113.3	182.1	177.3	61.9	42.4	72.7	49.4	65.3	58.2	37.0	48.4	**52.2**
1131021 Water distribution charges	152.7	155.9	20.8	201.6	225.9	117.6	121.2	98.5	90.1	56.6	100.5	34.3	45.3	44.0	**52.1**
1111092 Tea	309.5	243.3	198.5	132.8	174.7	185.9	77.0	79.5	285.5	244.5	76.9	58.3	27.0	41.6	**48.6**
1113011 Alcohol	102.1	102.4	66.7	94.9	92.8	76.0	121.6	139.0	225.4	60.3	70.4	199.1	15.0	39.3	**44.3**
1152011 Lenses and glasses	109.2	122.2	85.9	111.4	85.3	104.9	63.9	211.9	144.0	46.6	74.9	44.1	13.0	35.1	**44.1**
1172022 Charges for radio, television use	130.5	94.4	103.4	102.9	171.9	200.2	84.6	92.8	134.8	13.8	155.4	56.9	29.4	30.1	**43.5**
1153031 Dental services	130.6	91.9	93.6	77.7	105.6	110.1	50.1	71.1	137.2	26.4	99.5	17.2	16.4	27.4	**42.9**
1145022 Other household services	136.8	123.0	91.6	113.2	191.5	208.0	65.3	90.8	115.3	69.9	79.6	49.9	29.1	35.0	**41.8**
1164021 Telephone, telegraph and telex services	142.3	111.8	52.3	93.2	131.6	53.1	109.0	107.2	52.9	29.5	77.6	51.4	36.1	34.4	**41.5**
1186011 Legal services	77.5	113.2	68.9	101.5	74.3	70.1	170.2	82.1	67.9	46.3	75.8	41.9	20.1	34.2	**39.4**
1151021 Other pharmaceutical products	208.0	72.3	98.4	85.9	99.8	95.3	85.0	92.4	108.4	68.5	79.0	52.9	40.8	35.9	**38.7**
1111053 Edible oils	232.4	109.7	99.9	212.9	110.1	117.2	122.2	162.3	229.3	99.4	93.0	80.2	36.7	33.7	**38.3**
1163011 Local transport services	170.1	142.2	50.5	127.4	144.2	165.8	141.1	143.6	142.2	44.1	84.6	51.9	29.8	24.0	**37.8**
1141021 Repairs to furniture, furnishings, floorings	78.1	141.5	130.1	81.2	158.8	77.1	69.5	64.1	52.8	59.3	73.2	91.7	30.1	37.9	**36.8**
1121013 Children's clothing (age 3 to 13 years)	111.9	130.9	105.6	95.5	125.3	145.6	78.5	79.2	13.6	89.3	78.0	59.9	14.0	37.4	**36.6**
1111104 Ice cream	86.6	188.1	93.9	58.0	123.4	92.4	76.4	56.3	88.9	106.9	73.3	73.4	38.2	39.3	**36.5**
1142021 Repairs to household textiles	71.7	129.4	112.8	74.5	145.6	71.5	63.7	58.8	48.4	54.5	70.3	88.2	29.6	37.4	**35.8**
1111016 Other cereal based products	137.1	122.0	131.1	108.8	106.1	124.6	87.5	68.4	98.8	197.5	48.4	60.8	9.2	19.1	**35.7**
1111064 Fresh vegetables	150.3	111.0	83.2	145.8	104.5	143.9	125.5	142.5	225.8	67.7	83.1	73.9	20.4	27.7	**35.1**
1153021 Specialist medical services	62.9	147.6	133.8	117.2	115.9	80.9	98.0	90.4	139.9	83.2	99.8	19.5	26.7	24.6	**34.6**
1146011 Domestic services	120.8	124.6	66.7	147.2	104.6	98.8	93.7	76.6	155.5	65.2	102.0	33.3	22.6	25.7	**34.1**
1163021 Railway and road transport services	125.5	120.8	33.6	110.6	85.3	65.7	143.9	129.9	122.1	66.7	72.0	73.0	36.3	32.2	**34.0**
1183012 Expenditures in cafes, bars	158.1	148.5	65.6	157.2	139.7	106.1	100.7	97.5	174.5	94.6	82.9	47.3	25.8	26.8	**33.8**
1151011 Medicine	173.0	80.1	60.1	152.0	107.8	105.4	105.0	120.1	162.9	76.3	75.8	73.0	34.4	30.1	**33.6**
1111071 Potatoes	138.5	80.7	99.2	94.4	66.0	77.9	136.1	128.0	189.4	121.9	84.5	62.5	25.0	32.9	**33.4**
1153041 Nurse services	95.0	136.6	83.7	104.4	92.6	82.5	83.1	49.2	111.4	62.2	95.3	23.1	18.4	24.2	**33.4**
1111081 Sugar	116.2	94.7	102.9	110.5	107.7	107.2	99.9	98.4	214.5	82.9	82.5	68.0	6.2	30.0	**32.6**
1152021 Orthopaedic, therapeutic appliances and products	131.0	117.3	73.9	174.7	135.9	121.1	58.8	93.8	104.6	148.9	72.4	64.0	23.7	29.1	**32.4**
1122021 Repairs to footwear	124.0	109.9	71.6	170.4	131.2	148.0	113.7	89.1	166.1	75.3	81.9	57.3	24.5	25.1	**32.3**
1161011 Motor vehicles	91.0	103.4	103.3	108.9	84.3	79.1	120.0	113.6	157.9	200.0	74.9	78.4	11.5	20.7	**32.1**
1163031 Other expenses related to transport services	133.8	107.3	52.2	101.7	81.3	82.9	87.3	77.4	84.7	48.3	77.1	34.8	27.2	23.8	**32.0**
1111093 Cocoa	141.3	105.1	104.1	75.7	93.5	100.8	50.3	49.3	136.6	102.0	82.3	55.3	19.0	32.4	**31.9**
1143014 Heating and air conditioning appliances	88.6	147.6	83.4	130.0	113.0	108.8	88.6	99.3	133.8	114.1	72.7	216.3	19.9	19.4	**31.7**
1162012 Vehicle maintenance costs	125.8	91.4	67.6	142.5	121.2	120.9	142.6	97.2	123.4	56.8	79.2	43.8	22.2	20.3	**31.7**
1181011 Hairdressers, beauticians and other similar services	132.8	116.8	85.3	149.4	108.4	130.6	87.8	78.2	194.4	104.0	83.8	61.9	16.9	28.8	**31.6**
1143021 Repairs to heating, washing, kitchen appliances	132.1	121.1	59.0	109.4	108.1	99.2	137.4	93.6	120.4	62.8	88.1	32.5	21.9	20.4	**31.4**
1172011 Expenses related to cultural events and activities	109.8	115.5	94.4	122.5	121.0	59.1	146.3	115.3	121.5	50.5	89.3	43.4	21.2	20.2	**31.4**
1153011 General practitioner medical services	92.4	125.4	133.5	89.3	92.5	110.3	91.3	54.6	114.8	86.1	92.5	24.5	16.1	22.2	**30.8**
1132011 Electricity	110.4	104.5	45.5	122.1	124.6	77.4	128.3	84.9	103.6	63.8	77.5	50.1	28.6	25.2	**30.2**
1144014 Gardening equipment	106.5	92.0	97.4	37.2	118.3	114.7	98.3	92.4	45.1	93.6	64.4	61.4	28.8	30.4	**30.0**
1111066 Frozen vegetables	104.9	131.5	101.7	100.5	181.8	127.8	90.3	99.9	114.5	97.4	88.4	38.5	22.7	22.4	**30.0**
1182031 Paper and drawing supplies	113.5	135.1	50.0	120.0	125.6	111.8	128.7	159.3	112.5	60.9	77.3	72.6	25.3	23.6	**30.0**
1153051 Other medical and paramedical services	101.8	109.1	115.1	81.3	88.0	92.9	88.8	59.6	135.6	86.3	82.8	25.0	12.0	21.2	**30.0**

	D	F	I	NL	B	L	UK	IRL	DK	GR	E	P	Coefficients of price variation EU6	EU9	EU12
1113013 Beer	115.3	90.5	79.4	60.3	103.1	80.7	127.4	128.6	88.9	64.1	79.6	38.5	20.0	22.6	**29.6**
1171011 Radios	89.9	155.1	83.2	86.2	110.8	111.6	99.0	114.5	134.8	162.6	63.5	59.5	23.2	20.4	**29.6**
1145021 Laundry and dry cleaning	108.2	122.0	97.1	113.1	123.3	134.9	62.1	69.7	137.2	65.1	73.2	58.2	10.4	23.5	**29.5**
1171041 Repairs of recreational goods	94.8	132.9	104.9	93.7	96.1	105.0	121.0	107.4	150.8	29.0	80.9	81.2	12.9	16.4	**29.0**
1162031 Other expenses related to personal transport	103.5	109.5	70.5	135.6	154.5	107.2	108.2	128.2	135.7	152.1	75.2	47.7	23.2	19.7	**28.7**
1111021 Beef	129.7	114.9	82.4	143.1	113.4	128.1	108.1	89.5	151.9	54.9	61.0	83.2	16.0	18.4	**28.4**
1144011 Glassware and tableware	123.0	94.1	83.4	104.7	99.2	110.8	131.3	52.6	93.7	115.3	88.5	34.5	12.2	21.9	**28.2**
1111033 Other seafood	92.6	109.2	99.1	61.3	121.0	126.2	153.3	177.3	155.4	147.0	82.3	92.5	21.1	27.9	**28.2**
1121021 Repairs to clothing	113.2	135.9	66.4	129.2	155.3	146.5	97.3	66.9	149.2	93.6	78.2	92.7	23.4	27.4	**28.0**
1121014 Babies' clothing (age 0 to 2 years)	147.2	115.6	85.5	126.3	110.6	151.9	70.8	67.9	87.2	88.3	74.3	80.4	18.3	27.5	**27.9**
1111032 Dried or smoked fish	134.2	125.9	124.7	113.8	135.4	117.9	99.1	77.9	175.4	66.6	107.3	60.0	6.3	20.6	**27.8**
1111052 Margarine	102.8	117.3	129.6	92.8	120.4	121.2	133.1	87.6	48.3	121.5	91.7	48.1	10.9	23.8	**27.4**
1172023 Other services nec	100.4	121.7	92.5	115.5	112.9	93.6	85.0	84.3	87.6	43.8	75.7	43.8	10.5	13.4	**27.0**
1131013 General household maintenance costs	92.6	131.6	57.0	102.1	111.1	100.7	94.0	82.8	111.1	51.5	77.9	54.5	22.6	20.0	**27.0**
1122013 Children's and babies' footwear	108.8	117.2	107.2	132.8	118.2	142.1	79.1	99.1	179.4	74.1	74.9	87.8	10.4	22.5	**27.0**
1111013 Bread	122.0	134.1	65.7	102.6	122.5	120.0	117.8	99.8	141.2	62.5	80.1	60.7	20.1	18.5	**26.8**
1111022 Veal	124.6	123.3	98.6	177.0	150.0	128.1	93.6	170.6	148.2	74.9	87.8	93.7	18.3	20.3	**26.3**
1111024 Mutton, lamb and goat meat	101.2	151.1	76.4	127.9	146.1	119.4	103.5	103.7	148.2	78.1	87.1	64.0	21.4	20.3	**26.2**
1111054 Other animal or vegetable fats	114.6	174.9	106.6	101.3	115.8	108.3	76.8	97.4	124.5	127.3	78.3	61.2	20.7	22.3	**26.1**
1132022 Liquified gas	196.8	95.6	104.1	161.5	118.3	128.3	138.7	120.8	141.1	95.8	82.8	87.8	26.1	21.7	**26.1**
1143013 Cookers and stoves	99.5	139.5	84.9	112.2	116.7	107.5	145.9	126.8	134.1	164.0	60.1	72.0	15.1	15.8	**26.1**
1111101 Jams, marmalades, honey, syrups	124.0	95.0	106.0	100.2	101.8	83.7	75.7	73.9	155.1	91.9	73.3	59.4	11.9	23.6	**26.0**
1183013 Expenditures in canteens	114.9	90.5	59.9	70.4	74.4	97.3	114.0	124.0	79.4	109.9	116.2	48.9	21.8	23.1	**26.0**
1112012 Other soft drinks	101.7	84.7	85.7	87.8	99.6	87.8	130.1	135.3	134.7	69.1	77.8	54.6	7.4	19.6	**25.9**
1132041 Coal, coke and other solid combustibles	128.7	130.0	90.7	113.2	110.0	78.4	87.2	82.1	66.4	68.8	74.4	57.0	17.3	21.8	**25.8**
1111051 Butter	103.7	106.4	115.7	122.5	107.0	91.0	87.1	60.0	86.8	106.2	110.6	33.5	9.1	18.1	**25.7**
1113014 Other alcoholic drinks	98.3	123.4	64.0	70.0	82.2	81.6	105.9	133.9	122.1	70.0	75.1	69.6	22.7	24.2	**25.7**
1183021 Hotels and other lodging accommodations	103.8	82.6	112.5	102.6	96.6	80.8	143.2	118.3	109.9	65.1	80.2	49.8	11.9	16.9	**25.4**
1111067 Vegetables preserved, prepared, soups	113.1	113.5	83.0	96.7	137.2	95.6	82.5	93.3	144.0	102.2	77.3	49.0	16.3	19.7	**25.2**
1111043 Other milk products, except cheese	101.6	102.8	99.9	72.9	111.4	83.8	147.9	85.6	83.2	107.0	75.5	49.4	13.6	21.1	**25.1**
1111105 Condiments, sauces,spices,salt	98.3	161.4	74.6	80.8	96.0	118.4	104.4	141.7	86.1	98.8	70.4	99.1	27.5	25.5	**25.0**
1173012 Periodicals, newspapers	118.9	125.3	100.4	108.9	114.3	93.2	68.6	81.2	124.5	87.4	81.9	44.3	9.9	17.9	**24.6**
1111072 Products derived from potatoes	134.2	78.4	78.4	85.7	97.5	104.4	96.1	92.3	113.0	93.6	81.0	37.4	20.1	17.2	**24.4**
1183011 Expenditures in restaurants	111.5	106.1	94.4	141.2	132.7	121.9	96.7	113.1	133.9	68.7	81.0	56.1	13.4	13.5	**24.3**
1111103 Confectionery	130.8	114.5	76.3	92.1	99.8	109.1	103.4	97.9	157.7	81.4	80.5	68.2	16.6	20.4	**23.8**
1111015 Pasta, noodles	129.1	106.2	86.9	129.1	137.5	130.0	136.8	131.8	177.2	99.0	80.3	76.4	14.7	17.8	**23.7**
1111062 Dried fruits	105.5	170.0	88.3	96.7	108.5	111.7	92.9	94.4	148.2	96.1	72.7	108.3	23.3	23.2	**23.7**
1121015 Clothing accessories	118.9	125.3	61.7	107.8	113.0	119.9	100.1	75.5	136.0	104.3	78.2	65.7	19.8	21.3	**23.4**
1171013 Record players, tape and cassette recorders	91.6	120.2	84.4	94.9	107.5	98.7	100.7	108.7	140.2	165.3	65.9	100.2	11.6	15.0	**23.3**
1121011 Men's clothing	111.7	117.8	89.5	111.4	121.7	140.6	96.0	93.7	151.1	88.4	81.8	61.8	13.1	17.2	**23.0**
1111028 Other fresh or frozen meat	114.4	113.7	104.8	121.1	115.6	122.0	56.2	61.1	94.1	95.8	74.4	123.5	4.9	23.6	**22.9**
1121012 Women's clothing	112.2	124.0	86.0	94.8	121.3	127.8	85.9	90.1	133.4	88.0	79.4	54.1	14.0	16.7	**22.9**
1171012 Televisions	97.4	125.1	83.0	95.3	110.5	120.3	106.4	113.1	141.5	151.6	77.1	64.7	14.0	15.0	**22.9**
1164011 Postal services	105.4	121.0	66.6	124.9	97.4	67.4	103.7	86.7	86.1	64.1	71.8	75.1	23.9	20.6	**22.8**
1111102 Chocolate	98.4	94.0	133.8	117.8	92.4	96.3	102.2	107.3	177.2	133.5	75.8	113.0	14.4	22.8	**22.8**
1111011 Rice	146.4	102.4	88.1	127.3	116.4	126.7	121.6	123.8	161.6	98.9	95.6	60.1	15.9	16.5	**22.8**
1182022 Other personal articles nec	89.7	101.0	84.0	88.8	97.8	100.9	135.6	116.3	79.5	78.3	74.9	51.1	7.0	16.6	**22.5**
1111065 Dried vegetables	122.8	117.6	100.4	114.4	172.0	109.2	109.0	141.7	174.2	121.8	89.4	85.1	18.8	20.1	**22.4**
1111027 Meat preparations, other meat products	123.7	101.6	89.4	85.8	112.2	107.8	91.1	82.5	139.0	90.1	74.7	55.8	12.6	17.2	**22.3**
1122011 Men's footwear	112.0	119.4	78.4	106.3	122.3	128.6	99.9	93.6	140.3	71.6	77.5	71.5	14.7	16.1	**22.1**
1182021 Articles for travelling and personal luggage	107.0	96.1	102.7	92.3	94.4	88.1	97.8	111.1	144.1	137.2	78.1	158.0	6.5	15.2	**21.6**
1122012 Women's footwear	108.9	136.4	69.8	115.8	119.7	124.5	114.8	117.6	139.8	74.6	77.6	86.5	18.6	16.3	**21.5**
1185011 Insurance, banking and other financial services	117.4	91.5	77.4	108.0	71.7	52.7	85.7	64.0	78.4	102.3	72.3	96.0	25.4	23.2	**21.4**
1144013 Non-electrical kitchen and household utensils	96.3	97.7	79.4	111.1	83.8	87.6	135.9	91.6	114.2	85.2	73.9	56.3	11.3	16.9	**21.4**
1111044 Cheese	120.3	95.3	97.6	116.9	117.9	111.1	92.3	84.8	156.7	78.9	79.2	84.2	9.0	18.4	**21.2**

	D	F	I	NL	B	L	UK	IRL	DK	GR	E	P	Coefficients of price variation		
													EU6	EU9	EU12
1143016 Other household appliances	99.0	116.4	91.7	87.2	94.6	96.4	104.1	95.8	107.4	148.0	54.8	84.4	9.4	8.4	**21.2**
1171033 Games and toys	108.7	113.2	88.8	118.1	117.0	101.0	95.1	102.3	103.0	40.4	78.4	105.2	9.5	8.9	**20.9**
1111061 Fresh fruits	138.9	126.3	84.1	102.4	89.8	130.4	115.1	109.6	142.4	96.4	85.3	70.2	18.7	17.0	**20.9**
1143012 Washing machines, tumble dryers	102.7	130.2	79.8	102.7	116.3	113.3	113.2	105.6	132.8	153.1	76.3	76.1	14.4	13.5	**20.9**
1171035 Flowers, other recreational goods	115.8	122.9	91.4	61.4	91.6	114.5	89.1	99.1	87.2	74.1	73.3	68.0	21.0	18.3	**20.8**
1111026 Delicatessen	116.0	110.8	78.2	117.2	114.2	121.0	93.5	83.4	131.5	73.9	76.9	75.6	13.1	15.9	**20.3**
1111012 Flour, other cereals	116.2	117.8	85.6	100.0	101.7	106.6	93.9	92.6	135.3	95.6	83.6	51.8	10.3	13.8	**20.2**
1111045 Eggs	101.1	124.1	122.3	104.0	98.9	109.9	102.5	106.0	131.2	82.6	85.6	51.3	9.0	9.9	**20.2**
1111031 Fresh, frozen fish	106.4	125.7	108.8	93.8	154.4	136.1	107.4	84.8	125.0	89.0	82.2	87.2	16.8	17.6	**20.2**
1181022 Non-durable personal care products	105.6	118.1	98.1	110.5	87.0	92.3	96.4	88.8	137.0	65.5	78.2	73.8	10.4	14.7	**19.9**
1163022 Other transport services	121.5	110.6	85.0	107.7	106.7	130.8	110.6	96.2	104.7	57.8	72.1	91.6	12.8	11.5	**19.7**
1111034 Preserved, prepared fish and other seafood	112.1	118.4	96.1	85.4	111.1	102.3	82.4	84.5	128.0	93.6	79.5	58.0	10.6	15.0	**19.5**
1111091 Coffee	142.5	80.4	98.4	75.4	84.1	89.7	84.9	105.7	104.8	97.7	73.7	84.3	23.6	19.9	**19.2**
1111025 Poultry	120.9	105.2	105.5	105.4	116.4	113.3	104.9	110.2	125.9	59.7	85.1	68.3	5.5	6.5	**19.2**
1143011 Refrigerators, freezers	101.0	122.3	84.0	94.1	123.2	112.2	116.5	104.2	119.1	162.3	75.7	116.1	13.6	11.8	**19.2**
1142011 Household textiles	112.2	106.3	82.7	108.3	110.7	117.3	109.6	94.6	115.6	65.0	78.8	65.6	10.4	9.8	**19.0**
1111041 Fresh milk	105.4	101.7	97.5	102.2	98.5	103.6	118.7	73.9	110.7	102.0	88.6	46.8	2.7	11.3	**19.0**
1111023 Pork	108.2	111.9	94.0	122.2	99.2	102.4	94.9	94.7	135.8	65.7	76.4	81.8	8.6	12.6	**18.8**
1132031 Heating oil and other heating fuels	98.9	101.0	109.4	98.3	91.7	88.9	94.8	89.3	115.9	92.8	75.5	45.3	6.7	8.7	**18.7**
1111042 Preserved milk	110.9	106.4	118.2	108.9	88.9	102.0	121.7	83.8	120.1	94.0	85.0	55.4	8.5	11.8	**18.5**
1144015 Light bulbs and electrical accessories	102.6	107.1	78.1	106.0	95.7	89.0	93.7	95.2	109.8	62.7	69.6	62.9	10.7	9.8	**18.3**
1181021 Durable and semi-durable personal care products	92.2	108.4	135.2	111.0	94.4	81.1	95.1	93.8	131.3	112.0	71.8	85.8	16.7	16.6	**18.2**
1162011 Tyres, inner tubes, replacement parts for motor vehicles	95.4	104.4	79.4	121.9	125.6	105.8	116.1	104.1	106.7	88.0	74.8	66.6	14.8	12.4	**18.1**
1141012 Floor coverings	104.4	114.8	88.7	98.1	97.6	110.8	97.9	112.4	113.3	93.2	74.6	57.0	8.5	8.3	**17.0**
1145011 Cleaning and maintenance products	127.9	90.3	99.1	104.2	90.7	95.4	82.5	97.8	137.7	93.3	79.5	87.0	12.7	16.7	**16.9**
1171031 Records, cassettes, magnetic tapes and accessories	120.1	106.1	90.1	83.3	112.4	91.4	87.4	86.5	108.4	83.6	74.9	131.3	13.1	12.8	**16.9**
1111063 Fruits frozen, preserved, and as juice	102.5	111.3	110.5	90.1	102.9	129.2	99.2	83.7	103.3	86.3	70.0	73.0	11.0	11.9	**16.8**
1141011 Furniture and furnishing accessories	95.2	123.8	112.9	85.5	92.3	111.6	114.4	111.0	78.5	89.3	73.8	77.2	13.0	14.1	**16.7**
1111014 Cakes, biscuits	102.6	118.9	90.3	109.3	100.2	101.7	85.1	90.5	133.6	101.1	74.4	78.3	8.4	13.9	**16.3**
1145012 Other non-durable household articles	106.9	112.1	74.7	96.8	90.8	97.3	101.1	97.4	94.3	64.0	72.7	74.1	12.4	10.2	**16.1**
1171022 Other important leisure durables (incl. computers)	95.7	97.2	100.5	109.5	115.8	111.0	110.2	126.5	105.0	119.8	73.9	71.7	7.2	8.5	**15.5**
1161021 Other modes of personal transport	107.4	101.9	95.9	111.6	102.7	101.1	93.0	115.1	137.1	100.7	75.3	79.5	4.8	11.6	**15.2**
1171021 Photographic and cinematic equipment	93.9	113.7	103.8	100.6	110.6	99.6	115.1	123.1	123.6	102.7	67.2	131.2	6.5	9.1	**15.1**
1171034 Film and other photographic supplies	98.5	108.8	84.5	110.1	105.4	101.2	120.9	125.1	115.1	134.9	77.4	102.3	8.4	10.8	**14.5**
1144012 Cutlery	91.2	96.5	100.9	110.2	98.8	97.7	130.5	78.9	115.6	95.4	77.2	109.2	5.8	13.7	**14.3**
1162021 Fuels and lubricants for motor vehicles	93.4	109.4	118.0	98.6	108.9	78.0	100.8	94.3	115.1	107.9	75.6	83.7	12.9	11.6	**13.7**
1171032 Sports equipment	117.5	93.0	95.6	97.7	107.8	104.9	95.0	92.2	112.4	103.9	73.2	76.3	8.1	8.5	**13.0**

Appendix G.2: List of products/services ranked by EU-9 coefficient of price variation in 1980 (based on price excluding VAT)

	D	F	I	NL	B	L	UK	IRL	DK	Coefficients of price variation	
Final consumption										EU6	EU9
1111012 Flour, other cereals	133.1	87.9	58.9	119.5	97.4	85.0	258.5	466.8	168.1	24.9	**73.6**
1111013 Bread	128.9	97.1	68.2	325.1	77.5	142.6	67.5	102.8	75.6	62.1	**63.4**
1111022 Veal	133.3	80.1	75.9	152.1	134.0	103.4	320.1	300.6	206.5	25.3	**50.9**
1111024 Mutton, lamb and goat meat	124.2	110.0	38.7	108.9	171.8	173.8	61.9	42.4	60.1	37.5	**49.3**
1111016 Other cereal based products	85.4	106.7	124.0	100.9	235.9	150.6	81.9	42.8	69.0	37.3	**47.9**
1111015 Pasta, noodles	128.8	158.9	91.3	124.1	100.8	54.8	98.9	27.0	218.9	29.8	**47.5**
1111025 Poultry	144.1	145.7	19.6	193.8	213.1	112.0	121.2	98.5	74.5	45.4	**44.6**
1111026 Delicatessen	292.0	227.4	187.3	127.7	164.8	182.3	77.0	79.5	236.0	26.3	**38.8**
1111045 Eggs	73.7	132.2	122.7	78.1	149.8	73.4	69.5	64.1	43.6	29.5	**37.8**
1111051 Butter	99.0	122.3	102.5	91.8	118.2	142.7	78.5	79.2	11.2	15.2	**37.5**
1111053 Edible oils	67.6	120.9	109.5	71.6	137.4	68.1	63.7	58.8	40.0	29.2	**37.5**
1111011 Rice	80.3	75.1	150.8	89.6	73.3	72.5	182.0	139.3	77.8	30.7	**37.4**
1111041 Fresh milk	73.1	105.8	68.2	97.6	70.1	68.7	170.2	82.1	56.1	18.8	**37.0**
1111028 Other fresh or frozen meat	103.0	114.2	81.0	107.1	80.5	102.8	63.9	211.9	119.0	13.1	**36.6**
1111042 Preserved milk	196.2	67.6	92.8	82.6	94.2	93.4	85.0	92.4	89.6	40.3	**35.4**
1111034 Preserved, prepared fish and other seafood	134.2	104.5	50.8	89.6	124.2	50.6	109.0	107.2	43.7	35.4	**35.4**
1111033 Other seafood	129.1	115.0	88.9	108.8	180.7	198.1	65.3	90.8	95.3	28.8	**34.8**
1111052 Margarine	81.7	159.9	91.2	55.8	111.2	88.0	76.4	56.3	73.5	32.8	**34.1**
1111027 Meat preparations, other meat products	96.3	95.7	62.9	91.3	87.5	74.5	121.6	139.0	186.3	14.3	**33.5**
1111064 Fresh vegetables	118.4	112.9	31.7	106.3	80.5	62.6	143.9	129.9	100.9	36.1	**33.5**
1111014 Cakes, biscuits	135.9	98.2	57.7	84.7	86.0	72.0	119.4	93.5	173.7	27.4	**32.7**
1113012 Wine	94.2	78.2	91.9	31.5	94.6	109.2	85.5	75.1	37.3	29.8	**32.2**
1111023 Pork	133.8	115.5	107.9	78.6	122.7	114.8	75.0	189.4	191.1	15.2	**31.1**
1111043 Other milk products, except cheese	219.2	102.5	98.9	204.7	103.9	114.9	122.2	162.3	189.5	36.1	**30.9**
1111101 Jams, marmalades, honey, syrups	125.0	98.2	98.2	72.8	88.2	91.6	50.3	40.1	112.9	16.4	**30.2**
1122021 Repairs to footwear	130.3	98.3	78.4	121.4	95.3	138.1	61.6	55.2	72.1	19.2	**30.2**
1111067 Vegetables preserved, prepared, soups	130.7	75.4	93.6	90.8	62.3	74.2	136.1	128.0	156.5	24.9	**29.7**
1111031 Fresh, frozen fish	123.1	88.2	100.4	98.9	162.2	190.7	84.6	92.8	111.4	29.2	**29.4**
1111066 Frozen vegetables	163.2	74.9	56.7	146.2	101.7	100.4	105.0	120.1	134.6	34.8	**28.5**
1122012 Women's footwear	81.9	92.9	90.9	51.9	104.3	114.7	133.3	161.2	128.4	22.1	**28.4**
1131021 Water distribution charges	91.0	109.6	113.7	78.6	103.8	110.2	133.1	71.2	39.9	12.3	**27.8**
1153011 General practitioner medical services	87.1	94.0	133.8	99.8	79.7	87.5	102.2	107.3	177.2	18.2	**26.7**
1151011 Medicine	107.9	106.3	98.9	116.4	109.1	119.6	56.2	49.7	77.8	6.2	**26.2**
1111081 Sugar	123.6	109.6	71.7	148.1	128.2	110.1	58.8	93.8	86.4	20.2	**25.9**
1111104 Ice cream	117.5	109.2	80.5	126.6	102.3	118.7	87.8	63.6	160.7	13.7	**25.0**
1122013 Children's and babies' footwear	100.2	115.6	60.9	109.5	133.9	133.2	84.6	66.9	123.3	22.6	**24.8**
1111093 Cocoa	126.2	91.2	46.4	97.8	76.7	75.4	87.3	77.4	70.0	28.4	**24.7**
1144012 Cutlery	87.0	137.2	65.4	68.5	82.8	107.6	90.8	115.2	71.2	27.0	**24.7**
1111072 Products derived from potatoes	109.6	88.5	97.1	106.3	101.6	102.1	99.9	80.0	177.3	6.7	**24.6**
1162012 Vehicle maintenance costs	103.9	68.6	67.9	91.5	57.4	47.9	74.5	52.0	64.8	26.4	**24.5**
1111103 Confectionery	118.7	77.7	63.8	137.0	114.3	109.9	142.6	79.0	102.0	24.2	**24.3**
1111044 Cheese	160.5	132.9	49.0	122.5	136.0	157.9	141.1	143.6	117.5	29.4	**24.3**
1111065 Dried vegetables	149.2	138.8	61.9	151.2	131.8	101.0	100.7	97.5	144.2	25.9	**24.2**
1112012 Other soft drinks	87.2	117.2	125.9	85.9	79.7	105.0	91.3	44.4	94.9	17.1	**24.0**
1111032 Dried or smoked fish	123.2	85.9	90.9	74.7	99.6	104.9	50.1	71.1	113.4	15.9	**23.8**
1113011 Alcohol	97.7	88.9	42.9	103.5	99.7	70.4	111.6	69.0	85.6	25.3	**23.6**
1121011 Men's clothing	102.0	77.0	72.8	51.1	88.9	73.4	110.8	116.9	73.5	20.2	**23.5**
1111061 Fresh fruits	141.8	103.7	78.5	140.2	98.6	137.0	125.5	142.5	186.6	20.9	**23.2**
1111091 Coffee	117.0	102.7	67.5	163.8	123.8	141.0	113.7	89.1	137.3	25.2	**23.2**
1143011 Refrigerators, freezers	101.7	77.0	52.5	59.7	64.1	88.5	99.1	100.8	65.6	23.1	**23.0**
1142021 Repairs to household textiles	109.7	80.8	100.0	84.9	87.8	76.1	65.8	60.1	128.2	12.8	**23.0**
1111071 Potatoes	84.1	127.7	79.0	100.4	87.4	75.0	83.1	49.2	92.1	19.2	**22.9**

	D	F	I	NL	B	L	UK	IRL	DK	Coefficients of price variation EU6	EU9
1111063 Fruits frozen, preserved, and as juice	114.0	116.4	62.9	141.5	98.7	94.1	93.7	76.6	128.5	23.0	**22.7**
1141021 Repairs to furniture, furnishings, floorings	174.2	81.3	91.3	136.9	102.0	116.6	120.6	98.2	116.6	26.6	**22.7**
1113013 Beer	92.8	111.8	95.9	85.2	156.7	116.2	78.5	81.2	94.6	21.5	**22.6**
1111062 Dried fruits	59.3	137.9	126.2	112.7	109.3	77.0	98.0	90.4	115.6	26.3	**22.5**
1145012 Other non-durable household articles	93.4	144.6	77.5	81.9	93.5	101.5	80.8	76.7	122.5	22.3	**22.4**
1143013 Cookers and stoves	113.9	110.5	79.6	95.9	94.8	71.3	75.8	66.7	54.9	16.2	**22.4**
1152021 Orthopaedic, therapeutic appliances and products	99.4	121.0	65.9	120.1	91.9	64.2	103.7	86.7	71.2	24.3	**22.3**
1144011 Glassware and tableware	89.9	87.4	87.6	61.8	96.0	76.2	128.6	69.6	68.8	13.5	**22.1**
1143015 Cleaning equipment	87.0	104.9	56.1	59.3	70.9	74.2	92.1	108.9	100.9	22.0	**22.0**
1141012 Floor coverings	101.4	148.7	93.5	85.8	99.8	98.5	66.8	79.2	102.9	19.5	**21.9**
1114011 Cigarettes	90.1	81.8	108.6	68.9	80.7	91.1	77.2	48.5	112.1	14.0	**21.8**
1122011 Men's footwear	108.8	80.0	76.5	88.7	85.5	100.7	114.2	47.8	77.4	12.6	**21.7**
1112011 Mineral water	103.6	107.9	89.1	117.8	114.2	56.3	146.3	115.3	100.4	21.2	**21.7**
1145021 Laundry and dry cleaning	105.2	106.5	54.1	91.4	97.4	109.0	87.0	61.4	112.4	20.0	**21.6**
1111105 Condiments, sauces,spices,salt	124.6	113.2	55.7	92.7	102.0	94.5	137.4	93.6	99.5	22.2	**21.4**
1113014 Other alcoholic drinks	100.4	114.9	47.2	101.7	100.5	101.6	111.9	129.5	93.0	23.0	**21.3**
1111021 Beef	80.0	149.7	77.2	118.8	100.6	107.7	83.2	96.1	105.1	23.2	**20.9**
1131013 General household maintenance costs	118.8	107.1	109.4	96.4	127.7	107.2	86.2	63.3	145.0	8.9	**20.9**
1171032 Sports equipment	126.1	68.4	86.3	63.9	72.5	81.5	73.8	85.9	86.6	24.9	**20.8**
1132022 Liquified gas	96.3	99.7	93.2	127.7	108.4	135.3	79.1	90.1	148.3	14.5	**20.2**
1143021 Repairs to heating, washing, kitchen appliances	100.1	96.5	78.3	81.9	129.4	86.9	71.7	75.9	119.0	17.8	**20.2**
1143014 Heating and air conditioning appliances	91.8	90.5	109.2	103.8	92.2	82.7	75.7	48.8	71.7	9.3	**20.1**
1111102 Chocolate	83.6	137.9	74.1	125.0	106.6	98.9	88.6	80.7	110.6	21.2	**20.0**
1121021 Repairs to clothing	114.8	97.7	75.6	137.6	97.8	116.5	94.0	72.8	125.5	18.1	**19.9**
1144021 Repairs to glassware, tableware, household utensils	115.8	97.4	66.9	78.1	86.0	99.2	89.9	79.6	130.3	17.4	**19.8**
1114021 Other tobacco products	94.2	91.8	53.6	97.6	93.9	77.5	123.0	95.5	110.3	18.1	**19.7**
1141011 Furniture and furnishing accessories	89.6	128.5	67.0	108.4	125.9	108.5	90.0	84.3	122.5	20.3	**19.5**
1153041 Nurse services	108.7	117.6	100.4	114.4	148.3	99.3	109.0	141.7	174.2	14.3	**19.4**
1121013 Children's clothing (age 3 to 13 years)	95.8	103.7	89.1	95.8	106.3	122.6	62.1	69.7	113.4	10.5	**19.3**
1132021 Town gas and natural gas	81.9	111.9	49.6	98.2	101.9	95.9	94.0	75.3	91.8	22.4	**19.3**
1162031 Other expenses related to personal transport	106.5	71.5	85.6	99.1	94.3	101.0	80.3	68.9	129.5	12.4	**19.2**
1111054 Other animal or vegetable fats	129.3	103.7	123.7	104.6	100.1	122.2	87.5	68.4	81.7	10.0	**19.0**
1171013 Record players, tape and cassette recorders	94.2	94.3	80.6	79.5	133.1	123.7	93.4	77.1	103.3	20.3	**18.9**
1121012 Women's clothing	79.6	131.9	76.3	73.1	95.5	101.5	86.1	104.1	111.4	21.7	**18.8**
1151021 Other pharmaceutical products	105.8	115.9	81.1	91.2	114.4	125.3	74.7	73.3	110.2	14.4	**18.5**
1144014 Gardening equipment	118.8	66.7	68.8	72.6	84.1	94.9	83.6	75.0	93.4	21.6	**18.4**
1121015 Clothing accessories	91.6	93.1	64.7	114.9	133.2	97.5	94.1	116.5	112.1	21.4	**18.3**
1153031 Dental services	84.6	101.0	84.0	88.8	84.3	91.7	135.6	116.3	79.5	6.8	**18.2**
1146011 Domestic services	98.8	100.2	78.5	94.4	114.8	127.8	83.5	76.2	124.9	15.2	**18.1**
1132041 Coal, coke and other solid combustibles	110.3	104.8	93.0	150.0	137.6	122.0	93.6	155.1	122.5	16.2	**17.8**
1144013 Non-electrical kitchen and household utensils	105.2	106.5	88.1	92.3	98.5	84.7	59.7	66.0	102.9	8.6	**17.8**
1143012 Washing machines, tumble dryers	90.0	72.0	75.2	74.4	85.9	79.8	113.1	110.0	111.3	8.1	**17.7**
1181011 Hairdressers, beauticians and other similar services	113.2	67.7	86.9	88.3	78.2	86.7	71.7	79.5	113.8	15.8	**17.7**
1111092 Tea	85.8	96.6	97.5	104.7	79.5	75.3	120.0	113.6	130.5	11.6	**17.5**
1153021 Specialist medical services	129.6	102.4	88.1	107.9	100.3	115.2	121.6	123.8	161.6	12.0	**17.2**
1162021 Fuels and lubricants for motor vehicles	85.2	83.1	70.9	106.8	74.2	83.4	118.2	74.5	94.4	13.7	**17.1**
1164021 Telephone, telegraph and telex services	102.7	94.2	78.2	117.2	98.4	110.0	81.3	83.4	131.5	12.3	**16.8**
1173011 Books, brochures, other similar printed matters	87.0	92.2	130.0	106.7	89.1	77.2	95.1	76.3	108.5	17.7	**16.7**
1145011 Cleaning and maintenance products	114.2	90.3	76.2	109.4	118.5	118.2	119.0	107.2	146.4	15.2	**16.7**
1163022 Other transport services	131.0	118.0	84.1	98.5	84.7	118.5	115.1	109.6	142.4	16.9	**16.6**
1143016 Other household appliances	91.9	70.2	98.7	86.9	83.3	73.5	124.5	96.2	90.8	11.8	**16.5**
1153051 Other medical and paramedical services	109.5	101.6	89.4	85.8	96.7	98.0	91.1	82.5	139.0	8.0	**16.2**
1185011 Insurance, banking and other financial services	82.7	93.0	118.0	98.6	93.9	70.9	100.8	76.7	115.1	15.6	**16.0**
1172011 Expenses related to cultural events and activities	102.1	104.6	82.5	103.6	93.6	93.1	82.5	86.1	135.8	8.1	**15.9**
1121014 Babies' clothing (age 0 to 2 years)	83.9	113.0	96.2	79.4	82.8	95.5	121.0	107.4	124.6	12.4	**15.9**
1161021 Other modes of personal transport	94.7	72.1	90.1	78.2	75.5	80.1	85.0	101.0	119.1	9.8	**15.8**

Code	Item	D	F	I	NL	B	L	UK	IRL	DK	Coefficients of price variation EU6	EU9
1132031	Heating oil and other heating fuels	108.0	114.0	62.0	98.7	112.4	114.3	117.8	99.8	116.7	18.2	**15.7**
1164011	Postal services	109.2	104.5	91.4	59.0	86.4	104.1	89.1	99.1	87.2	18.3	**15.3**
1181021	Durable and semi-durable personal care products	106.3	90.2	66.7	70.6	96.9	83.1	76.0	70.3	89.6	16.3	**15.3**
1161011	Motor vehicles	99.1	89.6	68.8	90.1	97.8	116.9	86.9	85.1	116.0	15.3	**15.2**
1162011	Tyres, inner tubes, replacement parts for motor vehicle	96.4	102.3	61.2	98.1	95.8	113.2	99.8	95.6	115.5	16.9	**15.0**
1173012	Periodicals, newspapers	90.0	88.8	74.9	117.2	118.5	100.8	116.1	94.6	88.2	16.0	**14.7**
1183021	Hotels and other lodging accommodations	80.7	90.2	95.2	106.0	86.7	88.8	113.5	64.1	95.5	8.6	**14.7**
1171031	Records, cassettes, magnetic tapes and accessories	99.2	88.8	84.3	72.4	95.8	93.0	71.7	68.7	105.8	9.9	**14.4**
1171021	Photographic and cinematic equipment	93.5	88.6	72.7	93.6	75.0	83.9	83.8	72.2	113.2	9.8	**14.2**
1181022	Non-durable personal care products	90.7	83.5	81.9	86.6	88.7	117.5	86.3	68.0	85.4	13.1	**13.9**
1171022	Other important leisure durables (incl. computers)	107.5	94.0	74.6	91.3	92.0	118.9	96.2	78.2	86.5	14.4	**13.8**
1171011	Radios	102.8	88.4	72.5	84.7	87.7	96.9	81.7	75.3	111.8	10.7	**13.5**
1171034	Film and other photographic supplies	89.4	91.7	62.2	79.7	98.6	102.0	101.3	84.7	98.4	15.2	**13.5**
1142011	Household textiles	88.1	118.6	80.1	95.1	100.6	97.7	126.9	103.1	110.8	12.3	**13.5**
1171041	Repairs of recreational goods	99.4	86.5	85.5	98.3	84.9	94.2	103.2	60.1	91.5	6.6	**13.5**
1163031	Other expenses related to transport services	96.9	121.7	79.8	98.8	109.7	103.0	113.2	105.6	132.8	12.6	**13.4**
1182011	Jewellery, watches, precious stones	84.2	92.9	83.6	72.5	79.6	101.5	99.5	90.2	64.9	10.9	**13.3**
1144015	Light bulbs and electrical accessories	98.7	90.2	82.8	119.7	114.4	110.8	84.1	92.0	110.7	12.9	**13.0**
1182021	Articles for travelling and personal luggage	90.8	101.1	79.2	92.6	86.4	92.5	74.0	73.6	110.4	7.4	**13.0**
1145022	Other household services	81.1	102.2	79.6	80.4	101.4	89.7	87.6	88.4	115.9	10.8	**12.6**
1152011	Lenses and glasses	91.9	125.1	82.2	91.6	104.2	114.6	106.4	113.1	116.9	14.5	**12.6**
1172023	Other services nec	90.8	91.1	57.9	89.8	90.3	80.9	81.5	77.4	90.7	14.4	**12.4**
1171035	Flowers, other recreational goods	105.8	99.3	72.5	104.1	95.4	106.6	95.3	76.9	95.5	12.1	**12.1**
1172022	Charges for radio, television use	98.1	90.5	114.8	108.9	76.6	92.7	105.8	83.8	99.3	12.9	**11.9**
1172021	Expenses for sporting events and activities	87.5	85.9	96.0	83.3	86.5	80.8	82.4	89.3	115.9	5.4	**11.3**
1182022	Other personal articles nec	94.6	95.3	65.5	82.0	78.3	88.5	87.9	79.2	77.9	12.3	**10.7**
1174011	Tuition costs	92.4	114.8	88.7	98.1	84.1	100.7	97.9	112.4	113.3	10.2	**10.5**
1183011	Expenditures in restaurants	95.0	95.2	90.5	107.3	88.5	91.9	80.9	93.6	113.3	6.4	**9.7**
1132011	Electricity	88.8	103.5	87.3	97.9	97.3	89.1	85.0	84.3	72.4	6.3	**9.7**
1163011	Local transport services	93.4	108.8	91.7	83.8	89.2	87.6	104.1	95.8	107.4	8.6	**8.9**
1171012	Televisions	89.5	105.5	103.6	88.1	85.3	99.9	89.1	96.4	108.4	8.4	**8.4**
1183013	Expenditures in canteens	87.2	101.7	82.0	105.9	90.9	92.0	105.1	101.7	95.1	8.8	**8.2**
1163021	Railway and road transport services	102.5	105.8	88.8	113.6	110.4	91.8	95.1	102.3	103.0	8.9	**7.7**
1182031	Paper and drawing supplies	84.7	82.7	88.2	92.8	99.8	100.9	95.8	102.8	86.8	7.7	**7.6**
1186011	Legal services	104.0	79.1	83.9	93.9	92.9	95.4	95.0	92.2	92.9	8.8	**7.3**
1171033	Games and toys	107.0	89.5	92.5	89.3	100.3	103.0	91.2	89.6	104.0	7.1	**7.1**
1183012	Expenditures in cafes, bars	83.1	106.3	97.9	96.7	95.3	90.5	100.1	100.1	102.1	7.4	**6.6**

Appendix H.1: List of products/services ranked by EU-12 coefficient of price variation in 1985 (based on price including taxes)

	D	F	I	NL	B	L	UK	IRL	DK	GR	E	P	A	S	FIN	Coefficients of price variation			
Final consumption																EU6	EU9	EU12	EU15
1186011 Legal services	209.8	131.2	41.4	90.5	98.3	91.7	130.3	98.0	244.7	40.9	50.8	31.8	176.3	214.4	290.9	46.7	47.5	**60.7**	60.3
1112011 Mineral water	129.0	107.8	48.5	142.5	140.3	104.3	255.9	360.1	330.6	101.0	122.3	85.5	114.1	427.3	419.6	28.5	57.0	**59.2**	64.8
1113012 Wine	117.9	98.8	90.8	122.6	103.9	86.3	236.1	290.2	238.3	75.5	43.5	52.1	120.4	282.4	366.0	12.8	47.9	**59.1**	62.4
1173011 Books, brochures, other similar printed matters	118.8	64.0	127.9	232.6	67.9	95.4	105.1	104.9	255.9	82.1	68.4	23.2	128.9	125.1	404.7	48.0	49.3	**58.0**	69.6
1174011 Tuition costs	98.2	251.3	136.8	125.6	116.5	53.3	161.4	50.7	154.3	30.9	58.4	43.4	114.9	95.4	159.7	46.3	45.0	**57.8**	51.7
1131021 Water distribution charges	157.4	210.3	21.1	191.0	208.0	128.2	108.1	137.6	229.6	65.5	265.1	64.3	154.7	265.2	115.3	42.9	39.7	**48.2**	46.0
1153051 Other medical and paramedical services	246.4	129.0	191.2	95.3	55.1	252.1	55.3	69.6	232.5	235.2	152.7	117.1	83.3	290.8	387.7	46.0	53.5	**48.0**	55.4
1143021 Repairs to heating, washing, kitchen appliances	103.7	107.3	110.2	106.6	124.7	94.6	113.5	260.7	151.4	49.1	68.5	57.5	107.2	157.4	149.8	8.3	37.3	**46.7**	41.8
1114011 Cigarettes	123.7	73.3	89.9	100.1	87.1	69.7	154.2	176.2	199.1	50.2	48.0	62.3	132.3	152.6	141.1	19.8	37.2	**46.6**	41.4
1153041 Nurse services	89.4	171.6	213.6	52.2	44.0	110.1	54.9	121.3	211.4	202.3	136.7	187.6	94.6	70.3	67.8	54.1	52.8	**46.1**	48.7
1163021 Railway and road transport services	159.3	118.7	61.3	140.1	120.3	88.0	176.0	207.2	133.7	51.7	53.9	54.8	120.6	147.3	136.8	28.2	31.1	**44.1**	38.9
1164021 Telephone, telegraph and telex services	125.3	92.0	66.7	48.4	134.8	43.2	174.8	128.3	80.2	32.4	84.4	111.3	121.8	56.6	124.4	41.8	42.1	**43.8**	41.4
1144021 Repairs to glassware, tableware, household utensils	171.9	139.8	51.7	158.5	176.6	179.7	103.6	99.0	150.7	104.2	45.6	33.4	57.5	245.3	189.3	30.3	29.9	**43.0**	47.5
1172022 Charges for radio, television use	105.5	89.1	78.0	80.9	162.3	184.7	106.1	91.6	158.3	20.3	104.7	60.9	75.0	114.8	128.7	35.6	32.2	**42.6**	39.1
1113013 Beer	80.3	153.9	140.2	113.7	156.9	123.2	118.8	259.4	156.9	71.4	63.2	65.0	108.9	301.3	353.7	20.6	32.4	**42.3**	55.9
1113014 Other alcoholic drinks	83.0	117.3	80.4	64.1	79.0	64.2	114.4	186.5	133.4	53.5	53.1	73.5	114.4	199.5	187.3	21.8	36.7	**41.0**	45.1
1145021 Laundry and dry cleaning	104.3	93.0	208.9	63.3	83.1	95.8	62.6	74.9	99.9	74.3	97.8	62.0	94.5	137.7	192.0	43.4	42.3	**40.5**	41.6
1151011 Medicine	178.7	71.2	76.1	158.7	90.1	92.8	95.6	126.3	171.2	60.6	64.1	60.0	156.8	112.4	142.9	37.5	33.6	**40.5**	36.9
1144012 Cutlery	126.0	102.2	90.5	73.8	80.8	64.4	99.4	39.5	146.5	148.7	93.3	24.3	87.3	152.8	108.3	22.5	33.1	**40.3**	37.9
1144014 Gardening equipment	85.2	77.8	94.4	84.4	103.1	69.7	196.4	175.6	111.2	86.3	77.8	57.1	102.7	76.3	106.2	12.6	38.0	**39.7**	36.6
1111032 Dried or smoked fish	91.3	106.0	98.5	89.5	74.4	73.1	72.3	60.1	111.1	67.3	209.5	89.2	110.8	96.1	71.6	13.4	18.9	**39.5**	36.3
1111042 Preserved milk	91.9	122.4	241.1	96.3	93.9	82.4	84.2	93.7	93.6	86.1	113.9	156.0	206.8	131.0	198.2	45.3	42.5	**38.5**	39.1
1114021 Other tobacco products	107.1	77.4	87.2	80.0	62.4	51.4	149.6	175.5	123.9	120.2	52.3	85.8	143.6	101.3	74.9	22.9	38.3	**37.9**	35.8
1171041 Repairs of recreational goods	82.2	94.0	157.0	142.1	197.6	151.6	92.5	93.2	145.7	118.0	69.5	36.6	137.9	136.6	138.5	28.4	29.0	**37.5**	33.2
1153021 Specialist medical services	107.7	110.5	153.4	76.0	56.1	76.4	76.8	96.7	119.6	87.5	139.3	20.5	71.2	56.1	66.3	32.7	28.6	**37.2**	38.0
1163011 Local transport services	159.8	141.7	78.4	137.3	162.3	141.5	116.1	154.0	188.8	40.1	71.9	64.6	153.5	206.8	200.9	20.3	20.7	**36.8**	36.4
1172021 Expenses for sporting events and activities	84.4	161.6	89.7	130.6	123.9	109.1	90.9	65.0	119.3	68.0	187.7	47.0	133.2	99.7	116.6	22.4	25.4	**36.8**	33.0
1113011 Alcohol	93.7	97.4	62.8	97.6	93.7	76.8	134.3	155.8	185.0	68.9	51.7	102.9	79.5	219.5	250.6	14.8	33.6	**36.8**	48.6
1111064 Fresh vegetables	129.5	111.7	85.6	141.7	157.7	108.9	148.8	182.0	207.6	59.8	84.2	57.1	131.0	313.4	218.9	19.2	25.3	**36.7**	45.9
1141021 Repairs to furniture, furnishings, floorings	107.3	132.8	99.3	48.8	113.5	161.9	111.7	64.4	81.9	65.5	111.1	38.2	151.2	160.1	146.8	31.1	31.6	**36.4**	36.4
1111053 Edible oils	189.1	122.4	81.4	173.3	106.6	118.6	126.1	153.6	271.9	118.5	99.9	100.1	174.3	366.0	282.3	28.4	35.9	**36.3**	47.5
1172011 Expenses related to cultural events and activities	93.7	118.4	133.4	81.3	88.5	52.1	134.1	76.4	91.2	39.2	64.8	48.8	81.1	80.9	91.1	27.6	26.7	**35.5**	31.9
1183013 Expenditures in canteens	120.2	116.0	114.4	45.1	52.8	62.6	89.1	132.0	138.3	88.0	102.6	43.1	239.4	151.9	149.2	37.7	34.5	**35.4**	45.1
1183012 Expenditures in cafes, bars	141.3	146.4	90.1	130.4	123.7	99.1	108.8	133.0	221.0	109.0	76.2	42.8	171.7	241.2	205.3	17.0	27.1	**35.4**	38.9
1153011 General practitioner medical services	82.7	118.3	173.5	84.2	69.2	122.3	126.6	161.8	147.9	86.1	124.9	33.3	81.2	105.2	177.6	32.2	28.5	**35.3**	35.2
1132021 Town gas and natural gas	111.2	127.5	90.1	92.6	109.7	104.9	89.7	168.9	173.9	31.3	86.6	83.5	117.9	153.9	171.4	11.8	25.6	**34.8**	33.5
1146011 Domestic services	106.1	150.5	119.0	99.0	81.7	95.1	98.0	88.1	113.7	71.9	64.2	16.6	96.7	134.2	177.5	20.1	18.3	**34.2**	36.1
1111071 Potatoes	143.3	100.2	88.4	93.7	60.3	66.8	116.8	162.2	160.8	122.9	64.9	70.7	140.7	196.4	258.1	29.2	32.6	**33.9**	43.6
1163031 Other expenses related to transport services	134.5	108.9	79.0	86.5	147.1	72.4	100.7	73.0	59.4	53.0	67.2	64.3	160.3	140.6	73.4	26.8	29.3	**32.8**	35.9
1171021 Photographic and cinematic equipment	93.4	120.4	90.4	108.6	125.4	103.5	101.4	126.4	129.5	187.0	135.2	247.4	131.4	109.2	121.0	12.0	12.6	**32.8**	30.1
1111033 Other seafood	81.2	111.6	149.9	50.1	78.8	68.4	109.3	93.3	96.5	105.9	93.1	33.8	99.9	161.2	88.7	36.0	29.2	**32.6**	33.4
1181011 Hairdressers, beauticians and other similar services	100.9	109.8	97.6	120.5	120.0	104.8	118.2	90.9	173.2	85.4	56.8	39.2	146.6	188.1	165.1	8.1	19.8	**31.8**	34.6
1162012 Vehicle maintenance costs	124.5	103.9	89.3	141.9	108.6	86.8	129.5	101.9	155.9	69.7	71.0	36.8	138.9	188.5	208.8	17.7	19.3	**31.7**	37.8
1163022 Other transport services	113.1	113.8	81.0	61.0	104.9	112.5	98.5	171.7	189.8	101.1	86.2	119.7	59.2	134.9	105.4	20.4	33.0	**30.6**	31.1
1171013 Record players, tape and cassette recorders	95.6	103.7	88.7	81.3	109.4	90.2	94.1	111.7	123.9	217.4	123.3	141.2	115.5	122.5	97.3	9.9	12.7	**30.5**	27.7
1111065 Dried vegetables	101.0	92.0	78.4	116.4	208.7	120.1	110.7	135.2	168.3	75.4	117.9	104.2	115.4	176.1	275.1	35.4	30.4	**30.3**	39.0
1183021 Hotels and other lodging accommodations	75.8	95.3	139.2	85.7	74.1	85.4	146.2	81.3	114.6	62.9	86.4	49.9	121.4	145.4	115.8	23.8	25.7	**30.2**	29.6
1161011 Motor vehicles	89.6	99.1	93.0	99.2	80.3	76.2	114.5	136.0	166.9	197.0	111.1	129.3	99.1	98.6	168.1	9.8	25.8	**29.9**	29.3
1171011 Radios	93.9	123.8	97.0	101.7	130.4	107.2	89.3	106.7	151.6	230.2	122.3	126.5	125.3	109.3	117.6	12.5	17.1	**29.6**	26.9
1143014 Heating and air conditioning appliances	94.5	95.5	93.6	92.5	135.4	95.3	124.5	105.4	137.9	94.0	47.9	182.0	110.9	111.1	167.6	15.2	16.5	**29.4**	28.5
1111104 Ice cream	90.9	125.1	155.7	59.7	90.4	95.8	69.6	111.4	132.5	167.9	133.5	149.3	123.6	132.9	159.3	29.4	28.0	**28.7**	26.5
1143013 Cookers and stoves	99.4	113.6	101.2	88.1	112.2	105.4	87.7	95.0	125.0	94.4	108.1	211.1	109.6	110.2	116.2	8.3	11.3	**28.4**	25.4

	D	F	I	NL	B	L	UK	IRL	DK	GR	E	P	A	S	FIN	Coefficients of price variation			
																EU6	EU9	EU12	EU15
1182022 Other personal articles nec	85.4	86.0	84.1	83.6	72.9	79.1	140.1	170.3	114.0	74.4	101.0	101.6	89.9	98.7	116.8	5.6	30.8	**28.3**	25.7
1111061 Fresh fruits	149.0	112.8	83.9	105.5	138.8	115.5	127.9	137.6	164.4	70.1	94.7	52.7	106.6	198.3	151.1	18.2	18.3	**28.2**	30.3
1185011 Insurance, banking and other financial services	122.2	84.0	112.1	121.5	90.6	75.6	98.2	91.9	116.2	111.2	38.4	50.2	60.2	184.1	137.5	18.2	16.0	**28.1**	35.6
1111092 Tea	177.0	191.0	129.8	96.3	112.6	124.2	75.2	79.7	162.5	172.4	120.0	122.0	209.3	181.9	285.7	24.6	30.8	**28.0**	36.1
1152011 Lenses and glasses	120.9	121.2	132.4	100.8	110.1	117.6	37.4	121.3	157.9	89.3	70.8	97.1	158.2	76.5	117.0	8.4	27.1	**27.9**	28.3
1144015 Light bulbs and electrical accessories	94.1	121.7	73.8	99.2	125.1	83.0	114.5	105.2	185.6	70.3	114.9	90.2	104.5	93.1	147.8	18.9	27.6	**27.6**	26.4
1122021 Repairs to footwear	116.7	128.1	89.4	109.5	101.6	125.1	104.9	87.7	158.6	60.5	86.5	52.5	136.1	166.5	268.3	12.0	18.3	**27.6**	42.1
1151021 Other pharmaceutical products	121.8	86.5	72.1	98.1	113.7	81.6	117.9	137.0	83.9	45.5	84.6	63.5	105.6	122.2	91.7	18.4	20.5	**27.5**	25.3
1182011 Jewellery, watches, precious stones	180.9	143.6	69.0	140.1	146.7	137.0	127.6	132.7	187.2	98.3	88.0	86.6	209.6	191.6	165.8	24.5	22.8	**27.4**	28.9
1132041 Coal, coke and other solid combustibles	110.5	135.3	86.2	110.8	99.7	79.0	108.8	113.3	114.3	63.3	75.4	37.6	114.7	131.9	127.2	17.7	14.7	**27.4**	26.2
1171035 Flowers, other recreational goods	143.6	109.8	82.0	58.2	86.2	98.3	99.3	114.4	95.8	65.4	58.8	66.8	115.5	196.5	250.8	27.4	22.6	**27.4**	46.9
1172023 Other services nec	94.6	117.9	119.2	115.5	126.0	110.9	54.5	58.5	108.1	63.0	130.3	76.0	160.6	102.4	109.5	8.6	24.8	**27.1**	27.5
1121021 Repairs to clothing	95.6	169.3	80.3	164.8	150.9	162.4	158.6	118.3	198.9	93.6	119.3	100.8	168.1	255.8	239.6	25.9	25.0	**26.9**	33.2
1121014 Babies' clothing (age 0 to 2 years)	118.6	146.9	138.5	79.7	148.5	172.6	82.0	69.1	103.5	118.9	99.1	110.6	126.4	139.3	132.0	21.7	29.1	**26.0**	23.4
1164011 Postal services	115.0	105.6	78.1	92.2	131.3	65.1	106.7	112.2	101.5	60.0	71.3	54.9	95.1	133.2	103.8	22.7	18.6	**25.9**	24.9
1111103 Confectionery	87.7	98.4	177.6	89.3	82.5	90.3	92.1	108.2	152.4	101.9	101.1	104.2	99.9	229.5	195.2	31.7	28.9	**25.5**	36.4
1132022 Liquified gas	136.4	123.4	113.2	148.3	111.6	99.3	131.7	140.3	131.9	69.3	66.6	72.4	141.8	235.2	135.1	13.4	11.7	**24.8**	32.2
1153031 Dental services	106.2	93.6	147.0	62.1	90.7	79.5	82.0	103.2	125.7	67.0	91.5	77.1	62.6	58.7	56.7	27.3	24.3	**24.7**	28.7
1171012 Televisions	92.8	128.1	87.2	89.9	122.3	109.3	81.7	108.5	154.7	184.5	139.3	126.5	124.4	98.9	88.7	15.3	20.6	**24.6**	23.9
1152021 Orthopaedic, therapeutic appliances and products	108.4	90.6	97.7	107.9	81.5	67.6	76.8	90.9	45.4	74.6	57.6	56.2	95.2	56.2	70.8	15.7	22.3	**24.6**	24.3
1145012 Other non-durable household articles	88.8	115.2	83.1	73.6	92.1	101.6	112.3	166.7	92.7	70.3	105.2	97.9	80.6	148.4	185.9	14.4	25.1	**24.1**	30.5
1131013 General household maintenance costs	105.4	125.6	96.9	109.3	108.3	91.3	100.9	108.1	124.6	57.7	65.6	56.6	109.2	158.5	156.2	10.2	10.0	**23.8**	27.8
1111062 Dried fruits	73.8	134.2	124.9	112.5	173.4	121.7	94.2	104.2	136.2	81.7	133.3	158.5	83.4	163.3	170.8	23.9	22.4	**23.4**	25.5
1145022 Other household services	104.0	114.7	94.7	99.0	117.0	113.6	99.2	98.7	127.3	67.5	72.0	47.7	105.5	92.7	123.2	7.9	9.6	**23.0**	21.4
1142021 Repairs to household textiles	99.9	110.2	91.0	95.2	112.4	109.1	95.3	94.8	122.3	64.9	69.1	45.9	101.8	135.9	54.8	7.8	9.6	**23.0**	25.9
1162031 Other expenses related to personal transport	99.9	124.0	130.0	91.7	141.2	102.6	80.8	122.7	83.6	94.4	65.9	72.8	113.6	152.4	150.2	15.6	18.8	**22.8**	24.7
1111067 Vegetables preserved, prepared, soups	98.9	110.6	111.2	99.9	107.3	105.5	82.9	100.3	181.1	95.1	117.7	148.1	139.7	203.8	246.3	4.5	23.5	**22.4**	34.5
1111054 Other animal or vegetable fats	128.7	135.0	169.9	100.9	106.2	117.6	74.3	99.4	137.9	177.2	130.5	142.2	120.4	223.0	236.0	18.0	22.0	**22.3**	31.0
1111022 Veal	120.8	95.1	119.2	144.0	131.7	112.4	149.1	139.4	158.9	76.9	89.0	86.3	126.8	178.6	141.9	12.6	14.5	**21.9**	22.4
1112012 Other soft drinks	96.9	111.6	79.5	97.5	101.6	82.7	106.4	147.2	148.5	83.5	85.3	89.5	115.4	171.0	218.2	11.5	21.6	**21.8**	32.9
1111102 Chocolate	90.0	88.9	128.7	118.9	98.0	100.7	106.2	100.4	169.5	127.0	97.3	157.9	102.7	161.4	192.6	14.1	21.5	**21.8**	25.8
1111013 Bread	114.4	136.8	94.6	92.6	102.6	96.7	85.8	108.8	133.1	69.1	85.2	64.9	111.0	205.7	179.5	14.5	15.7	**21.5**	33.3
1143015 Cleaning equipment	101.5	112.4	99.4	84.3	110.1	96.6	85.6	98.4	117.0	177.1	130.2	108.3	101.0	98.2	103.8	9.2	10.5	**21.5**	19.9
1121015 Clothing accessories	111.8	133.0	94.4	86.9	109.4	105.9	83.0	70.6	123.1	77.1	71.1	76.3	107.8	160.6	121.5	13.6	18.5	**21.2**	24.4
1111016 Other cereal based products	111.2	112.2	149.8	76.1	82.1	104.3	81.8	93.2	101.4	146.1	117.6	127.7	124.2	152.6	191.0	22.6	20.9	**21.2**	25.8
1111025 Poultry	104.6	127.3	101.7	94.6	100.7	104.3	86.2	97.0	135.1	77.2	82.6	54.7	69.7	127.7	121.3	9.7	13.9	**21.1**	22.2
1111021 Beef	117.1	92.6	106.5	129.1	107.4	115.3	99.8	105.1	145.2	80.3	57.3	91.0	106.0	178.2	156.6	10.1	13.3	**21.0**	26.1
1111034 Preserved, prepared fish and other seafood	92.1	139.9	131.2	91.2	97.3	103.3	70.3	73.9	117.0	112.4	125.2	83.0	74.3	166.7	232.3	17.6	22.1	**20.8**	36.0
1111024 Mutton, lamb and goat meat	126.1	115.8	108.8	124.0	144.3	128.0	92.8	116.5	131.9	71.1	105.6	65.0	100.0	171.4	212.1	8.9	11.5	**20.8**	29.3
1111043 Other milk products, except cheese	76.2	122.0	123.2	73.5	121.0	82.6	105.3	120.2	80.6	106.0	119.3	70.8	105.1	140.2	120.6	22.5	20.6	**20.6**	20.5
1111051 Butter	96.2	99.9	114.6	99.1	101.0	90.7	92.3	82.5	107.7	114.0	171.9	111.3	131.8	122.7	178.0	7.2	9.1	**20.4**	23.5
1111028 Other fresh or frozen meat	110.6	108.1	119.5	99.1	102.2	113.0	65.2	79.5	84.4	75.1	62.8	93.9	127.4	129.3	167.3	6.2	17.3	**19.7**	26.1
1111093 Cocoa	108.3	92.1	96.5	95.8	67.6	128.8	158.4	125.6	114.0	111.3	105.6	109.7	53.1	114.7	172.1	18.7	22.5	**19.5**	26.3
1173012 Periodicals, newspapers	116.8	114.3	93.2	101.6	101.0	111.6	77.3	108.2	138.1	95.6	98.9	56.5	92.4	142.4	205.6	7.9	14.9	**19.4**	29.7
1122012 Women's footwear	114.8	118.9	86.9	86.4	127.9	125.6	102.3	104.2	132.8	80.6	88.5	72.2	119.5	154.8	150.7	15.5	14.6	**18.9**	21.9
1143012 Washing machines, tumble dryers	105.4	114.8	78.5	94.6	106.8	108.7	98.0	111.6	132.9	168.7	120.6	123.6	111.9	126.7	107.4	11.7	13.3	**18.9**	17.2
1111023 Pork	102.9	95.5	106.0	114.8	90.2	98.5	93.0	107.3	162.4	105.7	78.5	100.6	109.8	186.2	167.9	7.8	19.1	**18.8**	26.5
1111081 Sugar	102.5	117.6	83.7	121.1	113.5	114.3	96.4	119.5	162.6	134.3	109.8	82.6	110.9	150.3	229.0	11.6	18.0	**18.4**	28.5
1183011 Expenditures in restaurants	109.1	92.6	124.8	98.6	113.1	108.8	104.4	133.7	133.8	95.7	70.0	76.8	93.3	131.9	159.7	9.5	12.2	**18.3**	21.0
1111014 Cakes, biscuits	102.1	113.0	122.8	89.5	94.6	96.2	75.2	100.3	132.7	91.5	97.8	64.1	119.2	177.4	198.4	11.2	16.0	**18.3**	30.9
1181022 Non-durable personal care products	91.0	125.3	91.5	93.4	91.9	85.8	94.9	107.7	146.6	86.5	105.8	80.5	109.0	156.9	171.6	13.6	18.5	**18.1**	24.9
1111063 Fruits frozen, preserved, and as juice	90.5	92.8	121.4	116.2	112.7	106.9	84.6	95.4	157.7	95.3	111.4	131.6	100.2	147.2	163.4	10.8	19.3	**18.0**	20.8
1144011 Glassware and tableware	103.7	104.6	59.7	88.3	87.5	87.6	124.9	112.6	86.9	87.6	75.9	84.0	85.1	155.2	182.3	16.8	18.7	**17.9**	30.1
1142011 Household textiles	112.8	95.9	99.0	102.6	137.7	115.0	106.4	90.5	105.8	69.1	76.7	84.1	111.1	129.4	107.4	12.7	12.1	**17.7**	17.1
1182031 Paper and drawing supplies	98.4	104.4	79.7	103.6	84.5	90.5	115.1	124.8	131.7	84.8	86.8	74.8	136.3	176.7	181.8	10.0	16.1	**17.7**	28.8
1111027 Meat preparations, other meat products	137.8	96.6	142.4	92.5	120.9	109.3	86.5	102.1	154.2	109.4	121.2	106.0	120.4	217.7	217.8	16.3	19.7	**17.5**	30.4

	D	F	I	NL	B	L	UK	IRL	DK	GR	E	P	A	S	FIN	Coefficients of price variation			
																EU6	EU9	EU12	EU15
1145011 Cleaning and maintenance products	122.8	101.4	101.6	99.9	96.6	103.8	87.0	100.6	143.8	100.1	88.6	71.8	138.5	166.0	213.8	8.2	14.9	**16.9**	30.4
1111041 Fresh milk	79.1	92.9	119.3	83.3	85.8	83.6	100.5	111.5	119.0	108.3	112.9	68.6	118.5	115.9	120.3	14.8	15.5	**16.9**	16.7
1122013 Children's and babies' footwear	101.5	104.2	107.2	120.6	146.0	121.7	80.7	89.2	136.8	109.0	104.8	90.2	108.9	127.3	196.4	13.0	17.9	**16.9**	23.6
1111052 Margarine	90.4	130.5	114.0	78.0	128.5	115.3	101.2	95.1	104.3	113.6	145.3	96.6	120.6	194.4	238.6	17.5	15.4	**16.6**	32.6
1111045 Eggs	80.9	124.2	129.7	82.1	98.4	105.2	105.0	111.8	131.6	98.7	92.1	86.9	136.0	148.8	184.3	18.1	16.4	**16.2**	24.0
1181021 Durable and semi-durable personal care products	100.0	117.3	89.9	90.6	124.1	100.2	92.2	89.4	119.2	137.8	86.9	127.8	123.3	135.6	158.4	12.4	12.8	**16.1**	18.8
1111012 Flour, other cereals	88.7	128.4	112.2	95.8	85.1	91.4	98.2	80.1	117.7	123.4	119.7	84.6	141.9	113.1	170.8	15.2	15.3	**16.1**	21.9
1111105 Condiments, sauces,spices,salt	89.4	117.1	116.4	81.1	94.2	79.5	94.2	120.6	88.3	84.4	107.9	75.3	112.1	128.5	137.0	15.9	15.4	**15.9**	18.4
1122011 Men's footwear	115.1	106.6	98.1	98.7	126.5	120.4	84.9	92.3	142.4	89.6	97.7	94.7	116.7	194.1	157.9	9.6	15.8	**15.6**	24.9
1143016 Other household appliances	97.4	106.9	92.5	87.3	116.7	101.8	90.3	105.3	127.7	135.6	96.0	137.1	115.5	110.8	133.2	9.6	12.0	**15.5**	14.8
1121013 Children's clothing (age 3 to 13 years)	102.9	100.8	102.2	92.5	121.9	99.9	92.0	80.7	144.8	97.9	95.6	100.2	122.8	135.3	188.2	8.7	17.0	**15.2**	23.6
1171022 Other important leisure durables (incl. computers)	89.3	110.0	100.3	99.1	135.3	98.6	101.8	120.9	117.3	135.2	117.9	149.2	112.8	121.2	114.2	13.9	12.4	**15.2**	13.6
1141012 Floor coverings	90.5	109.3	144.4	116.1	103.2	113.1	99.8	85.1	121.3	84.1	115.9	113.4	139.6	68.7	127.7	14.5	15.3	**15.1**	18.5
1132011 Electricity	114.7	112.5	102.8	94.1	116.1	88.2	78.8	89.3	97.7	80.1	83.0	72.5	79.7	54.2	48.6	10.2	12.5	**15.1**	22.1
1111066 Frozen vegetables	100.1	114.0	133.3	105.6	113.7	98.6	89.6	123.9	115.0	84.2	83.6	88.4	114.3	116.1	231.1	10.5	11.5	**14.9**	30.2
1171034 Film and other photographic supplies	85.4	100.6	94.3	115.5	114.0	96.6	119.4	128.4	132.8	123.5	105.4	144.9	118.3	95.4	137.7	10.6	14.0	**14.8**	14.9
1111101 Jams, marmalades, honey, syrups	104.9	95.8	140.0	112.0	113.7	112.3	76.1	96.0	119.5	107.2	108.7	87.4	156.6	153.4	246.9	11.9	15.6	**14.7**	32.6
1182021 Articles for travelling and personal luggage	105.6	92.8	113.1	89.0	96.0	88.1	90.6	102.8	126.0	108.2	86.6	135.5	107.9	104.1	127.4	9.3	12.0	**14.6**	14.1
1143011 Refrigerators, freezers	98.1	114.0	87.7	91.1	108.1	106.0	90.6	104.9	105.0	134.1	118.1	138.4	108.1	106.0	109.9	9.3	8.5	**14.3**	12.8
1132031 Heating oil and other heating fuels	87.0	123.3	107.2	100.3	95.9	78.0	87.3	103.2	110.1	78.5	87.3	90.8	114.9	116.3	84.5	14.7	13.2	**13.6**	14.2
1162021 Fuels and lubricants for motor vehicles	98.7	115.0	106.9	98.2	92.3	82.1	89.7	117.6	99.3	71.8	85.8	95.3	120.5	94.1	105.4	10.5	10.9	**13.1**	13.2
1111015 Pasta, noodles	100.2	99.8	100.5	92.4	119.3	98.9	85.2	117.1	139.0	109.7	98.3	114.9	140.7	212.0	266.3	8.1	14.6	**13.1**	37.9
1121012 Women's clothing	112.2	102.5	99.8	85.5	115.3	111.0	82.9	99.1	97.5	87.7	110.5	74.3	116.4	147.3	131.9	9.6	10.6	**12.8**	17.6
1161021 Other modes of personal transport	96.1	95.4	107.9	99.2	97.1	90.7	91.7	105.0	138.0	87.4	112.5	109.1	105.5	113.0	142.2	5.3	13.4	**12.8**	14.5
1171031 Records, cassettes, magnetic tapes and accessories	102.7	115.4	88.9	92.3	112.0	94.7	97.8	110.4	140.0	99.3	96.9	113.6	128.1	127.2	145.0	9.8	14.0	**12.8**	15.2
1111031 Fresh, frozen fish	100.1	105.8	112.9	82.3	112.7	92.6	86.5	96.4	115.7	104.4	95.7	73.6	118.0	108.9	81.9	10.9	11.3	**12.7**	13.3
1111044 Cheese	106.7	98.0	93.9	112.8	114.3	101.7	97.4	127.5	139.7	94.3	114.4	125.5	132.8	173.4	151.7	7.1	13.0	**12.7**	18.7
1162011 Tyres, inner tubes, replacement parts for motor vehicles	86.2	113.4	95.7	111.7	115.2	101.3	106.1	118.3	140.5	98.6	107.3	118.2	130.7	123.1	127.3	10.1	13.2	**12.1**	12.3
1121011 Men's clothing	96.1	109.4	100.9	97.5	121.7	114.1	86.8	90.4	122.0	96.9	113.7	86.1	114.2	155.0	165.2	8.7	11.8	**11.9**	20.0
1144013 Non-electrical kitchen and household utensils	103.5	96.7	84.0	97.0	94.4	86.4	106.9	113.0	130.0	97.9	103.9	97.4	110.0	153.6	216.8	7.1	13.2	**11.6**	28.8
1111091 Coffee	114.7	93.0	98.9	85.4	81.3	104.8	92.4	119.2	99.1	87.4	98.9	109.5	91.7	131.5	106.3	11.8	12.0	**11.4**	13.1
1111026 Delicatessen	109.7	103.5	89.4	99.7	114.0	107.9	91.9	86.2	119.5	86.7	85.1	99.1	144.9	184.2	196.8	7.6	10.6	**11.3**	29.2
1111011 Rice	119.3	95.1	98.5	91.4	108.7	105.4	107.5	119.5	127.7	103.6	94.8	96.0	95.2	150.9	156.5	9.0	10.6	**10.4**	17.5
1171033 Games and toys	101.2	112.2	110.3	100.9	105.1	92.1	80.2	102.9	103.0	126.3	103.7	99.7	95.1	133.3	156.6	6.4	9.0	**10.3**	16.5
1141011 Furniture and furnishing accessories	92.2	117.8	94.6	96.0	107.1	107.9	109.1	115.5	105.6	89.7	84.0	109.7	82.0	80.1	105.6	8.9	8.1	**10.1**	11.8
1111072 Products derived from potatoes	112.1	98.5	121.5	81.2	107.7	105.5	96.8	107.7	113.7	118.2	108.0	105.7	155.8	209.0	262.0	12.0	10.5	**9.6**	36.5
1171032 Sports equipment	104.9	90.0	101.5	85.2	96.2	97.8	99.4	91.7	112.5	113.1	94.7	110.2	91.5	102.5	117.2	6.9	7.9	**8.6**	9.1

Appendix H.2: List of products/services ranked by EU-9 coefficient of price variation in 1985 (based on price excluding VAT)

Final consumption	D	F	I	NL	B	L	UK	IRL	DK	Coefficients of price variation EU6	EU9
1111012 Flour, other cereals	120.6	102.2	44.5	135.7	132.4	98.4	255.9	360.1	271.0	29.0	**57.3**
1111021 Beef	230.3	122.3	175.4	90.8	52.0	244.8	55.3	69.6	190.6	46.3	**52.0**
1111013 Bread	103.4	93.6	89.0	116.8	98.0	83.8	236.1	290.2	195.3	10.9	**49.3**
1111024 Mutton, lamb and goat meat	83.6	162.7	196.0	49.7	41.5	106.9	54.9	121.3	173.3	52.9	**49.2**
1111015 Pasta, noodles	86.1	238.2	134.1	119.6	109.9	50.3	161.4	50.7	126.5	47.2	**45.6**
1111014 Cakes, biscuits	111.0	60.7	125.4	221.5	64.1	85.2	105.1	104.9	209.8	49.0	**45.1**
1111026 Delicatessen	117.1	87.2	61.2	46.1	127.2	41.9	174.8	128.3	65.7	41.4	**45.0**
1111044 Cheese	85.9	116.0	236.4	91.7	88.6	77.7	84.2	93.7	76.7	47.5	**44.9**
1111033 Other seafood	97.5	88.2	204.8	60.3	78.4	90.4	62.6	74.9	81.9	45.4	**44.1**
1111011 Rice	196.1	124.4	38.0	86.2	92.7	86.5	130.3	98.0	200.6	46.5	**42.8**
1111042 Preserved milk	79.6	73.7	86.6	80.4	97.3	67.7	196.4	175.6	91.1	11.6	**41.9**
1111045 Eggs	100.1	73.4	80.0	76.2	58.9	48.5	149.6	175.5	101.6	22.4	**41.2**
1111022 Veal	96.9	101.7	101.1	101.5	117.6	91.8	113.5	260.7	124.1	7.8	**40.2**
1111032 Dried or smoked fish	77.6	111.2	78.8	61.0	74.5	60.6	114.4	186.5	109.3	21.8	**38.4**
1111016 Other cereal based products	147.1	199.3	19.4	181.9	196.2	120.9	108.1	137.6	188.2	43.2	**37.7**
1111023 Pork	115.6	69.5	82.5	95.3	82.2	67.7	154.2	176.2	163.2	19.1	**35.7**
1111031 Fresh, frozen fish	75.0	145.9	137.5	108.3	148.0	116.2	118.8	259.4	128.6	21.0	**34.9**
1111025 Poultry	148.9	112.5	56.2	133.4	113.5	83.0	176.0	207.2	109.6	28.5	**34.3**
1111066 Frozen vegetables	112.3	110.0	112.2	43.0	49.8	59.1	89.1	132.0	113.4	38.0	**33.6**
1111063 Fruits frozen, preserved, and as juice	100.3	125.9	97.4	46.5	107.1	152.7	111.7	64.4	67.1	30.7	**32.2**
1111091 Coffee	133.9	95.0	81.1	89.2	56.9	63.0	116.8	162.2	131.8	29.0	**32.2**
1111028 Other fresh or frozen meat	98.6	84.5	71.6	77.0	153.1	179.3	106.1	91.6	129.8	36.9	**31.4**
1111061 Fresh fruits	87.6	92.3	61.6	93.0	88.4	72.5	134.3	155.8	151.6	14.0	**31.1**
1111034 Preserved, prepared fish and other seafood	167.0	67.5	74.6	151.1	85.0	87.5	95.6	126.3	140.3	36.7	**30.9**
1111101 Jams, marmalades, honey, syrups	71.2	105.8	137.5	47.7	74.3	61.1	109.3	75.9	79.1	36.3	**30.9**
1111071 Potatoes	72.5	112.1	170.1	80.2	65.3	109.2	126.6	161.8	121.2	34.8	**30.7**
1111092 Tea	125.7	103.2	72.5	82.4	138.8	68.3	100.7	73.0	48.7	27.0	**30.4**
1111064 Fresh vegetables	176.7	116.0	79.8	165.0	100.6	111.9	126.1	153.6	222.9	27.7	**30.1**
1111052 Margarine	100.7	93.2	150.4	72.4	47.1	72.1	76.8	96.7	98.0	36.1	**30.0**
1112012 Other soft drinks	70.8	90.3	127.7	81.6	59.3	80.6	146.2	66.1	93.9	25.1	**29.9**
1113014 Other alcoholic drinks	79.7	105.5	142.8	50.2	72.3	85.5	60.5	90.6	108.6	32.5	**29.8**
1111027 Meat preparations, other meat products	160.7	132.5	47.4	151.0	166.6	174.5	103.6	99.0	123.5	30.9	**29.8**
1112011 Mineral water	94.4	87.2	71.9	110.9	196.9	113.3	110.7	135.2	138.0	35.8	**29.3**
1111051 Butter	72.1	89.1	153.9	135.3	186.4	147.2	92.5	93.2	119.4	29.8	**29.2**
1111065 Dried vegetables	87.6	112.2	130.8	77.4	83.5	49.2	134.1	76.4	74.8	28.8	**29.0**
1111041 Fresh milk	117.8	96.9	88.7	70.3	76.2	62.5	99.4	39.5	120.1	21.5	**28.9**
1132011 Electricity	104.0	123.9	127.1	67.0	126.9	162.8	82.0	69.1	84.8	24.3	**28.9**
1111104 Ice cream	99.2	107.9	74.3	51.3	99.0	100.4	98.5	139.6	155.6	22.2	**28.4**
1114021 Other tobacco products	74.9	64.5	77.2	70.3	68.8	74.6	121.8	138.5	93.4	6.0	**28.2**
1132022 Liquified gas	76.9	83.0	162.9	85.0	70.5	85.2	92.1	98.4	124.9	33.3	**28.0**
1121013 Children's clothing (age 3 to 13 years)	155.3	161.0	110.0	80.9	94.6	110.9	75.2	79.7	133.2	25.0	**27.5**
1131013 General household maintenance costs	83.0	99.4	101.0	97.1	118.9	99.0	47.4	47.6	88.6	10.5	**26.5**
1131021 Water distribution charges	83.9	160.5	68.1	138.5	142.4	145.0	158.6	96.2	163.0	27.9	**26.4**
1121014 Babies' clothing (age 0 to 2 years)	106.1	102.2	112.2	84.7	92.5	105.0	37.4	121.3	129.4	9.1	**25.5**
1142021 Repairs to household textiles	64.7	113.2	114.6	94.5	163.6	108.7	81.9	84.7	111.6	26.8	**25.4**
1121015 Clothing accessories	82.5	102.6	62.5	83.4	105.1	74.1	99.6	95.6	152.1	17.6	**25.3**
1132041 Coal, coke and other solid combustibles	93.2	78.9	134.9	52.2	85.6	75.0	82.0	93.8	103.0	28.9	**23.9**
1113011 Alcohol	78.6	83.6	85.3	83.4	64.2	68.0	99.6	110.6	136.8	10.6	**23.7**
1141021 Repairs to furniture, furnishings, floorings	77.9	97.1	70.4	61.8	77.4	90.7	97.7	135.5	76.0	14.9	**23.5**
1111062 Dried fruits	121.0	105.9	83.9	135.0	148.8	102.7	148.8	182.0	170.2	18.5	**23.1**
1153021 Specialist medical services	90.3	95.5	106.0	96.5	75.8	87.9	93.0	107.3	162.4	10.0	**22.9**
1122011 Men's footwear	106.8	72.9	61.1	82.4	95.5	72.9	102.5	124.5	68.8	18.7	**22.7**

	D	F	I	NL	B	L	UK	IRL	DK	Coefficients of price variation EU6	EU9
1141012 Floor coverings	95.1	76.4	82.8	90.7	68.5	60.4	66.8	73.9	37.2	15.3	**22.6**
1143015 Cleaning equipment	112.9	113.8	144.0	84.8	85.0	105.0	64.6	80.8	113.0	18.7	**22.4**
1145022 Other household services	66.8	102.9	113.0	61.8	114.2	73.8	91.6	97.7	66.1	24.6	**22.4**
1122012 Women's footwear	158.7	121.1	58.5	117.7	123.3	122.3	111.0	120.6	153.4	25.3	**22.3**
1143014 Heating and air conditioning appliances	86.8	93.3	102.0	83.9	85.8	94.2	72.1	81.5	148.4	6.8	**22.0**
1122021 Repairs to footwear	126.0	92.6	69.5	55.4	72.4	87.8	86.3	93.0	78.5	26.7	**22.0**
1111054 Other animal or vegetable fats	78.9	136.3	82.3	124.4	116.9	105.9	90.9	65.0	97.8	19.6	**21.9**
1145012 Other non-durable household articles	80.8	118.0	111.2	76.6	81.8	92.2	61.1	60.1	95.9	16.9	**21.9**
1144015 Light bulbs and electrical accessories	97.5	94.6	126.9	63.9	70.2	93.1	71.1	75.8	83.1	22.5	**21.2**
1111067 Vegetables preserved, prepared, soups	132.1	138.8	88.3	124.2	116.7	93.5	108.8	133.0	181.1	16.2	**21.0**
1151021 Other pharmaceutical products	101.2	86.1	88.5	91.2	63.8	125.0	137.7	102.1	93.4	19.8	**20.8**
1162031 Other expenses related to personal transport	120.9	72.5	120.7	77.7	96.7	97.6	75.2	83.0	126.4	19.2	**20.8**
1111103 Confectionery	116.4	87.6	81.9	135.1	102.5	77.5	129.5	82.8	127.8	20.4	**20.8**
1153031 Dental services	95.8	117.6	83.7	121.1	95.4	102.1	96.4	119.5	162.6	12.7	**20.0**
1144011 Glassware and tableware	78.9	75.0	109.1	99.9	82.4	89.9	92.3	81.6	138.9	13.5	**19.9**
1151011 Medicine	103.4	101.0	109.6	94.4	96.4	109.7	65.2	64.6	69.2	5.8	**19.6**
1162011 Tyres, inner tubes, replacement parts for motor vehicles	91.0	78.5	50.6	74.2	70.0	78.2	108.6	91.5	71.2	16.5	**19.5**
1141011 Furniture and furnishing accessories	81.4	108.0	73.9	75.5	102.8	97.6	71.0	88.2	126.8	15.0	**19.2**
1153051 Other medical and paramedical services	89.6	113.0	122.8	89.5	79.5	85.9	75.2	100.3	132.7	16.1	**19.1**
1111081 Sugar	99.2	142.7	109.2	83.2	77.1	84.9	98.0	88.1	93.2	22.3	**19.0**
1163021 Railway and road transport services	73.9	86.8	119.3	79.3	80.9	74.6	100.5	111.5	119.0	18.1	**18.9**
1144014 Gardening equipment	98.1	112.1	80.0	73.0	87.5	94.6	72.2	57.4	100.9	14.0	**18.7**
1161021 Other modes of personal transport	79.4	69.6	102.9	97.6	90.2	95.4	73.6	86.7	129.3	12.8	**18.5**
1164011 Postal services	75.6	104.7	129.7	78.2	92.8	93.9	105.0	111.8	131.6	18.9	**18.3**
1121011 Men's clothing	130.7	95.1	71.1	88.7	116.6	103.1	111.2	125.1	134.8	19.0	**18.3**
1111072 Products derived from potatoes	103.9	120.9	88.3	88.2	103.5	99.0	89.7	137.3	142.5	11.0	**18.1**
1121021 Repairs to clothing	102.4	108.0	75.8	104.3	85.4	111.7	91.2	71.3	130.0	13.2	**18.0**
1143021 Repairs to heating, washing, kitchen appliances	85.0	94.1	72.9	81.9	95.8	73.8	92.5	119.7	121.7	10.6	**17.9**
1111102 Chocolate	94.3	104.1	89.5	114.8	113.2	93.6	118.2	73.9	142.0	9.7	**17.9**
1111053 Edible oils	149.3	134.3	76.9	130.8	153.1	133.5	116.1	154.0	154.8	19.3	**17.7**
1132021 Town gas and natural gas	100.9	89.0	71.7	87.8	112.2	61.4	106.7	102.0	83.2	19.4	**17.4**
1163022 Other transport services	94.9	97.4	107.2	114.9	137.7	108.7	80.7	89.2	136.8	12.8	**17.4**
1143013 Cookers and stoves	87.6	104.6	110.2	77.1	113.0	91.6	70.3	99.8	68.5	13.3	**17.3**
1174011 Tuition costs	84.3	95.4	107.9	99.2	81.6	81.0	91.7	105.0	138.0	11.0	**17.1**
1153011 General practitioner medical services	92.5	114.8	78.5	79.5	89.7	97.1	98.0	111.6	132.9	13.2	**16.7**
1171012 Televisions	78.4	98.7	98.6	68.2	75.4	71.0	81.9	109.6	72.4	15.2	**16.7**
1161011 Motor vehicles	79.8	94.0	77.5	78.5	73.5	76.6	82.5	97.9	120.2	8.2	**16.3**
1171022 Other important leisure durables (incl. computers)	90.3	85.0	86.6	77.7	102.4	89.2	80.0	65.6	118.7	8.4	**16.2**
1172011 Expenses related to cultural events and activities	98.7	86.7	95.8	74.8	90.6	78.7	78.8	102.8	126.0	9.8	**16.1**
1171041 Repairs of recreational goods	98.0	80.8	118.6	106.7	97.2	100.3	66.2	78.0	98.0	11.3	**16.1**
1163011 Local transport services	114.8	94.8	101.6	95.1	91.1	92.7	87.0	100.6	143.8	8.2	**16.1**
1122013 Children's and babies' footwear	96.9	114.1	73.1	93.1	83.8	70.5	94.6	113.3	93.7	16.8	**15.5**
1171032 Sports equipment	79.4	92.2	122.4	97.6	86.7	101.0	86.8	69.2	99.4	14.0	**15.3**
1162021 Fuels and lubricants for motor vehicles	86.3	88.0	67.5	98.7	67.6	85.4	100.1	101.5	108.0	13.7	**15.3**
1111043 Other milk products, except cheese	85.3	100.5	90.4	85.2	70.2	71.0	72.3	60.1	91.1	12.7	**15.1**
1121012 Women's clothing	107.2	70.8	95.0	102.1	76.1	67.5	85.4	83.5	95.2	18.0	**15.0**
1153041 Nurse services	95.7	92.6	124.8	98.6	95.0	97.1	104.4	133.7	133.8	10.9	**15.0**
1171013 Record players, tape and cassette recorders	101.0	80.0	83.1	82.9	101.2	107.5	73.8	83.9	116.7	11.7	**15.0**
1113013 Beer	82.9	80.5	85.9	77.7	113.8	85.1	108.3	85.7	113.0	13.7	**14.9**
1172022 Charges for radio, television use	76.3	104.0	105.1	100.3	80.6	69.6	75.9	103.2	90.2	15.9	**14.9**
1144012 Cutlery	100.4	115.3	80.2	77.8	86.2	86.3	74.6	88.5	109.1	14.3	**14.7**
1163031 Other expenses related to transport services	84.5	122.0	114.0	74.3	121.2	102.9	101.2	95.1	104.3	17.6	**14.7**
1113012 Wine	82.4	104.4	89.0	85.5	104.3	101.1	77.7	86.7	124.3	9.6	**14.6**
1182011 Jewellery, watches, precious stones	75.6	85.1	69.3	93.9	86.6	90.4	92.3	96.2	115.2	10.1	**13.7**
1143016 Other household appliances	106.0	80.2	101.0	121.0	105.4	100.4	129.7	113.3	130.2	11.8	**13.7**
1162012 Vehicle maintenance costs	98.9	71.9	83.9	86.2	110.2	102.7	92.5	73.6	86.7	13.9	**13.5**

	D	F	I	NL	B	L	UK	IRL	DK	Coefficients of price variation EU6	EU9
1111105 Condiments, sauces,spices,salt	89.3	98.3	81.4	68.3	103.2	85.1	94.1	111.7	101.6	13.0	**13.4**
1171011 Radios	77.8	96.3	95.1	80.5	68.1	81.6	85.4	65.1	96.5	11.8	**13.3**
1185011 Insurance, banking and other financial services	98.3	83.1	121.5	81.2	90.5	94.2	96.8	87.6	113.7	14.1	**13.2**
1181022 Non-durable personal care products	93.6	73.5	86.1	107.4	107.8	90.8	84.7	103.7	114.5	12.8	**13.2**
1144021 Repairs to glassware, tableware, household utensils	91.8	107.3	86.2	79.5	84.6	93.1	75.0	78.9	110.7	9.7	**13.1**
1132031 Heating oil and other heating fuels	119.6	104.0	103.9	141.2	105.3	93.7	131.7	127.5	108.1	13.8	**12.9**
1111093 Cocoa	87.3	101.5	82.9	103.4	118.3	92.4	101.4	126.4	106.1	12.0	**12.9**
1145011 Cleaning and maintenance products	102.7	78.1	90.3	108.5	90.3	102.9	86.8	85.4	119.0	10.8	**12.8**
1172021 Expenses for sporting events and activities	86.1	96.1	74.3	76.6	102.0	94.6	78.8	104.9	105.0	11.6	**12.8**
1114011 Cigarettes	87.2	85.2	85.8	74.0	105.8	99.4	76.3	77.2	102.5	11.6	**12.7**
1183013 Expenditures in canteens	88.8	104.9	108.1	96.1	89.8	82.2	69.7	83.7	84.4	9.6	**12.5**
1152021 Orthopaedic, therapeutic appliances and products	107.3	118.9	85.2	82.3	120.7	118.5	102.3	104.2	108.9	15.2	**12.5**
1182031 Paper and drawing supplies	100.6	78.4	83.8	71.8	68.3	93.6	80.3	96.9	81.2	13.8	**12.5**
1173011 Books, brochures, other similar printed matters	93.6	84.1	98.5	88.0	112.5	93.3	85.2	117.1	113.9	9.5	**12.3**
1181011 Hairdressers, beauticians and other similar services	90.1	86.6	75.3	77.6	94.1	84.6	85.0	89.8	114.8	7.8	**12.2**
1171033 Games and toys	100.6	94.9	87.1	79.1	92.9	78.8	68.5	72.6	80.1	9.1	**12.1**
1181021 Durable and semi-durable personal care products	87.8	89.2	103.6	69.2	94.7	82.7	75.2	78.4	94.8	12.0	**11.9**
1145021 Laundry and dry cleaning	110.6	97.6	92.2	104.2	123.3	114.3	80.7	94.7	108.1	9.7	**11.9**
1182021 Articles for travelling and personal luggage	84.3	92.2	85.5	81.9	102.3	101.9	75.5	73.5	100.0	9.0	**11.8**
1171035 Flowers, other recreational goods	79.8	94.0	79.9	110.0	91.2	86.3	103.8	104.4	108.9	11.4	**11.8**
1182022 Other personal articles nec	90.8	81.5	71.2	81.5	79.3	77.1	93.0	91.9	106.6	7.3	**11.7**
1164021 Telephone, telegraph and telex services	87.7	98.9	89.9	90.6	104.3	89.5	80.2	89.4	119.2	6.4	**11.5**
1173012 Periodicals, newspapers	104.9	86.4	97.8	81.4	108.8	104.7	82.9	90.1	79.9	10.4	**11.4**
1152011 Lenses and glasses	109.2	114.3	91.4	96.8	95.3	105.3	77.3	108.2	113.2	8.0	**11.3**
1183011 Expenditures in restaurants	96.2	96.7	82.0	95.0	97.4	96.3	79.9	70.1	98.0	5.7	**10.6**
1171021 Photographic and cinematic equipment	85.4	80.2	78.4	73.4	93.4	90.9	78.5	85.6	104.7	8.4	**10.5**
1171034 Film and other photographic supplies	87.8	85.5	113.0	88.7	91.0	88.0	77.9	100.7	94.3	10.1	**10.3**
1146011 Domestic services	84.4	84.2	97.1	83.3	95.3	81.0	80.3	67.1	88.3	7.1	**9.9**
1171031 Records, cassettes, magnetic tapes and accessories	78.3	82.5	92.0	83.3	108.2	88.0	88.5	98.3	96.1	11.0	**9.6**
1144013 Non-electrical kitchen and household utensils	89.0	94.8	84.2	70.8	88.1	86.3	74.4	80.0	95.9	8.6	**9.5**
1143011 Refrigerators, freezers	91.2	96.7	80.3	83.2	93.6	101.4	86.3	80.2	104.3	8.1	**9.3**
1143012 Washing machines, tumble dryers	87.6	92.9	77.1	80.0	89.9	97.4	82.9	77.1	100.2	8.0	**9.3**
1183021 Hotels and other lodging accommodations	80.9	110.1	86.8	91.4	101.0	96.3	94.9	93.9	86.6	10.1	**8.7**
1172023 Other services nec	86.6	97.0	90.6	82.5	87.1	73.3	78.0	95.6	81.4	8.4	**8.6**
1142011 Household textiles	92.5	105.9	88.9	91.8	102.2	81.5	87.7	87.9	102.1	8.7	**8.3**
1186011 Legal services	92.0	75.9	86.0	81.1	80.8	87.3	99.4	91.7	92.2	6.2	**7.9**
1183012 Expenditures in cafes, bars	104.6	88.9	90.4	87.0	92.9	94.1	93.5	97.2	104.7	6.2	**6.3**

Appendix I.1: List of products/services ranked by EU-12 coefficient of price variation in 1990 (based on price including taxes)

	D	F	I	NL	B	L	UK	IRL	DK	GR	E	P	A	S	FIN	Coefficients of price variation			
Final consumption																EU6	EU9	EU12	EU15
1186011 Legal services	70.7	147.7	97.5	114.8	77.9	61.6	178.8	159.9	282.6	70.3	74.6	52.5	109.7	327.2	305.2	30.9	49.7	**55.4**	62.8
1144021 Repairs to glassware, tableware, household utensils	117.2	96.3	32.7	81.0	123.0	119.9	136.9	47.5	78.1	36.6	20.5	18.0	102.4	217.6	167.1	33.2	36.4	**54.9**	59.2
1153041 Nurse services	120.9	82.7	295.7	87.0	86.6	90.0	37.6	130.1	173.5	168.8	105.9	57.7	178.5	182.1	248.6	60.1	57.7	**54.8**	50.6
1153051 Other medical and paramedical services	114.6	164.6	71.6	134.8	167.9	187.3	27.6	92.0	108.7	104.0	27.6	35.5	90.9	131.8	157.0	27.6	40.5	**51.2**	46.0
1145021 Laundry and dry cleaning	78.3	81.5	161.6	67.5	73.2	86.4	37.9	61.0	203.8	73.7	124.2	52.7	70.0	136.9	100.3	35.0	52.8	**50.1**	45.9
1111053 Edible oils	172.1	112.4	89.3	142.0	103.0	129.7	113.7	121.8	333.3	99.2	107.8	85.2	175.0	478.0	512.4	21.8	47.7	**47.9**	73.0
1113012 Wine	122.9	115.7	66.5	146.2	146.7	163.3	204.8	300.2	258.5	139.5	63.2	65.7	173.9	277.5	425.3	24.7	40.8	**47.8**	54.7
1111065 Dried vegetables	70.3	89.2	92.3	137.2	272.3	102.5	97.5	115.8	171.6	82.7	132.7	50.1	123.3	137.2	269.6	53.3	45.7	**47.5**	48.3
1151011 Medicine	190.7	74.6	87.2	212.2	113.7	117.5	119.2	160.8	230.0	56.1	72.9	72.2	148.1	120.8	171.0	38.6	36.2	**45.2**	40.3
1172022 Charges for radio, television use	109.4	113.0	132.7	96.5	147.5	92.5	81.2	76.9	188.9	22.7	76.5	38.5	106.4	171.6	196.9	16.8	29.3	**44.4**	44.4
1112011 Mineral water	119.2	92.5	75.0	155.7	130.0	101.9	100.4	254.1	261.7	94.5	138.0	92.6	97.3	392.6	353.5	23.4	45.3	**44.0**	60.0
1132021 Town gas and natural gas	97.8	113.2	103.6	92.1	98.8	82.1	93.6	161.2	224.5	20.9	121.8	82.2	102.0	114.6	103.0	9.8	36.4	**43.4**	39.0
1143021 Repairs to heating, washing, kitchen appliances	154.6	99.8	88.7	209.2	91.3	112.6	108.3	112.6	136.8	37.4	81.2	38.6	188.7	169.0	144.9	34.3	29.2	**42.6**	40.6
1141021 Repairs to furniture, furnishings, floorings	150.2	97.1	123.2	50.0	69.3	122.3	86.0	37.3	96.2	28.0	100.0	54.4	180.6	207.5	120.0	33.4	37.2	**42.6**	48.8
1131021 Water distribution charges	229.3	123.3	57.4	116.1	209.8	165.2	170.0	95.4	180.4	81.0	66.2	91.9	204.7	243.4	206.6	39.0	35.1	**41.5**	40.5
1162012 Vehicle maintenance costs	129.5	106.6	82.2	109.8	92.3	98.1	118.3	90.1	220.9	55.0	75.2	49.6	122.1	237.8	121.9	14.5	33.9	**41.4**	44.5
1153011 General practitioner medical services	94.3	95.6	219.5	92.7	68.6	110.8	107.1	111.4	177.0	144.3	239.9	90.3	74.5	195.0	271.1	43.1	37.5	**40.5**	44.9
1144012 Cutlery	111.3	83.0	93.2	142.8	127.0	110.1	92.4	71.7	200.5	98.9	62.6	30.5	95.0	234.3	190.4	17.9	32.0	**40.3**	45.8
1111033 Other seafood	124.3	120.5	166.1	56.9	59.9	88.4	72.5	49.3	62.5	65.7	76.7	63.1	153.9	99.8	89.1	37.6	42.1	**40.2**	38.8
1174011 Tuition costs	104.0	171.4	134.9	103.5	87.3	47.1	93.9	72.3	129.0	47.1	68.9	49.6	170.0	133.3	164.8	35.7	33.0	**40.2**	40.4
1111071 Potatoes	120.7	139.9	86.8	127.6	62.4	67.1	122.1	108.1	206.9	75.8	82.8	48.1	153.5	151.1	145.8	29.9	35.5	**40.0**	36.7
1163021 Railway and road transport services	131.5	131.0	57.3	124.8	108.5	79.4	170.5	123.8	120.5	45.1	60.5	43.7	102.6	133.7	121.7	26.6	26.3	**39.5**	35.2
1164021 Telephone, telegraph and telex services	139.4	84.8	89.2	64.3	145.2	51.9	126.1	141.6	80.0	36.1	69.2	71.7	151.4	75.1	69.7	36.7	33.0	**39.0**	38.9
1114021 Other tobacco products	109.0	85.5	87.9	79.1	69.3	74.0	121.1	220.5	103.5	114.6	124.2	60.0	78.0	119.4	145.9	15.2	41.4	**38.9**	36.3
1172021 Expenses for sporting events and activities	80.1	113.3	149.8	102.7	86.5	68.6	73.4	56.5	71.4	54.9	181.5	104.1	112.2	91.2	162.7	26.5	30.3	**38.4**	36.7
1132022 Liquified gas	169.3	147.3	158.2	149.5	114.0	102.8	147.6	158.2	244.1	56.7	66.5	73.1	168.7	188.9	217.5	17.0	24.3	**38.3**	36.0
1114011 Cigarettes	120.1	81.3	89.3	91.3	98.1	73.1	127.9	140.4	198.5	60.4	66.7	65.6	113.5	150.3	165.8	16.0	32.5	**37.9**	36.0
1111042 Preserved milk	94.3	92.0	223.5	86.7	91.1	101.3	70.6	86.6	87.1	82.9	143.5	148.7	134.6	162.9	137.9	42.5	41.5	**37.8**	34.4
1113011 Alcohol	96.1	100.1	76.5	102.8	106.7	89.6	129.6	148.8	212.2	79.1	66.7	75.0	96.1	271.7	351.2	10.5	33.0	**36.4**	59.5
1145022 Other household services	103.9	88.3	92.3	114.9	152.3	125.2	130.2	70.2	161.1	65.3	131.6	23.2	129.5	224.1	100.9	19.2	24.5	**36.0**	39.6
1111092 Tea	164.2	123.9	160.3	70.5	122.6	121.7	64.0	60.5	123.1	107.4	94.4	209.6	142.0	136.6	177.8	24.3	32.8	**35.8**	32.8
1111012 Flour, other cereals	92.1	125.1	129.6	92.7	89.8	95.2	86.9	96.0	222.9	167.5	150.8	69.6	146.1	159.1	171.8	15.9	35.8	**35.5**	32.6
1171041 Repairs of recreational goods	100.0	85.0	88.9	110.7	146.7	120.6	125.4	75.2	155.1	62.9	126.8	22.3	125.8	217.8	98.1	19.2	23.2	**35.3**	39.2
1146011 Domestic services	85.5	78.1	127.6	90.7	111.6	121.2	109.3	153.6	172.8	59.3	121.8	34.7	158.0	187.3	197.3	18.2	25.3	**35.0**	37.6
1163031 Other expenses related to transport services	90.6	137.2	104.9	111.2	138.4	96.5	122.8	52.8	134.8	43.4	60.8	61.5	72.6	123.8	152.6	16.4	23.8	**34.4**	33.9
1172011 Expenses related to cultural events and activities	91.8	104.4	158.7	71.5	104.2	48.0	113.5	50.4	84.5	50.2	92.8	95.0	89.3	109.0	97.7	35.4	35.1	**34.1**	30.4
1181011 Hairdressers, beauticians and other similar services	91.5	125.0	104.1	112.8	138.1	120.6	77.9	73.0	169.5	72.0	122.7	33.5	104.9	184.9	182.6	13.0	25.5	**33.5**	36.1
1151021 Other pharmaceutical products	142.8	141.0	71.0	109.5	151.4	101.3	94.3	95.8	139.3	43.5	97.9	51.0	128.7	110.8	106.3	23.7	22.8	**33.3**	29.7
1132031 Heating oil and other heating fuels	70.8	120.5	163.6	96.4	59.3	57.4	108.7	86.6	152.9	77.9	98.6	136.6	105.2	133.0	80.2	40.1	35.6	**32.9**	30.7
1113014 Other alcoholic drinks	85.9	104.0	96.7	88.6	100.1	87.0	110.6	200.5	146.9	90.1	83.3	69.1	116.1	255.3	384.5	7.4	31.3	**32.4**	61.2
1173011 Books, brochures, other similar printed matters	115.8	61.8	106.9	201.3	105.3	78.0	86.3	93.3	155.1	98.1	109.6	101.2	132.8	163.4	225.4	39.7	36.1	**32.1**	36.1
1153021 Specialist medical services	116.8	106.1	112.3	76.7	51.2	45.7	65.8	141.7	139.5	120.7	134.7	98.1	76.6	189.0	267.0	33.9	36.1	**32.0**	47.1
1171035 Flowers, other recreational goods	129.7	146.1	170.0	47.1	113.5	125.3	65.1	118.4	73.0	108.7	109.8	77.5	146.3	178.8	289.8	31.1	34.5	**31.8**	44.8
1183012 Expenditures in cafes, bars	108.1	120.6	92.4	112.8	120.9	100.2	91.8	109.2	193.8	86.2	113.5	37.1	144.4	248.5	225.8	9.5	24.9	**31.6**	42.3
1132041 Coal, coke and other solid combustibles	114.7	142.9	109.2	121.2	129.2	83.8	100.6	124.2	77.4	43.3	76.6	50.0	99.0	148.5	108.1	15.6	18.0	**31.0**	29.4
1172023 Other services nec	98.3	141.7	89.2	115.9	104.3	103.0	48.1	55.4	119.1	48.7	129.0	93.9	170.1	116.6	146.5	15.4	28.9	**30.9**	32.5
1183013 Expenditures in canteens	128.0	111.5	135.9	83.8	62.5	107.1	82.7	110.0	160.3	86.7	158.4	56.8	191.6	194.5	178.7	24.0	26.0	**30.6**	35.6
1185011 Insurance, banking and other financial services	126.5	111.6	108.1	95.2	89.5	143.6	78.9	95.4	105.2	57.5	63.3	39.4	123.3	137.9	119.5	16.3	17.5	**30.5**	29.1
1122021 Repairs to footwear	105.8	120.4	109.8	103.8	94.7	121.8	110.7	81.4	158.4	54.2	72.4	47.4	106.9	147.2	197.1	8.6	18.0	**30.1**	34.5
1113013 Beer	83.7	117.4	133.9	108.1	123.7	105.6	149.8	203.3	157.1	87.0	123.6	59.1	110.6	294.8	392.1	14.1	25.3	**30.1**	56.3
1163011 Local transport services	117.7	110.4	93.1	119.6	115.3	103.4	134.5	127.4	154.8	35.1	79.1	63.2	109.4	124.7	147.7	8.4	14.2	**30.0**	27.8
1152011 Lenses and glasses	99.9	98.0	139.8	94.6	71.1	90.8	89.9	96.4	149.5	73.5	101.6	42.5	132.1	116.2	118.9	20.7	22.8	**28.5**	26.5
1111104 Ice cream	111.9	98.0	156.8	49.2	81.5	88.2	70.3	109.4	133.6	108.9	115.5	72.3	114.6	104.4	129.6	33.5	30.8	**28.4**	25.8

	D	F	I	NL	B	L	UK	IRL	DK	GR	E	P	A	S	FIN	Coefficients of price variation EU6	EU9	EU12	EU15
1111062 Dried fruits	75.2	166.9	103.3	101.2	200.8	102.3	101.5	122.4	151.3	85.2	135.8	119.8	95.9	135.6	173.8	35.1	30.2	**28.4**	27.7
1171013 Record players, tape and cassette recorders	98.3	125.7	99.4	90.3	123.3	100.3	64.0	111.4	108.7	180.5	124.8	62.3	139.2	119.0	146.6	12.6	17.1	**27.7**	26.0
1111054 Other animal or vegetable fats	138.7	173.7	180.4	82.1	99.8	143.3	74.4	88.6	150.7	143.2	161.7	104.8	162.3	245.0	319.1	26.2	30.2	**27.5**	41.2
1161011 Motor vehicles	90.7	98.7	96.8	106.8	86.5	80.4	102.9	138.3	182.0	171.0	121.3	147.8	100.0	101.2	171.7	9.2	27.5	**27.3**	27.3
1144013 Non-electrical kitchen and household utensils	94.0	103.0	87.4	100.8	91.8	91.8	104.9	93.0	176.1	66.6	106.9	66.1	114.4	157.3	169.9	5.7	24.6	**27.0**	30.0
1142011 Household textiles	109.0	150.8	100.3	81.8	103.8	104.6	89.8	150.4	82.1	67.2	87.4	66.4	89.7	89.4	74.5	19.2	22.7	**26.5**	25.4
1153031 Dental services	131.1	79.0	92.4	75.5	140.6	113.3	80.3	129.1	153.9	68.1	138.9	97.2	74.4	197.5	222.8	23.6	25.3	**26.3**	37.4
1171021 Photographic and cinematic equipment	90.4	111.3	116.7	110.3	104.5	94.4	100.7	119.3	105.5	213.2	117.4	124.9	111.5	94.7	122.6	9.0	8.6	**26.0**	24.1
1144015 Light bulbs and electrical accessories	101.1	107.0	74.4	94.6	93.0	90.4	129.7	86.1	148.3	62.7	81.7	60.7	103.3	93.3	119.2	10.8	21.1	**25.9**	23.6
1111064 Fresh vegetables	105.7	113.0	85.6	118.1	120.7	82.2	128.1	153.8	169.9	62.7	100.9	98.1	82.9	212.8	195.8	14.5	22.6	**25.7**	34.4
1131013 General household maintenance costs	95.9	98.8	122.6	107.3	108.0	114.5	99.7	99.1	145.6	66.0	86.6	42.4	112.9	194.0	204.3	8.4	13.6	**25.4**	36.0
1111061 Fresh fruits	151.8	134.5	79.8	123.7	132.6	123.6	104.9	137.1	167.2	75.7	109.0	66.5	104.3	154.9	146.4	17.7	18.6	**25.4**	24.2
1111103 Confectionery	89.5	101.4	153.7	92.0	87.3	93.4	91.2	101.9	168.4	92.9	122.6	80.7	123.8	220.3	215.2	22.5	26.2	**25.0**	36.5
1182031 Paper and drawing supplies	115.0	116.0	112.0	100.9	109.4	101.2	82.1	117.5	153.7	71.1	95.3	47.7	96.3	140.5	198.3	5.6	16.1	**25.0**	30.9
1111043 Other milk products, except cheese	75.0	110.6	150.3	71.2	119.6	115.0	122.4	116.7	91.6	166.8	145.5	90.5	99.3	126.0	118.5	25.4	21.8	**24.7**	22.5
1111052 Margarine	79.9	120.1	167.0	93.7	137.0	121.1	92.3	116.4	115.1	104.4	179.1	89.9	130.2	221.6	297.4	23.6	21.2	**24.7**	40.9
1111024 Mutton, lamb and goat meat	134.9	125.0	108.6	130.7	144.8	118.9	80.2	90.6	136.1	60.5	121.5	69.6	89.6	153.0	223.8	9.1	17.3	**24.5**	32.6
1111015 Pasta, noodles	99.9	89.1	105.8	87.6	113.3	95.8	80.2	100.0	161.6	108.6	114.1	52.6	140.0	185.9	203.8	9.2	21.7	**24.3**	33.9
1142021 Repairs to household textiles	104.3	103.5	104.7	77.8	80.3	110.4	94.3	61.1	106.0	45.9	89.6	57.4	123.3	150.3	142.5	13.2	16.9	**24.2**	29.5
1111072 Products derived from potatoes	105.9	104.2	135.7	89.4	105.8	165.3	92.5	126.8	175.5	100.8	176.3	138.4	139.3	215.8	219.4	21.5	23.9	**24.1**	29.5
1144014 Gardening equipment	83.7	94.5	135.0	107.6	83.4	101.2	145.9	69.5	122.5	78.6	81.6	76.0	126.0	97.2	104.4	17.4	22.9	**24.1**	22.2
1111022 Veal	113.7	114.2	111.7	150.0	124.4	119.7	94.0	104.5	170.8	68.3	83.9	90.1	110.5	139.9	136.4	10.7	18.2	**24.0**	22.2
1111051 Butter	83.5	106.4	134.3	94.1	104.4	98.1	84.5	92.7	118.0	117.4	184.8	120.8	119.5	126.8	174.0	15.2	15.1	**23.8**	24.3
1121015 Clothing accessories	110.3	128.8	112.9	76.9	93.5	94.1	89.7	87.3	117.2	50.9	85.9	60.8	103.9	100.0	102.1	16.2	15.7	**23.6**	21.1
1121014 Babies' clothing (age 0 to 2 years)	99.6	121.6	125.7	74.7	98.5	109.1	73.2	48.6	76.8	110.4	118.6	91.6	82.9	72.0	127.9	16.1	26.1	**23.5**	23.9
1111028 Other fresh or frozen meat	109.8	113.6	117.8	102.4	103.4	113.5	71.7	67.3	66.3	57.4	72.7	90.0	94.5	137.7	148.8	5.1	21.0	**23.4**	26.7
1111016 Other cereal based products	98.3	104.9	164.7	78.5	90.5	88.5	93.6	98.5	145.0	137.1	105.1	92.6	125.7	175.2	214.1	27.1	25.2	**23.3**	31.2
1162031 Other expenses related to personal transport	106.8	109.0	116.5	94.7	94.7	127.7	90.5	82.3	113.9	65.7	84.8	45.8	133.6	143.3	124.2	10.8	13.1	**23.3**	24.8
1111021 Beef	121.7	103.5	98.0	135.3	113.4	116.4	90.7	102.3	160.8	76.7	68.1	88.2	109.6	164.2	170.3	10.6	17.6	**23.1**	26.3
1111091 Coffee	123.8	52.6	116.6	76.4	92.6	100.2	106.7	145.1	105.0	94.2	98.2	132.1	112.5	97.7	121.2	25.6	24.8	**22.8**	20.7
1164011 Postal services	116.0	95.2	98.2	88.8	100.5	73.9	94.9	95.8	111.3	59.0	85.1	43.2	105.3	113.4	109.4	13.3	11.8	**22.6**	21.4
1122011 Men's footwear	113.3	139.1	116.2	111.7	115.4	118.6	76.0	89.1	142.1	81.1	71.6	80.0	108.7	108.6	148.0	7.7	17.4	**22.2**	21.7
1111102 Chocolate	85.1	105.9	158.9	122.7	106.6	106.4	87.3	86.7	167.3	107.3	128.6	130.9	105.0	197.3	220.3	19.9	25.1	**22.1**	30.9
1111027 Meat preparations, other meat products	140.2	120.2	156.5	116.7	134.5	130.4	79.4	112.1	208.4	134.9	153.1	126.3	164.8	271.8	199.1	9.9	25.1	**22.0**	30.3
1173012 Periodicals, newspapers	108.6	103.1	115.4	93.4	100.5	92.2	72.3	107.9	152.6	114.9	129.0	62.5	100.4	140.7	182.3	8.0	19.5	**21.9**	26.2
1112012 Other soft drinks	95.3	92.8	119.2	98.9	135.5	101.8	94.4	136.9	178.8	89.3	108.5	114.3	105.2	195.9	196.2	14.2	23.3	**21.8**	29.0
1152021 Orthopaedic, therapeutic appliances and products	98.3	97.2	120.9	86.4	97.3	88.0	100.9	84.0	62.9	53.7	71.8	62.8	128.5	89.4	108.1	11.5	15.9	**21.8**	22.6
1122013 Children's and babies' footwear	113.5	122.0	112.0	138.9	126.7	123.4	67.5	66.2	97.6	99.0	88.6	90.7	77.7	89.2	104.1	7.3	22.5	**21.2**	20.8
1111013 Bread	112.3	123.3	88.4	101.6	108.3	111.0	77.8	98.5	139.3	68.5	117.1	65.8	117.2	209.3	208.9	9.9	16.1	**21.2**	35.4
1143015 Cleaning equipment	99.6	119.8	110.6	96.3	103.3	102.2	77.2	107.7	109.5	175.9	142.0	109.4	127.1	107.6	139.2	7.4	10.9	**21.2**	19.7
1111031 Fresh, frozen fish	100.9	102.4	135.0	73.5	98.4	109.7	81.5	80.9	130.5	94.9	88.8	63.5	112.1	122.6	93.9	17.5	19.9	**21.2**	19.9
1121013 Children's clothing (age 3 to 13 years)	100.3	131.5	99.1	84.3	111.6	81.5	67.2	73.6	107.1	91.9	133.6	84.2	84.2	75.5	121.2	16.6	20.2	**20.8**	20.9
1122012 Women's footwear	108.6	120.8	109.1	114.9	117.8	112.1	81.7	79.4	133.0	78.1	75.7	69.2	111.1	97.6	125.5	3.9	15.2	**20.7**	19.3
1171011 Radios	109.9	134.6	135.5	102.0	136.0	126.3	70.8	108.0	137.1	167.3	123.4	87.4	143.6	118.4	167.8	10.8	17.9	**20.6**	20.6
1183021 Hotels and other lodging accommodations	84.1	89.6	124.7	97.1	90.6	93.3	113.8	95.7	134.1	84.0	117.9	56.3	93.2	108.3	126.3	13.6	16.0	**20.6**	19.5
1181022 Non-durable personal care products	95.4	111.4	106.7	94.4	102.1	94.2	85.6	102.6	160.4	83.8	115.4	73.7	106.0	141.5	180.9	6.6	19.5	**20.5**	25.7
1111045 Eggs	77.5	124.8	109.9	85.8	86.8	94.5	110.7	126.5	141.7	91.8	101.9	69.0	132.6	156.1	168.1	16.7	19.3	**20.4**	25.2
1111066 Frozen vegetables	96.8	105.9	122.7	81.2	100.6	89.9	88.9	88.3	130.1	75.1	112.9	57.3	100.0	128.0	194.8	13.1	15.5	**20.4**	29.4
1145012 Other non-durable household articles	82.4	129.9	120.8	74.0	93.8	100.5	84.3	109.6	119.4	65.5	99.4	79.1	66.6	126.0	168.4	19.7	18.1	**20.2**	26.9
1163022 Other transport services	117.5	96.0	95.3	76.6	89.0	99.9	111.1	84.6	96.7	54.7	78.3	63.3	102.9	82.9	118.1	12.8	12.3	**19.8**	19.4
1111034 Preserved, prepared fish and other seafood	92.5	110.2	117.2	93.2	105.4	110.2	73.4	79.1	135.0	117.4	138.7	77.9	83.1	141.1	146.9	8.7	17.9	**19.8**	22.0
1111026 Delicatessen	92.2	119.8	113.7	117.2	103.9	111.6	71.4	69.3	128.0	84.3	95.3	74.3	122.5	187.3	173.3	8.5	19.3	**19.7**	29.7
1141012 Floor coverings	95.9	117.3	145.0	102.9	117.5	135.2	87.7	92.6	135.6	81.9	119.5	79.7	161.3	151.9	178.0	14.3	17.2	**19.5**	24.5
1111023 Pork	98.9	106.7	116.1	120.3	97.2	115.2	88.9	95.0	146.1	78.1	83.5	73.6	85.0	167.6	169.6	8.1	15.0	**19.4**	26.9
1111105 Condiments, sauces,spices,salt	100.4	107.0	103.4	70.6	100.9	92.1	92.1	105.8	87.9	111.7	109.8	47.7	143.0	176.7	179.3	12.6	11.3	**18.9**	31.1
1171012 Televisions	100.3	106.8	98.8	88.6	113.5	104.8	85.2	107.9	149.2	140.4	109.3	76.9	118.3	106.0	122.0	7.5	16.5	**18.7**	17.0

	D	F	I	NL	B	L	UK	IRL	DK	GR	E	P	A	S	FIN	Coefficients of price variation EU6	EU9	EU12	EU15
1121011 Men's clothing	99.7	111.5	105.4	87.1	118.5	103.0	67.7	87.0	119.5	78.2	134.1	88.2	88.0	87.5	128.7	9.4	15.9	**18.4**	18.5
1144011 Glassware and tableware	117.3	94.4	72.5	90.9	109.8	90.9	90.2	64.6	99.1	76.4	80.1	64.8	70.9	135.3	140.9	15.0	16.8	**18.2**	24.7
1111067 Vegetables preserved, prepared, soups	94.5	98.5	138.3	99.0	114.2	89.2	77.0	79.0	131.3	117.9	119.2	123.7	103.5	147.5	162.2	15.6	19.9	**18.1**	21.2
1143014 Heating and air conditioning appliances	97.3	120.5	111.2	100.6	111.3	109.1	80.4	107.7	163.3	126.9	122.4	91.4	127.8	111.6	142.2	7.0	19.1	**17.9**	17.2
1111032 Dried or smoked fish	100.1	104.7	124.5	92.6	94.8	116.4	95.4	71.1	136.6	73.2	102.7	96.0	87.5	121.4	94.3	10.9	17.6	**17.9**	17.3
1111014 Cakes, biscuits	102.5	102.7	122.6	94.4	99.8	102.0	73.8	95.2	143.7	104.0	120.1	77.1	116.7	190.3	218.2	8.5	17.6	**17.7**	32.5
1143011 Refrigerators, freezers	91.9	128.7	85.2	97.2	119.9	123.8	85.5	98.0	138.4	114.3	132.0	85.0	126.3	117.3	157.9	15.7	17.6	**17.7**	18.9
1111044 Cheese	104.5	100.7	94.7	108.5	114.0	99.4	81.2	120.4	153.5	93.5	129.4	135.1	126.4	167.4	181.5	6.1	17.6	**17.5**	23.0
1111093 Cocoa	101.5	130.0	67.2	87.5	85.0	99.9	94.9	97.6	95.0	66.5	105.0	88.0	58.4	110.5	149.9	20.2	16.5	**17.4**	23.8
1132011 Electricity	120.8	90.3	85.7	84.6	124.2	107.5	90.1	85.8	118.1	92.5	141.0	98.0	104.6	70.2	68.5	15.9	15.6	**17.4**	20.0
1111063 Fruits frozen, preserved, and as juice	102.3	105.4	127.1	98.9	127.5	100.5	68.5	85.7	123.4	102.1	111.5	136.3	76.4	123.0	130.1	11.1	17.8	**17.1**	18.2
1161021 Other modes of personal transport	95.4	101.2	103.9	107.2	100.1	94.7	91.3	92.2	153.9	93.0	116.1	84.4	104.4	134.6	151.9	4.4	17.4	**16.9**	19.4
1111025 Poultry	100.2	114.7	109.0	103.2	112.8	101.7	88.2	96.5	122.0	82.6	91.8	58.0	85.5	169.4	156.7	5.2	9.2	**16.6**	25.4
1121012 Women's clothing	105.0	117.1	108.0	90.5	100.6	111.8	73.5	99.3	135.6	82.7	102.0	78.7	106.6	91.8	144.5	8.0	15.6	**16.6**	18.2
1162021 Fuels and lubricants for motor vehicles	99.2	104.8	127.1	95.3	97.6	75.1	95.5	96.4	103.7	64.2	87.1	83.5	101.4	119.8	111.3	15.3	12.8	**16.1**	15.9
1162011 Tyres, inner tubes, replacement parts for motor vehicle	76.9	103.8	107.7	103.0	109.5	97.3	116.6	87.3	124.6	86.9	138.2	122.6	91.1	137.7	126.1	10.9	13.3	**15.9**	16.7
1171033 Games and toys	113.4	128.3	104.8	96.4	126.1	100.3	70.8	121.5	127.4	127.0	138.4	111.6	138.5	168.0	157.3	11.0	16.3	**15.6**	19.2
1111101 Jams, marmalades, honey, syrups	110.1	79.1	143.8	99.7	113.1	104.1	84.9	92.7	100.6	97.0	117.8	101.3	120.5	141.7	174.9	17.8	17.2	**15.5**	21.6
1182022 Other personal articles nec	85.5	77.2	111.9	75.1	95.0	90.5	103.8	123.3	85.7	78.6	95.1	81.4	106.7	90.1	123.6	13.8	16.1	**15.4**	16.1
1182021 Articles for travelling and personal luggage	102.9	88.3	112.5	97.4	93.4	89.3	85.9	99.9	145.2	111.4	100.8	91.0	108.7	109.1	165.2	8.6	17.0	**15.3**	19.7
1111041 Fresh milk	76.8	97.3	130.4	85.4	84.3	88.8	97.7	103.9	111.6	105.3	104.5	78.2	104.2	110.5	106.8	18.6	15.9	**15.2**	14.0
1145011 Cleaning and maintenance products	116.0	97.8	100.1	101.7	101.6	98.1	90.2	86.2	130.7	74.0	99.7	76.9	121.7	177.0	205.1	6.0	12.4	**15.2**	31.0
1182011 Jewellery, watches, precious stones	110.8	125.3	87.3	129.8	110.1	101.6	98.2	116.1	125.2	87.7	88.4	84.9	106.1	111.2	131.8	12.8	11.9	**14.9**	14.4
1143016 Other household appliances	90.9	108.2	110.0	86.3	99.5	102.6	81.6	91.6	96.3	135.1	113.6	82.4	110.4	113.1	126.8	8.6	9.5	**14.7**	14.7
1111011 Rice	119.2	88.8	104.4	93.8	100.7	112.1	119.0	110.7	122.3	112.9	126.6	70.2	83.2	116.1	132.1	10.0	10.3	**14.5**	15.5
1121021 Repairs to clothing	83.3	111.3	96.4	99.5	91.4	104.8	108.7	89.6	97.0	83.6	129.0	75.5	114.4	194.2	209.8	9.2	8.8	**14.3**	33.4
1183011 Expenditures in restaurants	86.6	100.5	117.2	98.1	105.2	102.4	93.8	98.7	122.7	93.1	103.5	64.4	95.5	148.1	176.9	8.9	10.2	**14.2**	24.0
1143012 Washing machines, tumble dryers	105.8	121.9	96.2	95.8	113.9	111.1	77.7	104.7	128.5	127.5	131.4	98.3	122.6	114.9	138.4	8.7	13.5	**14.2**	14.1
1171032 Sports equipment	110.8	83.3	120.7	95.9	98.4	109.1	76.7	79.2	115.8	96.3	111.3	100.1	115.8	88.1	129.8	11.7	15.6	**13.8**	15.0
1171022 Other important leisure durables (incl. computers)	93.0	101.4	116.9	85.5	119.2	103.5	90.5	102.7	117.7	105.0	136.8	96.1	104.1	121.7	131.9	11.6	11.3	**13.2**	13.4
1141011 Furniture and furnishing accessories	97.5	106.8	103.3	106.3	110.9	108.0	86.0	97.4	120.7	80.7	96.0	80.4	91.8	86.4	125.4	4.0	8.9	**11.9**	13.2
1171034 Film and other photographic supplies	88.4	98.8	90.6	106.5	110.0	94.8	102.5	111.1	132.0	99.6	115.4	88.4	125.3	128.0	151.8	8.0	12.1	**11.9**	16.1
1171031 Records, cassettes, magnetic tapes and accessories	99.4	100.4	98.7	86.9	91.7	88.7	104.0	90.6	120.9	118.7	115.5	98.4	104.5	111.8	124.8	5.7	10.1	**11.0**	11.4
1181021 Durable and semi-durable personal care products	95.1	106.8	96.0	83.4	110.7	96.6	103.5	88.3	107.3	110.3	112.6	80.1	107.6	113.1	135.9	9.0	8.8	**10.7**	13.1
1143013 Cookers and stoves	90.7	116.4	108.1	96.4	102.5	103.0	105.2	101.0	128.9	112.7	121.2	116.1	127.5	119.0	144.0	7.9	10.0	**9.6**	12.0
1111081 Sugar	104.9	105.2	93.8	94.1	94.5	101.6	95.3	108.6	121.2	89.4	109.6	104.9	110.2	126.4	165.8	5.1	8.4	**8.4**	16.9

Appendix I.2: List of products/services ranked by EU-9 coefficient of price variation in 1990 (based on price excluding VAT)

Final consumption	D	F	I	NL	B	L	UK	IRL	DK	GR	E	P	A	S	FIN	Coefficients of price variation EU6	EU9	EU12	EU15
1111013 Bread	106.1	78.4	284.3	82.1	81.7	87.4	37.6	130.1	142.2	157.3	99.9	57.7	162.3	146.9	213.4	61.7	**58.3**	54.8	49.5
1111015 Pasta, noodles	68.7	77.3	155.4	63.7	69.1	83.9	37.9	61.0	167.0	68.7	117.2	52.7	63.6	110.4	86.1	36.6	**47.6**	45.3	41.6
1111051 Butter	95.6	81.0	84.5	74.6	65.4	71.8	121.1	220.5	84.8	106.8	117.2	55.6	70.9	96.3	125.2	12.3	**45.3**	42.3	39.2
1111011 Rice	66.1	140.0	89.4	108.3	73.5	59.8	178.8	159.9	231.6	65.5	70.4	52.5	99.7	263.9	262.0	30.9	**45.0**	50.7	56.3
1111022 Veal	65.7	84.5	84.7	129.4	256.9	99.5	97.5	115.8	140.7	77.1	125.2	50.1	112.1	110.6	231.4	53.4	**44.7**	46.2	46.1
1111025 Poultry	111.4	87.7	68.8	146.9	122.6	98.9	100.4	254.1	214.5	88.1	130.2	92.6	88.5	316.6	303.4	23.6	**43.4**	41.9	53.8
1111041 Fresh milk	116.2	114.2	159.7	53.7	56.5	85.8	72.5	49.3	51.2	61.2	72.4	63.1	139.9	80.5	76.5	37.9	**42.9**	40.7	39.2
1111061 Fresh fruits	88.1	87.2	214.9	81.8	85.9	98.3	70.6	86.6	71.4	77.3	135.4	148.7	122.4	131.4	118.4	43.4	**42.7**	39.2	34.6
1111021 Beef	114.9	109.7	61.0	137.9	138.4	158.5	204.8	300.2	211.9	130.0	59.6	65.7	158.1	223.8	365.1	25.8	**41.6**	48.1	51.6
1111014 Cakes, biscuits	107.1	156.0	68.8	127.2	158.4	181.8	27.6	92.0	89.1	96.9	26.0	35.5	82.6	106.3	134.8	28.1	**41.2**	51.4	46.2
1111016 Other cereal based products	160.8	106.5	81.9	134.0	97.2	125.9	113.7	121.8	273.2	92.5	101.7	85.2	159.1	385.5	439.8	22.0	**39.5**	39.9	65.1
1111012 Flour, other cereals	109.5	91.3	30.0	76.4	116.0	116.4	136.9	47.5	64.0	34.1	19.3	18.0	93.1	175.5	143.4	33.8	**38.4**	56.2	55.6
1111072 Products derived from potatoes	85.8	99.0	152.6	67.5	98.3	46.6	113.5	41.0	69.3	46.8	87.5	88.0	81.2	87.9	83.9	35.8	**38.2**	36.7	32.8
1111028 Other fresh or frozen meat	140.4	92.0	113.0	47.2	65.4	118.7	86.0	37.3	78.9	26.1	94.3	54.4	164.2	167.3	103.0	33.2	**36.8**	41.9	45.1
1111101 Jams, marmalades, honey, syrups	101.6	58.6	98.1	189.9	99.3	75.7	86.3	75.9	127.1	91.4	103.4	93.7	120.7	131.8	193.5	39.9	**35.8**	31.6	33.9
1111045 Eggs	130.3	80.4	81.8	60.7	137.0	50.4	126.1	141.6	65.6	33.6	65.3	71.7	137.6	60.6	59.8	36.3	**35.2**	40.6	41.0
1111031 Fresh, frozen fish	214.3	116.9	52.7	109.5	197.9	160.4	170.0	95.4	147.9	75.5	62.5	91.9	186.1	196.3	177.3	39.0	**34.6**	40.8	37.9
1111103 Confectionery	121.2	123.2	156.0	44.4	107.1	121.7	65.1	96.3	59.8	92.7	103.6	71.8	133.0	144.2	248.8	30.0	**34.5**	31.7	42.4
1111033 Other seafood	88.1	90.6	201.4	87.5	64.7	107.6	107.1	111.4	145.1	134.5	226.3	83.6	67.7	157.3	232.7	41.4	**34.1**	38.9	41.9
1111093 Cocoa	80.3	87.7	88.7	83.6	94.4	84.5	110.6	200.5	120.4	76.8	78.6	64.0	105.5	205.9	330.0	5.2	**33.9**	35.1	57.3
1111023 Pork	178.2	70.7	80.0	200.2	107.3	114.1	119.2	160.8	188.5	52.3	68.8	72.2	134.6	97.4	146.8	38.5	**33.3**	42.4	38.3
1111092 Tea	66.2	114.2	150.1	90.9	55.9	55.7	108.7	86.6	125.3	66.4	93.0	126.5	95.6	107.3	68.8	38.7	**32.4**	30.9	29.0
1111064 Fresh vegetables	153.5	117.4	154.1	66.5	115.7	118.2	64.0	60.5	100.9	100.1	89.1	209.6	129.1	110.2	152.6	24.3	**32.1**	37.1	33.4
1114021 Other tobacco products	98.2	78.4	143.9	41.5	76.9	83.2	61.1	88.9	109.5	80.1	103.1	61.8	104.2	84.2	111.2	35.2	**31.6**	29.6	27.1
1111042 Preserved milk	97.2	162.5	123.8	97.6	82.4	45.7	93.9	72.3	105.7	43.9	65.0	49.6	154.5	107.5	141.5	35.3	**31.5**	38.5	38.0
1111026 Delicatessen	91.4	107.3	95.0	86.9	93.2	79.7	93.6	161.2	184.0	19.5	114.9	82.2	92.7	92.4	88.4	9.1	**31.2**	39.1	35.9
1111052 Margarine	74.9	95.5	144.0	96.9	72.7	66.6	73.4	56.5	58.5	51.2	171.2	96.4	102.0	73.5	139.7	28.3	**31.2**	39.5	37.3
1111102 Chocolate	109.2	100.6	103.0	72.4	48.3	44.4	65.8	115.2	114.3	102.9	127.1	90.8	69.6	152.4	229.2	33.0	**31.1**	28.5	42.9
1111043 Other milk products, except cheese	112.8	132.6	79.6	120.4	58.9	65.1	122.1	108.1	169.6	70.6	78.1	48.1	139.5	121.9	125.2	29.8	**30.7**	35.5	32.4
1111054 Other animal or vegetable fats	112.2	68.5	81.9	86.1	92.5	71.0	127.9	140.4	162.7	56.3	62.9	65.6	103.2	121.2	142.3	17.1	**29.6**	34.9	32.4
1111027 Meat preparations, other meat products	144.5	94.6	81.4	197.4	86.1	109.3	108.3	112.6	112.1	34.9	76.6	38.6	171.5	136.3	124.4	34.3	**28.8**	42.0	39.1
1121011 Men's clothing	66.0	140.7	86.8	85.4	168.7	91.3	88.3	111.3	124.0	72.6	121.3	102.4	79.9	109.4	149.2	33.7	**28.6**	27.2	26.9
1111065 Dried vegetables	86.1	118.6	124.6	87.5	84.7	92.4	86.9	96.0	182.7	156.1	142.3	69.6	132.8	128.3	147.5	16.4	**28.4**	29.9	27.2
1111062 Dried fruits	89.8	94.9	73.6	97.0	100.7	87.0	129.6	148.8	173.9	73.7	62.9	75.0	87.4	219.1	301.5	9.7	**28.2**	32.0	52.6
1111044 Cheese	122.9	124.2	55.1	117.7	102.4	77.1	170.5	123.8	98.8	42.0	57.1	40.5	93.3	107.8	104.5	25.8	**28.0**	40.9	36.3
1112011 Mineral water	91.9	134.3	81.8	109.3	98.4	100.0	48.1	55.4	97.6	45.4	121.7	86.9	154.6	94.0	125.8	16.0	**27.4**	30.0	31.1
1121013 Children's clothing (age 3 to 13 years)	121.7	146.5	151.6	69.3	83.9	139.1	74.4	88.6	123.5	122.1	144.4	89.6	135.3	197.6	273.9	26.5	**27.3**	25.5	38.9
1111032 Dried or smoked fish	121.0	101.0	75.4	103.6	87.1	95.2	118.3	90.1	181.1	51.3	70.9	49.6	111.0	191.8	104.6	14.6	**27.0**	35.5	37.3
1121014 Babies' clothing (age 0 to 2 years)	79.6	83.2	81.3	90.1	72.7	78.1	102.9	138.3	149.2	145.8	108.3	126.3	83.3	81.6	147.4	6.5	**27.0**	26.0	26.7
1143013 Cookers and stoves	87.4	102.5	105.6	63.0	78.8	97.4	63.7	39.5	63.0	94.1	105.9	78.3	69.1	58.1	109.8	16.6	**27.0**	24.6	25.4
1111034 Preserved, prepared fish and other seafood	104.0	78.7	85.5	134.7	119.8	106.9	92.4	71.7	164.3	92.2	59.1	30.5	86.4	189.0	163.4	18.2	**26.1**	35.4	39.3
1122011 Men's footwear	115.0	66.6	77.6	63.7	118.2	110.0	69.8	117.4	126.1	58.1	124.0	83.1	62.0	159.3	191.2	25.1	**25.4**	26.9	36.6
1132011 Electricity	78.5	85.5	141.0	77.6	74.6	88.1	91.2	92.6	138.0	79.2	109.5	74.7	112.5	177.7	215.2	25.2	**24.7**	23.7	37.1
1143015 Cleaning equipment	86.2	88.4	138.4	66.2	72.4	79.0	81.4	80.1	118.9	116.9	93.8	79.1	104.8	141.3	183.8	26.7	**24.4**	22.6	30.7
1144011 Glassware and tableware	108.6	44.4	98.0	64.5	77.8	89.5	92.8	118.0	86.1	80.3	87.7	112.9	93.8	78.8	104.0	26.6	**24.3**	22.4	20.6
1112012 Other soft drinks	119.6	105.7	124.7	79.1	52.5	104.0	82.7	89.4	131.4	80.8	141.4	48.5	159.7	156.9	153.4	25.4	**24.1**	29.5	32.2
1144014 Gardening equipment	74.6	89.3	133.5	103.5	85.3	95.0	75.9	70.5	137.1	100.0	114.8	111.9	87.5	159.1	189.1	19.2	**24.1**	21.2	30.0
1153021 Specialist medical services	83.7	111.4	106.7	79.7	85.8	84.1	85.6	102.6	160.4	78.1	103.0	73.7	88.3	141.5	180.9	13.4	**24.0**	23.6	29.8
1132022 Liquified gas	65.8	93.3	137.9	67.2	102.2	108.5	122.4	106.1	75.1	142.2	129.9	77.4	90.3	101.6	118.5	25.9	**23.9**	25.4	23.2
1141021 Repairs to furniture, furnishings, floorings	92.9	87.9	114.0	75.4	88.9	147.6	80.4	115.3	143.9	85.9	157.4	118.3	116.1	174.0	188.3	23.5	**23.9**	24.8	28.9
1144015 Light bulbs and electrical accessories	123.0	101.3	131.5	98.5	115.0	116.4	69.0	91.1	170.8	115.0	136.7	107.9	137.3	219.2	170.9	10.1	**23.9**	21.2	28.4
1111024 Mutton, lamb and goat meat	102.2	107.1	121.7	91.0	139.2	89.8	81.2	76.9	154.8	21.2	72.2	38.5	96.7	138.4	169.0	16.0	**23.5**	40.0	39.3
1143014 Heating and air conditioning appliances	96.3	95.8	108.1	86.4	82.7	101.3	62.3	54.7	54.3	48.9	64.9	76.9	78.8	111.0	127.7	9.0	**23.4**	25.1	27.2

		D	F	I	NL	B	L	UK	IRL	DK	GR	E	P	A	S	FIN	Coefficients of price variation			
																	EU6	EU9	EU12	EU15
1111067	**Vegetables preserved, prepared, soups**	79.9	74.0	122.7	85.6	105.3	117.7	109.3	153.6	141.6	55.3	114.9	34.7	143.6	151.0	169.4	19.2	**23.4**	33.5	33.8
1145021	**Laundry and dry cleaning**	99.6	102.9	94.1	117.2	108.3	110.2	58.7	53.8	80.0	92.3	79.1	77.5	64.8	78.9	89.4	7.1	**23.4**	21.5	21.1
1121021	**Repairs to clothing**	95.6	127.2	84.3	77.2	87.2	93.4	78.1	136.7	67.3	62.6	78.0	56.8	74.8	72.1	63.9	16.9	**23.3**	26.5	26.0
1111071	**Potatoes**	79.5	130.0	100.9	104.9	130.6	93.7	122.8	52.8	110.5	40.4	57.4	56.9	66.0	99.8	131.0	17.4	**23.2**	33.9	32.7
1113013	**Beer**	73.4	99.0	122.8	91.2	103.9	94.3	130.3	165.3	128.8	74.2	110.4	54.7	92.2	237.7	336.6	15.2	**23.1**	27.7	54.9
1153031	**Dental services**	72.4	124.8	109.9	85.8	72.9	84.4	110.7	126.5	141.7	85.6	91.0	69.0	110.5	156.1	168.1	21.1	**23.1**	23.6	28.0
1151021	**Other pharmaceutical products**	93.7	124.6	90.9	79.5	105.3	79.1	58.4	59.8	87.8	85.6	126.0	84.2	70.2	60.9	121.2	16.5	**22.7**	22.6	24.6
1142011	**Household textiles**	73.4	79.7	113.4	90.8	78.7	90.4	126.9	56.5	100.4	67.0	72.9	65.0	105.0	78.4	89.6	14.9	**22.4**	23.5	21.7
1121015	**Clothing accessories**	82.5	86.8	73.4	85.1	77.1	82.0	91.2	84.5	144.3	56.8	95.4	56.5	95.3	126.9	145.8	5.6	**22.2**	25.3	28.4
1122021	**Repairs to footwear**	92.7	95.3	71.9	111.4	101.4	73.4	111.4	139.8	139.3	58.4	90.1	83.8	69.1	171.6	168.1	15.7	**22.2**	24.7	32.3
1132031	**Heating oil and other heating fuels**	70.1	101.3	153.2	88.4	129.2	114.2	92.3	105.8	94.3	89.0	159.9	83.2	118.4	178.7	297.4	24.7	**21.9**	24.9	43.9
1111063	**Fruits frozen, preserved, and as juice**	97.1	83.7	88.8	108.4	143.7	121.6	130.2	70.2	132.0	60.9	124.2	23.2	117.7	180.7	86.6	19.2	**21.8**	34.2	35.2
1153051	**Other medical and paramedical services**	72.3	129.9	120.8	74.0	78.8	89.7	84.3	109.6	119.4	61.0	88.8	79.1	55.5	126.0	168.4	24.2	**21.6**	23.0	30.7
1153011	**General practitioner medical services**	73.8	89.6	124.7	81.9	76.1	83.3	113.8	95.7	134.1	78.3	105.3	56.3	77.7	108.3	126.3	19.4	**21.4**	23.6	23.1
1111091	**Coffee**	133.5	133.6	65.1	103.3	142.8	98.3	94.3	95.8	114.2	40.5	92.4	47.2	117.0	89.4	91.2	23.8	**21.3**	32.4	29.5
1164021	**Telephone, telegraph and telex services**	87.8	88.3	124.5	92.6	79.7	103.9	83.0	71.1	136.6	62.4	91.7	88.9	87.5	97.9	94.3	15.2	**21.1**	21.6	19.4
1111081	**Sugar**	85.5	118.5	95.5	106.4	130.3	117.1	77.9	73.0	138.9	67.1	115.8	31.0	95.4	149.1	156.7	13.8	**21.0**	30.7	31.5
1164011	**Postal services**	90.9	101.6	111.2	94.9	105.0	97.4	80.4	107.7	163.3	108.2	109.3	91.4	127.8	111.6	142.2	6.7	**20.9**	18.7	18.7
1163031	**Other expenses related to transport services**	88.3	93.4	138.3	93.4	107.7	86.6	77.0	79.0	131.3	109.9	112.5	114.5	103.5	130.5	162.2	17.7	**20.9**	18.4	21.4
1145011	**Cleaning and maintenance products**	83.6	78.2	100.2	83.5	113.9	96.0	82.1	111.3	146.6	83.2	96.9	97.7	87.7	158.0	168.4	13.2	**20.8**	18.9	26.5
1172011	**Expenses related to cultural events and activities**	106.0	121.6	88.1	81.4	119.0	97.4	61.6	121.5	127.4	118.4	130.6	95.4	125.9	168.0	157.3	14.6	**20.5**	19.2	23.3
1111066	**Frozen vegetables**	93.5	80.6	85.5	104.4	138.4	117.1	125.4	75.2	127.1	58.6	119.6	22.3	114.4	175.6	84.2	19.2	**20.4**	33.5	34.8
1113011	**Alcohol**	111.0	94.1	99.2	80.3	71.6	128.2	68.6	77.6	86.2	42.3	56.5	30.3	102.8	111.2	102.6	19.2	**20.3**	33.8	31.1
1114011	**Cigarettes**	87.6	78.4	117.5	79.8	67.1	85.7	78.2	78.4	122.5	54.0	90.7	36.3	110.1	93.7	102.1	18.1	**20.2**	27.8	25.8
1111104	**Ice cream**	94.8	114.3	84.8	106.4	114.1	97.3	91.8	88.8	158.9	73.5	107.1	34.4	131.3	200.4	193.8	10.5	**20.1**	28.7	37.5
1141011	**Furniture and furnishing accessories**	87.6	75.1	88.9	73.9	95.2	85.5	69.7	81.3	132.5	92.6	101.9	45.0	116.7	149.9	174.9	9.0	**20.0**	23.3	32.8
1111105	**Condiments, sauces,spices,salt**	107.2	135.5	100.2	114.3	121.9	81.4	100.6	124.2	63.4	40.4	72.3	46.3	90.0	119.8	92.8	15.4	**20.0**	32.4	29.4
1172022	**Charges for radio, television use**	75.0	73.2	107.6	75.1	79.8	80.8	90.3	123.3	70.2	67.0	84.9	69.6	97.0	72.7	123.6	14.4	**19.7**	19.4	21.1
1111053	**Edible oils**	158.2	139.6	152.1	141.0	107.5	99.8	147.6	158.2	200.1	52.8	62.7	73.1	153.4	152.3	186.7	16.4	**19.1**	34.6	32.0
1151011	**Medicine**	94.3	100.3	123.9	69.3	92.8	106.5	81.5	65.8	107.0	88.4	83.8	63.5	93.4	98.9	93.9	16.7	**18.9**	19.5	17.4
1162011	**Tyres, inner tubes, replacement parts for motor vehicle**	80.9	95.8	95.5	98.9	83.1	99.6	62.1	56.3	104.9	71.9	85.1	63.5	102.1	151.0	148.8	8.1	**18.8**	19.0	28.6
1113012	**Wine**	92.8	101.5	100.7	87.6	75.8	114.9	96.3	66.2	129.8	50.5	64.6	43.9	89.1	118.7	169.2	12.8	**18.8**	29.0	33.3
1122013	**Children's and babies' footwear**	88.7	90.2	62.5	79.8	78.2	87.8	112.8	86.1	121.6	53.5	72.9	51.9	86.1	75.2	102.3	11.7	**18.7**	24.5	22.6
1141012	**Floor coverings**	91.5	87.3	88.0	65.7	67.5	98.6	82.0	49.7	86.9	39.1	80.0	49.1	102.8	121.2	122.3	14.7	**18.4**	25.0	29.0
1171031	**Records, cassettes, magnetic tapes and accessories**	89.7	84.3	116.6	83.5	102.0	89.7	59.6	69.7	101.1	87.0	99.6	116.5	63.7	99.2	111.7	12.4	**18.3**	17.7	18.7
1153041	**Nurse services**	84.9	105.9	122.7	81.2	84.5	80.3	88.9	88.3	130.1	70.0	100.8	57.3	83.3	128.0	194.8	16.9	**18.3**	21.8	32.3
1144021	**Repairs to glassware, tableware, household utensils**	95.3	86.9	97.0	78.8	84.5	82.3	62.9	98.1	125.1	98.0	115.2	53.4	83.7	113.5	156.5	7.6	**17.9**	21.2	25.6
1163011	**Local transport services**	93.7	101.2	98.8	83.6	107.1	101.7	85.2	107.9	149.2	130.8	103.1	71.2	118.3	85.5	122.0	7.6	**17.6**	19.4	18.7
1162012	**Vehicle maintenance costs**	84.1	93.8	121.8	86.8	94.0	120.7	76.3	75.3	111.1	69.8	106.7	68.1	134.4	151.9	178.0	15.3	**17.6**	19.7	29.4
1131021	**Water distribution charges**	133.2	127.5	67.1	104.4	125.1	120.0	104.9	111.5	137.0	64.5	97.3	56.8	94.8	124.9	146.4	19.8	**17.5**	25.5	24.6
1161021	**Other modes of personal transport**	81.1	88.2	98.5	78.6	84.3	98.4	63.8	64.3	110.7	86.3	104.3	66.6	63.0	113.8	126.1	8.9	**17.3**	17.5	21.6
1144013	**Non-electrical kitchen and household utensils**	99.4	117.3	97.6	94.3	92.3	105.9	66.1	72.4	116.5	69.1	63.9	68.4	90.6	87.6	127.0	8.3	**17.2**	21.4	21.3
1171012	**Televisions**	80.6	108.5	71.6	82.0	95.9	110.5	74.3	79.7	113.4	84.0	117.9	72.6	105.3	94.6	135.5	15.9	**17.2**	18.2	19.7
1171011	**Radios**	89.9	82.2	103.0	79.7	79.8	91.1	64.2	77.4	117.8	76.5	107.2	65.9	97.3	153.5	187.3	9.4	**17.0**	18.1	32.9
1152021	**Orthopaedic, therapeutic appliances and products**	102.7	134.6	130.3	96.2	128.3	119.2	70.8	108.0	112.4	155.9	110.2	87.4	119.7	95.5	144.0	12.1	**16.9**	19.3	18.9
1173011	**Books, brochures, other similar printed matters**	71.8	82.0	125.4	80.6	79.5	86.2	97.7	103.9	91.5	98.1	98.6	78.2	94.7	89.1	91.7	19.9	**16.8**	15.5	13.8
1172021	**Expenses for sporting events and activities**	96.6	66.7	120.8	84.1	106.7	101.1	73.8	92.7	100.6	90.4	105.2	86.6	100.4	141.7	174.9	17.8	**16.8**	15.2	25.3
1121012	**Women's clothing**	86.2	106.0	83.5	76.2	103.6	89.6	55.7	101.3	89.1	153.9	111.4	53.2	116.0	96.0	125.8	11.7	**16.8**	27.6	25.7
1145012	**Other non-durable household articles**	86.2	82.0	101.6	72.9	81.8	78.6	87.7	68.3	51.6	45.8	64.1	53.7	107.1	72.1	92.8	10.6	**16.7**	22.0	22.5
1172023	**Other services nec**	90.3	74.5	112.5	82.2	88.1	79.7	74.7	90.8	119.0	95.0	90.0	77.8	90.6	88.0	165.2	13.9	**16.5**	15.0	23.7
1162021	**Fuels and lubricants for motor vehicles**	86.8	90.0	97.6	113.5	77.8	108.7	77.3	77.2	119.8	57.4	74.6	68.1	77.3	135.2	145.6	13.0	**16.4**	21.0	26.4
1171022	**Other important leisure durables (incl. computers)**	106.0	76.1	72.0	71.4	104.4	96.0	78.3	69.8	96.8	78.9	125.9	83.8	87.2	56.6	58.8	17.0	**16.4**	19.0	21.7
1142021	**Repairs to household textiles**	99.7	96.3	93.9	126.6	117.4	106.9	81.7	95.0	140.0	58.2	74.9	77.0	92.1	112.8	117.1	11.0	**16.3**	22.8	20.9
1182022	**Other personal articles nec**	97.2	70.2	101.4	80.9	82.7	97.4	66.7	64.4	94.9	82.1	99.4	85.6	96.5	71.0	111.4	12.6	**16.2**	14.7	15.9
1171013	**Record players, tape and cassette recorders**	91.7	80.6	79.6	91.6	91.2	88.8	70.6	97.9	125.8	68.8	115.5	115.5	105.3	135.0	155.8	5.9	**16.1**	18.5	23.6
1171021	**Photographic and cinematic equipment**	89.0	104.0	56.5	73.8	68.0	89.2	82.5	79.3	77.9	48.9	93.8	75.2	48.7	89.1	128.7	19.6	**16.1**	18.9	25.1

	D	F	I	NL	B	L	UK	IRL	DK	GR	E	P	A	S	FIN	Coefficients of price variation EU6	EU9	EU12	EU15
1143012 Washing machines, tumble dryers	96.8	108.6	94.9	64.9	74.8	84.0	78.0	71.0	96.1	43.4	76.7	52.0	86.6	80.6	87.6	16.7	**15.9**	23.4	20.9
1171032 Sports equipment	83.7	85.3	87.3	90.5	84.1	84.6	79.4	75.0	126.1	79.3	103.7	72.1	87.0	108.5	130.4	2.7	**15.8**	15.9	18.5
1163021 Railway and road transport services	93.2	105.7	105.4	82.2	111.8	100.0	67.7	87.0	119.5	72.9	126.5	81.7	88.0	77.4	128.7	9.7	**15.7**	18.4	19.3
1132041 Coal, coke and other solid combustibles	118.3	105.4	99.6	110.3	136.6	112.2	80.2	82.4	111.6	51.6	108.5	64.4	81.5	123.4	223.8	10.3	**15.5**	23.6	35.6
1143016 Other household appliances	93.7	91.9	97.9	79.9	75.8	114.0	78.7	66.9	93.4	56.0	75.7	39.1	111.3	115.6	106.6	13.5	**15.1**	24.0	24.6
1163022 Other transport services	109.6	89.5	72.5	85.8	103.6	88.3	90.2	64.6	99.1	71.2	75.6	60.0	70.9	119.7	140.9	13.3	**15.0**	17.7	24.0
1161011 Motor vehicles	103.1	76.8	80.1	64.6	71.2	89.2	96.6	68.8	79.3	51.0	58.9	54.1	78.0	66.9	101.4	15.5	**15.0**	21.0	20.7
1174011 Tuition costs	97.2	125.3	87.3	129.8	92.5	90.7	98.2	116.1	125.2	87.7	83.4	78.6	106.1	111.2	131.8	16.5	**15.0**	17.2	16.7
1143021 Repairs to heating, washing, kitchen appliances	106.8	87.3	89.9	114.2	107.0	103.9	78.9	93.0	131.8	65.4	64.2	75.4	91.3	132.4	146.2	9.5	**14.9**	21.0	23.9
1185011 Insurance, banking and other financial services	79.6	98.1	108.1	96.4	86.1	92.0	105.2	82.1	128.9	96.1	108.2	116.1	127.5	119.0	144.0	9.7	**14.8**	13.8	16.9
1152011 Lenses and glasses	101.5	120.8	104.9	108.4	111.1	105.8	71.0	79.4	109.0	72.8	67.6	59.1	92.6	78.7	107.7	5.7	**14.8**	21.7	20.2
1171034 Film and other photographic supplies	92.1	93.7	90.8	76.4	80.5	99.8	63.9	90.3	111.1	70.5	91.1	67.3	88.8	74.0	124.0	9.0	**14.6**	15.8	18.0
1143011 Refrigerators, freezers	73.2	89.7	112.9	79.4	83.5	87.6	73.5	75.4	96.7	100.1	165.0	103.2	99.6	102.3	149.4	14.2	**14.2**	25.6	25.7
1145022 Other household services	98.5	104.0	81.1	85.7	102.2	99.1	67.7	89.5	114.2	63.8	110.5	56.2	97.7	168.8	179.3	9.0	**14.1**	20.2	32.5
1182021 Articles for travelling and personal luggage	92.8	102.8	80.8	80.8	95.7	99.2	67.6	85.1	105.3	108.7	117.3	84.0	102.2	92.7	118.8	9.2	**12.9**	14.6	14.5
1131013 General household maintenance costs	84.1	83.3	103.0	90.5	101.9	102.2	86.7	80.6	119.3	61.5	77.3	36.2	94.1	156.5	175.4	9.0	**12.7**	24.2	34.1
1113014 Other alcoholic drinks	103.2	93.1	85.4	100.9	92.2	92.3	117.0	103.6	126.9	29.9	70.6	48.6	91.2	100.6	126.8	6.3	**12.2**	29.6	27.6
1171035 Flowers, other recreational goods	92.7	99.3	106.8	89.9	78.1	70.8	83.0	78.4	85.0	54.7	77.8	71.4	92.2	96.6	95.5	13.6	**12.2**	16.2	15.3
1144012 Cutlery	101.8	80.3	82.5	74.9	84.5	66.0	82.5	77.9	91.2	50.3	76.0	36.9	87.8	91.5	93.9	13.3	**11.5**	22.2	20.7
1132021 Town gas and natural gas	100.9	97.8	102.8	95.2	93.5	95.5	82.1	106.8	126.0	60.6	85.1	44.2	87.5	113.3	198.3	3.4	**11.3**	22.5	32.9
1181021 Durable and semi-durable personal care products	104.6	74.9	95.8	79.2	84.6	100.1	103.5	90.0	100.2	96.2	113.0	60.0	69.3	93.6	113.4	12.2	**11.1**	15.5	16.4
1146011 Domestic services	87.4	101.0	92.9	81.3	97.5	91.3	67.1	97.9	89.8	163.9	126.8	93.5	105.9	107.6	139.2	7.0	**10.9**	23.8	22.7
1162031 Other expenses related to personal transport	88.1	85.6	86.9	59.6	80.7	82.2	80.1	86.0	72.0	104.1	98.0	40.8	119.2	142.5	153.9	12.1	**10.7**	20.0	30.6
1182031 Paper and drawing supplies	81.6	85.5	98.2	72.2	100.2	92.4	78.7	83.5	96.5	97.9	122.1	82.1	86.8	98.1	113.2	11.0	**10.4**	14.0	13.9
1171041 Repairs of recreational goods	71.9	87.5	90.5	97.2	93.6	94.5	101.4	79.4	102.1	81.0	123.4	104.8	75.9	111.0	126.1	9.3	**10.4**	13.9	16.2
1183012 Expenditures in cafes, bars	77.5	93.6	83.1	100.5	94.0	84.6	89.1	101.0	108.2	92.8	108.9	81.9	104.4	113.3	151.8	8.8	**10.0**	10.5	17.7
1183021 Hotels and other lodging accommodations	83.4	101.2	88.1	78.7	104.4	93.8	90.0	80.3	88.0	102.8	106.2	74.2	89.7	100.1	135.9	10.1	**9.3**	11.4	15.5
1181011 Hairdressers, beauticians and other similar services	79.7	86.6	92.4	72.8	83.6	91.6	71.0	74.5	78.9	125.9	101.4	70.4	92.0	113.1	126.8	8.1	**9.1**	17.7	19.9
1181022 Non-durable personal care products	73.1	89.0	88.4	84.0	86.2	93.6	94.5	72.8	79.5	61.5	115.2	64.5	95.3	156.6	180.1	7.4	**8.9**	16.8	33.0
1183011 Expenditures in restaurants	85.5	101.2	94.8	100.3	94.8	96.4	74.8	88.5	98.9	75.2	90.6	74.4	76.5	76.5	125.4	5.4	**8.7**	10.7	15.0
1173012 Periodicals, newspapers	108.4	82.5	96.3	95.9	95.8	95.2	90.2	86.2	107.1	69.0	94.1	76.9	110.6	177.0	205.1	7.8	**8.5**	12.0	33.4
1122012 Women's footwear	79.3	93.8	98.1	93.1	87.8	91.7	87.6	108.5	86.5	181.8	104.8	106.8	92.9	76.4	105.2	6.5	**8.4**	25.2	23.9
1182011 Jewellery, watches, precious stones	76.0	80.4	84.9	82.8	79.1	91.4	81.6	80.2	100.6	79.4	77.8	55.0	79.6	119.4	151.8	6.0	**8.4**	12.5	24.5
1183013 Expenditures in canteens	87.2	95.2	94.9	82.0	78.4	79.2	90.4	82.4	99.1	110.6	109.0	98.4	87.1	98.9	124.8	8.0	**8.2**	11.3	13.3
1171033 Games and toys	87.9	96.7	91.6	87.1	90.2	90.8	76.7	78.5	100.0	70.4	82.0	49.6	71.3	136.6	134.5	3.4	**8.0**	15.6	24.2
1186011 Legal services	92.0	88.7	78.8	88.8	79.4	90.7	95.3	88.3	99.3	83.3	97.9	89.7	110.2	126.4	165.8	6.1	**7.1**	7.0	21.8

APPENDIX J

The soft drinks and mineral water sector

J.1. List of information sources

J.1.1. Interviews

Group marketing director, German mineral water manufacturer
Group marketing manager, large food and beverage multinational
Chief water buyer, supermarket company
Senior consultant, research agency and consultancy specializing in beverages market in Europe
Account director, international advertising agency handling major water brand in Europe
Account manager, French agency handling major water brand
Product manager, European/US soft drinks manufacturer

J.1.2. Other main information sources

Agra-Alimentation
Bates Dorland Advertising
Beverage Industry
BSN
Business de France
Cadbury Schweppes
Dagens-Naeringsliv
Datamonitor
Economist Intelligence Unit
Euromonitor
Eurofood
Financial Times
Food-Manufacture
Frost & Sullivan
Gerolsteiner Brunnen
Key Note
LFRA
Nestlé
Packaging Week
Parfums-Cosmétiques-Arômes
Projection 2000
Süddeutsche-Zeitung
SwissBusiness
The Grocer
UNESDA
Wall Street Journal

J.2. Other statistical material

Figure J.2.1. Sales of soft drinks and mineral water – France

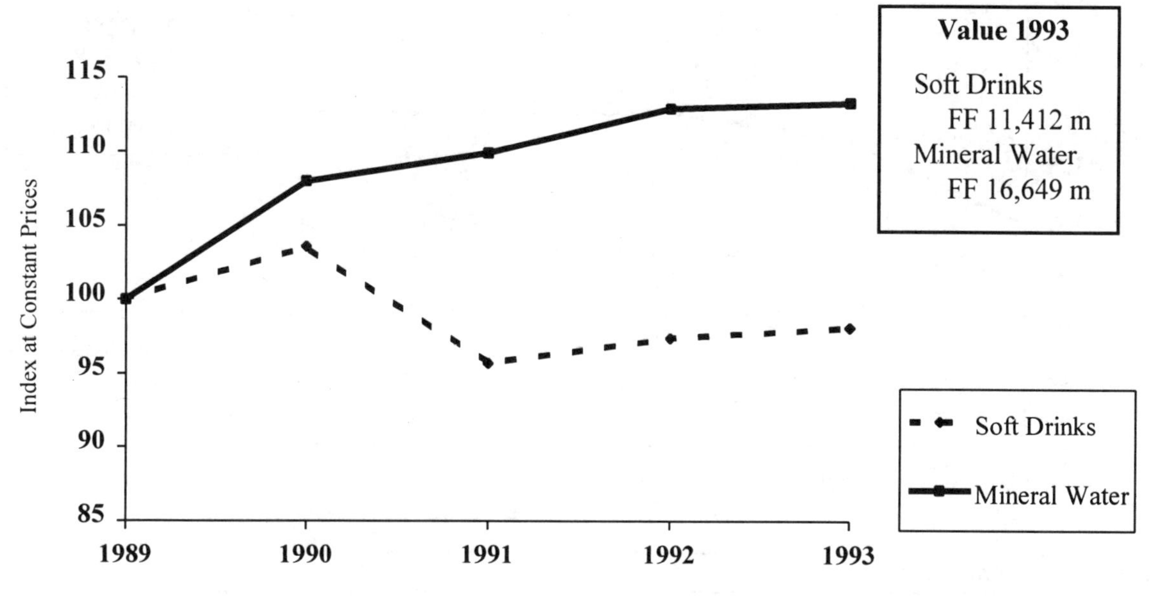

Source: Euromonitor.

Figure J.2.2. Sales of soft drinks and mineral water – Germany

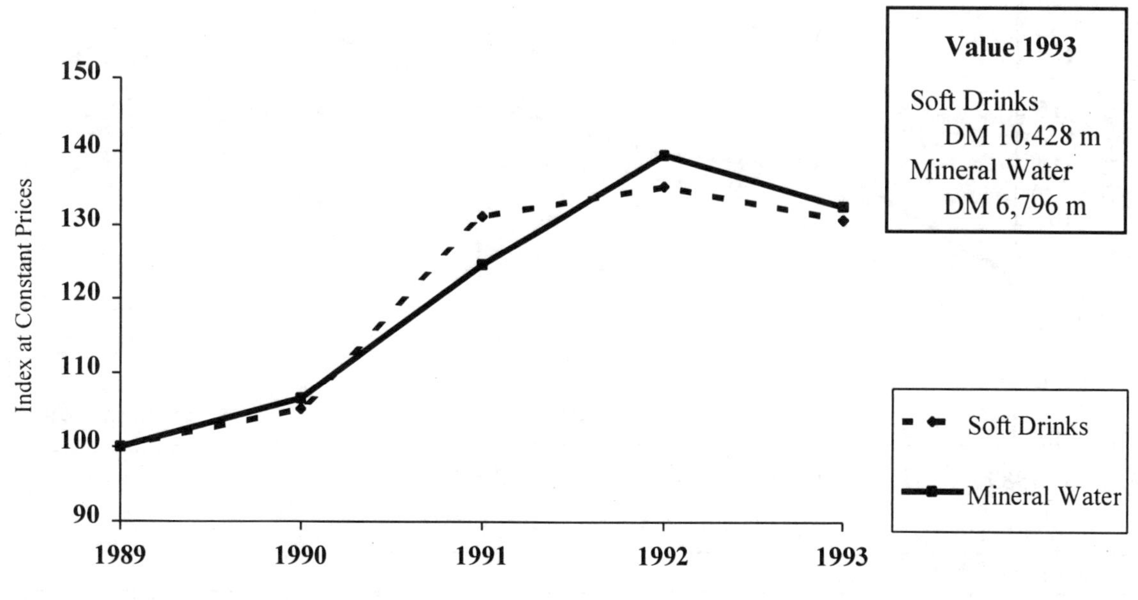

Source: Euromonitor.

Figure J.2.3. Sales of soft drinks and mineral water – Spain

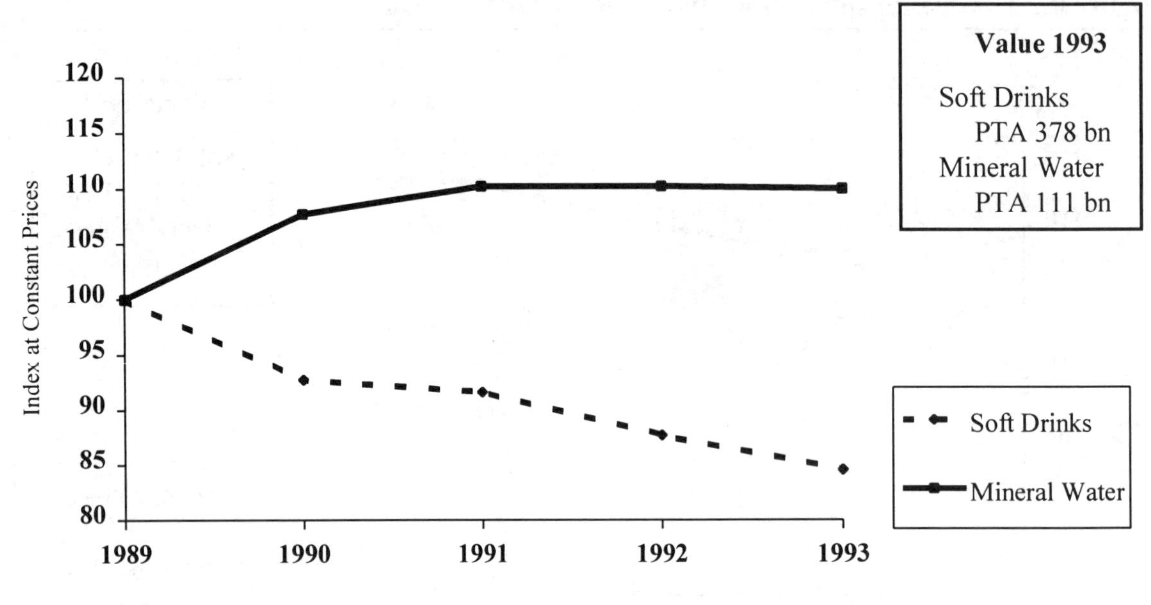

Source: Euromonitor.

Figure J.2.4. Sales of soft drinks and mineral water – Italy

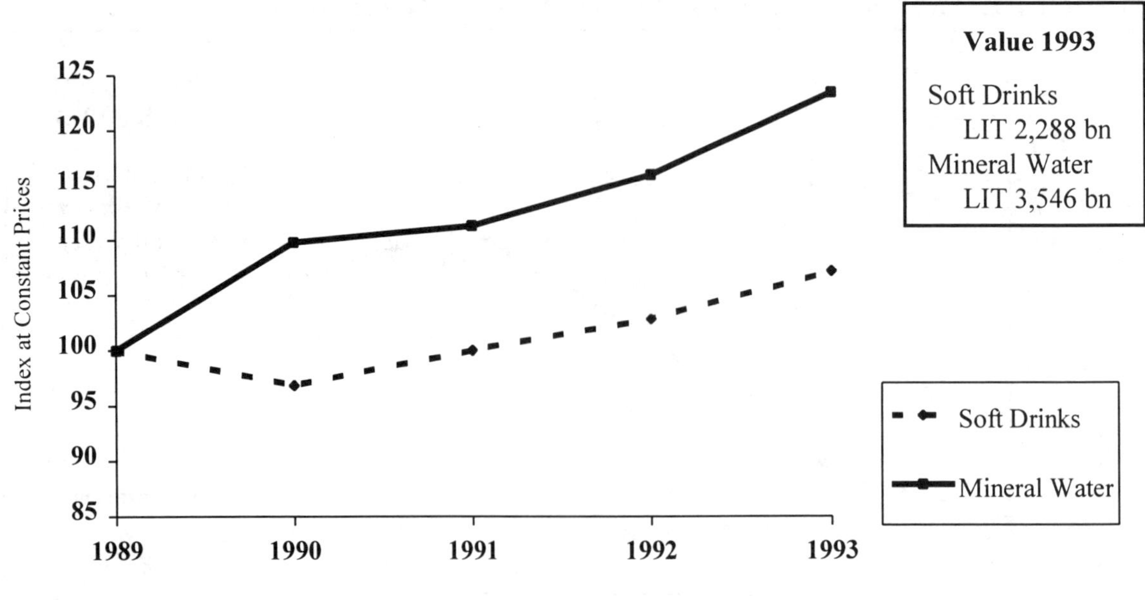

Source: Euromonitor.

Figure J.2.5. Sales of soft drinks and mineral water – UK

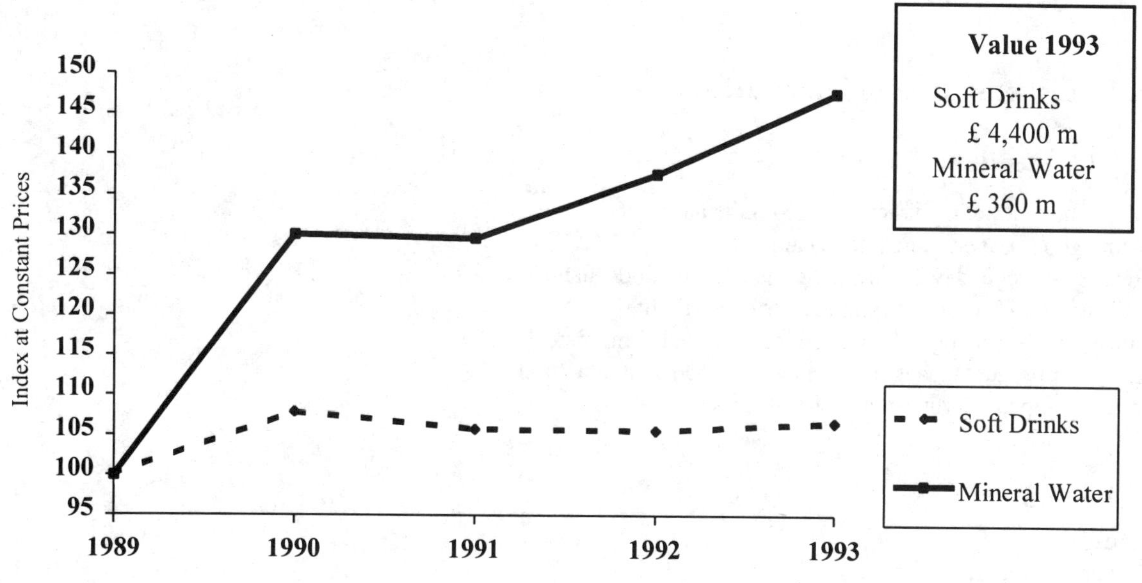

Source: Euromonitor.

APPENDIX K

The white goods sector

K.1. List of sources of information

K.1.1. Interviews

Divisional marketing director, large retail chain
White goods buyer, large retail chain
Head of strategic development, German white goods manufacturer
Industry 'guru', academic and industry consultant
European electrical goods analyst, international firm of stockbrokers
European product manager, Italian white goods manufacturer
Industry expert, European industry association

K.1.2. Data sources

ANIE
Appliance Manufacturer
Baron's
Business Age
CECED
Chambre de Commerce et d'Industrie de Paris
Company Reports
Confortec
EIU
Euromonitor
Financial Times
Frankfurter Allgemeine Zeitung
Handelsblatt
National Statistics
Professional Engineering
Strategic Management Journal
The European
The Economist
Works Management HBR
Le Nouvel Economiste
Les Echos
London Business School
Management Today
Marketing Week

APPENDIX L

The construction service sector

L.1. List of sources of information

L.1.1. Interviews

Managing director, European international architect/designer
Professor at Paris University, French industry expert
Director general, representative of European industry association
Senior partner, multinational law practice specializing in construction and contracting
Special advisor to Board on EU Business, large Swedish contractor
Italian project finance specialist
Partner, UK based quantity surveyor with large international practice
UK based international consulting engineer
Procurement manager, large UK contractor/builder
Business development director, large European contractor/builder
Managing director, large German construction business
Commercial director, large French contracting firm

L.1.2. Other main information sources

Bernard Williams Associates/Financial Times
Building Magazine
Centre for Strategic Studies in Construction, Reading University
Construction Europe
Construction Forecasting and Research
Construction News
Construction Industry Research Association
DEBA (Data for European Business Analysis)
DOE
DTI
Engineering News Record
European Construction Institute
EuroConstruct
Eurostat
European International Contractors
FIEC (European Construction Industy Federation)
National Economic Development Council
W S Atkins/European Commission DG III

L.2. Other statistical material

Figure L.2.1. Efficiency of the EU construction industry (total EU construction output/total EU employment)

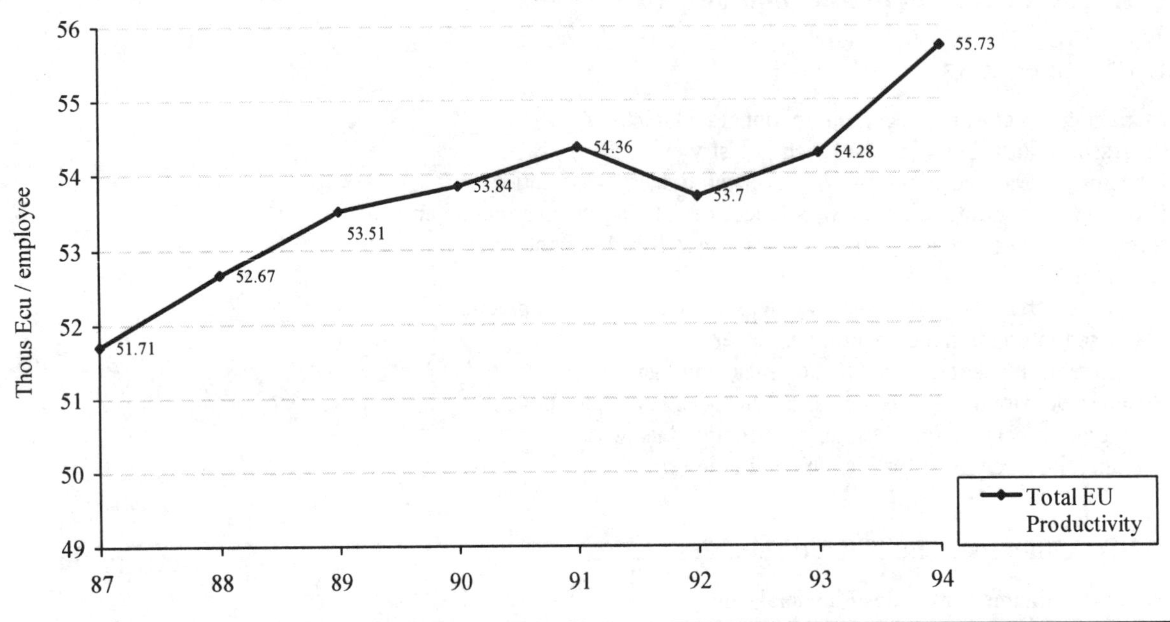

Source: FIEC, EuroConstruct, HAA Research.

Figure L.2.2. European international contracts won as a percentage of total EU construction output (1987–94)

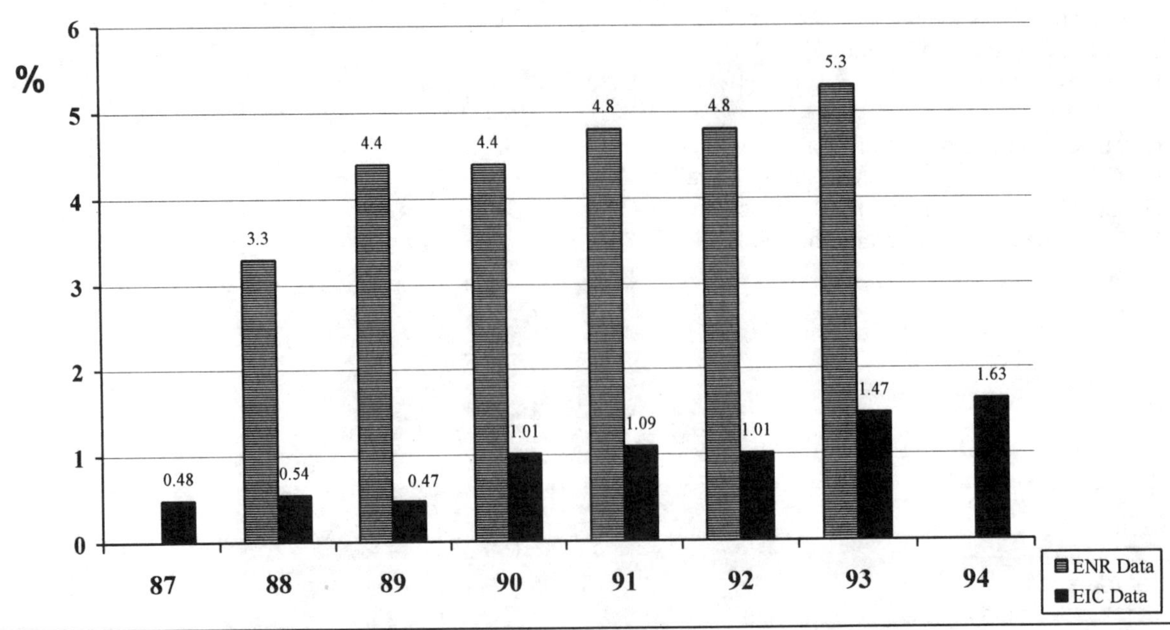

Source: EIC.

Figure L.2.3. Volume of new contracts in million US$ – France

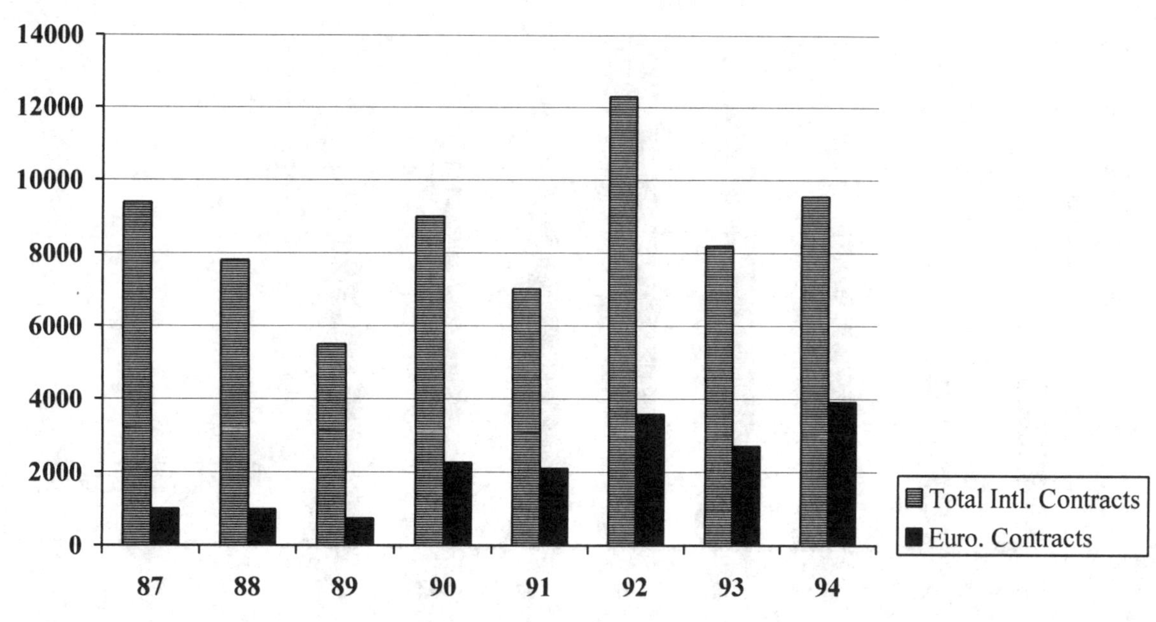

Source: EIC.

Figure L.2.4. Volume of new contracts in million US$ – Germany[1]

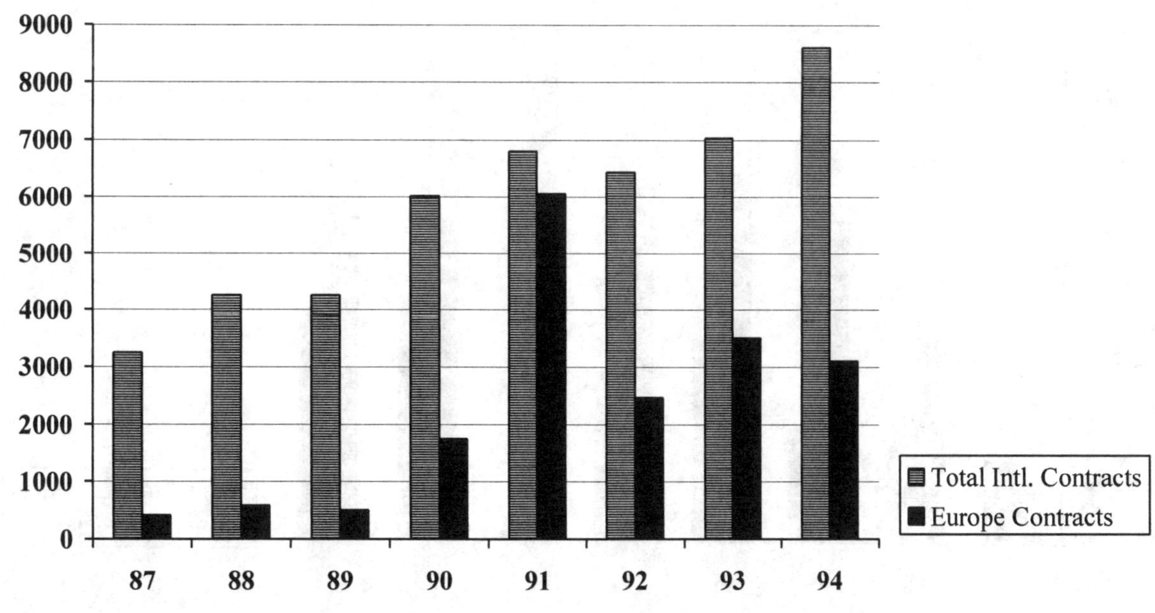

Source: EIC.
[1] All figures include new contracts won by subsidiaries.

Figure L.2.5. Volume of new contracts in million US$ – Italy

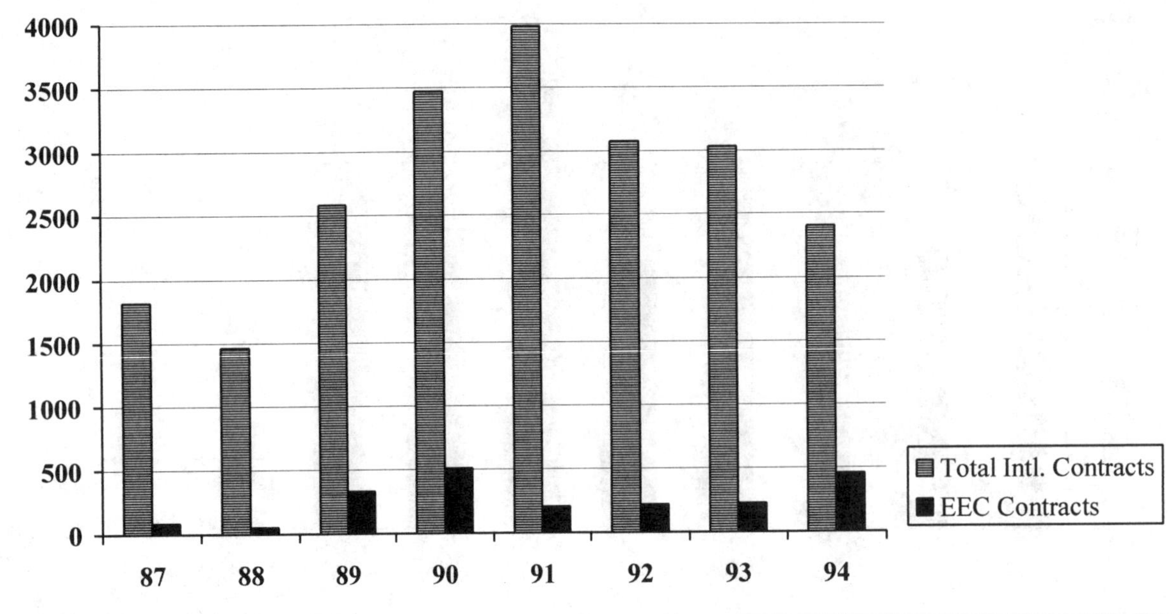

Source: EIC.

Figure L.2.6. Volume of new contracts in million US$ – Netherlands

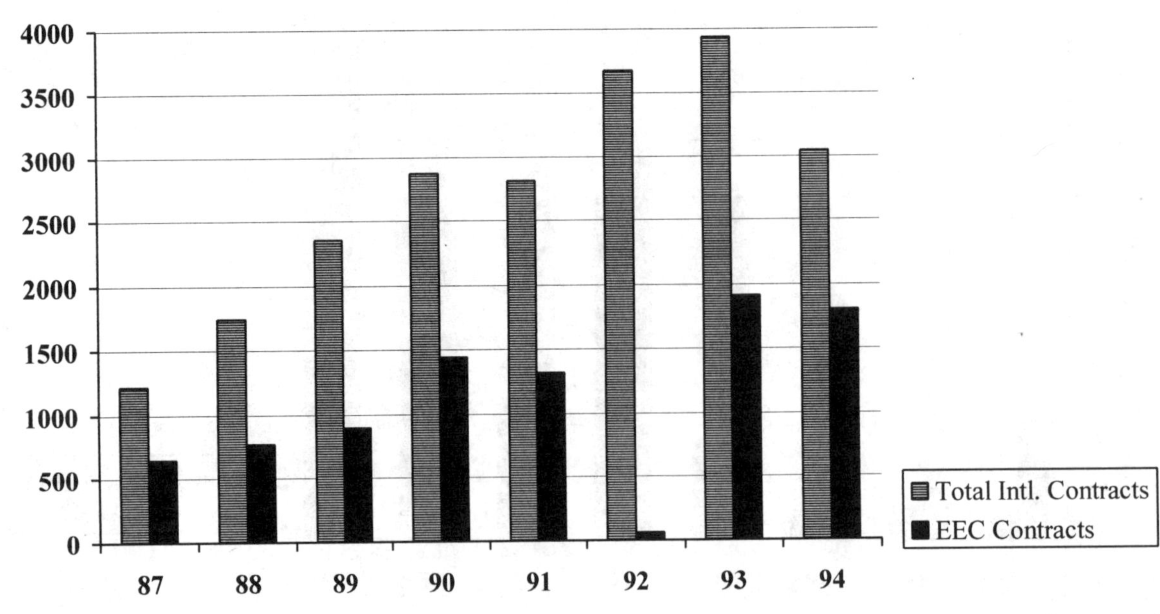

Source: EIC.

Figure L.2.7. Volume of new contracts in million US$ – Spain

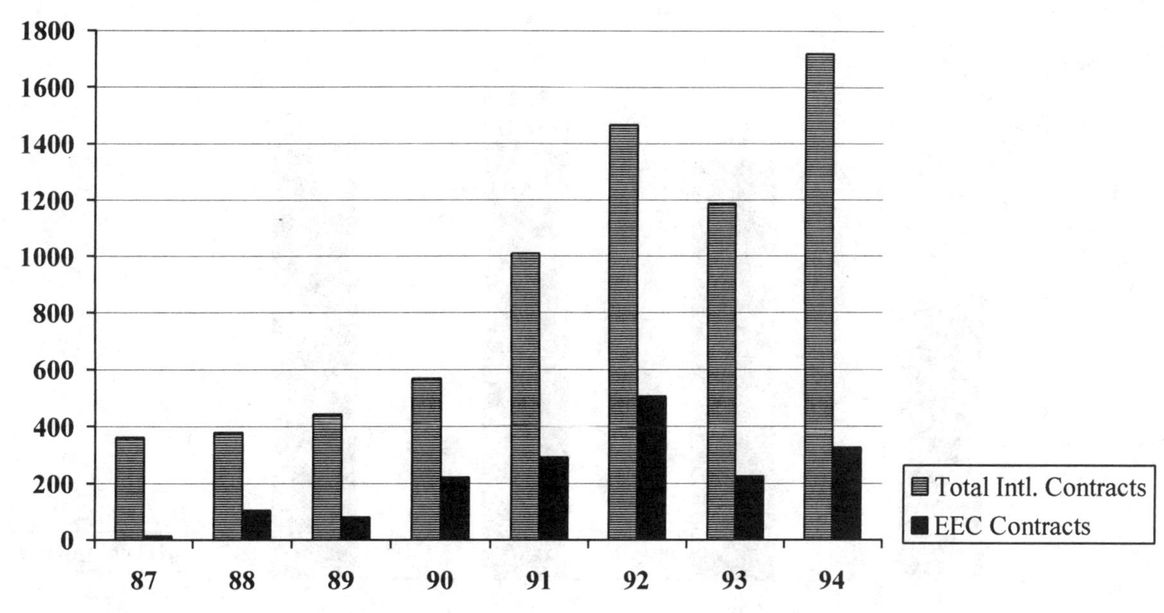

Source: EIC.

Figure L.2.8. Volume of new contracts in million US$ – Denmark

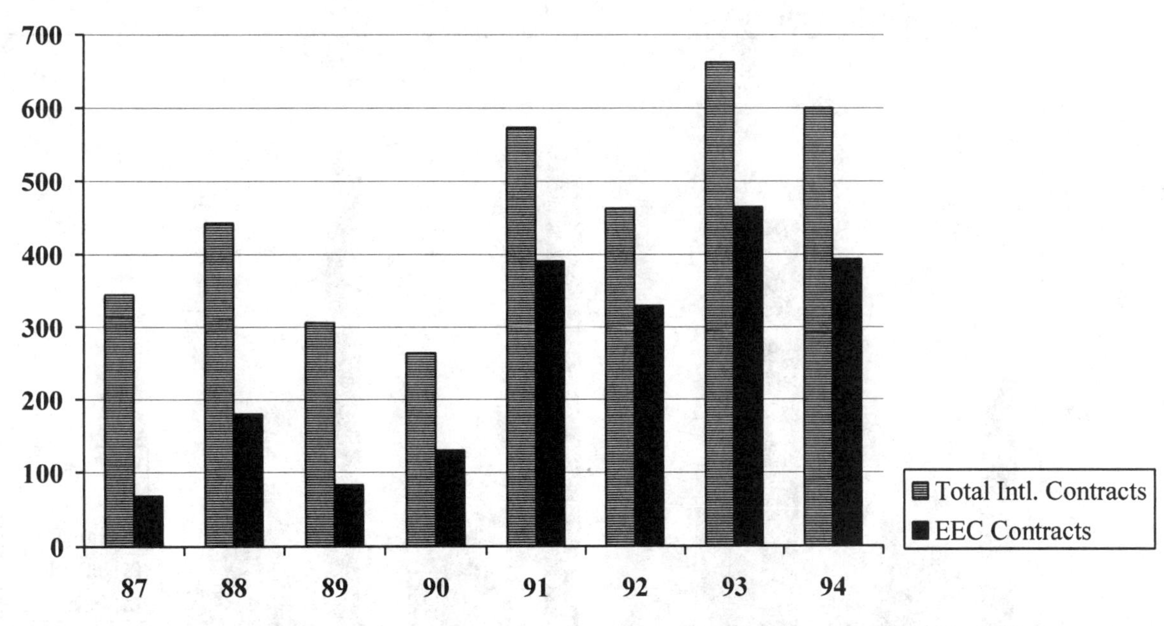

Source: EIC.

Figure L.2.9. The total number for Europe of recorded holdings in other countries (1991–94)

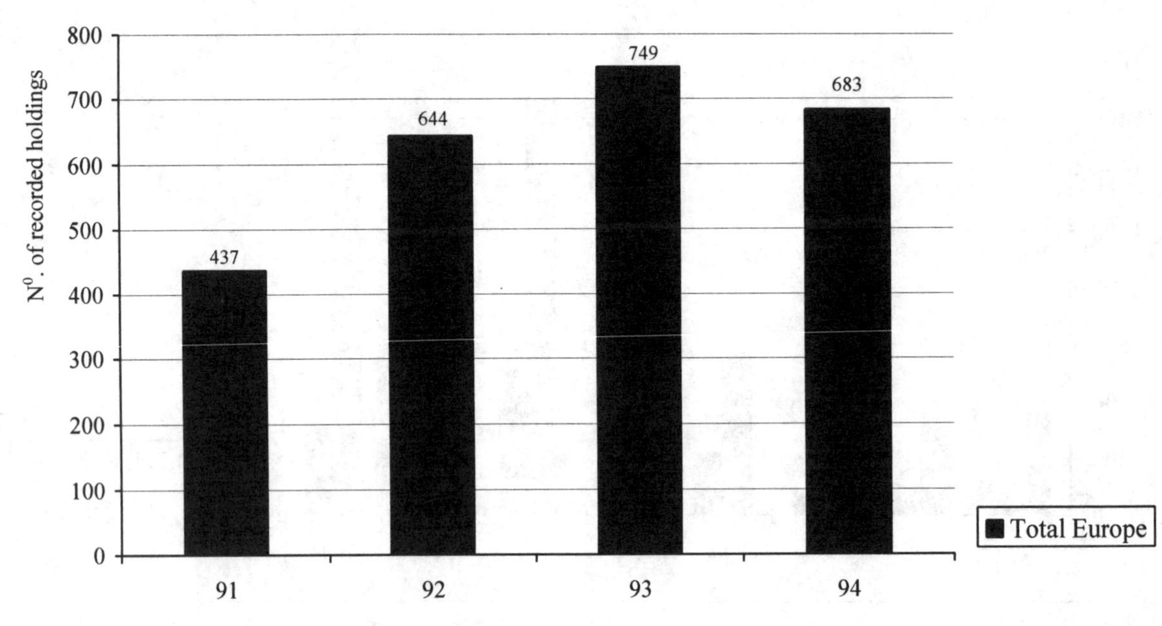

Source: EIC.

Figure L.2.10. The total number of recorded holdings in other countries by five European countries

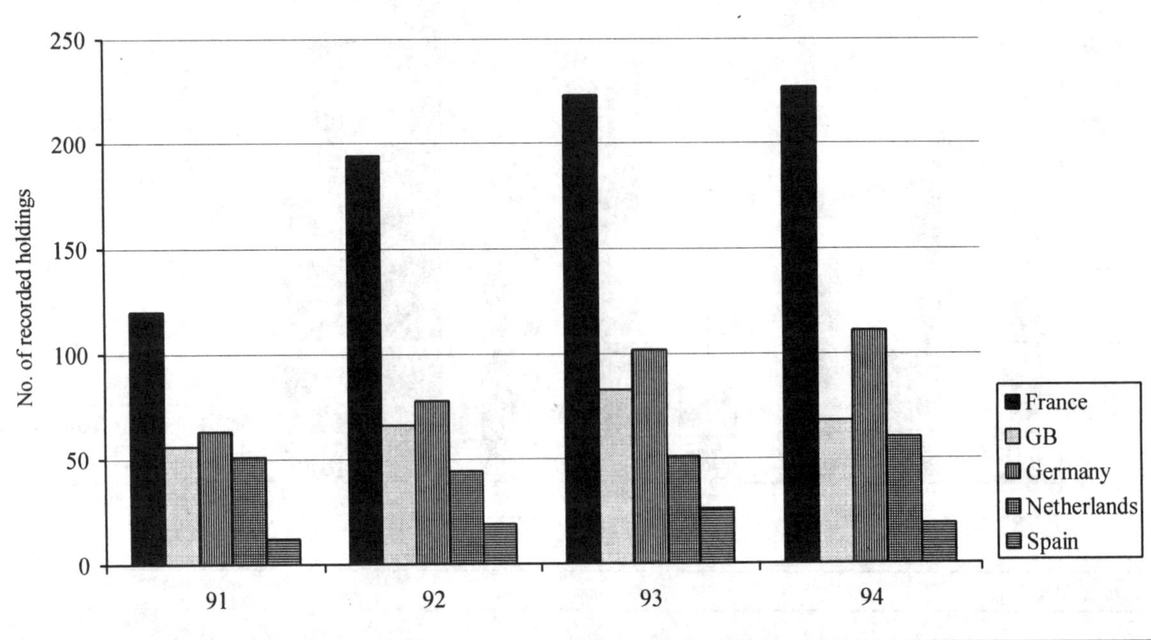

Source: EIC.
NB. GB = UK

APPENDIX M

The chocolate confectionery sector

M.1. List of sources of information

M.1.1. Interviews

Product manager, major international confectionery manufacturer
Account manager, large advertising agency handling major confectionery brand
Head of international trade, large chocolate manufacturer
Head of corporate strategy, confectionery division of major food company
Industry 'guru', head of industry association
Account manager, specialist in food and confectionery at international advertising agency
Head of corporate communications, food company

M.1.1. Data sources

BISCOFA
Biscuit, Cake and Chocolate Confectionery Alliance
Brillat-Savarin
Caobisco
Confectionery Production
Dagens-Naeringsliv
Economist Intelligence Unit
Panorama of EU industry 1994
Euromonitor
Euroglaces
Financial Times
Harvard Business School
IMEDE
Kraft Jacobs Suchard
Leatherhead Food Research Association
Lebensmittel-Zeitung
The Manufacturing Confectioner
Market Research Europe
Market Assessment Publications
Mars Inc
Nestlé Rowntree
Studiecentrum Snacks en Zoetwaren
Swiss Bank Corporation/Warburg

Bibliography

Buigues, P. and Ilzkovitz, F. (1988), 'The sectoral impact of the internal market', European Commission document, Vol. 2, No 335, Office for Official Publications of the EC, Luxembourg.

Buigues, P., Ilzkovitz, F. and Lebrun, J.-F. (1990), 'The impact of the internal market by industrial sector: the challenge for the Member States', in *European Economy*, Special Edition, Office for Official Publications of the EC, Luxembourg.

Central Statistical Office (1992), 'Report on the census of production: 1990, summary volume', in *Business Monitor*, December.

Centre Régional de la Consommation Nord-Pas de Calais (1994), 'Etude de prix transfrontalière Belgique - France - Royaume-Uni en 1993 et 1994', October.

CEPII (1996), 'The development of intra- versus inter-industry trade flows inside the EU due to the internal market programme', report prepared for the European Commission (DG II/DG XV).

Davies, S. and Lyons, B. (1996), *Industrial Organization in the European Union*, Oxford University Press.

DRI (1995), 'Survey of the trade association's perceptions of the effects of the single market', report prepared for the Commission of the European Communities (DG III).

Engel, C. (1993), 'Real exchange rates and relative prices: an empirical investigation', *Journal of Monetary Economics*, Vol. 32, pp. 35–50.

Engel, C. and Rogers, J. (1994), 'How wide is the border?', *National Bureau of Economic Research (NBER) Working Paper*.

European Commission (1988), 'The Economics of 1992', in *European Economy*, No 35, March 1988, Part D (The effects of market integration), p. 118, Office for Official Publications of the EC, Luxembourg.

European Commission, 'Survey of car prices within the European Union', May 1993 to May 1995.

European Commission (1994 and 1995), *Panorama of EU industry,* Office for Official Publications of the EC, Luxembourg.

Eurostat (1995), *Comparison in real terms of the aggregates of ESA, results for 1992 and 1993*, Office for Official Publications of the EC, Luxembourg.

Fishwick, F. and Denison, T. (1992), 'The geographical dimension of competition in the European single market', Office for Official Publications of the EC, Luxembourg.

Frost and Sullivan (1994), *European food and drink strategies, market overview and company profiles,* October.

Goodall, John (1995), 'The Role of the Construction Economist is Raising the Relative Efficiency of the National Construction Industry in Europe', Brussels, May.

Groupe MAC (1988), 'Technical barriers in the EC: Illustration in six industries', in *Research on the cost of non-Europe, Basic findings,* Vol. 1, Office for Official Publications of the EC, Luxembourg.

INSEE (1990), 'Les prix dans 23 agglomérations en 1989', *INSEE Première*, No 69.

Institut für Angewandte Verbraucherforschung (1994), 'Cross-border price comparison', study prepared for the European Commission (Consumer Policy Service).

Jacquemin, A. and Sapir, A. (1991), 'Competition and imports in the European market,' in Winters and Venables, *European integration: trade and industry*, Cambridge University Press.

Jacquemin, A. and Sapir, A. (1996), 'Is a European hard core credible?: a statistical analysis', *CEPR Discussion Paper,* No 1242.

Knetter, M. (1989), 'Price discrimination by US and German exporters', *American Economic Review*, Vol. 79, No 1.

Knetter, M. (1993), 'International comparisons of pricing-to-market behaviour', *American Economic Review*, Vol. 83, No 3.

Latham, M. (1994), 'Constructing the Team', HMSO, July.

Malueg, D. and Schwartz, M. (1994), 'Parallel imports, demand dispersion and international price discrimination', *Journal of International Economics*, Vol. 37, No 3/4.

Ministère de l'Agriculture (1990), 'Enquête annuelle d'entreprise de l'industrie agro-alimentaire: résultats sectoriels et régionaux'.

Ministère de l'Agriculture (1993), 'Enquête annuelle d'entreprise de l'industrie agro-alimentaire: résultats sectoriels et régionaux'.

Ministère de l'Industrie, des Postes et Télécommunications et du Commerce extérieur (1994), 'La dispersion des performances des entreprises en 1993', in *SESSI statistiques*, No 152, January.

Ministère de l'Industrie, des Postes et Télécommunications et du Commerce extérieur (1995), 'La situation de l'industrie en 1993: résultats détaillés de l'enquête annuelle d'entreprise – Tome 1', in *SESSI statistiques*, No 153, March.

NEDC European Public Purchasing Working Party (1992), 'European Community Public Works Directive: A Study of the Application in Practice'.

Nerb, G. (1988), 'The completion of the internal market: a survey of European industry's perception of the likely effects,' in *Research on the cost of non-Europe, Basic findings,* Vol. 3, Office for Official Publications of the EC, Luxembourg.

Ohno, K. (1989), 'Export pricing behaviour of manufacturing: A US-Japan comparison', *IMF Staff Papers*, Vol. 36, No 3.

de Reuver, T. (1996), 'Concentration of the European snack and confectionery industry', *The Manufacturing Confectioner*, January.

Rogers, J. and Jenkins, M. (1995), 'Haircuts or hysteresis? Sources of movements in real exchange rates', *Journal of International Economics*, Vol. 38, pp. 339–360.

Services des statistiques industrielles (SESSI) du Ministère de l'Industrie (1994), 'La dispersion des performances des entreprises en 1993'.

Statistisches Bundesamt (1994), 'Zwischenörtlicher Vergleich des Verbraucherpreisniveaus in 50 Städten', *Wirtschaft und Statistik*, June.

Stepford, J. and Baden Fuller, C. (1991) 'Globalization frustrated: the case of white goods', *SMJ,* Vol. 12.

Stigler, G.J. and Sherwin, R.A. (1985), 'The extent of the market', *Journal of Law and Economics*, Vol. XXVII.

Sutton, J. (1991), *Sunk Costs and Market Structure*, MIT Press.

Weiss, P. (1994), 'Price differentials in Western Europe', *EFTA Economic Affairs Department*, March.

Winters, L.A. (1992), 'Trade flows and trade policy after 1992', *CEPR.*